Strategic Planning
for
Public Relations

Ronald D. Smith, APR
Buffalo State College

2002

LAWRENCE ERLBAUM ASSOCIATES, PUBLISHERS
Mahwah, New Jersey   London

Acquisitions Editor: Linda Bathgate
Textbook Marketing Manager: Marisol Kozlovski
Editorial Assistant: Karin Wittig Bates
Cover Design: Kathryn Houghtaling Lacey
Textbook Production Manager: Paul Smolenski
Full-Service Compositor: TechBooks
Text and Cover Printer: Hamilton Printing Company

This book was typeset in 10/12 pt. Times, Italic, Bold, Bold Italic. The heads were typeset in ACaslon Regular, ACaslon Bold, ACaslon Italic, and ACaslon Bold Italic.

Lawrence Erlbaum Associates, Inc., Publishers
10 Industrial Avenue
Mahwah, New Jersey 07430

Library of Congress Cataloging-in-Publication Data

Strategic planning for public relations / edited by Ronald D. Smith.
        p. cm.
    Includes index.
    ISBN 0-8058-4233-0
    1. Public relations.   I. Smith, Ronald D., 1948-

HM 1221 .S77 2002   2001055584
659.2—dc21

Books published by Lawrence Erlbaum Associates are printed on
acid-free paper, and their bindings are chosen for strength and durability.

Printed in the United States of America
10 9 8 7 6 5 4 3

Brief Contents

Contents

Preface

*S*trategic Planning for Public Relations offers college and university students a new way to deepen their understanding of public relations and other kinds of strategic communication. It is intended for people serious about entering a profession that is rapidly changing, shedding a past that often involved merely performing tasks managed by others and taking on a newer, more mature role in the management of organizations.

This book provides an in-depth approach to public relations planning, more comprehensive than can be found anywhere else. It is built on a step-by-step unfolding of the planning process most often used in public relations, with explanations, examples and exercises that combine to guide students toward a contemporary understanding of the profession.

The approach used in *Strategic Planning for Public Relations* is rooted in the author's belief and observation that students learn best through a three-fold pattern of being exposed to an idea, seeing it in use, and then applying it themselves. This is the rhythm of this book, its cadence if you will. This is the design that takes a complex problem-solving and decision-making process and turns it into a series of easy-to-follow steps.

Note to Students

Thank you for allowing me to share my ideas and insights into a profession that I have found to be challenging and rewarding. I wish you much success as you proceed toward a career that I hope you, too, will discover to be exhilarating.

I stumbled into public relations somewhat by accident, at least not by my own conscious design. I began my career as a newspaper reporter, and later as an editor, with some side trips into television writing and producing. I then made the transition into public relations—at first building on a familiar base of media relations, publicity and newsletters, and only later navigating into issues management, crisis response, integrated communication, and a host of related areas. Frankly, I wish there had been a book like this to guide me toward an understanding of how to do public relations, especially the research and planning parts. So I'm pleased to be able to share with you some of the insights I've picked up along the way.

With this book and the practical exercises that go with it, you are proceeding along the road to professional success. I wish you the best of luck.

You should be aware that this book is intended for group development and class activities. While you certainly can use it alone, you will find that it comes more fully alive as a text to guide group projects. Even if you are not a student in a traditional classroom, try to use this book in the context of your own project task force or professional work team.

Note to Instructors

Thank you for choosing this textbook for your students. Thanks especially for the opportunity to share with them some of my thoughts and observations on an exciting profession. I trust that you will find the information contained in this book to be well within the framework of contemporary professional practice and academic principles.

Strategic Planning for Public Relations grew out of my observation that students seem to learn best when they understand concepts, have patterns to follow and adapt, and have the opportunity to work individually and in groups on tasks that gradually unfold to reveal the bigger picture. This is my intention with this book—to provide a structure, yet to give you much flexibility in leading your students through the planning process.

Acknowledgments

John Dunne was right that no one is an island. Neither does an author write alone, but instead reflects in some way the insight of others in the field who write, teach and engage in the practice.

Strategic Planning for Public Relations enjoys the input of many people. As the author of this textbook, I'll take personal responsibility for any errors or omissions, but I'm confident these are fewer because of the advice and assistance of many knowledgeable people who helped with this book.

Collectively, my students have been major contributors to this book. It is in the classroom that I have tested and refined the ideas contained herein. My students have prodded me to articulate my ideas and to bolster them with plenty of real-world examples.

My academic colleagues at Buffalo State emphasize practical, applied communication, and I have benefited from ongoing professional conversations with them, Marian Deutschman in particular. My professional colleagues within the Public Relations Society of America consistently have helped me with their insight and constructive criticism. In particular, Ann Reynolds Carden APR and Stanton H. Hudson APR have helped me refine some of my ideas.

Two publishing teams have been helpful and supportive throughout the progress of *Strategic Planning for Public Relations*. Marisa L'Heureux at NTC/Contemporary Publishing was invariably encouraging as she guided the conceptual development of this book. After a corporate transition landed me in the lap of Lawrence Erlbaum Associates, Linda Bathgate fortuitously became the book's pilot, steering it to its final form. My special thanks go to Elizabeth MacDonnell, who as editor has read this book far more than anybody ought to. Liz has been a gentle editor, allowing me the freedom to say what I believe needs to be said, while guiding me to use language clearly and effectively. If you find this book to be lucid and unconfused, much of the credit belongs to Liz.

Authors appreciate the comments and criticism of their peers, and I am particularly grateful to faculty across the country who took time from their busy teaching schedules to review this book: Ron Anderson of University of Texas at Austin, M. L.

Cornette of the University of South Dakota, Rick Fischer of Memphis State University, Larissa Grunig of the University of Maryland, Lawrence Lamb of the University of North Carolina, Ruth Ann Weaver Lariscy of the University of Georgia, Kathleen Martinelli of San Jose State University, Shirley Serini of Ball State University, and Bill Sledzik of Kent State University.

Personal Dedication

Like the entirety of my life, this book is dedicated to my family.

Though they don't realize it, my three sons have been an inspiration as I worked on this book. We sometimes would sit across the desk from each other, me working at my computer, one of them at theirs.

As he progressed through college and now in his job in Japan, Josh has challenged me to explain public relations every time I suggested he consider it as a career. As Aaron maneuvers his way through college, he has settled in as a public relations major. With his writing talents and his gift of being able to analyze any situation, he'll be good if he pursues this field. Matt is still in high school, safe for the time being from having to make career decisions. But he, too, is a fine writer and an organized thinker, skills that will come in handy if Plan A (playing in the NBA) doesn't work out.

My greatest appreciation goes to my wife, Dawn Minier Smith. During the evolution of this book, indeed during my entire teaching career, Dawn has been my sounding board. A teacher herself, she has lent her ear as I tested ideas, tried out new ways to present lessons, and attempted to make sense of theories, cases and observations. Since she doesn't see any domestic value in a wife fawning over her husband, Dawn's constructive criticism has been always trustworthy and thus most valuable. I always take her suggestions seriously. Sometimes I've even had the good sense to follow them.

An Invitation

This book is the result of much dialogue with others, particularly feedback from my students. But reader reaction inevitably is useful. I invite all readers—students, teachers and practitioners—to share your thoughts with me. Give me comments and suggestions for future editions. Share your success stories and your frustrations with this book. I also invite you to use my Web site, where I have included an expanding number of pages and links related to public relations and other aspects of strategic communication.

Ron Smith
smithrd@bscmail.buffalostate.edu
faculty.buffalostate.edu/smithrd

About the Author

Ronald D. Smith, APR, is a professor of public communication at Buffalo State College, the largest college within the State University of New York. He teaches public relations planning, writing and related classes to undergraduate and graduate students. He also is active as a consultant in public relations and strategic communication, assisting businesses and nonprofit organizations with planning, research, communication management and media training.

In this book, Smith draws on considerable professional experience. In addition to 12 years as an educator, he worked for 10 years as a public relations director and eight years as a newspaper reporter and editor. He also has been a Navy journalist.

Smith holds a bachelor's degree in English education from Lock Haven State College and a master's degree in public relations from Syracuse University. He has presented numerous workshops and seminars and has published research on public relations and persuasive communication. He also is the author of *Becoming a Public Relations Writer* (2nd edition in press, Lawrence Erlbaum Associates) and co-author of *MediaWriting* (2000, Longman).

Smith is an accredited member of the Public Relations Society of America and has served as president of PRSA's Buffalo/Niagara chapter and chair of the Northeast District. In 1998, he was honored as "Practitioner of the Year" by the Buffalo chapter, which has given him several other awards and citations.

Cases and Examples

Following is an index of actual cases, organizations and events cited within *Strategic Planning for Public Relations* as examples of various principles, strategies, and techniques.

Introduction

Why a book on strategic planning for public relations? Because effective and creative planning is at the heart of all public relations and related activity. And because the field is changing.

No longer is it enough merely to know *how* to do things. Now the effective communicator needs to know *what* to do, *why* and how to *evaluate* its effectiveness. Public relations professionals used to be called upon mainly for tasks such as writing news releases, making speeches, producing videos, publishing newsletters, organizing displays and so on. Now the profession demands competency in conducting research, making decisions and solving problems. The call now is for strategic communicators.

To put it another way, *communication technicians* traditionally focus on tasks to be accomplished. These technician-level specialists in public relations and marketing communication perform entry-level jobs or specialized tasks, often directed by others. *Communication managers,* meanwhile, make decisions. Consider the complementary roles of two categories of communications managers: tactical and strategic.

Tactical managers make day-to-day decisions on many practical and specific issues. Should they send a news release or hold a news conference? Are they better off with a brochure or a web page? Should they develop a mall exhibit, or would it be more effective to create a computer presentation? Do they need another advertisement, and if so, for which publication or station, and with what message using which strategy?

Strategic managers, on the other hand, are concerned with management, trends, issues, policies and corporate structure. What problems are likely to face the organization over the next several years, and how might they be addressed? What is the crisis readiness of the organization? Should senior personnel be offered an advanced level of media training? What should be the policies for the Web page?

In the workplace, public relations practitioners often find themselves functioning in both the technician and the managerial roles, but the balance is shifting. Today's environment—and more importantly, tomorrow's—calls for greater skill on the management side of communication. The job of strategic communication planning calls for four particular skills: (1) understanding research and planning, (2) knowing how to make strategic choices, (3) making selections from an expanding inventory of tactical choices and (4) completing the process by evaluating program effectiveness.

A premise underlying this book is that public relations and marketing communication are becoming more strategic, more scientific. It is this strategic perspective that will differentiate the effective practitioner from the one who simply performs tasks and provides basic services.

Strategic Planning for Public Relations is about making such decisions—not by hunches or instinct, but by solid and informed reasoning that draws on the science of communication as well as its various art forms. This book tries to make the complex process of strategic communication easily understandable by taking you through the process step by step. You'll find nine steps, each presented with three basic elements:

1. *Explanations* that are clear and understandable, drawn from contemporary theory and current practice.
2. *Examples* that help you see the concept in action, drawn from both nonprofit and forprofit organizations.
3. Hands-on *exercises* in both short form and expanded versions that help you apply the process in your own situation.

Experience shows that this hybrid format—part textbook, part workbook—can make it easier to learn about the planning process because it helps you think, see and do. *Strategic Planning for Public Relations* gives you a solid, proven process that works. It doesn't offer any secrets of the trade, because there really are no secrets. Effective managers in public relations and marketing communication use this kind of a process everyday, and that's not much of a secret. This book makes field-tested procedures available to you in an understandable way so you can apply them yourself.

Strategic Communication

Ask executives in business and nonprofit organizations what kind of employee they value, and they'll probably refer to someone who can effectively and creatively solve problems and exploit opportunities.

An effective practitioner understands a problem and manages it to its successful conclusion. How do we manage problems? Sometimes by making them go away. Sometimes just by helping them run their course with the least harm to the organization. Public relations practitioners face all kinds of problems: low visibility, lack of public understanding, opposition from critics and insufficient support from funding sources. Marketing communicators face similar problems: unfamiliarity of companies or products, apathy among consumers, product recalls and other liabilities. Both may deal with indifference among workers and misunderstanding by regulators.

Practitioners also deal with opportunities, such as promoting new products and services or enhancing already effective programs. In most organizations, it is this positive communication that accounts for most of the time practitioners spend on the job. Meanwhile, forward-looking practitioners try to transform even obstacles into opportunities for their organizations and clients.

Strategic communication is the name for such planned communication campaigns. More specifically, it is intentional communication undertaken by a business or nonprofit organization, sometimes by a less structured group. It has a purpose and a plan, in which alternatives are considered and decisions are justified. Invariably, strategic communication is based on research and subject to eventual evaluation. It operates within a particular environment, which involves both the organization and groups of people who affect it in some way.

Old, Yet New

The ancient and enduring wisdom that nothing is new under the sun applies even to contemporary communication.

Building credibility, maintaining trust, repairing misunderstandings and promoting ideas are part of the human impulse. Today's public relations practitioner deals with the same kind of problems that faced our predecessors last year, last decade, last century. Nothing is new but the timing, the tools and perhaps our insight into the problem-solving process.

Strategic communication often is either informational or persuasive. Its common purpose is to build understanding and support for ideas and causes, services and products.

Where do we find examples of strategic communication? They're all around us. Public relations is the most common embodiment of strategic communication, so much so that this book uses the two terms interchangeably. Actually, however, strategic communication is the concept and public relations is its primary example. In earlier days, much public relations activity was haphazard and reactive. But most current public relations activity is strategic, and most practitioners see themselves as strategic communicators.

However, not all strategic communicators practice public relations. Marketing communication also is an embodiment of the concept of strategic communication. Still other examples are public health and social marketing campaigns, diplomacy and international relations, constituent relations, political campaigns, and ecumenical or interreligious affairs.

Meanwhile, public relations itself is sometimes known by alternative names, often linked to subsidiary areas such as media relations, or employee communication. Nevertheless, a research-based strategic planning process is necessary for effective management of all the various aspects of public relations—regardless of their names—including community relations, special events planning and promotion, political campaigns, nonprofit events, and fund-raising and development (Austin and Pinkleton, 2001). To that list we can add other elements of strategic public relations: public affairs, issues management, crisis communication, public information, consumer and customer relations, lobbying, investor relations, and so on. Additionally, there are some new names on the field: litigation public relations, risk communication and reputation management.

Regardless of the label, we look to public relations for leadership and insight in the practice of strategic communication, because most of the related fields and specialties have adopted the set of skills and approaches that public relations has developed over the last 75 years or so (Botan, 1997; Botan & Soto, 1998). Meanwhile, public relations is beginning to more cousciously borrow some of the techniques and approaches developed by other fields, particularly marketing and one of its primary communication tools, advertising.

Integrated Communication

Public relations and marketing are distinct yet overlapping fields. Each has its own focus and its own particular tools, and each discipline fulfills different purposes within an organization. Yet more and more, it is becoming evident that the coordination of public relations and marketing communication can increase an organization's efficiency and effectiveness. Let's look first at the common distinctions between public relations and marketing communication and then at how they complement each other.

In its classic sense, **public relations** focuses on long-term patterns of interaction between an organization and all of its various publics, both supportive and nonsupportive. Public relations seeks to enhance these relationships, thus generating mutual understanding, goodwill and support. **Marketing communication** focuses more immediately on products and services that respond to the wants and needs of consumers. It seeks to foster an economic exchange between the organization and its consumers.

Both disciplines deserve a seat at the management table. Both identify wants, interests, needs and expectations of key groups of people, and both structure ways to communicate with them. Both disciplines rely on research and are rooted in the organization's mission and directed toward its "bottom line." Finally, public relations and marketing communication share a concern about both the short-term and long-term interests of the organization.

The lines between marketing and public relations have never been neat and clean. Laypeople and the media use the terms more or less interchangeably, and distinctions have been built more on stereotypes than on a reality. Consider, for example, the stale notions that advertising is solely a marketing tool or that public relations is only about publicity. In truth, public relations traditionally has engaged in public service advertising, and it is a public relations perspective that drives image and advocacy advertising. Marketing, meanwhile, has used media relations, publicity and special events while launching new or modified products, and many marketing concepts have proven useful to public relations practitioners in nonprofit organizations attempting to recruit volunteers or participants, lobby regulators and raise funds.

Some organizations are consciously blending the concepts and the tools of public relations and marketing communication, not always smoothly. Purists argue against diluting the disciplines, often fearing that integration will demote public relations to just another piece of the marketing mix or subsume public relations under the advertising tent. Others accept integration in principal but dread lopsided implementation, such as the "full-service" advertising agency that claims to offer integrated communication while allocating most of the client's budget to advertising.

And guaranteed to send shivers down the spines of most public relations practitioners are articles such as one about a British survey reporting that public relations is "no longer a peripheral activity when it comes to marketing communication" but rather "an integral part of the marketing ethos" and "one of the most important aspects of the marketing mix" (Gray, 1998). Such language can ignite turf battles because it portrays public relations as merely a part of marketing that is finally being recognized as valuable. Yet this same "Future of Public Relations" study by Countrywide Porter Novelli, one of the United

Kingdom's top five public relations agencies, reports some positive trends. Among marketing and corporate affairs directors, 92 percent said public relations is integral to business objectives, 58 percent said public relations is of equal importance with advertising and 66 percent expect to increase public relations spending over the next three years.

Conflicting advice has come from the academic community. A report by the Association for Education in Journalism and Mass Communication (AEJMC) suggested integrating public relations and advertising into a shared curriculum to reflect new practices in the field. The Educational Affairs Committee of the Public Relations Society of America (PRSA) reacted quickly to oppose such a blending.

Controversy exists even on naming rights. Some people call the blending "integrated marketing communication." Others dub it "integrated communication," "marketing public relations" or "total communication." Some bulky new terms being kicked around are "marketing-based public relations" and "integrated communications (advertising and public relations)."

One study reports that while the educational community may have mixed feelings about integrating the disciplines, practitioners seem to be accepting, even embracing, the opportunities it can bring. That was the observation of two practitioners-turned-professors at Florida International University: Debra Miller, a former PRSA president, and Patricia Rose, former president of the Miami Advertising Federation. The two reported that "public relations professionals support integrated marketing communications and accept it as a reality and necessity" because it makes sense and leads to broader skills that can enhance their careers (Miller & Rose, 1994).

The 1998 appointment of a public relations executive to head Young & Rubicam's international advertising network dispelled some fears within the public relations community about integrated communication. Thomas Bell, former head of Y&R's sister agency, Burson-Marsteller Worldwide, vowed to be "someone who can deliver integrated thinking" so the ad agency will consider "all the persuasive disciplines" in servicing clients (Holmes, 1998).

Some people are working mightily to coordinate the complementary fields while maintaining the autonomy and distinctive role of each. Interestingly, some of these people are outside the formal structures of public relations and marketing. They include CEOs who direct their marketing and public relations teams to collaborate in a new-product campaign, and university presidents who enjoin their media relations people to be attentive to recruiting and fund-raising needs.

As organizations set out to create such a cooperative environment, the political task can be dicey, but the potential rewards are huge. Often it is enlightened organizational leaders who see the big picture, recognizing the value of a coordinated and strategic approach to communication. Some of the most successful corporations in North America integrate their communication, blending the traditional disciplines of public relations and advertising to creatively present a clear and consistent message to their various publics. For example, when McDonald's introduced its McLean sandwich, it first used public relations to create awareness through the media, followed by advertising messages to reinforce the publicity and promotion. Additionally, it was publicity that enabled Goodyear to sell 150,000 new Aquatred tires before the first advertisements ran. Meanwhile, Pfizer used publicity alone to sell $250 million of Viagra before any consumer advertising began.

The integrated approach also has been used by nonprofit organizations such as the American Cancer Society in its campaign for sunblock. The approach has been adopted by more loosely organized social campaigns dealing with bicycle safety, teen smoking, animal rights, birth control, utility deregulation and AIDS research. One study suggested that nonprofit organizations are particularly open to the coordinated use of public relations and marketing communication techniques (Nemec, 1999).

Communication integration seems to be happening globally. Philip Kitchen and Don Schultz (1999) reported that the concept is gaining momentum not only in the United States but also in the United Kingdom, New Zealand, Australia and India. The integrated model, they observe, has become "acceptable," though not yet the "established norm."

Gronstedt (2000) cited Saturn, Xerox, Motorola, Hewlett-Packard and Federal Express as examples of companies that have effectively integrated their communication. Companies such as these use integrated communication on three levels: external communication, focusing on customers; vertical internal communication between senior management and frontline workers; and horizontal internal communication across departments, business units and geographic boundaries (Hiebert, 2000).

Some folks say the concept of integrated communication is wrapped in the history of public relations itself. Porter Novelli vice president Helen Ostrowski (1999) believes that marketing-based public relations lies at the very roots of public relations. After all, public relations founding father Edward Bernays engineered the debutante march in New York City's Easter parade to make smoking fashionable among women so Lucky Strike could sell more cigarettes.

Tom Harris is a leading proponent of integrated communication, which he calls an outside-in process that begins with an understanding of the consumer publics, particularly their wants, interests, needs and lifestyles. Harris (2000) pointed out that public relations is particularly effective in building brand equity, which is based on the organization's reputation. The practical benefit of reputation is seen in the 1992 Los Angeles riots, when none of the 30 McDonalds restaurants in the riot area were touched while more than 2,000 buildings were destroyed. Harris said that is because McDonalds had long been involved and visible in the community.

In their influential book, *Managing Public Relations,* James Grunig and Todd Hunt (1984) identified four now-famous evolutionary models of public relations. The first two—exemplified by press agentry and public information—rely on one-way dissemination of information. The latter models—an asymmetrical one associated with persuasion, a symmetrical model dealing with dialogue and relationship-building—feature two-way communication for both dissemination and research/feedback. Each of the models is evident today, often used by the same organization. Each can be effective in achieving particular organizational objectives.

An interesting tug-of-war exists between the persuasion and relationship models. In subsequent research, Grunig (1992) himself noted that many organizations still primarily practice the persuasion model. With only anecdotal evidence, it seems safe to

Attributes of a Strategic Communication Program

Rather than manufacture definitions, *Strategic Planning for Public Relations* focuses on the characteristics of strategic communication. An effective communication program includes the following attributes, which apply equally to corporations and nonprofit organizations and to large and small endeavors:

- Spurred both by regulation and customer demand, organizations must be *accountable* to their publics. Most publics are increasing their expectations for *quality performance* and *open communication*. Organizations are successful in the long run only to the extent that they have high performance, delivering quality products and services. Strategic communication enhances reputations by accurately reflecting the organization's performance.

- All organizations operate in a *competitive environment*. Publics besought by rivals will remain loyal to those organizations that earn loyalty consistently and continuously.

- Effective communication involves *cooperation* between public relations and marketing. Just as each knight was an equal participant at the round table in King Arthur's court, so too at today's management table both disciplines have effective and equal voices.

- The consumer philosophy has taken hold of all aspects of society, and organizations must answer with a *customer-driven response,* focusing on benefits for their publics. People support organizations they believe serve their interests and needs.

- Organizational communication adheres to *high ethical standards* of honesty, accuracy, decency, truth, public interest and mutual good. Growing numbers of organizations have developed clear credos or codes of ethics.

- Mergers, downsizing and restructuring have led both businesses and nonprofits to seek ways to operate with *lean resources,* and the duplication that exists amid the isolation of

marketing from public relations often is too great a price for organizations to pay.

- Strategic communication is part of an organization's *management function* and decision-making process, based on careful planning that identifies issues, gathers data, considers alternatives and determines action. It is rooted in the organization's mission as lived out through its bottom line. Note that this bottom line goes beyond money earned or raised; it focuses on the organization's fundamental purpose or mission. Organizational goals and positioning statements are carried out through specific and measurable objectives that chart the course for desired levels of awareness, acceptance and action. Strategists plot courses and measure results.

- Many *media changes* are affecting the way organizations communicate. The "mass media" have fragmented to the point that none rules supreme anymore. Lines are blurring between news and entertainment. Meanwhile, increasing advertising costs and tighter promotional budgets have led organizations to look at the more cost-effective communication and promotional tools from the public relations side of the house.

- Strategic communication uses *multiple tools,* drawing from all communication-related disciplines to talk with various groups of people. New technologies make it easier to supplement general media with more personal and interpersonal targeted communication vehicles.

- The strategy of choice in a competitive environment is *proactive, two-way communication,* in which organizations plan for and initiate relationships with the people important to their success, emphasizing dialogue over monologue and using various techniques to interact with their publics and markets.

- Organizations are successful to the extent they enjoy a strong *reputation,* which results from neither accident nor luck. Strategic planning can identify and evaluate an organization visibility and reputation. No organization can afford to be a "best-kept secret" among a relatively small number of supporters; continuing effectiveness requires the development and maintenance of a strong and positive reputation.

- All kinds of organizations are realizing more keenly the need for long-term, mutually beneficial *relationships* between the organization and its various publics and market segments. Public relations practitioners long have recognized this, and marketing more recently has been discussing the need for relationship marketing.

suggest that most of today's public relations agencies are hired to engage in persuasion on behalf of their clients, who believe their problems can be solved if only they can gain the support of their publics. Persuasion isn't necessarily bad: The same principles and techniques that persuade people to buy this CD or that perfume can be deployed on behalf of responsible sexual behavior or nutritional literacy, volunteerism or other social virtues. Public relations students are exposed to this model through case studies and campaigns courses, through practicums and senior seminars, and especially through professional internships.

Perhaps we need to envision public relations anew, seeing it as serving the persuasive needs of client organizations as well as fostering more productive and beneficial relationships between organizations and their various publics. Public relations practitioners should be prepared to help organizations engage their publics both in word and deed.

This is the vision that guides *Strategic Planning for Public Relations*. The planning process this book presents can be used for persuasion or dialogue, because each is a strategic activity and each helps practitioners influence behavior and generate consensus. The planning process also can help organizations both overcome obstacles and capitalize on opportunities. Additionally, the process works equally well for businesses and nonprofits, whether they be large or small, international or grassroot, richly endowed or impoverished.

Nine Steps of Strategic Public Relations

Most textbooks dealing with public relations encourage a four-phase process. Some use the RACE acronym (research, action, communication, evaluation) articulated by John Marston (1963) in *The Nature of Public Relations*. In *Public Relations Cases,* Jerry Hendrix (2000) used the acronym ROPE (research, objectives, programming, evaluation). In *Public Relations Campaign Strategies,* Robert Kendall (1992) offered another formula—RAISE (research, adaptation, implementation strategy, evaluation).

Most public relations textbooks, however, simply refer to a four-stage process without constraining it with an acronym. Marketing communication books also present a step-by-step process, but with little consistency about the number of steps involved. While acronyms can be useful mnemonic devices, they can be too confining. The four stages of public relations planning are more complex than the acronyms indicate.

Strategic Planning for Public Relations offers a model that seems a bit more logical. The steps are grouped into four phases that are both descriptive and accurate, but their names don't lend themselves to an acronym. So without a great deal of fanfare, this model is called, simply, the Nine Steps of Strategic Public Relations.

Phase One: Formative Research
> Step 1: Analyzing the Situation
> Step 2: Analyzing the Organization
> Step 3: Analyzing the Publics

Phase Two: Strategy
> Step 4: Establishing Goals and Objectives
> Step 5: Formulating Action and Response Strategies
> Step 6: Using Effective Communication

Phase Three: Tactics
> Step 7: Choosing Communication Tactics
> Step 8: Implementing the Strategic Plan

Phase Four: Evaluative Research
> Step 9: Evaluating the Strategic Plan

The process of these steps is deliberate, and they must be taken in sequence. After identifying a problem, our tendency too often is to skip ahead to seeking solutions, leaping over research and analysis. This can result in unwarranted assumptions that later prove to be costly, counterproductive and embarrassing. Careful planning leads to programs that are proactive and preventative, rather than to activities that are reactive and remedial. At the same time, the steps in this process are flexible enough to allow for constant monitoring, testing and adjusting as needed.

Ask experienced communication managers, and you may find that they don't necessarily articulate their planning specifically along the lines of these nine steps. But talk with them about their work, and you are likely to find that they go through a process pretty much like the one being presented here, whether they identify "steps" or not.

A few practitioners may admit (somewhat guiltily) that they don't do much planning. If they are being honest, they'll tell you they know they've been lucky so far with their hunches. Perhaps they don't do formal planning because they don't have the time or because the environment is so unstable that all they can do is react. Some practitioners may tell you their bosses and clients want action rather than planning (though such shortsighted bosses and clients often don't remain in business very long). If you could observe how professionals work, however, you'd probably find that effective communication managers do plan. The good ones have learned how to build the research and planning components into their work and "sell" it to their clients and bosses.

Formative Research

During the first phase of the nine steps, Formative Research, the focus is on the preliminary work of communication planning, which is the need to gather information and analyze the situation. In three steps, the planner draws on existing information

The Jargon of Strategic Public Relations

Consider the following terms that distinguish among various types of public relations activities:

- **Projects** are single and usually short-lived public relations activities designed to meet an objective. Examples: A news release or a few closely related tactics surrounding an open house.
- **Programs** are ongoing public relations activities dealing with several objectives associated with a goal. Programs have a continuing commission within the organization and focus on its relationship with a particular public. Examples: An organization's programs in community relations or employee relations.
- **Campaigns** are systematic sets of public relations activities, each with a specific and finite purpose, sustained over a length of time and dealing with objectives associated with a particular issue. Examples: A campaign to reduce accidents associated with drunk driving, or a campaign to improve employee morale and productivity.

available to the organization and, at the same time, creates a research program for gaining additional information needed to drive the decisions that will come later in the planning process.

Step 1: Analyzing the Situation.   Your analysis of the situation is the crucial beginning to the process. It is imperative that all involved—planner, clients, supervisors, key colleagues and the ultimate decision makers—are in solid agreement about the nature of the opportunity or obstacle to be addressed in this program.

Step 2: Analyzing the Organization.   This step involves a careful and candid look at three aspects of the organization: (1) its internal environment (mission, performance and resources), (2) its public perception (reputation) and (3) its external environment (competitors and opponents, as well as supporters).

Step 3: Analyzing the Publics.   In this step you identify and analyze your key publics—the various groups of people who interact with your organization on the issue at hand. *Strategic Planning for Public Relations* provides an objective technique for setting priorities among the various publics, helping you select those most important on the particular issue being dealt with. This step includes an analysis of each public in terms of their wants, needs and expectations about the issue, their relationship to the organization, their involvement in communication and with various media, and a variety of social, economic, political, cultural and technological trends that may affect them.

Strategy

The second phase of the planning process, Strategy, deals with the heart of planning: making decisions dealing with the expected impact of the communication, as well as the nature of the communication itself.

Step 4: Establishing Goals and Objectives.   Step 4 focuses on the ultimate position being sought for the organization and for the product or service. This step helps you develop clear, specific and measurable objectives that identify the organization's hoped-for impact on the awareness, acceptance and action of each key public. A good deal of attention is given to objectives dealing with acceptance of the message, because this is the most crucial area for public relations and marketing communication strategists.

Step 5: Formulating Action and Response Strategies.   A range of actions is available to the organization, and in this step you consider what you might do in various situations. This section includes typologies of initiatives and responses.

Step 6: Using Effective Communication.   Step 6 deals with the various decisions about the message, such as the sources who will present the message to the key publics, the content of the message, its tone and style, verbal and nonverbal cues, and related issues. Lessons from research about persuasive communication and dialogue will be applied for the ultimate purpose of designing a message that reflects the information gained through Step 3.

Tactics

During the Tactics phase, various communication tools are considered and the visible elements of the communication plan are created.

Step 7: Choosing Communication Tactics.   This inventory deals with the various communication options. Specifically, the planner considers four categories: (1) face-to-face communication and opportunities for personal involvement, (2) organizational media (sometimes called controlled media), (3) news media (uncontrolled media) and (4) advertising and promotional media (another form of controlled media). While all of these tools can be used by any organization, not every tool is appropriate for each issue. Following the menu review, the planner packages the tactics into a cohesive communication program.

Step 8: Implementing the Strategic Plan.   In Step 8, you develop budgets and schedules and otherwise prepare to implement the communication program. This step turns the raw ingredients identified in the previous step into a recipe for successful public relations and marketing communication.

Evaluative Research

The final phase, Evaluative Research, deals with evaluation and assessment, enabling you to determine the degree to which the stated objectives have been met and thus to modify or continue the communication activities.

Step 9: Evaluating the Strategic Plan.   This is the final planning element, indicating specific methods for measuring the effectiveness of each recommended tactic in meeting the stated objectives.

Effective Creativity

Before we begin putting a plan together, a word about creativity. Most communications professionals are creative people, visual or verbal artists who bring imaginative ideas to the task at hand. But mere novelty doesn't guarantee success. We all have seen people whose creative ideas seem to flop around without any sense of direction, artists who can't seem to apply their artistic concept. For creativity to be effective, it must have relevance; innovative ideas need to serve a purpose. Too many campaigns never get off the ground because they are built more on novelty than on effectiveness. Some are just too cute for words; others are downright bizarre. An inside joke in the advertising industry is that sometimes agencies win creative awards but lose the account, because their innovative advertising programs didn't sell the product or their imaginative approach didn't achieve the desired results.

In the not-so-distant past, some practitioners worried that strategic planning might interfere with their creativity. But things are changing. In a crowded field of competitors all courting the same audiences, communication professionals have turned to greater use of research as a complement to the creative approach. Practitioners who once flew by the seat of their pants have found that careful planning can raise an organization's messages above the commotion of everyday life.

One thing has become clear: it really is counterproductive to separate creative and research people, because each can help the other. They share the common purpose of helping their client or their organization solve a problem. Research can nurture creative inspiration, develop ideas, keep things on target and evaluate the effectiveness of the creative endeavors.

Strategic Planning for Public Relations is built on two notions that can help make you creatively effective. First, a step-by-step system of planning is essential to learning how to develop an effective communication program. And second, effective creativity is more likely to result from careful and insightful planning than from a bolt of inspiration.

This book is for people who appreciate road maps. A map doesn't tell you where you must go; rather, it helps you explore possibilities. You consider options, make choices, select alternatives and develop contingencies. In short, you plan. Then you implement the plan by getting behind the wheel and beginning the road trip.

Creativity and Structure

Are you easily creative? *Strategic Planning for Public Relations* will help transform your artistry, insight and spontaneity into something more than mere novelty. It will lead you to consider every aspect of a strategic communication plan, helping you be creative within an effective framework.

Are you analytical and well organized? This book will enhance your innate sense of organization and structure, freeing your creativity to enhance your program effectiveness.

So it is with *Strategic Planning for Public Relations.* This book won't tell you what has to be done to develop your communication program, but it will lead you through the various decision points and options. The resulting program will be as unique as each individual student or practitioner and as tailored as each organization needs it to be. It will be a comprehensive, well thought-out program that is both deliberate and creative. Use this book to nurture your creativity and channel it to make your work more effective.

Every person is both deliberate and creative, each to a greater or lesser degree. *Strategic Planning for Public Relations* tries to help you cultivate both qualities. It helps creative people become more organized in their planning, and it helps methodical people bring more creative energy to their work. This book gives you a model—one to be considered, adapted to fit your particular circumstances and used to the extent that it helps you be both effective and creative in your communication planning.

Citations and Recommended Readings

Austin, E. W., & Pinkleton, B. E. (2001). *Strategic public relations management: Planning and managing effective communication programs.* Mahwah NJ: Lawrence Erlbaum Associates.

Botan, C. H. (1997). Ethics in strategic communication campaigns: The case for a new approach to public relations. *Journal of Business Communication, 34 (2),* 188–202.

Botan, C. H. & Soto, F. (1998). A semiotic approach to the internal functioning of publics: Implications for strategic communication and public relations. *Public Relations Review, 24 (1),* 21–44.

Burnett, J. & Moriarty, S. (1998). *Introduction to marketing communications: An integrated approach.* Upper Saddle River, NJ: Prentice Hall.

Caywood, C. L. (1995). *International handbook of public relations and corporate communications.* Hillsdale, NJ: Lawrence Erlbaum.

Caywood, C. L. (1997). *The handbook of strategic public relations and integrated communications.* New York: McGraw-Hill.

Cutlip, S. M., Center, A. H., & Broom, G. M. (2000). *Effective public relations* (8th ed.). Upper Saddle River, NJ: Prentice Hall.

Goldman, J. (1984). *Public relations in the marketing mix: Introducing vulnerability relations.* Lincolnwood, IL: NTC Business.

Gray, R. (1998). PR does the business. *Marketing (June 11),* 24–26.

Gronstedt, A. (2000). *The customer century: Lessons from world class companies in integrated marketing and communications.* New York: Routlege.

Grunig, J. E. (Ed.). (1992). *Excellence in public relations and communication management.* Hillsdale, NJ: Lawrence Erlbaum.

Grunig, J. E. & Hunt, T. (1984). *Managing public relations.* New York: Holt, Rinehart, Winston.

Harris, T. L. (2000). *Value added public relations: The secret weapon of integrated marketing.* Chicago IL: NTC Business.

Harris, T. L. (1991). *The marketer's guide to public relations: How today's top companies are using the new PR to gain a competitive edge.* New York: Wiley.

Hendrix, J. (2000). *Public relations cases* (5th ed.). Belmont, CA: Wadsworth.

Hiebert, R. W. (2000). The customer century: Lessons from world class companies in integrated marketing and communications. *Public Relations Review, Fall, 26 (3),* 381.

Holmes, P. (1998). With Bell's appointed, Y&R's commitment to integration now goes beyond lip service. *Inside PR (Sept. 28), 5 (9),* 2,10.

Kendall, R. (1999). *Public relations campaign strategies: Planning for implementation (3rd ed).* New York: HarperCollins.

Kitchen, P. J. & Schultz, D. E. (1999). A multi-country comparison of the drive for IMC. *Journal of Advertising Research, 39 (7),* 21–38.

Marston, J. E. (1963). *The nature of public relations.* New York: McGraw-Hill.

McElreath, M. (1997). *Managing systematic and ethical public relations campaigns* (2nd ed.). Madison, WI: Brown & Benchmark.

Miller, D. A. & Rose, P. B. (1994). Integrated communications: A look at reality instead of theory. *Public Relations Quarterly, 39 (11),* 13–16.

Nemec, R. (1999). PR or advertising: Who's on top? *Communication World, 16 (3),* 25–28.

Newsom, D., Turk, J. V., & Kruckeberg, D. (1999). *This is PR: The realities of public relations* (7th ed.). Belmont, CA: Wadsworth.

Ostrowski, H. (1999). Moving the measurement needle. *The Public Relations Strategist, 5 (2),* 37–39.

Schultz, D. E., Tannenbaum, S. I., & Lauterborn, R. F. (1993). *Integrated marketing communications: Pulling it together and making it work.* Lincolnwood, IL: NTC Business.

Seitel, F. P. (1998). *The practice of public relations* (7th ed.). Upper Saddle River NJ: Prentice-Hall.

Simon, R. & Zappala, J. (1996). *The public relations workbook: Writing and techniques.* Lincolnwood, IL: NTC Business.

Sirgy, M. J. (1998). *Integrated marketing communications: A systems approach.* Upper Saddle River, NJ: Prentice Hall.

Wilcox, D. L., Ault, P. H., Agee, W. K. & Cameron, G. T. (2000). *Public relations: Strategies and tactics* (6th ed.). New York: Longman.

Wilson, L. (2000). *Strategic program planning for effective public relations campaigns* (3rd ed.). Dubuque, IA: Kendall-Hunt.

FORMATIVE RESEARCH

Have you heard the phrase "shooting in the dark"? It refers to trying to hit a target without being able to see it. As a reference to strategic communication planning, "shooting in the dark" means trying to design a program without doing any research. In more common language, it means not doing your homework. In any context, it's not a good idea!

Research is the planner's homework. It's the foundation of every effective campaign for public relations and marketing communication. Your communication tactics might be innovative, but they will probably be ineffective if you don't have adequate research. Without research, you will probably end up sending messages of little value to your organization and little interest to your publics (who most likely won't be listening anyway).

How common is research in public relations and marketing communication? In a special issue of his professional newsletter *pr reporter,* Patrick Jackson summarized information from Ketchum Public Relations. The newsletter noted that 75 percent of practitioners use research to plan new programs, 58 percent to monitor progress and make mid-course revisions and 58 percent to measure outcomes (Jackson, 1994). Even during crises, when reaction time is minimal, 36 percent do research to get a quick read on public opinion. Virtually all practitioners report that they are doing more research than ever before.

The first of the four phases of the strategic planning process deals specifically with gathering and analyzing **formative research,** which is the data on which you will build your communication program. Fran Matera and Ray Artigue (2000) call this **strategic research,** the systematic gathering of information about issues and publics that affect organizations, particularly as the organization engages in the two-way models of public relations that were outlined in the Introduction of this book. In contract, they also note a second category, **tactical research,** which is information obtained to guide the production and dissemination of messages. Whereas tactical research helps public relations practitioners do their job effectively, strategic research more directly impacts on the organization's overall mission.

Step 1
Analyzing the Situation

Step 2
Analyzing the
Organization

Step 3
Analyzing the Publics

During this formative research phase, focused as it is on strategy, you will conduct a comprehensive situation analysis to gather the information needed to make wise decisions.

To accomplish this, you will gather information in three key areas: (1) the issue you are facing, (2) your organization or client, and (3) your intended publics. Specifically, you will obtain background information on the issue, assess the organization's performance and reputation and catalogue its resources, and identify and analyze key publics.

Don't let the idea of research scare you. Research begins with informal and often simple methods of gathering relevant information. Often you can look to a three-prong research program for most public relations projects:

- *Casual Research.* Recollect what is already known. Think about the situation; "pick the brains" of clients, colleagues and other helpful individuals. Interview other people with experience and expertise. Brainstorm alone or with other planners.

- *Secondary Research.* Look for existing information. Investigate organizational files to learn what already exists on the issue. Search the library for information from books, periodicals and special reports. Check for similar material on the Internet (but be wary about the validity of what you find out there). Review and analyze how other organizations handled similar situations.

- *Primary Research.* If necessary, conduct your own research. Appendix A: Applied Research Techniques will help with the basic primary research techniques such as surveys, focus groups and content analysis. The appendix also discusses the ethics of research.

As you conduct formative research, keep one thing in mind: The information you obtain through research will help in planning, but research does not offset the need for common sense. Your professional judgment remains the strongest resource you bring to the planning process. Use research to inform your professional judgment, but make decisions on relevant information as well as on your own reliable experience and professional insight.

Let's look at the three areas in which you will conduct your research, starting with an analysis of the issue.

Step 1

Analyzing the Situation

The first step in any effective public relations plan or marketing communication program is to carefully and accurately identify the situation facing your organization. This seems simple enough. Common sense, right? But sense isn't all that common, and people sometimes have different ideas about what the situation is.

Public Relations Situation

Put simply, a **situation** is a set of circumstances facing an organization. A situation is similar in meaning to a problem, if by "problem" you use the classic definition of a question needing to be addressed. For example, a situation for an automotive manufacturer might be the availability of side air bags (rather than front placement) in its new model-year cars. For a small nonprofit organization dealing with at-risk youth, a situation might be the misunderstanding and fear that some people have of these youths.

Without an early and clear statement of the situation to be addressed, you will not be able to conduct efficient research or define the goal of your communication program later in the planning process.

Note that situations are stated as nouns—*availability* of air bags, *fear* of youths. Later when we talk about organizational goals, we will add the verbs to indicate how we want to impact on these situations—*promoting* consumer acceptance of the air bags, *dispelling* the notion that all at-risk youth are dangerous. For now, simply identify the situation without commenting on it.

A situation is approached in either a positive or negative vein. That is to say, it may be identified as an *opportunity* to be embraced because it offers a potential advantage to the organization or its publics (such as the side air bags), or it may be an *obstacle* to be overcome because it limits the organization in realizing its mission (such as the fear of at-risk youth). Depending on how they assess the situation and its potential impact on the organization, two planners may look differently at the same situation—one calling it an obstacle, the other an opportunity.

Even in crisis situations, obstacles can be approached as opportunities—if the problem was not self-inflicted. Organizations under attack may use the public attention generated by the crisis to explain their values and demonstrate their quality. Pepsi fought the 1993 syringe hoax by issuing video news releases showing how its production process made it impossible to contaminate the product before it left the plant. Similarly,

The Zen of Public Relations

Sometimes a new paradigm—a different perspective—can enhance our understanding. And what could be farther from the practicality of public relations than spirituality? To better understand an important public relations concept, consider the principle of interconnectedness—the duality in which everything is related. What appears to be opposite is not separate; it is only the other end of the pole, the other side of the lake.

When we think of public relations issues, our tendency often is to identify them as either obstacles or opportunities. But such words mask an important relationship. The spirituality associated with Zen values

harmony. A problem is not necessarily something negative but rather something lacking harmony, a point of yet-unrealized potential. An obstacle puts us at a crossroads, allowing us to go this way or that, with consequences based on the choice we make.

The ultimate public relations problem is a crisis. Yet even that word gives us philosophical pause. Interestingly, the Chinese term *wei ji* and the parallel Japanese word *kiki,* both of which translate as "crisis," are made up of two characters—one meaning "danger," the other meaning "opportunity." A crisis, then, is a decision point where choices point to consequences.

Johnson & Johnson used satellite news conferences when it reintroduced Tylenol after several people were killed in 1982 when someone tampered with the over-the-counter medicine. In doing so, the company, which already enjoyed a good reputation, emerged from the crisis with even more consumer respect and confidence.

Whether the issue is viewed as an opportunity, as an obstacle or simply as an unrealized potential, the communication team and the organization's or client's leadership must come to a common understanding of the issue before it can be adequately addressed. Consider the following example of mixed signals: The executive director of an agency dealing with drug abuse wanted a public relations consultant to focus on communication between the agency and external publics such as the courts, police and probation personnel. The board of directors, on the other hand, wanted a plan for better communication among the board, staff and executive director. Significantly different expectations, to say the least! How do you think you might handle this?

In this case, the consultant asked both the director and the board to reach consensus about the central issue and to re-think what they wanted. They asked themselves what the real issues were and concluded that the focus should be on the agency's visibility and reputation with its external publics. Once this was clarified, the consultant developed a strategic plan and helped the agency implement it. The Strategic Planning Exercise on page 25 will help you clarify the issue at hand for your organization.

Ongoing communication with the research client is imperative. In their book *Applied Research Design,* Terry Hedrick, Leonard Bickman and Debra Rog (1993) recommended at least four research touch points:

1. An initial meeting with the client to develop a common understanding of the client's research needs, resources and expected uses.

2. A meeting to agree on the scope of the project, particularly its costs and other resources.

3. Following an initial review of literature and other secondary sources, a meeting to refine the research questions and discuss potential approaches and limitations.

4. A meeting for agreement on the proposed study approach.

The Background of Issues Management

F. J. Aguilar (1967) explained environmental scanning as a process of seeking "information about events and relationships in a company's outside environment, the knowledge of which would assist top management in its task of charting the company's future course of action."

W. Howard Chase (1977) coined the term "issues management," though the concept has been around since the days of Ivy Lee. But Chase pushed the concept forward, away from a catch-as-catch-can approach and toward a more systematic technique, which he outlined in five steps (Jones & Chase, 1979). Raymond Ewing (1997) expanded this into a seven-step process.

Here is a newer synthesis of the various steps in issues management:

1. Identify future issues that are likely to affect an organization. Develop an early warning scanning system that considers where the organization wants to go and looks at potential roadblocks and other outside economic, political, technological, social and other kinds of pressures on the organization. Look for forces that could help move the organization along its path.

2. Research and analyze each issue. Carefully gather as many facts as possible about these issues. Consult specialists who are particularly familiar with the issues.

3. Consider options in responding to each issue. Use creative problem-solving techniques to discover as many alternatives as possible to deal with the issue at hand. Establish your standards for success and the criteria that your organization should use to make choices among the various alternatives.

4. Develop an action plan for the best option. Select the most appropriate alternative, usually in terms of cost-effectiveness, practicality and organizational fit. Then develop a specific plan to address the issue.

5. Implement this plan, giving as much energy and resources as it warrants.

6. Evaluate the effectiveness of the response, both during its implementation when there is still time to make appropriate adjustments and when the program is completed.

Archie Boe (1979), then CEO of Allstate Insurance Companies, explained that "issues management and strategic planning are both born of the dynamic tradition in American business management that rejects the passive approach of hoping to know the future and merely adjusting to it, for an affirmative posture of *creating* the future and *fitting* the corporate enterprise into it."

After interviewing 248 public relations managers, Martha Lauzen (1997) found a link between two-way public relations and both the early detection and accurate diagnosis of issues: "The answer lies in the confluence of public relations and issues management as they become true boundary-spanning functions, acting as the eyes and ears of organizations, serving as parts of an early warning system."

For practitioners, the conclusion is that two-way public relations, which inherently involves issues management, leads to more effective outcomes and ultimately will move the practitioner into the "dominant coalition" of managers who wield power and make decisions within organizations.

Issues Management

Issues are situations that present matters of concern to organizations. **Issues management** is the process by which an organization tries to anticipate emerging issues and respond to them before they get out of hand. Like many other aspects of public relations, issues management involves potential change. For example, insurance companies, hospitals and health maintenance organizations all are trying to predict trends within the health-care industry and to have some kind of impact on the future.

Some organizations use a "best practices" approach as they weigh their options during issues management. This approach to organizational problem-solving, also known as **benchmarking,** involves research into how other organizations have handled similar situations. Peter Schwartz and Blair Gibb (1999) note three benefits of benchmarking: (1) the organizational initiative that prevents internal inertia from taking over, (2) the continual awareness of innovations coming from competitors, and (3) the introduction of fresh air from outside the organization.

Despite its name, issues management does not focus on control; neither does it involve one-way communication nor manipulation of a public. Rather, issues management helps the organization interact with its publics. It helps an organization settle the issue early or divert it, or perhaps even prevent its emergence. More likely, however, the organization will have to adjust itself to the issue, trying to maximize the benefits or at least minimize the negative impact. Public relations often drives this early warning system within an organization.

The purpose of issues management, as noted above, is to deal with issues before they get out of hand. When that happens, the issue becomes a crisis. **Crisis management** is the name given to the process by which an organization deals with out-of-control issues. But "management" is a bit of a misnomer. It's more about coping with crises.

Consider this analogy: Issues management is like steering a sailboat. You run with the wind when it happens to be blowing in the direction you want to go, and you tack to make some progress against the wind. Sometimes you stall when there is no wind. But always, you adapt to an ever-changing environment. In a crisis situation, the analogy is more like trying to ride out a storm. Often the best you can do is drop your sail, hang on, and hope the vessel is strong enough to survive without too much damage.

One thing to remember about crises: They may be sudden and unpredicted, but they seldom are unpredictable. Crises are more like volcanoes that smolder for awhile before they erupt. Warning signs abound, at least to the trained eye.

A study by the Institute for Crisis Management found that only 14 percent of companies' crises burst suddenly onto the scene, while 86 percent had been smoldering situations that eventually popped. Catastrophes represented only 9 percent of the cases. The biggest crisis categories were white-collar crime, labor disputes and mismanagement. Environmental problems, defects and recalls, and class-action lawsuits were other significant categories. All of these represent areas in which organizations should be paying attention to the quality of their performance and its impact on their reputation.

An organization committed to the concept of strategic communication is probably engaged in an ongoing issues management program that identifies crises in their early stages. Less nimble organizations that always seem to be in reactive mode are the ones likely to be caught off guard by a crisis.

Preparedness, then, is the key to effective issues management, particularly in crisis situations. James Lukaszewski (1997) focuses on a six-step program of preparedness, including early and competent leadership, a prioritized approach, strategies to preserve and/or recover the organization's reputation, implementation of effective plans, pre-authorization for the organization to act quickly on its own, and a response based on openness, responsiveness, truthfulness and empathy.

The strategic approach to crisis management might be encompassed in the following six principles.

1. *Principle of Existing Relations.*   During a crisis, communicate with employees, volunteers, stockholders, donors, community leaders, customers, government and professional authorities, and other constituent groups, as well as with colleagues. Minimally, keep everyone informed, because their continued support will be important in your rebuilding activities following the crisis. Ideally, enlist the help of some of these publics during the crisis to communicate credibly and effectively.

2. *Principle of Media-as-Ally.*   Crises invite scrutiny because they have a potential impact on a large number of people. So treat the news media as allies that provide opportunities to communicate with key publics. If the media become intrusive and/or hostile, this often is because the organization has not been forthcoming in providing legitimate information to the media and its other publics. A good pre-existing program of media relations can minimize media hostility.

3. *Principle of Reputational Priorities.*   Your top priority after safety issues is to your own reputation. Remembering this can help you focus on doing what's best for your customers, employees and other key publics. Set objectives that deal with maintaining (or if necessary, restoring) your credibility. Use the crisis as an opportunity to enhance your reputation for social responsibility with your various publics.

4. *Principle of Quick Response.*   Be accessible to your publics as quickly as possible. A standard guideline for crises that capture the immediate attention of the news media is the one-hour rule. Within an hour of learning about a crisis, the organization should have its first message available to its publics, particularly the media (which generally is the most compelling public in the early stages of an active crisis). For less attention-getting crises, an organization might be able to prepare for five or six hours before going public.

5. *Principle of Full Disclosure.*   Silence is not an acceptable response during a crisis. Without admitting fault and without speculating about facts not yet known, the organization should provide as much information as possible. The presumption should be that everything the organization knows should be made available. Specific justification should be considered internally for not releasing certain information.

Phase One

Step
1

Phase One

Step
1

6. *Principle of One Voice.* A single, trained spokesperson should represent the organization. If multiple spokespersons are needed, each should be aware of what the others are saying, and all should work together from the same set of facts and the same coordinated message.

Public Relations and Ethics

Part of your research into the situation should involve an examination of ethical aspects, particularly the basis on which practitioners and their organizations or clients make ethical decisions. You might begin by considering three classic approaches to making such determinations: deontological ethics, teleological ethics and ethical relativism.

The *deontological approach* to ethical decision making is rooted in a standard or moral code. In essence, this approach says that certain actions are, in and of themselves, good; others are bad. An example of such a code is the Public Relations Member Code of Ethics (see Appendix B: Ethical Standards), which proclaims the intrinsic value of honesty, integrity, fairness, accuracy and so on.

The *teleological approach,* on the other hand, is focused more on the impact that actions have on people. It is rooted in the notion that good results come from good

---

Ethics by Committee

Hospitals have their ethics committees, so why not public relations agencies? One agency has such a panel. At Ruder-Finn, the company's ethics committee brings together account executives with outside ethical experts such as rabbis, ministers and priests, theologians and philosophers. Their goal: to struggle with the ethical dimension of issues and then to advise management.

R-F special projects coordinator Emmanuel Tchividjian, who coordinates the committee, says the ethics team has reviewed issues such as whether the agency should continue a favorite account with the Greek National Tourist Office after a military coup in Greece. After the committee (including an ethics professor at a theological seminary) went to Greece to investigate, Ruder-Finn resigned the account because it did not want to assist a military dictatorship.

The agency also considered whether to accept a book-promotion account involving the Church of Scientology. That account was rejected because the firm did not want to be involved with what it considered a religious cult.

But Ruder-Finn did accept an account with the Swiss government over the issue of money and gold that the Nazis took from Jews during the Holocaust—a particularly sensitive issue for an agency where most of the managers and staff are Jewish. That account was accepted on the belief that much could be gained by open communication, said Tchividjian.

The committee serves to remind employees that "the bottom line is not the most important thing," explained Tchividjian. "We do have to make money, but there are values that have a higher priority."

Another ethical innovation by Ruder-Finn was borrowed from the legal profession. When the company is approached by a potential client with an issue that raises ethical concerns, the agency conducts discovery research at the client's expense, soliciting information from industry insiders and ethicists about the moral dimension of the issue. Based on the findings, Ruder-Finn may reject the client, or it may use the information to help frame the client's position on the sensitive issue.

actions; thus something is ethical when it produces good consequences. An example of this also is implied in the PRSA code, which connects the need for ethical behavior and conduct with the public interest.

A third approach, *ethical relativism,* suggests that actions are ethical to the extent they reflect particular social norms. While an advantage of this approach is respect for cultural diversity, it has the mirrored disadvantage of dominance of mainstream culture and an inability to judge the basic rightness or wrongness of actions.

Communication strategists help themselves and their organizations when they anticipate how they will approach ethical decisions. Without advance thinking, the planner often is left either with no guidelines on determining whether something is ethical or simply with an unexamined personal feeling. Neither of those choices is particularly useful.

Don't presume that you have to decide ahead of time which of the classic approaches to use. In truth, most organizations—as most individuals—slip back and forth among the three styles of ethical decision making. The value of advance thinking is that you can recognize the different foundations for determining ethical actions and responses and you can consider each approach as you make your decisions.

David Finn of Ruder-Finn public relations agency in New York City has observed that ethical decision making is not a choice between good and bad but rather a choice between two conflicting goods. The challenge is first to discern the difference and then to make an appropriate choice. In a column on ethics that he writes for *Reputation Management* magazine, Finn observed that "addressing ethical issues intelligently calls for a probing as well as an open mind" (1998).

Strategic Planning Example: Analyzing the Situation

Because it has received state permission to expand from a two-year to a four-year program, Upstate College wants to develop a strategic communication plan to deal with student enrollment and retention, financial contributions and community support.

■ ■ ■

In the wake of the highly publicized recall of a defective crib toy, Tiny Tykes Toys needs a strategic communication plan focusing on consumer confidence and the eventual expansion of its customer base.

Strategic Planning Exercise: Analyzing the Situation

To participate in this exercise, select an organization that has both your personal interest and your firsthand knowledge. For example, you might select your current business, nonprofit organization or client; a volunteer project; or an enterprise in which you were once involved. If you are a student, you might select an issue related to the college or university you attend.

Start with the basic planning questions. Careful consideration of these may satisfy your informational needs. You also may find it useful to address the more complete set of expanded planning questions. Use these to the extent that they help you get a better understanding of the situation facing your organization. If some of these questions don't seem to address your specific planning needs, skip over them.

Basic Planning Questions

1. What is the situation facing the organization?
2. What is the background of the situation?
3. What is the significance or importance of the situation?

Expanded Planning Questions

A. Existing Information

Answer the following questions based on what you know directly or what you can learn from your client or colleagues within your organization.

Background on the Issue

1. Is this the first time your organization has dealt with this situation or are you setting out to modify an existing communication program? If the latter, is this a minor modification or a major one?
2. What is the cause of this situation?
3. Is there any dispute that this is the cause?
4. What is the history of this situation?
5. What are the important facts related to this situation?
6. Does this situation involve the organization's relationship with another group?
7. If yes, what group(s)?

Consequences of the Situation

1. How important is this situation to the organization's mission?
2. How consistent is this situation with the mission statement or vision statement?
3. How serious of a response is warranted to this situation?
4. What is the likely duration of this situation: one-time, limited/short-term or ongoing/long-term?
5. Who or what is affected by this situation?
6. What predictions or trends are associated with this situation? (These can be organizational, industry-related, community relations, nation-related, etc.)
7. What potential impact can this situation make on the organization's mission or bottom line?
8. Do you consider this situation to be an opportunity (positive) or an obstacle (negative) for your organization? Why? If you consider this an obstacle, how might you turn it into an opportunity?

Resolution of the Situation

1. Might information (quality or quantity) affect how this situation is resolved?
2. How can this situation be resolved to the mutual benefit of everyone involved?
3. What priority does this situation hold for the public relations/communications staff and for the organization's top management?
4. How strong is the organization's commitment to resolving this situation?

B. Research Program

If there are any significant gaps in the existing information, you may have to conduct research to learn more about the issue. This section will guide you through consideration of that option.

1. What is the basis for the existing information noted above: previous formal research, informal or anecdotal feedback, organizational experience, personal observation, presumption/supposition by planner(s) and/or something else?
2. How accurate is this existing information?
3. How appropriate is it to conduct additional research?
4. What information remains to be obtained?
5. If the existing information is not highly reliable, consider additional research, such as the following:
   ✓ Interviews with key people within the organization
   ✓ Review of organizational literature/information
   ✓ Additional personal observation
   ✓ Interviews with external experts or opinion leaders
   ✓ Surveys with representative publics
6. What research methods will you use to obtain the needed information?

C. Research Findings

After you have conducted formal research, indicate here your findings as they shed light on the issue facing your organization, and write a brief summary of the issue facing your organization. ∎

Consensus Check

Does agreement exist within your organization about the recommended strategies within this phase of the planning process?

    If "yes," proceed to the next section.

    If "no," consider the value and/or possibility of achieving consensus before proceeding.

Step 2

Analyzing the Organization

The basis of effective communication is self-awareness. As such, strategists must have a thorough and factual understanding of their organization—its performance, its reputation and its structure—before a successful strategic communication plan can be created. They also seek to understand any factors that might limit the plan's success.

The second step of the strategic planning process involves a **public relations audit,** an analysis of the strengths and weaknesses of your organization or client. A traditional method drawn from marketing is called SWOT analysis, because it considers the organization's strengths, weaknesses, opportunities and threats. What follows here is a more elaborate analysis that focuses on three aspects of the organization: its internal environment, its public perception and its external environment.

Before moving on to the details of the analysis, it is important to point out that candor is the key to this step. To create an effective communication program, you must take an honest look at your organization, identifying its weaknesses and limitations as well as its strengths. If your organization is second best, admit it to yourself and proceed from that basis. Don't delude yourself by pretending that your organization is something it's not. No successful public relations program has ever been built on fiction, and it does not serve your purposes to overlook flaws or shortcomings within your organization. However, temper your candor with tact. Brutal or indiscriminate honesty may turn off a client or a boss.

Exhibit 2.1 shows the relationship among the various elements of a public relations audit.

Internal Environment

Because public relations involves more than words, begin the audit by looking at the organization's performance and structure, and any internal impediments to success.

Performance includes the quality of the goods and services provided by the organization, as well as the viability of the causes and ideas it espouses. The audit looks at this quality both as it is now and as it was in the past; it also considers the level of satisfaction that the organizational leadership has with this quality.

Within the topic of performance, the internal audit also looks at the organization's *niche*—its specialty, the function or role that makes the organization different from

Exhibit 2.1   The Public Relations Audit

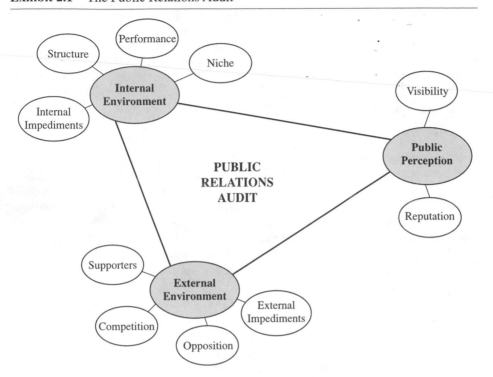

similar organizations. The word *niche* originally referred to a wall recess or alcove for displaying a vase of flowers, a religious statue, a bust or some other accent piece. In the context of public relations and marketing, a niche retains some of that original notion. It is a viewing point, the nook or cubbyhole that an organization occupies in a position for all to see.

The audit also considers the *structure* of the public relations operation within the organization. Specifically it reviews the purpose or mission of the organization as it relates to the situation at hand, as well as the role public relations plays within the organization's administration. The audit inventories organizational resources that can be marshaled for the communication program, including personnel, equipment, time and budgets. No decisions or commitments are being made at this point as to what resources to use; during the audit stage, you merely are identifying the organization's available resources as they relate to the situation to be addressed.

Internal impediments are the final part of the internal audit. Here you consider any impediments or obstacles within the organization that might limit the effectiveness of the public relations program. For example, many practitioners have expressed that their college education did not prepare them for the lack of organizational support, the need for continuing vigilance and the amount of political in-fighting that goes on within some organizations. Wounded egos, shortsighted executives, company favorites and other barriers must be considered as you develop the program.

The term *impediment* is chosen with care. An impediment is not an insurmountable barrier, such as a road blocked off for repaving. Rather it is a hindrance, more like a slow-moving truck on a country road. You can allow the truck to set the pace and remain behind it, or you can carefully and safely pass the truck and continue on your way.

Public Perception

What people think about the organization is the key focus for the public relations audit. This perception is based on both visibility and reputation.

Visibility refers to the extent to which an organization is known. More subtly, this includes whether people know about an organization, what they know about it, and how accurate this information is. Public relations practitioners can do a great deal to affect the visibility of their organization or client.

Reputation is based on visibility, but it deals with how people evaluate the information they have. It is the general prevailing sense that people have of an organization. Reputation is based on both word and deed—on the verbal, visual and behavioral messages, both planned and unplanned, that come from an organization. Though we speak of reputation as a single perception, it really can be inconsistent, varying from one - public to another and from one time to another. Reputation generally lags behind an organization's conscious attempt to affect the way people perceive it.

Generally, the stronger the organization's visibility and the more positive its reputation, the greater the ability it has to build on this positive base. On the other hand, low visibility suggests the need to create more awareness, and a poor reputation calls for efforts to rehabilitate the public perception of the organization, first by making sure the organization is offering quality performance, and then by trying to bring awareness into harmony with that performance.

Writing in Communication World, Pamela Klein noted that "psychologically, a company with a solid reputation earns the benefit of the doubt in times of crisis" (Klein, 1999). Supporting her claim, she pointed to a 1977 Ernst & Young study, "Measures That Matter," which found that 40 percent of a company's market value is based on non-financial assets, including reputation. Klein also cited a 1988 Burson-Marsteller study, "Maximizing Corporate Reputations," which reported that the CEO's reputation accounts for 40 percent of how a company is viewed by stakeholders and other publics.

This chapter's Strategic Planning Exercise: Analyzing Public Perception (page 30) contains an Image Index, a tool developed to help you determine the public perception of an organization. The index is a series of contrasting characteristics or attributes—fun or tedious, expensive or inexpensive, risky or safe—that can be applied to any organization. Obviously there is no right or wrong response to any of these characteristics, and the index does not lead to a numerical "answer." Rather, it is meant to stimulate your insights. By considering your organization in relation to these terms, you may come to an inference or a conclusion that perhaps you did not have before. In the planning process, you can use the index twice, first based on what the organization thinks of itself and later based on what its publics think of it.

External Environment

The analysis of the organization concludes with an examination of its external environment. This includes a careful look around. Who are the *supporters*—the people and groups who currently or at least potentially are likely to help the organization achieve its objectives? What groups share similar interests and values?

Also ask questions such as: Who is your competition? Who is your opposition? Are there any external impediments to your success? Research suggests that in a highly competitive environment, public relations activities often use messages and communication tactics to be persuasive, while lower levels of competition may lend themselves less to advocacy and more to relationship building. But an organization's environment also may be uneven; it may be competitive with one public while cooperative with another.

An important aspect of the external analysis is to consider the nature of any rivalry that may exist. There's a big difference between a *competitor,* who provides a similar product or service, and an *opponent,* who is fighting your organization. Consider a store selling fur coats: A competitor might be the other fur store across town, while animal-rights activists would be opponents. But even opponents come in different shapes and sizes, and planners have some important questions to ask about the nature of opposition. Are they opposed to your organization specifically or rather to a particular product or service associated with it? Do they exist primarily to work

---

Where to Get Information for an Audit

You can get information for a public relations audit from several different sources. Consider the following steps in gathering the information you will need:

1. See if past research has addressed some of the relevant issues, and obtain copies of that information.

2. Check the public information about your organization, such as your annual reports, past news releases and clipping files of published stories about your organization.

3. Ask people close to your organization if they can provide some of the necessary information from their own experience. Talk with

managers and long-term employees. Talk especially with your front-line staff, such as clerks and sales representatives, and with the key service providers, such as nurses in a hospital or teachers in a school. Ask all of these sources what customers and other people outside the organization are asking and saying.

If additional information still is needed, conduct more formal research. Begin by broadening your resources for informal research. Eventually you may find that you require more formal research techniques. (See Appendix A: Applied Research Techniques for more information on secondary and primary research.)

against you and put you out of business, or is their opposition a by-product of a product, service or cause they support? Are they mainly vocal advocates or are they activists? Are they reasonable in their opposition, or are they zealots who undertake a no-holds-barred fight?

Additionally, consider any *external impediments* such as social, political or economic factors that might interfere with your organization's ability to address the situation.

Strategic Planning Example: *Analyzing the Organization*

UPSTATE COLLEGE

Internal Environment
Upstate College is a private liberal-arts college with 2,000 students, primarily commuters and residents from within a 100-mile radius. Most of the students had average grades in high school. They selected Upstate because of its reputation for small classes, reasonable tuition and practical programs. In the past, about half the graduates went into the workforce and half transferred to four-year colleges and universities. The college has a news bureau and marketing office with a one-person staff assisted by freelancers and alumni volunteers. The office has equipment for desktop publishing, and the college publishes a weekly student newspaper and a quarterly alumni newsletter and oversees a Web site. It has only a token advertising budget.

Public Perception
Upstate College sees its reputation as being beneficial, relatively inexpensive, practical and an essential ingredient in the educational mix of this part of the state.

External Environment
Higher education has been a relatively noncompetitive environment until recent years, when lower numbers of students, fewer funds and more alternatives for students have combined to create a climate that is somewhat competitive, though not unfriendly. Competition includes a private four-year college with very high entrance standards and even higher tuition, a large state university with entrance standards similar to Upstate's and about half the tuition, and a community college with only token costs, minimal entrance requirements and a background (and continuing reputation) as a trade school. Upstate City recently has lost several major employers, and weakening family finances have begun to affect the ability of some Upstate College students to remain full-time students. Research reveals declining numbers of students in most area high schools, indicating a shrinking pool of traditional-aged candidates for college. Additionally, general research reveals growing educational opportunities for Web-based distance learning.

■ ■ ■

Internal Environment
Tiny Tykes Toys manufactures toys for infants and toddlers. It recently voluntarily recalled one of its crib toys, a plush animal doll with a shiny nose. When babies chewed on the nose, it secreted an indelible green dye into their mouths and on their faces that

lasted for several months. The dye was harmless, but the consumer lawsuits (minor) and resulting publicity (major and sensationalized) have caused a decrease in sales of other Tiny Tykes toys. The company has 130 union workers and 27 management staff. It also has a two-person public relations/marketing staff. Unrelated to the recall, but happening around the same time, a small but vocal group of employees began agitating for increased pay and shorter working hours.

Public Perception
The recall endangered the company's reputation for quality among stockholders, consumers, pediatricians and other interest groups. The defect has been eliminated in new versions of the toy. The company perceives its image as fun, low tech, inexpensive, beneficial and safe.

External Environment
The business environment for children's toys is highly competitive, and it has become more so due to increasing international rivals and the expansion into the toy market of domestic companies once associated primarily with children's clothing.

Tiny Tykes has several competitors, some of them nationally known companies with huge promotional budgets. Several of these companies have products of similar quality and cost to Tiny Tykes'; they currently enjoy a more favorable reputation because of the recall. The overall business environment for toys is a growing and highly competitive market. The dissident employee faction has the potential for contributing to a wider consumer backlash against the company.

Strategic Planning Exercise: *Analyzing the Internal Environment*

Basic Planning Questions

1. What is the quality of your organization's performance?
2. What communication resources, including budget, are available?
3. How supportive is the organization of public relations activity?

Expanded Planning Questions

A. Existing Information
Answer the following questions based on what you know directly or what you can learn from your client or colleagues within your organization.

Performance
1. What service/product do you provide related to the issue identified in the Strategic Planning Exercise in Step 1?
2. What are the criteria for determining its quality?
3. What is its quality?
4. Within the last three years, has the quality improved, remained unchanged or deteriorated?

5. How satisfied is organizational leadership with this quality?
6. What benefit or advantage does the product/service offer?
7. What problems or disadvantages are associated with this product/service?
8. What is the niche or specialty that sets you apart from competitors?
9. How has the service/product changed within the last three years?
10. How is the service/product likely to change within the next two years?
11. Should changes be introduced to improve the service/product?
12. Are organizational leaders willing to make such changes?

Structure

1. What is the purpose/mission of your organization related to this issue?
2. How does this issue fit into the organizational vision?
3. Is this expressed in a strategic business plan for your organization?
4. What communication resources are available for potential public relations/marketing communication activity: personnel, equipment, time, money and/or something else?
5. Within the next three years, are these resources likely to increase, remain unchanged or decrease?
6. How strong is the public relations/communication staff's role in the organization's decision-making process?

Internal Impediments

1. How supportive is the internal environment for public relations activities?
2. Are there any impediments or obstacles to success that come from within your organization:

   Among top management?
   - Are these impediments caused by policy/procedure?
   - Are these impediments deliberate?

   Among public relations/marketing staff?
   - Are these impediments caused by policy/procedure?
   - Are these impediments deliberate?

   Among other internal publics?
   - Are these impediments caused by policy/procedure?
   - Are these impediments deliberate?

3. If you have identified impediments, how can you overcome them?

B. Research Program

If there are any significant gaps in the existing information, you may have to conduct research to learn more about the internal environment. This section will guide you through consideration of that option.

1. What is the basis for the existing information noted above: previous formal research, informal or anecdotal feedback, organizational experience, personal observation, presumption/supposition by planner(s) and/or something else?

2. How accurate is this existing information?

3. How appropriate would it be to conduct additional research?

4. What information remains to be obtained?

5. If the existing information is not highly reliable, consider additional research, such as the following:

    ✓ Interviews with key people within the organization

    ✓ Review of organizational literature/information

    ✓ Additional personal observation

    ✓ Interviews with external experts or opinion leaders

    ✓ Surveys with representative publics

6. What research methods will you use to obtain the needed information?

C. Research Findings

After you have conducted formal research, indicate your findings as they shed light on the internal environment of your organization and write a brief summary of the internal environment. ∎

Strategic Planning Exercise: *Analyzing Public Perception*

Basic Planning Questions

1. How well known is your organization?

2. What is the reputation of your organization?

3. How do you want to affect this reputation?

Expanded Planning Questions

A. Existing Information

Answer the following questions based on what you know directly or what you can learn from your client or colleagues within your organization.

Reputation

1. How visible is your service/product?

2. How widely used is your service/product?

3. How is the product/service generally perceived?

4. How is your organization generally perceived?

5. Is the public perception about your organization correct?

6. What communication already has been done about this situation?

7.   Within the last three years, has your organization's reputation improved, remained unchanged or deteriorated?

8.   How satisfied is organizational leadership with this reputation?

Image Index
Place an "X" at the appropriate location in the following listing:

Does your organization consider its product(s) or service(s):

Contemporary	__ __ __ __ __	Traditional
Fun	__ __ __ __ __	Tedious
High Tech	__ __ __ __ __	Low Tech
Ordinary	__ __ __ __ __	Distinguished
Inexpensive	__ __ __ __ __	Expensive
Practical	__ __ __ __ __	Idealistic
Modest	__ __ __ __ __	Pretentious
Abundant	__ __ __ __ __	Scarce
Beneficial	__ __ __ __ __	Worthless
Efficient	__ __ __ __ __	Inefficient
Routine	__ __ __ __ __	Innovative
Essential	__ __ __ __ __	Luxury
Safe	__ __ __ __ __	Risky
High Quality	__ __ __ __ __	Low Quality

B. Research Program
If there are any significant gaps in the existing information, you may have to conduct research to learn more about the public perception of your organization. This section will guide you through consideration of that option.

1.   What is the basis for the existing information noted above: previous formal research, informal or anecdotal feedback, organizational experience, personal observation, presumption/supposition by planner(s) and/or something else?

2.   How reliable is this existing information?

3.   How appropriate would it be to conduct additional research?

4.   If the existing information is not highly reliable, consider additional research, such as the following:
   ✓ Interviews with key people within the organization
   ✓ Review of organizational literature/information
   ✓ Additional personal observation
   ✓ Interviews with external experts or opinion leaders
   ✓ Surveys with representative publics

C. Research Findings
After you have conducted formal research, indicate your findings as they shed light on the public perception of your organization and write a brief summary of the public perception.

Strategic Planning Exercise: *Analyzing the External Environment*

Basic Planning Questions

1. What is the major competition for your organization?
2. What significant opposition exists?
3. Is anything happening in the environment that can limit the effectiveness of the public relations program?

Expanded Planning Questions

A. Existing Information

Answer the following questions based on what you know directly or what you can learn from your client or colleagues within your organization.

Competition

1. How competitive is the external environment of your organization?
2. What other organizations compete on this issue?
3. What are their performance levels?
4. What are their reputations?
5. What are their resources?
6. What does the competition offer that you don't?
7. How has the competition changed within the last three years?
8. Within the next three years, is the competition likely to increase, remain unchanged or decrease?

Opposition

1. What groups exist with a mission to resist or hinder your organization?
2. How effective have these groups been in the past?
3. What is their reputation?
4. What are their resources?
5. How have these groups changed within the last three years?
6. How have their tactics changed?
7. Within the next three years, is the opposition likely to increase, remain unchanged or decrease?

External Impediments

1. Is the environment in which you are operating currently growing, stable, declining or unpredictable?
2. What changes, if any, are projected for this environment?
3. What impediments deal with customers?
4. What impediments deal with regulators?
5. What impediments have financial or economic origins?
6. What impediments have political origins?
7. What impediments originate in society at large?

B. Research Program

If there are any significant gaps in the existing information, you may have to conduct research to learn more about the external environment of your organization. This section will guide you through consideration of that option.

1. What is the basis for the existing information noted above: previous formal research, informal or anecdotal feedback, organizational experience, personal observation, presumption/supposition by planner(s) and/or something else?

2. How reliable is this existing information?

3. How appropriate would it be to conduct additional research?

4. What information remains to be obtained?

5. If the existing information is not highly reliable, consider additional research, such as the following:
   - ✓ Review of organizational literature/information
   - ✓ Review of other published information (books, periodicals, etc.)
   - ✓ Review of electronic information (Internet, CD-ROM, etc.)
   - ✓ Interviews with key people within the organization
   - ✓ Interviews with external experts or opinion leaders
   - ✓ Focus groups with representative publics
   - ✓ Surveys with representative publics
   - ✓ Content analysis of materials

6. What research methods will you use to obtain the needed information?

C. Research Findings

After you have conducted formal research, indicate your findings as they shed light on the external environment of your organization and write a brief summary of the external environment.

Consensus Check ✓

Does agreement exist within your organization about these observations on the internal and external environment?

   If "yes," proceed to the next section.

   If "no," consider the value and/or possibility of achieving consensus before proceeding.

Step 3

Analyzing the Publics

The planner's ability to identify and analyze publics is the cornerstone of an effective integrated communication campaign. The two elements of this—identification and analysis—are equally important. First, the planner needs to address the right group of people, so as not to squander organizational resources or miss opportunities to interact with important publics. Second, the planner must carefully examine each public in order to develop a strategy to communicate effectively.

What Is a Public?

What do we mean by the term *public?* One definition that still holds true is the classic definition given by social philosopher John Dewey in *The Public and Its Problems* (1927): A **public** is a group of people that shares a common interest vis-à-vis an organization, recognizes its significance and sets out to do something about it. Publics are homogeneous in that they are similar in their interests and characteristics. They usually are aware of the situation and their relationship with the organization. They think the issue is relevant, and they are at least potentially organized or energized to act on the issue.

Publics, Markets and Audiences

Don't confuse publics with *markets* (also called *market segments*), which are a particular type of public. Think of the difference as that between family and friends.

A public is like your family. You don't pick them; they just are—like generous Cousin Ezekiel and crazy Aunt Bertie. Publics may be helpful or annoying, friendly or not, but an organization must deal with them regardless. Publics exist because of their interaction and interdependency with an organization or because both they and the organization face a common issue.

A market, on the other hand, is more like your friends. You pick them; they pick you. Most people select friends on the basis of shared interests and common values. Organizations develop their markets among those publics with whom they intend to conduct business or generate support and participation. As segments of a particular population, markets include people with characteristics (age, income, lifestyle and so on) that can help the organization achieve its bottom line. For public relations purposes, *bottom line* is a term that identifies an organization's mission or fundamental goal (selling cars, educating students, serving patients and so on).

Also, don't confuse publics with *audiences,* which merely are people who pay attention to a particular medium of communication and receive messages through it. An organization's relationship with an audience is usually brief, such as the length of time it takes to read an article or listen to a speech—much more temporary than its relationship with a public.

Let's take the example of a presidential candidate. The audience includes people who actually hear a speech or watch a television commercial. Some members of these audiences may be part of one of the candidate's wider publics, such as registered party members. But other registered members may not be among any of the candidate's audiences, though they remain part of an important public. Additionally, other members of the candidate's audiences may be members of a different public, such as voters registered with the opposing political party.

Usually audiences are not homogeneous but more often are *aggregates*—mere assortments of individuals with perhaps nothing in common other than their use of a particular communication medium. However, the more specialized the communication medium is, the more likely its audiences are to have in common both demographic characteristics (such as age and income) and psychographic characteristics (such as lifestyles and values). So the audience of very specialized media may coincide with your public.

Audiences are relatively unimportant to your planning for strategic communication. Most organizations want to develop mutually beneficial relationships with their various publics, such as a company that hopes to create satisfactory business relationships with its customers. Strategic communicators try to reach those audiences who also happen to include their publics and markets.

Characteristics of a Public

When you begin to identify publics, how do you know what to look for? Here are five important characteristics of a public:

1. *A public is distinguishable.* It is a recognizable grouping of individuals, though not necessarily a recognized organization or formal group. For example, a jewelry company might want to promote itself to "everyone who wants to buy expensive jewelry." But that isn't a public, because it does not identify a particular group of people. Rather the jeweler might identify its public as "people with incomes above $50,000 who are marking life events such as birthdays, anniversaries, graduations and so on."

2. *A public is homogeneous.* Its members share common traits and features. They may not know each other, but they have enough in common for you to treat them as a group. For example, all college professors who teach criminal justice courses do not know each other and may not even agree on specific

issues within the discipline. But their collective interest in and knowledge of criminal justice warrant their identification as a public by an organization such as the National Association of Chiefs of Police. Consumer publics identified as market segments traditionally have been identified by common traits, such as the baby boomers, ethnics, seniors, Generation Xers and so on.

3. *A public is important to your organization.*   Not every identifiable group and certainly not every isolated individual is important to your organization's success. Some can safely be overlooked or deferred. Strategists for public relations and marketing communication are most interested in those publics that can significantly impact on an organization's bottom line and affect its progress toward achieving its mission.

4. *A public is large enough to matter.*   Make sure your public is large enough to warrant strategic attention and the possible use of public media. If you are dealing with only a few people, they don't constitute a public and your programming tactics would probably be limited to personal communication tools. Having said that, don't hesitate to treat a small group of individuals as a public if they are vital to the organization. For example, a lobbying effort may be directed at a handful of members of an important senate committee.

5. *A public is reachable.*   A public is a group with which you are able to interact and communicate. For example, it is easy for a community college to reach potential students, because most are concentrated within a small geographic area. It is more difficult for a university of world renown to reach potential students, because they are thinly scattered throughout the world.

Identifying Publics

Good communication planning calls for the identification of an organization's various publics. As pointed out at the beginning of this section, there is no such thing as a *general public*. Rather, each public is linked with the organization in a unique relationship.

Four Categories of Publics

Over the years, sociologists studying organizations have developed the useful concept of *linkages,* which are the patterns of relationships that exist between an organization and its various publics (see Esman, 1972; Evan, 1976; and Grunig & Hunt, 1984). While various categories of linkages have been suggested, this book presents four useful categories of linkages: customers, producers, enablers and limiters. If you consider these linkages, you are likely to identify each relevant public for your program. Exhibit 3.1 shows the relationship among the various public relations linkages.

Customers are those publics that receive the products or services of an organization, such as current or potential consumers, purchasers, clients, students, patients, fans, patrons, shoppers, parishioners, members and so on. This category also includes *secondary customers,* who are the customers of your customers, such as the companies and graduate schools to which a college's graduating seniors apply.

Exhibit 3.1   Categories of Publics

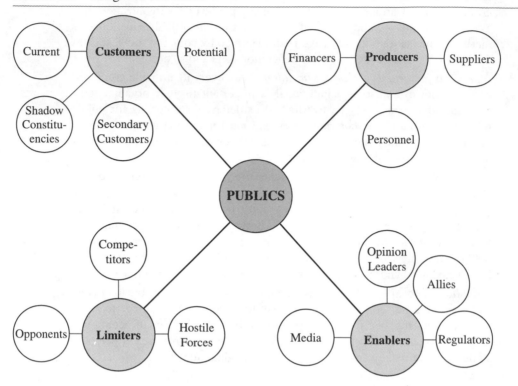

The category of customers also includes what has been called *shadow constituencies* (Mau & Dennis, 1994), people who may not have a direct link with the organization's products or services but who can affect the perception of an organization. For example, if hard times force a high-tech company known for its philanthropy to cut back on charitable contributions to the arts, members of the arts community may vocally criticize the company, adding to its problems.

Those publics that provide input to the organization are called **producers.** These include personnel such as employees, volunteers and unions; producers of needed materials such as suppliers; and producers of the financial resources such as backers, donors and stockholders.

Enablers are those publics that serve as regulators by setting the norms or standards for the organization (such as professional associations or governmental agencies), opinion leaders with influence over potential customers (such as stockbrokers and analysts), and groups that otherwise help make the organization successful (such as the media). Other groups of publics include allies, which the organization may be able to work with on cooperative projects and to construct parallel interests.

Those publics that in some way reduce or undermine the success of an organization (such as competitors, opponents and hostile forces) are known as **limiters.** The same

A Typology of Publics

Here are some examples of the common families of publics appropriate to various public relations or marketing communication situations. Let this list spark your creative thinking about identifying publics relevant to your organization.

Customers

    Occasional/Regular

    Current/Potential/Former

    Competitive/Loyal

    Age, Ethnicity, Spending Potential or another variable

    Members/Casual Customers

    Secondary Customers

    Shadow Constituencies

Producers

    Employees/Volunteers

    Veteran/Novice

    Volunteers: Leadership/Grassroot

    Line/Staff

    Management/Nonmanagement

        Management: Upper/Mid

        Nonmanagement: Supervisory/Staff/
            Maintenance/Production/Uniformed

    Management/Union

    Families/Retirees

    Investors/Shareholders

    Donors/Foundations/Grantors

    Current/Potential/Former

Enablers

    Community Leaders:

        Governmental/Professional/Business/Union/
            Educational/Religious/Ethnic

Organizations: Service/Professional/Religious/
    Social/Ethnic/Cultural/Political/Environmental/
    Activist

Industry Association/Regulatory Agencies/
    Accreditation Bodies

Professional Experts/Consultants/Analysts

Government Bodies

    Town/City/County/State/Federal

    Elective/Appointive

    Legislative/Executive/Judicial

    Staff/Advisory/Committee/Departmental

Diplomatic: Embassy/Consulate

Military/Civilian

Media: Local/State/Regional/National/
    International

    Specialized:

        Professional/Financial/Consumer/
            Religious/Ethnic/Trade/Advocacy/
            Academic

    Availability: General/Limited/Restricted

    Print/Broadcast/Computer

    Print: Newspapers/Magazines/Newsletters

    Newspapers: Daily/Nondaily

    Electronic: Television/Radio

        Television: Broadcast/Cable

        Radio: AM/FM; Commercial/Public

    Computer: News Groups/Web Sites

Limiters

    Competitors

    Opponents

    Activists

    Hostile Forces

activist groups that were cited above as potential enablers can become limiting publics when the organization is unable to walk in step with them. Likewise, an unfriendly newspaper or television station can become a limiting public.

Having identified major categories of publics, the next step is to look at each of them in more detail. By more narrowly identifying our publics, we can understand them better. For example, a university embarking on a recruiting campaign can't simply identify potential students as a public. That is too broad a category, because there are so many different kinds of potential students. Rather, it might classify its publics as high-school students, junior-college transfers, returning adult learners, employed people seeking retraining and professional development, underserved minorities, perhaps even recreational learners. Each of these publics might have very different characteristics, and if the university is to be effective it must deal with each public individually.

We also want to eliminate from consideration groups that are not publics, having no present or impending relationship with an organization and thus no mutual consequences. For example, college students would not be a public for a travel agency specializing in senior-citizen bus tours. The best advice in dealing with groups that are not publics is don't—don't waste time and money trying to communicate with people who have no reasonable or relevant relationship with your organization or no interest in your products or services.

Key Publics

Sometimes the task of selecting publics for a strategic communication program is an easy one. In many situations, the appropriate public is quite evident—a manufacturing plant seeking to increase productivity looks to its employees; a church wanting to increase contributions looks to its congregation; a politician seeking re-election targets voters in his or her district.

A major part of developing an effective communication campaign is to identify the appropriate specific publics, called **key publics** or **strategic publics.** (This book generally uses the term "key publics" to classify those specific publics that the planner identifies as being most important to the public relations activity. Other books sometimes use the term "target public," though this seems to suggest that the public is merely a bull's-eye for the organization's darts rather than part of a reciprocal relationship.)

Key publics are the people you want to engage in a communication process. Don't allow yourself to be general here. The manufacturing plant may not need to address all of its employees. Some already are very productive; others are new and still learning their responsibilities, so an accent on productivity could hinder their progress. Instead, the company may focus on a particular work shift to increase productivity. Likewise, the church may raise funds primarily among its affluent parishioners, and the politician may aim the re-election campaign particularly toward senior citizens who vote.

If key publics are not readily obvious to your planning team, the examples and exercises that follow can help you identify them systematically and objectively. After you have identified your many publics, you will select those that are particularly important for the situation you are working on. These key publics often number from two to five, though this could increase considerably with complex issues.

Readers coming from a background in marketing should be forewarned: The tendency in marketing has been to identify objectives before selecting key publics.

However, *Strategic Planning for Public Relations* uses the publics-before-objectives order for three reasons: (1) the first two steps in the planning process have already helped you identify the focus for your planning; (2) publics exist in a relationship with an organization even prior to any objectives for impacting that relationship; and (3) objectives are relevant only when they link an organization's goals with a particular public.

Intercessory Publics and Opinion Leaders

In everyday situations, it is not uncommon to ask a friend to put in a good word for us with someone we want to impress. We do this to get dates, jobs and good deals on stereos. This practice is often called *networking*. But the more appropriate term is *intercession,* which basically means using an influential go-between. Accordingly, an *intercessor* is a person who presents your case to another, especially to someone with whom the intercessor has some influence.

What's common in everyday life is also found in public relations activity. An organization often will address itself not only to its key publics but also to groups who already are in contact with that public. These **intercessory publics** serve as an influential bridge between an organization and its publics. In many planning situations, some of the publics listed as enablers can function as intercessory publics, because they already have the attention and respect of the ultimate public.

Take the news media, for example. In most public relations activities, the media are not the public you are finally trying to reach. Rather they are a first point of contact, providing a means to reach another public, such as music lovers whom an opera company might identify as one of its key publics. In this case the media, particularly their music critics, already have the attention of the music lovers, who presumably read and appreciate the reviews. So the public relations practitioner sets out to inform, interest and impress the critic.

As another example, consider an organization providing job training to high-school dropouts in an inner-city area. The organization might find through research that coaches in community centers and ministers in urban churches can be intercessory publics. These people share the organization's interest in helping the young adults who left school early, and they often hold the confidence of the young people. The job-training agency could direct some attention toward coaches and ministers, increasing their knowledge of the program and the benefits it offers the community and the participants. Properly orchestrated, coaches and ministers could become vocal supporters and even unofficial recruiters for the job-training program.

In addition to intercessory publics, we sometimes deal with intercessory individuals. Usually we call these people **opinion leaders,** men and women who have a particular influence over an organization's publics. Research provides some guidance into working with people who will carry an organization's messages to others. Paul Lazarsfeld's two-step flow of communication theory (Lazarsfeld et al., 1944) and the multi-step flow theory that evolved from it observe that the media influence opinion leaders, who in turn influence other people. Everett Rogers' diffusion of innovations theory (1995) noted that people who are quick to try new ideas or products are influential with latecomers to the innovation.

An opinion leader is an influential role model who has the respect and confidence of the public. Members of publics look to opinion leaders as they obtain information, form attitudes and opinions, and determine action. Opinion leaders are particularly useful because they generate *word-of-mouth support,* perhaps the most effective type of communication precisely because opinion leaders are independent. That is, they do not speak under the auspices of the organization, nor do they directly benefit from it. Because of this independence they are often quite believable.

Where can you find an opinion leader? Ask. Look around. Research the publics. You will find *formal opinion leaders* with structured roles, such as elected or appointed officials, and *informal opinion leaders,* who exert influence simply because they are informed, articulate and recognized leaders on a particular issue. For both, their influence is based on existing relationships, real or perceived. Examples of these are family, neighborhoods, political parties, ethnicity and shared lifestyle, social or professional interests. Opinion leaders may be global or local. For example, informal opinion leaders might include talk-show hosts such as Oprah Winfrey or Dr. Laura Schlesinger, or they might be local people like an opinionated clerk at the corner store or a well-read neighbor.

Some opinion leaders fall into the category of *vocal activists,* people who are linked to particular issues and who are known are advocates for their cause. While some activists can be dismissed as single-issue zealots, most are perceived as both independent and critical, and their support can add credibility to an organization's message.

Opinion leaders may have some characteristics different from your publics. Researchers with the Roper Organization found that people who are identified as opinion leaders prefer reading over television as a source of their information ("Opinion leaders," 1992). They also initiate action on topics of interest, such as by writing letters to the editor, attending public meetings and rallies, or working with activist groups.

Strategic Planning Example: Identifying Publics

- *Customers* include students and in most cases parents. Potential customers are academically average high-school students or employed people seeking an education. Secondary customers include eventual employers and (with the program expansion) graduate schools.
- *Producers* include the faculty and administration, alumni and other donors, as well as banks and other financial aid programs.
- *Enablers* include the state education department and the media (state and local). Opinion leaders include guidance counselors and career counselors.
- *Limiters* include other area colleges and universities as well as banks cutting back on student loans.

After due consideration, *key publics* for this campaign are identified as students, guidance counselors and alumni.

■ ■ ■

- *Customers* include parents, grandparents and other purchasers of baby toys.
- *Producers* include employees (both union and management), stockholders and suppliers.
- *Enablers* include other members of the American Toy Institute, financial media, family-and child-oriented media and consumer protection agencies (which are increasing their regulation of toy manufacturers). Opinion leaders for customers include pediatricians, early childhood educators, child psychologists and consumer groups.
- *Limiters* include other toy companies (especially importers of cheap toys), a consumer activist group threatening a boycott and a faction of disgruntled employees challenging the union and encouraging a walkout.

After due consideration, *key publics* for this campaign are identified as employees, parents and other purchasers, family and child media and consumer protection agencies.

Phase One

**Step
3**

Strategic Planning Exercise: *Identifying Publics*

Basic Planning Questions

1.   Who are the major publics for your organization?
2.   Who are the key publics for this situation?
3.   Who are the intercessory publics or major opinion leaders?

Expanded Planning Questions

A. Existing Information
Answer the following questions based on what you know directly or what you can learn from your client or colleagues within your organization.

Customers
1.   Who are your primary customers?
2.   Who are your secondary customers (who uses the products or services of your primary customers)?
3.   How have your customers changed within the last three years?
4.   How are your customers likely to change within the next three years?

Producers
1.   Who produces your service/product?
2.   Who provides your organization with services and materials?
3.   Who provides money?
4.   How have your producers changed within the last three years?
5.   How are your producers likely to change within the next three years?

Enablers
1.   Who are opinion leaders among your customers?
2.   Who are your colleagues?

3. Who are your regulators?

4. How have regulators helped you within the last three years?

5. With whom do you have contracts or agreements?

6. What media are available to you?

7. How have the media helped you in the last three years?

8. How have your enablers changed within the last three years?

9. How are your enablers likely to change within the next three years?

Limiters

1. Who are your competitors?

2. Who are your opponents?

3. What type of opponents are they: advocates, dissidents, activists or zealots?

4. Who can stop you or slow you down?

5. How have your limiters changed within the last three years?

6. How are your limiters likely to change within the next three years?

Intercessory Publics and Opinion Leaders

1. What publics are in a position of influence with your key publics?

2. How likely is it that they will speak for your organization's position?

3. Who are formal opinion leaders for this audience: elected government officials, appointed government officials or someone else?

4. How likely is it that they will speak for your organization's position?

5. Who are informal opinion leaders for this audience: family leaders, neighborhood leaders, occupational leaders, religious leaders, ethnic leaders and/or community leaders?

6. How likely is it that they will speak for your organization's position?

7. Who are vocal activists on this issue?

8. How close is their position on this issue vis-à-vis the organization's?

9. How likely is it that they will speak for your organization's position?

B. Research Program

If there are any significant gaps in the existing information, you may have to conduct research to learn more about your organization's various publics. This section will guide you through consideration of that option.

1. What is the basis for the existing information noted above: previous formal research, informal or anecdotal feedback, organizational experience, personal observation, presumption/supposition by planner(s) and/or something else?

2. How reliable is this existing information?

3. How appropriate would it be to conduct additional research?

4. What information remains to be obtained?

5. If the existing information is not highly reliable, consider additional research, such as the following:

    ✓ Review of organizational literature/information

    ✓ Review of other published information (books, periodicals, etc.)

    ✓ Interviews with key people within the organization

    ✓ Interviews with external experts or opinion leaders

    ✓ Focus groups with representative publics

    ✓ Surveys with representative publics

6. What research methods will you use to obtain the needed information?

C. Research Findings
After you have conducted formal research, indicate your findings as they shed light on the organization's publics.

Identifying Key Publics

Based on the issue you identified in Step 1: Analyzing the Situation, as well as the above information and insights about your various publics, select several that warrant particular attention. These become your key publics as you address this issue.

While all your publics are important for some situations, not all are worth your attention as you deal with the situation at hand. For example, the college's recruiting program may not need to involve its graduates, and the toy company's competitors may not be a significant public in a campaign to regain consumer confidence.

The Strategic Planning Example and Exercise that follow present a worksheet which can help you be objective in identifying key publics. This worksheet can also be a useful tool any time you must set priorities among various options. It provides a process for objectively ranking the importance of various items under consideration. Use it now to establish priorities among the publics you identified. You may find it appropriate to rearrange your listing of publics, either by dividing a public that seems be too general or by grouping several related publics.

The score that emerges from the worksheet is the basis on which you will identify your key publics. Generally, you will select the publics with the highest scores, subject of course to some second-guessing based on common sense.

Strategic Planning Example: **Identifying Key Publics**

Eleven publics were identified for Upstate College: students, parents, eventual employers, graduate schools, faculty, alumni and donors, state education department, media, other colleges and universities, banks, and administration. These are listed and

UPSTATE COLLEGE

Exhibit 3.2   Upstate College Priority Worksheet

K Administration	J Banks	I Other Schools	H Media	G State Education Dept.	F Alumni and Donors	E Faculty	D Graduate Schools	C Employers	B Parents	
A^2	A^2	A^2	A^1	A^2	A^1	A^2	A^2	A^2	A^1	**A** *Students* ⑰
B^1	B^1	B^1	H^2	B^1	F^1	B^1	D^1	B^1	X	**B** *Parents* ⑥
C^3	C^3	C^1	H^3	C^1	F^2	E^2	C^1	X	X	**C** *Employers* ⑨
D^1	D^1	D^2	H^3	G^1	F^3	E^3	X	X	X	**D** *Graduate Schools* ④
E^2	E^3	E^3	E^1	E^3	F^1	X	X	X	X	**E** *Faculty* ⑰
F^3	F^3	F^3	H^1	F^3	X	X	X	X	X	**F** *Alumni and Donors* ⑲
G^1	G^1	G^1	H^3	X	X	X	X	X	X	**G** *State Education Dept.* ④
H^2	H^3	H^3	X	X	X	X	X	X	X	**H** *Media* ⑳
K^1	I^1	X	X	X	X	X	X	X	X	**I** *Other Schools* ①
K^1	X	X	X	X	X	X	X	X	X	**J** *Banks* ⓪

prioritized in Exhibit 3.2. (What the numbers mean in Exhibit 3.2 and how they were assigned will be explained in the following Strategic Planning Exercise.)

On the issue of expanding to a four-year program, Upstate College's key publics score as follows:

Key Public	Prioritized Score
Media	20 points
Alumni and other donors	19 points
Students	17 points
Faculty	17 points
Eventual employers	9 points

Other publics not selected as being particularly important on this issue include parents (6 points), who can be addressed along with students; graduate schools (4 points), which can be addressed along with eventual employers; administration (2), which can be addressed along with faculty; the state education department (4 points), which already has been addressed through the expansion process; and other colleges (1 point) and banks (2 points), which do not need to be addressed in this program.

■ ■ ■

Eight publics for Tiny Tykes Toys were identified: parents and other purchasers, child-care professionals (including pediatricians, educators and psychologists), consumer groups/consumer protection agencies, employees, stockholders, American Toy Institute, media and competitors—a regrouping of publics previously identified. These are listed and prioritized in Exhibit 3.3. (Again, the numbers in the exhibit will be explained in the pages that follow.)

On the issue of increasing consumer confidence and expanding customer base in the wake of the crib toy recall, Tiny Tykes's key publics and their scores are:

Key Public	Prioritized Score
Child-care professionals	13 points
Parents and other purchasers	10 points
Consumer organizations/agencies	10 points
Media	9 points
Employees	9 points

Other publics not selected as being strategic on this issue include stockholders (5 points), who could be addressed in part through the media or in combination with employees; the American Toy Institute (3 points), which could be addressed through the media; and competitors (0 points), which do not need to be addressed specifically except through the media.

Exhibit 3.3 Tiny Tykes Toys Priority Worksheet

K	J	I	H Competitors	G Media	F American Toy Institute	E Stockholders	D Employees	C Consumer Groups	B Child-Care Professionals	
			A^3	G^1	A^2	A^2	A^2	C^2	A^1	**A** Parents/Purchasers ⑩
			B^3	G^1	B^3	B^3	B^3	B^1	X	**B** Child-Care Professionals ⑬
			C^3	G^1	C^3	C^2	D^1	X	X	**C** Consumer Groups ⑩
			D^3	D^1	D^3	D^1	X	X	X	**D** Employees ⑨
			E^2	E^1	E^2	X	X	X	X	**E** Stockholders ⑤
			F^3	G^3	X	X	X	X	X	**F** American Toy Institute ③
			G^3	X	X	X	X	X	X	**G** Media ⑨
			X	X	X	X	X	X	X	**H** Competitors ⓪
		X	X	X	X	X	X	X	X	**I**
	X	X	X	X	X	X	X	X	X	**J**

Strategic Planning Exercise: *Identifying Key Publics*

A. Directions for Use

1. On the Priority Worksheet (Exhibit 3.4), first assign a letter from A to K to each public you want to compare. The worksheet will accommodate 11 choices at a time; the order of listing is of no consequence. List each of the publics in the spaces marked A, B, C . . . J along the right-hand column and the spaces marked B, C, D . . . K along the top row. Note that choices A and K are not duplicated in the listings. Also record the key public names on the Scoring Chart (Exhibit 3.5).

2. Comparing each possible combination of items—AB, AC, AD, AE . . . BC, BD, BE, BF, etc.—mark the letter of the item you think is the more important public. In each box, also enter a comparative rating number (for example, A^1 or C^3) using the following scale: 1 = slightly stronger preference; 2 = moderately stronger preference; 3 = much stronger preference.

3. When all possible pairs are considered, add the rating numbers for each letter. Enter this number on the Scoring Chart. If just one person is setting the priorities, enter the number in the Total column. If more than one person is setting the priority, enter the numbers for each person in columns in the Scoring Chart, beginning at the left. Add these and enter the sum in the Total column. For the average, divide this total by the number of persons.

4. The resulting sore provides a sense of the priority being given to each individual item.

Exhibit 3.4 Priority Worksheet

K	J	I	H	G	F	E	D	C	B	
										A
									X	B
								X	X	C
							X	X	X	D
						X	X	X	X	E
					X	X	X	X	X	F
				X	X	X	X	X	X	G
			X	X	X	X	X	X	X	H
		X	X	X	X	X	X	X	X	I
	X	X	X	X	X	X	X	X	X	J

Exhibit 3.5   Scoring Chart

		Rating 1	Rating 2	Rating 3	Rating 4	Rating 5	Rating 6	Rating 7	Total	Average
	A									
	B									
	C									
	D									
	E									
	F									
	G									
	H									
	I									
	J									
	K									

Phase One

Step 3

B. Interpreting the Data

The highest scores in the Priority Worksheet indicate those publics that you consider most important. These generally become your key publics. If you are inclined to add publics that you did not score high, or disregard publics that you did score high, reconsider your criteria. Select a manageable number of key publics to be addressed by this campaign. As a general rule, try to select between two and five different publics. To offset bias or shortsightedness among planners, it is always an advantage to have a team discuss the various publics and rank them, rather than for an individual to do this alone. ■

Consensus Check ✓

Does agreement exist within your organization about the appropriateness of these key publics as groups to be addressed by an integrated communication campaign?
   If "yes," proceed to the next section.
   If "no," consider the need and/or possibility of achieving consensus before proceeding.

Analyzing Key Publics

Careful analysis of each key public is the cornerstone of the research phase. The more information and insight you bring to this step, the more effective your overall program will be. The idea behind this step is to allow the planner to "get inside the mind" of the organization's key publics. Much of this information can be obtained through informal research such as interviews and brainstorming; some of it may require more formal research techniques such as focus groups and surveys. (See Appendix A:

Applied Research Techniques for more information on these research methods.) Through formal and informal research, as well as good sense, the planner carefully examines each public.

One of the most important ways of analyzing a public is to consider the consequences it has on the organization and, conversely, the consequences the organization has on the public—actively or at least potentially. In a very real way, consequences create publics, and our public relations involvement with publics often is guided by an analysis of how real and obvious those consequences are.

In this step, you will reconsider the general information uncovered in Step 2: Analyzing the Organization and apply it to each key public. You'll want to note the public's stage of development and its key characteristics. Each of these topics is discussed below.

Stages of Development

Publics are not fixed in concrete; rather, they are fluid and evolving. Grunig and Hunt (1984) identified four stages of publics: nonpublics, latent publics, aware publics and active publics. To this list, a fifth type can be added: apathetic publics. The relationship of each stage can be seen in Exhibit 3.6, where the solid arrow points to the changes that can be encouraged by effective public relations activity, and the dotted arrow shows changes that may evolve, with or without public relations input. Let's look at each type of public.

Exhibit 3.6   Stages of Publics and Their Relationships

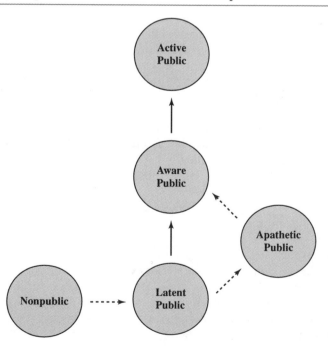

Nonpublic.   A **nonpublic** is a group that does not share any issues with the organization, and no real consequences exist to or from the organization. At this level and this time, this group simply is of no significance to the organization. For example, a nonpublic for an animal adoption shelter would be people who live in apartments that don't allow pets. The logical public relations response for this public is observation, periodically monitoring the situation to see if it changes.

Latent Public.   A **latent public** shares an issue with the organization but does not yet recognize this situation or its potential. You might call it an embryonic public, because it has much potential but as yet no self-awareness. For the animal adoption shelter, senior citizens who would appreciate companionship would be a latent public. An organization's public relations response is to plan communication to enhance its relationship with this public.

Apathetic Public.   A public that faces an issue, knows it and simply doesn't care is an **apathetic public.** To this public, the issue is not important enough to warrant its attention, and the consequences are not perceived as being important. This can be frustrating for an organization, but properly identifying an apathetic public may help the organization reframe its message to overcome the apathy. An apathetic public for the animal adoption shelter might be people who don't particularly like pets. The public relations response to such a public is to monitor the situation carefully, for it could change quickly if the issue begins to capture the public imagination. Meanwhile, the organization also should develop plans to communicate with the apathetic public, trying to transform its apathy into interest. But realize that changing negative attitudes and opinions is a difficult task.

Aware Public.   An **aware public** recognizes that it shares an issue and perceives the consequences as being relevant, but it is not organized to discuss and act on the issue. An aware public for the animal adoption agency may be people who have learned that psychologists believe the companionship of pets improves the quality of life for senior citizens. The public relations response is to initiate proactive communication, providing information about the issue, stressing its significance to the public and presenting the organization's opinion or intended action. At this stage the organization can control the tone and themes of the message.

Active Public.   In the final stage of its development, an **active public** has reached the fullness of what we identify as a public. It is discussing and acting on the shared issue. For the animal shelter, an active public might be the local chapter of a senior citizen organization that is actively encouraging senior citizens to adopt pets. In friendly circumstances such as the one described above, this can be an opportunity for building coalitions. In confrontational situations, on the other hand, an organization's response to an active public generally is reactive communication, responding to questions and often to accusations or even active opposition. At this stage the tone or message themes are no longer controlled by the organization but instead by the active public.

Publics may be active on all of the issues important to the organization, active only on some popular issues, or active on single and often controversial issues. One animal-rights group, for example, may confine its activism to local issues involving impounding of stray animals, neutering, credentialing of pet owners and other issues related to a particular shelter, while a similar group may be active on a wider range of issues, including testing of medicines and cosmetics on animals, fur and leather fashion, hunting and fishing, and vegetarianism.

Key Characteristics

After noting the stages of development, look at each public in reference to the following five key characteristics: the public relations situation, the organization, the public's communication behavior, its demographics and its personality.

- **Public Relations Situation.**   Assess the public's wants, interests, needs and expectations related to the issue, as well as what it does not want or need. Consider relevant attitudes of the public. Maslow's hierarchy of needs (1970) and Packard's hidden needs (1964) outlined on subsequent pages in this chapter, can be useful aids in considering the interests and needs of publics.

- **Organization.**   Consider each key public's relationship with the organization—how your organization impacts on the public and vice versa. Also consider the visibility and reputation of your organization with this public.

- **Communication.**   Study the public's communication habits, such as the media or communication channels it uses. Identify people who might be credible message sources for this public and who are its opinion leaders. Also indicate whether the public is seeking information on the issue. This assessment will have major impact later when you choose your communication tools, because information seekers are likely to initiate communication or make use of tactics that require their direct involvement.

- **Demographics.**   Identify demographic traits such as age, income, gender, socioeconomic status or other relevant information about this public.

- **Personality Preferences.**   Consider the psychological and temperamental preferences of this key public. Appraise the relative merits of logical versus emotional appeals. Knowing something about the personality of the key public and then tailoring messages to fit such psychological preferences can make communication more persuasive and more effective. During this step of the planning process, use the Personality Preferences Index, located in Strategic Planning Exercise: Analyzing Key Publics, to look more closely at each of your key publics. Later in the process you will consider ways to craft messages that complement these preferences.

Like other aspects of this research phase, your answers to the questions posed in this exercise may be tentative and based on presumptions or common sense. However, insight from the organization's experience can prove useful as you begin to understand

Maslow's Hierarchy of Needs

Psychologist Abraham Maslow (1970) developed a drive-motive theory or a theory of human motivation, commonly known as the *hierarchy of needs*. This theory offers an understanding not only of what people need but also of what Maslow called *prepotency,* the ordered internal relationship among needs by which more basic needs must be addressed first. His theory is presented visually as a two-part pyramid of five levels, with the stronger needs at the base.

The base of the pyramid includes four levels of needs:

- Basic physiological needs deal with oxygen, food and water, and sleep, as well as with basic sexual urges.
- Safety needs include shelter, employment, economic stability and other kinds of security.
- Love needs focus on belonging, family, friends and group identity.
- Esteem needs deal with respect and appreciation.

The top of the pyramid includes the fifth level of needs, self-actualization. This category deals with achieving potential and with the pursuit of ideals such as spirituality and perfection, beauty and art, peace and understanding.

Note that the self-actualization needs are in a category by themselves, separated from the others. Whereas a deficiency in any of the four levels in the

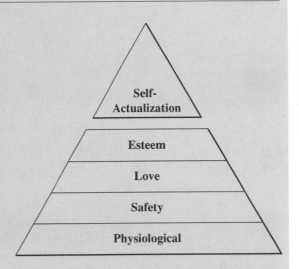

base of the pyramid can create tension within a person, the final level adds to the person's freedom to explore and achieve his or her greatest ambitions.

Needs at each level of Maslow's pyramid are interrelated and can be fulfilled in different ways, and recent research suggests that Maslow's categories of motivations are more appropriate than their particular order. For example, while the sex urge is a basic physiological need, it is an urge that can be controlled. For some people, sex also can have application to a feeling of security; for others, it may be less associated with basic physiological needs and more with a sense of love and belongingness, self-esteem, even spirituality.

the communication preferences of your key publics. Eventually you may decide that formal research is needed; if so, consult Appendix A: Applied Research Techniques for some research suggestions.

Rethinking Your Publics

Occasionally, this part of the process may point out a problem in your earlier identification of key publics. If you find it difficult to identify traits common to your public, perhaps you have defined the public in terms that are too general.

Packard's Hidden Needs

In his book *The Hidden Persuaders,* Vance Packard (1964) noted that advertising and public relations agencies sometimes turn to psychology to gain insight into why people react to messages in certain ways. He identified eight motivations that persuaders often tap to sell products, social messages and political candidates:

- Need for emotional security
- Need for reassurance of worth
- Need for ego gratification
- Need for creative outlets
- Need for love objects
- Need for a sense of power
- Need for roots
- Need for immortality

Consider the plight of a group of planners developing a program to raise awareness, generate interest and obtain funds to help save the African elephant from human predators. The planners misidentified as one of their key publics "people with incomes above $50,000." As they analyzed their publics, the planners were having difficulty because they could not identify the mindset of this public, which was too broad and had no common traits other than income. It wasn't really a public at all but rather a demographic description, and not a very comprehensive one at that.

So the planners redefined their public more specifically as "people with incomes above $50,000 who have a pre-existing interest in issues of conservation and endangered animals." With that criteria, the planning team then could develop a profile of its public: people who want to help animals, expect a workable plan for doing so, want an organization with a proven track record, have an altruistic spirit to make the world a better place and have the financial ability to contribute to this cause. This redefinition also helped the planners avoid wasting resources by trying to convert people to a cause in which they had no interest.

Review the analysis of each of your publics and consider whether the information you have generated should lead you to make any changes in the lineup. For example, a public that earlier seemed to be key may now be shown to be too apathetic to justify your action at this time.

Remember: Planning is a flexible process. The conclusion of Step 3 is one point along the way where you should rethink your plans so far, adjusting them based on the information becoming available to you through continuing research.

Benefit Statement

Conclude your analysis of the publics with a **benefit statement** that briefly indicates the benefit or advantage your product or service can offer this public, or how you can help satisfy its need or solve its problems. For example, the benefit a community foundation might offer its donors could be stated as follows:

*Equity Foundation offers donors the opportunity to pool their money with the
donations of others, thereby compounding small donations into larger, more
effective grants.*

In more of a marketing vein, the benefit an online bookstore might offer college and
university students could be written as:

*Cyber Booksellers can assure university students that it can provide class textbooks at
discount prices with immediate delivery.*

This concludes the Formative Research phase of the strategic planning process.
Having completed these steps, you now should have some clear insights about your
issue, the status of your organization as it relates to this issue and your various publics
and their relationship to your organization. You are probably already beginning to get
ideas about how to communicate with these publics. Jot down whatever may come to
mind, but don't worry yet about developing specific program tactics. The next phase of
the planning process addresses strategic questions, such as the outcomes you want to
accomplish and the approach you will take.

Strategic Planning Example: Analyzing Key Publics

Upstate College alumni and other donors are a latent public that can quickly become an
active one.

Analysis of Key Characteristics
Issue: The alumni/donor public will appreciate this program expansion; this public
needs only basic information to instill appreciation.

Organization: This key public provides continued support for the college, while the college provides this public with a sense of pride and value of the academic degree. This
public has high knowledge of the college and thinks favorably about it. It can be called
upon for action. It shares the college's self-image as a high-quality institution.

Communication: This public occasionally participates in on-campus activities and
has access to general news media as well as the college newsletter. The college
has a mailing list of alumni and donors. This public is not actively seeking
information because an announcement has not yet been made, but it could be
expected to be attentive to information. Credible sources include famous alumni and
respected donors.

Personality Preferences: This is a diverse group, with some members having a
preference for messages that are factual, logical and reality based, while others prefer
messages focused on ideas, sentiment and vision.

Demographics: Wide range. Higher than average in education. No particular significance in demographics other than geographic proximity to college.

Benefit Statement

Upstate College can provide information to alumni about the college's successes and strengths, giving alumni a sense of pride in their alma mater and an opportunity to help build on those strengths.

(Note: Similar analyses would be made for each individual key public you have identified.)

Tiny Tykes Toy Company employees are an active public.

Analysis of Key Characteristics

Issue: The employee public wants to see the company reputation improved and wants to see the employer regarded as a leader in the industry. Morale has been affected negatively by the recall: employee public does not want to feel bad about making an inferior infant product, needs information on quality and safety, and cautiously expects leadership from the company in improving quality and reputation.

Organization: This employee public ultimately affects the quality and productivity of the company, knows the company intimately and has organized for action through unions and through work teams. The company affects this public through continuing employment. Employees do not share management's self-image of being beneficial and safe.

Communication: The employee public gets its information in an interpersonal setting with management and supervisors, can be reached through direct mailings and newsletters, and also receives information from local news media. This public is actively seeking info on this issue. Credible sources include management officials, veteran employees and union leaders.

Personality Preferences: Rank-and-file employees are accustomed to receiving messages based on fact, certainty and logical analysis. Managers may be more disposed to messages that also deal with vision.

Demographics: The employee public spans age groups but has in common lower-middle class socioeconomic/educational background; there are many ethnic workers. Most members of this public do not personally use company products, but often in the past they have given the products as gifts to family and friends.

Benefit Statement

Tiny Tykes can provide information that will give employees renewed purpose and pride about the quality and safety of its products.

(Note: Similar analyses would be made for each individual key public you have identified.)

Strategic Planning Exercise: *Analyzing Key Publics*

Basic Planning Questions

1. What is the nature and type of each key public?
2. What are the major wants, interests, needs and expectations of each public?
3. What benefits can you offer this public?

Expanded Planning Questions

A. Existing Information

Answer the following questions based on what you know directly or what you can learn from your client or colleagues within your organization.

1. Who is your key public?
2. Indicate the category below that best describes that key public at this time and consider the public relations response indicated.

Category	Response
Latent public Faces an obstacle or opportunity vis-à-vis the organization Does not yet recognize this situation or its potential	Monitor the situation, anticipating change toward awareness. Meanwhile, begin to plan a communication process to provide information about the issue, explain its significance to the public and present your organization's opinion or intended action.
Apathetic public Recognizes an obstacle or opportunity vis-à-vis the organization Does not perceive this issue as important or interesting	Monitor the situation, looking for any change toward perceiving the relevance of the issue. Meanwhile, begin to plan a communication process to provide information about the issue, explain its significance to the public and present your organization's opinion or intended action.
Aware public Recognizes an obstacle or opportunity vis-à-vis the organization Not yet organized for action	Initiate a communication process to present the issue, explain its significance to the public, and present your organization's opinion or intended action.
Active public Recognizes an obstacle or opportunity vis-à-vis the organization Preparing to organize or already organized for action	Because you did not communicate sooner, you must now engage in reactive communication, responding to questions and perhaps to criticism and accusations without being able to control the tone or themes of the messages.

Phase One

Step
3

Analysis of Key Characteristics
Issue

1.   What does this key public know about this issue?
2.   What does this public think about this issue?
3.   What does this public want on this issue?
4.   What does this public not want on this issue?
5.   What does this public need on this issue?
6.   What problem(s) does this public have related to this issue?
7.   What does this public expect from the organization vis-à-vis this issue?
8.   How free does this public see itself to act on this issue?

Organization (including product/service)

1.   How does or how might the key public affect your organization?
2.   How does or how might your organization affect this public?
3.   What does this public know about your organization?
4.   How accurate is this information (compared to information in Step 2)?
5.   What does this public think about your organization?
6.   How satisfied are you with this attitude?
7.   What does this public expect from your organization?
8.   How much loyalty does this public have for your organization?
9.   How organized or ready for action on this issue is this public?
10. How influential does this public see itself as being within the organization?
11. How influential does the organization see this public as being?
12. Place an "X" at the appropriate location in the following listing:

Does this key public think the image of your organization's product(s) or service(s) are:

Contemporary	—	—	—	—	—	Traditional
Fun	—	—	—	—	—	Tedious
High Tech	—	—	—	—	—	Low Tech
Ordinary	—	—	—	—	—	Distinguished
Expensive	—	—	—	—	—	Inexpensive
Idealistic	—	—	—	—	—	Practical
Modest	—	—	—	—	—	Pretentious
Scarce	—	—	—	—	—	Abundant
Worthless	—	—	—	—	—	Beneficial
Efficient	—	—	—	—	—	Inefficient
Ordinary	—	—	—	—	—	Innovative
Essential	—	—	—	—	—	Luxury
Risky	—	—	—	—	—	Safe
High Quality	—	—	—	—	—	Low Quality

13. What are the similarities and the differences between your organization's self-image in the exercise on page 36 and the image of it held by this public?

Communication

1. What media do this public use among each of the following: personal communication channels, organizational media, news media and advertising/promotional media?
2. Is this public actively seeking information on this issue?
3. How likely is this public to act on information it receives?
4. Who are credible sources and opinion leaders for this public?

Demographics/Psychographics

1. What is the average age of members of your key public?
2. Where is your key public located geographically?
3. What is the socioeconomic status of your key public?
4. What products or services does your key public commonly use?
5. What are the cultural/ethnic/religious traits of your key public?
6. What is the education level of your key public?
7. What lifestyle traits does your key public have?
8. Are there other relevant characteristics about your key public?

Personality Preferences

Place an "X" at the appropriate location in the following listings:

Information Presentation: Is this public more likely to prefer messages:

that present.............................facts	___ ___ ___ ___ ___	or ideas
that deal with.....................certainty	___ ___ ___ ___ ___	or possibility
that point toward..................what is	___ ___ ___ ___ ___	or what might be
that give information..........literally	___ ___ ___ ___ ___	or figuratively
that depict................common sense	___ ___ ___ ___ ___	or a vision

Information Content: Is this public more likely to prefer messages:

that are addressed to..........the head	___ ___ ___ ___ ___	or the heart
that are based on.....logic and reason	___ ___ ___ ___ ___	or sentiment
that seek to.........convince the mind	___ ___ ___ ___ ___	or touch the emotions
that lead one to....................analyze	___ ___ ___ ___ ___	or sympathize
that focus on..........things or groups	___ ___ ___ ___ ___	or individuals

Benefits

1. What benefit or advantage does your organization offer each public?
2. How does this benefit differ from the benefits available from other organizations?

B. Research Program

If there are any significant gaps in the existing information, you may have to conduct research to learn more about your organization's various publics. This section will guide you through consideration of that option.

1. What is the basis for existing information noted above: previous formal research, informal or anecdotal feedback, organizational experience, personal observation, presumption/supposition by planner(s) and/or something else?
2. How reliable is this existing information?
3. How appropriate would it be to conduct additional research?
4. What information remains to be obtained?
5. If the existing information is not highly reliable, consider additional research, such as the following:
    ✓ Interviews with key people within the organization
    ✓ Interviews with external experts or opinion leaders
    ✓ Review of organizational literature/information
    ✓ Review of other published information (books, periodicals, etc.)
    ✓ Review of electronic information (Internet, CD-ROM, etc.)
    ✓ Focus groups with representative publics
    ✓ Surveys with representative publics
6. What research methods will you use to obtain the needed information?

C. Research Findings

After you have conducted formal research, indicate your findings as they shed light on the organization's publics. Also, write a benefit statement about how the organization can satisfy the wants and needs, address the interests, and solve the problems of this particular key public.

Consensus Check ✓

Does agreement exist within your organization on the analysis of these key publics?
    If "yes," proceed to the next section.
    If "no," consider the need and/or possibility of achieving consensus before proceeding.

Citations and Recommended Readings

Aguilar, F. J. (1967). *Scanning the business environment*. New York: Macmillan.

Boe, A. R. (1979). Fitting the corporation to the future. *Public Relations Quarterly, (Winter), 24*, 4–6.

Chase, W. H. (1977). Public issue management: The new science. *Public Relations Journal, 33 (10)*, 25–26.

Dewey, J. (1927). *The public and its problems*. Chicago: Swallow.

Esman, M. J. (1972). The elements of institution building. In J. W. Eaton (Ed.), *Institution building and development* (pp. 78–90). Beverly Hills, CA: Sage.

Evan, W. H. (1976). *Interorganizational relations*. New York: Penguin.

Ewing, R. P. (1997). Issues management: Managing trends through the issues life cycle. In C. C. Caywood (Ed.), *The handbook of strategic public relations and integrated communications* (pp. 173–188). New York: McGraw-Hill.

Finn, D. (1998). How ethical can we be? www.ruderfinn.com/persp/how_ethical.html.

Grunig, J. E. & Hunt, T. (1984). *Managing public relations*. New York: Holt, Rinehart, Winston.

Hedrick, T. E., Bickman, L., & Rog, D. J. (1993). *Applied social research methods: 32. Applied research design: A practical guide*. Newbury Park, CA: Sage.

Jackson, P. (Ed.). (1994). *Practical, actionable research for public relations purposes. Exeter*, NH: PR Publishing.

Jones, B. L. & Chase, W. H. (1979). Managing public policy issues. *Public Relations Review, 5*, 2–23.

Klein, P. (1999). Measure what matters. *Communication World, 16 (9)*, 32+.

Lauzen, M. (1997). Understanding the relation between public relations and issues management. *Journal of Public Relations Research, 9 (1)*, 65–82.

Lazarsfeld, P. F., Berelson, B., & Gaudet, H. (1944). *The people's choice*. New York: Columbia University.

Lukaszewski, J. E. (1997). Establishing individual and corporate crisis communication standards: The principles and protocols. *Public Relations Quarterly, 42 (fall)* 7–14.

Maslow, A. (1970). *Motivation and personality* (2nd ed.). New York: Harper & Row.

Matera, F. R. & Artigue, R. J. (2000). *Public relations campaign and techniques, Building bridges into the 21st century*. Boston: Allyn & Bacon.

Mau, R. R. & Dennis, L. B. (1994). Companies ignore shadow constituencies at their peril. *Public Relations Journal, (May)*, 10–11.

Opinion leaders: New study outlines how to reach them. (1992). *PR Reporter, (Oct. 5), 35 (38)*, 1–3.

Packard, V. (1964). *The hidden persuaders*. New York: Pocket Books.

Rogers, E. (1995). *The diffusion of innovations* (4th ed.). New York: Free Press.

Schwartz, P. & Gibb, B. (1999). *When good companies do bad things: Responsibility and risk in an age of globalization*. New York: John Wiley & Sons.

STRATEGY

Strategy is the heart of planning for public relations, marketing communication and related areas. All the embodiments of strategic communication are rooted in the research already undertaken in the previous phase and growing toward the eventual choice of communication tactics. Just as rushing through the research phase would have jeopardized the foundation on which to build your public relations or marketing communication plan, failing to give adequate attention to strategy can result in weak messages and pointless activity.

Phase Two deals with mapping your course toward your overall destination, deciding both where to go and how to get there. By building on research from Phase One of the planning process, you will anchor your program in the mission or vision of the organization and you will maintain a fixed gaze on your chosen publics.

The entire strategic process is interrelated and interdependent: Goals guide the development of objectives, which in turn help drive decisions about what persuasive strategies to use and what tactics to employ to address the problem or opportunity. In their classic book *Public Relations Management by Objectives*, Norman Nager and T. Harrell Allen (1984) used the analogy of transportation: Goals provide the direction while objectives pinpoint the destination.

Step 4
Establishing Goals
and Objectives

Step 5
Formulating Action
and Response Strategies

Step 6
Using Effective
Communication

Establishing Goals and Objectives

What is strategy? Simply stated, **strategy** is the organization's overall plan. It is how the organization decides what and how it wants to achieve. It has a dual focus: the action of the organization (both proactive and responsive) and the content of its messages (theme, source, content and tone). Refer to strategy in the singular, because each program should have a single, unifying strategy. To better understand strategy, you first need to understand the twin concepts of goals and objectives.

Before we begin, it should be noted that public relations and marketing strategists generally make the distinction that goals are general and global while objectives are specific. However, some advertisers and other specialists rooted in business disciplines either reverse the meanings of the terms or use them interchangeably. In your actual practice, you may find people applying different definitions to these terms, so make sure you understand what the words mean. In *Strategic Planning for Public Relations,* we use the terms as they are outlined below.

Goals

A **goal** is a statement rooted in the organization's mission or vision. Using everyday language, a goal acknowledges the issue and sketches out how the organization hopes to see it settled. A goal is stated in general terms and lacks measures; these will come later in the objectives.

In general, communication goals can be categorized as relating to three different types of management situations: **reputation management goals,** which deal with the identity and perception of the organization; **relationship management goals,** which focus on how the organization connects with its publics; and **task management goals,** which are concerned with getting certain things done. It is unnecessary, even unlikely, that every campaign will have each type of goal. Planners mix and match these as they consider appropriate to their specific campaign.

Who sets an organization's communication goals? Public relations managers do, usually as an implementation of the organization's strategic plans, which ideally the public relations people have had a hand in developing. These overall plans may be identified in global documents, such as the strategic business plan, or in implementation guidelines, such as an annual strategic plan or a statement of priorities or directions.

Examples of Public Relations Goals

Reputation Management Goals

- Improve the company's reputation within the industry.
- Enhance the hospital's prestige as the leading center for sports medicine.
- Reinforce the organization's image with potential donors or investors.
- Strengthen the agency's standing within the environmental movement.

Relationship Management Goals

- Promote better appreciation of the firm among potential clients.
- Enhance the relationship between the company and its customers.

- Maintain a favorable relationship amid social or organizational changes.

Task Management Goals

- Increase public support for organizational goals.
- Advance social change on a particular issue.
- Impact public behavior on matters associated with the organization's mission.
- Create a favorable climate for our client among regulatory agencies.
- Attract a sell-out crowd to a fundraising concert.

Whatever source they use, strategic communication planners first should note how the organization defines what it means to be successful and then develop goals that grow out of this definition.

Positioning

Before you set the specific objectives, it is useful to determine the position you seek with your publics. Having previously identified the relevant public relations situation in Step 1 and now having set your goal, ask yourself this simple question: What do we want people to think about us?

A successful approach to strategic communication in a competitive environment is to position the organization according to its own particular niche. **Positioning** is the process of managing how an organization distinguishes itself with a unique meaning in the mind of its publics—that is, how it wants to be seen and known by its publics, especially as distinct from its competitors.

The concept of distinctiveness is an important one for all organizations—large and small businesses, educational and charitable organizations, political and human service groups, hospitals, churches and sports teams. In most settings, organizations are known more by their distinctiveness than by their similarities. For example, in the field of higher education, a dozen or more schools might be located in a particular metropolitan area. Each is likely to be identified by its unique characteristics: the large public university, the small church-affiliated college, the high-priced two-year private school, the community college with an open admissions policy, the mid-sized public institution that

---

Examples of Positioning Statements

Here are some examples of how various organizations might try to position themselves. Note how each statement highlights a desired attribute of the organization by implying a distinction from competitors.

- The leader that sets industry standards
- The best value, reflecting low cost and high quality

- The most economical
- The most expensive and most prestigious
- The hospital preferred by women
- The family-friendly restaurant
- The environmentally friendly brand

---

used to be a teachers college and so on. Problems can occur when the niche is not unique. For example, if your school is one of two small church-affiliated colleges in the area, you will emphasize what distinguishes it from the other, such as lower costs, a suburban campus, graduate degrees, evening/weekend programs or the particular denomination or religious community that sponsors the college.

Organizations have found that the concept of positioning is fluid, and some organizations have made successful attempts to reposition themselves to keep pace with a changing environment. Consider Oldsmobile's "Not Your Father's" campaign, which tried to reposition Olds from a line of cars popular with middle-aged and senior drivers to one fashionable for a younger generation.

How does an organization position itself? First it conducts and analyzes research to determine just how it is perceived by various publics; it also considers the position held by its major competitors. The organization then identifies the position it would like to hold, seeking to distinguish itself from its competition. Having done all this, the organization develops a strategy to modify its current position or perhaps simply to maintain the niche it already holds.

Don't confuse the public relations concept of positioning with its use in marketing, where the term refers to the competitive approach for a persuasive message (i.e., positioning according to features such as customer focus, competitive advantage, social responsibility, lifestyle or product attribute). When we talk about positioning in public relations, we refer less to the presentation of the products or services and the messages about these, and more to perception—how we want our organization to be seen by our publics. As Al Ries and Jack Trout explained in *Positioning: The Battle for Your Mind* (1987), "Positioning is not what you do to a product. Positioning is what you do to the mind of the prospect."

Objectives

An **objective** is a statement emerging from the organization's goals. It is a clear and measurable statement, written to point the way toward particular levels of awareness, acceptance or action. Objectives often are established by communication managers

Phase Two

Step
4

responding to broader organizational goals. Like goals, objectives deal with intended outcomes rather than procedures for reaching them. A single goal may be the basis for several objectives.

Management by objectives (MBO) is the process by which effective and efficient organizations plan their activities. While the term MBO has somewhat gone out of favor, the approach remains useful. From this perspective, organizations don't merely do things because they *can* be done; rather, they act because managers have determined that they *should* act in order to further the work of the organization in some strategic and measurable way.

For instance, a reactive and nonstrategic public relations or marketing communication department may decide that because the company has just purchased desktop publishing software, a scanner and a color printer, the department should prepare new promotional brochures and flyers. But a proactive and strategic department would first determine what needs to be done, say, to promote more understanding among potential customers. Then it might conclude that it should produce new brochures and buy the equipment with which to do so. This is managing by objectives, not by whim.

As you can see by this example, objectives help direct the organization to act in ways that make sense. Objectives also serve another purpose: They give the planner a reference point for evaluation. When you measure the effectiveness of your strategic communication program in Step 9, you will look back to your objectives and ask whether your messages and actions have had the effect you wanted. You will then scrutinize each objective to determine if you have been successful.

Standards for Objectives

Eleven specific criteria can be identified for public relations objectives. These will become the elements of effective and practical objectives.

Goal-Rooted.   Objectives are rooted in goals. They are based on the organization's goal statements, which themselves grow out of the mission or vision that the organization has defined for itself. Thus, objectives are responsive to a particular issue that the organization has recognized as important to its effectiveness. Public relations objectives often reflect organizational strategic plans and they may parallel financial projections, marketing ambitions, advertising or promotional expectations and objectives associated with other aspects of the organization.

Public-Focused.   Objectives are linked firmly to a particular public and are based on the wants, interests and needs of that public. Objectives for one public may be similar to those for another public, but each must be distinct.

Impact-Oriented.   Objectives are oriented toward the impact they can achieve. They define the effect you hope to make on your public, focusing not on the tools but on intended accomplishments. In writing objectives, avoid statements that deal with disseminating news releases, producing brochures, holding open houses and other activities that belong with an eventual tactical response to the objectives. Such nonobjective language is dangerous; it confuses activity with achievement and can lull you into a false belief that because you are *doing* something, you are also *accomplishing* something.

Linked to Research.   Good objectives aren't just pulled out of the air; they are tied to research. For example, if research shows that 40 percent of your key public is familiar with your organization's products or services, your objective might be to increase that to 50 percent—not because 50 percent is a magic number, but because it represents a reasonable ambition based on the current situation, as seen through research.

Explicit.   Objectives are explicit and clearly defined. There is no room for varying interpretations; everyone involved in the public relations activity must share a common understanding of where the objective is leading. Don't use ambiguous verbs such as *educate, inform, promote,* or *encourage.* Instead use strong action verbs to state your objective specifically. For example, instead of saying you want "to enhance knowledge of recycling," say your objective is "to increase residents' understanding of the benefits of recycling by 25 percent."

Measurable.   Objectives are precise and quantifiable, with clear measures that state the degree of change being sought. Avoid adjectives such as *appropriate* or *reasonable.* Instead state, for example, that you want "to effect a 20 percent increase in recycling of paper products during the next six months."

Time-Definite.   Objectives are time-definite. Objectives include a clear indication of a time frame—*by December 31, within six months, during the spring semester* and so on. Avoid ambiguous phrases such as "in the near future" or "as soon as possible." Some objectives may indicate a graduated or multi-stage approach to the time frame. For example, you might indicate that a certain effect is expected in two stages: a 50 percent increase within six months, a 75 percent increase after the first year.

Singular.   Objectives are singular, focusing on one desired response from one public. Don't state in an objective that you want "to increase awareness *and* generate positive attitudes." You may be successful in the first effort but unsuccessful in the latter, making it difficult to evaluate your effectiveness. Most strategic communication programs will have multiple objectives, but each objective should be stated separately.

Challenging.   Objectives are challenging. They stretch the organization a bit and inspire people to action. Don't aim at too safe a level of achievement or you might find that you haven't really achieved anything worthwhile. Instead, set your sights high.

Attainable.   Though challenging, objectives also need to be attainable and doable according to the organization's needs and resources, so don't set your sights *too* high. Seldom is it realistic to aim for 100 percent of anything, whether you are trying to expand your customer base or reduce opposition. Don't create a recipe for failure by setting objectives that are unattainable.

Acceptable.   Objectives are acceptable. They enjoy the understanding and support of the entire organizational team—public relations or communication staff, managers, right up to the CEO. The value of objectives is not that they are written but rather that they are used. They need the strength of consensus if they are to be useful to both your organization's planners and its decision makers.

Hierarchy of Objectives

An ordered hierarchy exists among communication objectives, growing out of a logical progression through three stages of persuasion: awareness, acceptance and action. Awareness begins the process, increasing gradually; interest then builds in stages, and attitudes bloom into an acceptable choice; verbal and physical actions are modified in steps. Note how this model parallels the AIDA pattern (*a*ttention, *i*nterest, *d*esire and *a*ction), the hierarchy of effects associated with advertising since the 1920s (Lipstein, 1985). This model also echoes the standard communication effects of cognitive, affective and conative changes (Ray, 1973).

   Whatever formula you use, remember: In your enthusiasm to resolve the issue, don't let your expectations get ahead of themselves. Develop a plan that will take your communication with each of your publics through each of the necessary steps. Make sure your message first will reach your target publics, who will then agree with this message and finally act on it.

Examples of Awareness Objectives

- To have an effect on the awareness of senior citizens in Lake County, specifically to increase their understanding of the advantages Upstate Health Program offers senior patients (60 percent of senior residents within six months)
- To have an effect on the awareness of legislators from the Southern Tier, specifically to

increase their understanding of the environmental impact that House Bill 311 will have on their constituents (all 15 Republican and 7 Democratic members of the House Committee on Environmental Affairs within two months)

Examples of Acceptance Objectives

- To have an effect on the acceptance of senior citizens in Lake County, specifically to increase their positive attitudes toward membership in Upstate Health Program (30 percent within six months)
- To have an effect on the acceptance of legislators from the Southern Tier, specifically to gain

their interest in the environmental issues addressed by House Bill 311 (10 of the 15 Republican members and 6 of the 7 Democratic members of the House committee within two months)

Examples of Action Objectives

- To have an effect on the action of senior citizens in Lake County, specifically to obtain an increase in their membership in Upstate Health Program (10 percent within six months, and an additional 10 percent within a year)
- To have an effect on the action of legislators from the Southern Tier, specifically for them to

vote in favor of House Bill 311 (6 of the 15 Republican members of the House and 6 of the 7 Democratic members of the House committee when the bill comes to a vote next spring)

Awareness Objectives. **Awareness objectives** focus on information, providing the *cognitive,* or thinking, component of the message. These objectives specify what information you want your publics first to be exposed to and then to know, understand and remember. Awareness objectives particularly deal with dissemination and message exposure, comprehension and retention.

When would you use awareness objectives? They are appropriate for transmitting purely functional information, for communicating on noncontroversial issues, and for the early stages of any communication campaign. Awareness objectives also are particularly useful for publicity and public information models of public relations. In general, awareness objectives impact on *what* people know about an organization and its products, services and ideas.

Acceptance Objectives. **Acceptance objectives** deal with the *affective,* or feeling, part of the message—how people respond emotionally to information they have received. These objectives indicate the level of interest or the kind of attitude an organization hopes to generate among its publics. Acceptance objectives are useful in several situations: forming interests and attitudes where none existed before, reinforcing existing interests and attitudes, and changing existing positive or negative attitudes.

Acceptance objectives are particularly important amid controversy and in persuasive situations using the advocacy (or asymmetrical) model of public relations. They impact on *how* people feel about the organization and its products, services and ideas. Notice how the examples of acceptance objectives above differ from the earlier examples of awareness objectives.

Action Objectives. **Action objectives** take aim at expression and conduct, providing the *conative,* or behavioral, element of the message. These objectives offer two types of action: opinion (verbal action) and behavior (physical action). Action objectives may attempt to create new behaviors or change existing ones, positively or negatively. They should be focused on the organization's bottom line, such as customer buying, student enrollment, donor giving, fan attendance and so on. Remember that action objectives serve not only as persuasive objectives that encourage audiences to act according to the wishes of the organization but also as objectives for building consensus and enhancing the relationship between the organization and its publics. Note how the action objectives shown in the example box differ from the earlier examples of awareness and acceptance objectives.

Just as most issues will have more than one goal, so too will each goal have a full set of objectives, at least one in each of the above categories for each of the identified publics. Too often, efforts in public relations and marketing communication fail because they pursue the awareness objectives and then jump quickly to action, forgetting the important bridge step of generating acceptance.

Indeed, acceptance is the key to effective public relations, and its importance has been obvious since Edward Bernays first talked about engineering consent. This implies more than merely disseminating information. We must take time to foster the public's acceptance of both our organization and its messages, through means that are both practical and ethical. For example, in a political campaign, news releases and debates may be useful tools to achieve awareness. But awareness doesn't guarantee acceptance, and through the release or the debate voters may actually learn that they disagree with the candidate on important issues. Thus successful awareness efforts could actually hinder your client—just one of life's little ironies.

Another paradox: As this hierarchy moves along the awareness–acceptance–action path from least important to most important objectives, the impact on the public will inevitably decrease. You might achieve an 80 percent awareness level among the public,

---

Writing Public Relations Objectives

Public   Objective for _____

Category   To have an effect on   ❏ Awareness
                                              ❏ Acceptance
                                              ❏ Action

Direction   Specifically, to   ❏ Create, Generate
                                              ❏ Increase, Maximize
                                              ❏ Maintain, Reinforce
                                              ❏ Decrease, Minimize

Effect   (w/ awareness category)   ❏ Attention   or   ❏ Comprehension
                (w/ acceptance category)   ❏ Interest   or   ❏ ± Attitude
                (w/ action category)   ❏ Opinion   or   ❏ Behavior

Focus   About _____

Performance Measure _____

Time Period _____

for example, but perhaps only 40 percent will accept the message favorably, and only 15 or 20 percent may act on it.

Writing Public Relations Objectives

In writing objectives, keep your language simple and brief. Avoid jargon. Use everyday language and strong action verbs. As part of the planning for a strategic communication campaign, objectives are not meant to be presented publicly, so don't worry if they begin to sound repetitious and formulaic. The guidelines listed below will help you deal with each important element of a well-stated objective.

Step 1: Public. Indicate the public to whom the objective is addressed.

Step 2: Category. Indicate the category of the objective: awareness, acceptance or action.

Step 3: Direction. Indicate the direction of movement you are seeking—that is, to *create* or *generate* something new that did not exist before; to *increase* or *maximize* a condition; to *maintain* effects or *reinforce* current conditions; or to *decrease* or *minimize* something.

Notice that *elimination* is not an option because a public relations undertaking is seldom able to completely remove an unwanted effect; the best we can hope to do is minimize it.

Another observation: Public relations and other strategic communication programs too often don't pay enough attention to maintaining current support. While

Phase Two

Step
4

Examples of Poorly Worded Objectives

Here are two examples of poorly worded objectives. Note how each can be improved.

- To interest more people in recycling as soon as possible

Critique: No public is indicated, merely a vague reference to "people"; "interest" is a nonspecific term; "recycling" is a very broad concept; the focus is on communication activity rather than impact on the public; measurement is nonexistent and the time frame is imprecise, thus making the objective impossible to measure.

Restatement: To have an effect on the action of Allen County residents, specifically to generate telephone inquiries to the CLEAN-UP help line (100 telephone calls during the first two months of the campaign; 400 telephone calls within six months)

- To prepare a new brochure about recycling

Critique: No public is indicated; the focus is on communication activity rather than impact on the public; measurement and time frame are not included.

Restatement: To have an effect on the awareness of students at Oxford State University, specifically to increase the awareness of students about the benefits of recycling on campus (45 percent during the fall semester) generating new support is important, don't overlook those who currently help you and agree with you.

Step 4: Specific Effect. Indicate the specific effect that you will address. If you are writing an awareness objective, the specific effect should deal with receiving the message, understanding it or perhaps remembering it. If you are focusing on the acceptance level, deal with generating interest, reducing apathy or fostering attitudes (usually positive attitudes, such as support for wearing a helmet while bicycling; sometimes negative attitudes, such as a sentiment against drinking alcohol during pregnancy). For action objectives, focus on evoking a particular opinion or drawing out a desired action.

Step 5: Focus. Indicate the focus of the specific effect you hope to achieve. Provide some detail about what you are seeking. However, don't move away from objectives by providing information about either strategy or tactics. That will come later in the planning process.

Step 6: Performance Measure. Indicate the desired level of achievement in measurement terms. Raw numbers or percentages usually do this well. The number itself should reflect baseline research and/or desired outcomes. For example, a university library might calculate that 35 percent of students use the library facility in any two-week period. However, guidelines from the Association of College and Research Libraries might suggest that 50 percent is the desired usage pattern, including both in-person use and internet connections. Therefore the campus library's public relations campaign might aim for a performance increase of 50 percent of the students. Stated other ways, the objective might specify a 40 percent increase over the present usage, or an increase from the present 2,800 students to 4,000 out of a total student population of 8,000.

Step 7: Time Period. Indicate the desired time frame, either within a single period or in multiple stages.

Strategic Planning Example: **Establishing Goals and Objectives**

Goals

Reputation Goal

- To recreate the college's image into a four-year institution

Task Goals

- To recruit more students
- To generate new donor support

Position

Upstate College wants to be known for its quality education and for its accessibility in terms of both cost and admission standards.

Objectives for High-School Students in a Three-County Area

- To have an effect on awareness, specifically to increase their knowledge that Upstate College is expanding into a four-year college (75 percent of students during their junior year)

- To have an effect on acceptance, specifically to generate interest in attending a growing institution (25 percent of students during their junior and senior years)
- To have an effect on action, specifically to obtain inquiries from an average of 15 percent of students in the college's primary three-county area during their junior or senior year
- To have an effect on action, specifically to obtain applications from an average of 5 percent of all graduates in the college's primary three-county area during their senior year

(Note: You also will have objectives for each of your other key publics.)

■ ■ ■

Goals

Reputation Goal

- To regain customer confidence

Task Goal

- To recapture the company's previous sales rates

Position

Tiny Tykes wants to be known as the company that cares about babies more than about its own profitability.

Objectives for Parents

- To have an effect on awareness, specifically that 75 percent of parent-customers will learn about the redesign of the baby toy within six weeks
- To have an effect on awareness, specifically that 65 percent of the parents will understand the sacrifices and commitment that the company has made by re-calling and redesigning the toys
- To have an effect on acceptance, specifically that 40 percent of these parents will regain trust that the company has acted responsibly in redesigning the toy
- To have an effect on acceptance, specifically that 30 percent of the parents will be interested in buying toys from the company within the next two years
- To have an effect on action, specifically that 25 percent of the parents will purchase toys from the company within the next two years

(Note: You also will have objectives for each of your other key publics.)

Strategic Planning Exercise: *Establishing Goals and Objectives*

Basic Planning Questions

1. What are the goals?
2. What position do you seek?
3. What are the specific objectives (awareness, acceptance and action for each public)?

Expanded Planning Questions

A. Goals

1. What are the organization's reputation goals on this issue?
2. What are the organization's relationship goals on this issue?
3. What are the organization's task goals on this issue?
4. Do any of these goals contradict another goal? If "yes," which goal(s) will you eliminate?
5. What is the relative priority among the viable goals?
6. Does the organization have resources (time, personnel, money, etc.) to achieve these goals? If "no," can resources be obtained? From where?
7. Does the organization have willingness to work toward these goals? If "no," how can willingness be generated?
8. Are there any ethical problems with these goals? If "yes," how can you modify the goals to eliminate the problems?

B. Position

1. What is a key public for this product/service/concept?
2. What position do you seek for your product/service/concept for this public?
3. Is this desired position appropriate? If "no," reconsider the position.
4. What is your current position?
5. What change do you need to make to achieve desired position?
6. What is the competition?
7. What is its position?

(Note: Replicate the above position questions for each public.)

C. Objectives

1. Write at least one awareness objective for each key public, such as "To have an effect on awareness, specifically . . ."
2. Write at least one acceptance objective for each key public, such as "To have an effect on acceptance, specifically . . ."
3. Write at least one action objective for each key public, such as "To have an effect on action, specifically . . ."
4. Answer the following questions for each individual objective:
   - Is this objective linked to the organization's mission or vision statement?
   - Is this objective responsive to the issue/problem/opportunity/goal?
   - Is this objective focused on a particular public?
   - Is this objective clearly measurable?
   - Does this objective indicate a time frame?

- Is this objective challenging to the organization?
- Is this objective realistically attainable?

(Note: You should be able to answer "yes" to each of these questions. If not, revise the objectives.)

Consensus Check

Does agreement exist within your organization about the recommended objectives included within this step of the planning process?

If "yes," proceed to the next section.

If "no," consider the value and/or possibility of achieving consensus before proceeding.

Phase Two

Step
4

Step 5

Formulating Action and Response Strategies

Effective public relations involves deeds as well as words, and strong programs can be built only on solid and consistent action. Ideally, action and messages work hand in hand, complementing each other as the organization interacts with its publics. This step of the planning process will focus on your decisions about action strategies as you prepare to achieve your objectives.

Strategic communication planners have many options about what their organization can do and say on any particular issue. These actions can be either proactive or reactive. In a *proactive* measure, the organization can launch a communication program under the conditions and according to the timeline that seem to best fit the organization's interests. Conversely, a *reactive* measure responds to influences and opportunities from its environment.

Proactive strategies include both communication and action. Response strategies include preemptive action, offensive and defensive responses, diversion, commiseration, rectifying behavior and strategic inaction. Let's look at each type.

Proactive Public Relations Strategies

Public relations strategies initiated by the organization are called **proactive strategies.** These can be the most effective strategies because they are implemented according to the planning of the organization, rather than because of a need to respond to outside pressure and expectations from publics. Proactive action strategies include the enhancement of organizational performance, audience participation and special events, development of alliances and coalitions, sponsorships and sometimes activism. Key proactive communication strategies include the presentation of newsworthy information and the development of a transparent communication process.

Action Strategies

The first category of proactive public relations strategies involves **action strategies**—tangible deeds undertaken by the organization in an effort to achieve its objectives. Let's look at the six categories.

Organizational Performance.   The performance of the organization is the first and most important area to consider when weighing various strategic communication

---

A Typology of Proactive Public Relations Strategies

Action Strategies   **Communication Strategies**
   Organizational performance   Newsworthy information
   Audience participation   Transparent communication
   Special events
   Alliances and coalitions
   Sponsorships
   Activism

---

initiatives. Ensure that the organization is working at its highest possible level of quality for its customers. One of the first questions in the Formative Research phase of this planning process (Step 2: Analysis of the Organization) was designed to identify the quality of the product or service associated with the issue being addressed. Public relations can't be expected to promote the good name of an organization that doesn't give good performance, and products or services should reflect a level of quality that meets the wants, interests, needs and expectations of key publics.

What do customers want? Quality products. Value. Customer service. Reasonable prices. They also expect the organizations they choose to patronize to be responsible members of society. For example, some companies have been unpleasantly surprised to find that customers won't buy products made by exploiting child laborers or cosmetics developed through animal testing. Consumers also may avoid firms with poor records on safety, pollution and discrimination. In his book *Building Your Company's Good Name* (1996), Davis Young noted that a good reputation—an organization's most valuable asset—is built on performance rather than on mere words.

One of the principles of effective public relations is **adaptation,** the willingness and ability of the organization to make changes necessary to create harmony between itself and its key publics. Some organizations use strategic communication to convince their publics to conform to the offerings of the organization; this is the persuasive model of public relations. Another model of public relations aims to enhance the mutual relationship between the organization and its publics, which means that sometimes the organization will need to change.

If a college or university wants to promote registration at summer school, for example, one of the first activities should be to research key publics (such as currently registered students, incoming freshmen and people who applied to the school and were accepted but who did not register), identifying the courses they want and the schedules they prefer. In other words, the school would create the summer program around its key publics' needs, rather than building it around the convenience of the faculty and administrators. Similarly, if a dental office wants to attract a professional clientele, it might

---

How to Make Ethical Judgments

In considering various proactive and reactive strategies, it's worth asking one of those sometimes uncomfortable ethical questions, the kind that doesn't have an easy answer and may give rise to more questions than answers. "To whom is moral duty owed?" asked Clifford Christians, Mark Fackler and Kim Rotzoll (1997) in their book *Media Ethics*. In response to this question, they suggest that communication strategists—journalists and editors, public relations practitioners and advertisers—clarify who will be influenced by their decisions and what obligations we have to them. Good advice.

Here are five obligations or duties, along with some thoughts on relevant considerations:

1. **Duty to ourselves.** Be careful to distinguish between following your conscience and simply acting on your own careerist self-interest. One way to do this is to pause and reflect on the basis of your own moral values.

2. **Duty to our clients.** Our clients, as well as our publics and audiences, deserve our best efforts, especially when they are paying the bills. But don't just blindly go where a client would send you without giving some thought to the client's motives and moral base and how these intersect with your own.

3. **Duty to our companies or bosses.** Strike a balance between company loyalty and stoogism. Stick to the recurring advice: Consider motivations and the impact that a company's policies and actions are likely to have.

4. **Duty to our professional colleagues.** Consider how your work is enhancing the prestige of your profession and the reputation of your fellow practitioners. Consider especially the commitments implied in the codes of ethics of the various professional organizations. (See Appendix B: Ethical Standards for the text of these codes.)

5. **Duty to society.** This is the ultimate ethical test: What does an action do *for* people? What does it do *to* them?

In an ideal world, ethical decisions would be simple and clear-cut. But the world isn't an ideal place, so be prepared to carefully discern among competing loyalties and differing values.

---

schedule office hours on weekends and evenings, perhaps with a couple of nights with appointments as late as 10 or 11 P.M. to accommodate busy executives.

Audience Participation.   Another important strategy initiative for the public relations planner is audience participation. This involves using strong two-way communication tactics and engaging your audiences and publics in your communication activities.

One way to do this is to communicate about the audience's relevant interests rather than the needs of the message source or the sponsoring organization. The formal term for this is **saliency** of the information—the degree to which information is perceived as being applicable or useful to the audience. Use examples and applications that address a key question of your public: "What's in it for me?" In a fundraising letter for AIDS research, for example, tell your readers that they can help make a cure possible, rather than merely citing the researchers' need for financial support. When possible, base your message on values shared by the organization and the public.

Audience participation also can be built on activities that bring individual members of your publics into direct contact with the products and services of your organization. For example, police departments in many cities routinely use ride-along programs to give citizens a firsthand look at their communities from inside a patrol car. Cosmetic companies give free samples, health clubs give low-cost trial memberships and private schools have shadow programs for prospective students.

Several years ago the Union of American Hebrew Congregations, the denominational leadership of Reform Judaism in the United States, wanted to strengthen bonds with Reform Jews around the country ("The Lives We Touch," 1992). Invoking the principle of audience participation, UAHC invited its 800 member congregations to participate in a video project by sharing their success stories. More than 200 congregations responded and asked to be included in the documentary, gaining a sense of solidarity with the national association.

Another way to foster audience participation is by generating feedback. Create convenient ways your audience can respond to your message and engage in dialogue. Use techniques such as toll-free phone numbers, surveys, question-answer sessions, interactive Web sites and similar tools.

A company may look to research in determining whether to establish a consumer-complaints hotline as a form of feedback. A complaints department can gauge customer satisfaction, minimize the loss of customers, and perhaps identify ways to prevent problems. Recent studies (Nyer, 2000; Nyer, 1999; Kowalski & Erickson, 1997) suggest that soliciting complaints can actually help an organization reduce customer dissatisfaction. It seems that people feel better about the source of their complaints when they actually have an opportunity to voice those complaints. After venting, they also feel better about the product or service they had complained about, according to the studies.

You also can build into your program **triggering events**—activities that generate action among your key publics. Examples of triggering events are speeches that conclude with an invitation for the audience to sign a petition or an open house that ends with an opportunity to join. Sometimes the triggering element is built into an event, such as election day as the triggering event for a political compaign.

Special Events.   *Special events* are another useful way to generate audience participation. These are staged activities that give the organization an opportunity to gain the attention and acceptance of key publics. Special events should be legitimate, meaning they are designed primarily as a means of engaging your publics and encouraging their interaction with your organization, with the potential for media attention being secondary.

Opposite of this type of special event is the *pseudoevent,* a gimmick or mere publicity stunt planned mainly to gain publicity and having little value beyond that. Avoid self-serving pseudoevents, but don't dismiss the news value of legitimate special events. An appropriate event can attract the attention of reporters and generate interest among your publics. To distinguish a legitimate special event from a pseudoevent ask yourself: Even if the news media don't report this activity, would it still be worthwhile? If you can answer "yes" to this question, then you probably are dealing with a real special event.

Another important requirement for effective special events is that they should be creative, with a spark of originality that sets them apart from the ordinary and the routine. Brainstorming with your colleagues sometimes can suggest an approach that would be distinctive enough so that the special event can become literally "the talk of the town."

There are many types of special events, which are outlined in the next section on Tactics. For now, simply consider the wide range of possibilities:

- Artistic programs, such as recitals and art shows
- Competitions, such as sporting events and essay contests
- Community events, such as parades, festivals and fairs
- Holiday celebrations for civic, cultural, ethnic, religious and other occasions
- Observances, such as anniversaries, birthdays, special days or months
- Progress-oriented activities, such as groundbreaking ceremonies, cornerstone placements and grand openings

A later section on activism deals with special events of a more polemic or confrontational nature.

Alliances and Coalitions.   When two or more organizations join together in a common purpose, the combined energy offers a real opportunity for strategic communication initiatives. *Alliances* tend to be less formal, more loosely structured, and perhaps smaller than *coalitions,* but both seek to forge relationships, often new ones, with groups that share similar values and concerns. Using this strength-in-numbers approach, organizations try to compound their influence toward meeting objectives and to enhance their ability to break through barriers while trying to relate to their publics.

The nature of alliances is that they generate energy and cooperation around a single and often narrow issue. For example, when Walt Disney Corporation announced plans in 1993 to create an American history theme park in the rolling hills of northern Virginia, an alliance was quickly formed by environmentalists, preservationists, journalists, historians, land owners, taxpayers and others. This alliance was so successful that it sent Disney scurrying back to Florida.

Alliances sometimes are made with internal publics, such as when a company convenes a task force of its employees to consider workplace concerns. Other alliances focus on external publics. For example, a health-care system facing unprofitable duplication of services among several of its hospital sites might hold public hearings to discuss the problem and invite community input toward finding a solution, thus building an alliance with its publics.

Sometimes organizations seek alliances with influential individuals, particularly with community leaders who are respected among the organization's publics. An organization trying to encourage African Americans to participate in a bone-marrow screening, for instance, may look to respected minority leaders in the community or perhaps to influential organizations such as the NAACP or Urban League, professional sports teams, black professional fraternities or sororities, or similar groups.

Organizations that recognize they have a poor reputation with their public sometimes seek alliances with organizations having a better standing with the public. For example, when the U.S. Immigration and Naturalization Service (INS) declared an
amnesty for illegal aliens who met certain residency requirements, in several communities it turned to churches that had an existing credibility within the Hispanic community,
on the belief that the aliens' distrust of the INS would be overcome by their greater trust
in the churches. The third-party endorsement the churches were able to provide the INS
opportunity helped many people become legal residents.

At times, coalition building can lead to some unlikely bedfellows. In some communities, for example, coalitions advocating sexual responsibility or access to prenatal and
postnatal care bring together pro-life and pro-choice activists who otherwise would have
little in common.

Sponsorships.   *Sponsorships* offer another proactive step that organizations can take to
gain visibility and respect among their key publics. Sponsorship is a significant strategy
for programs oriented toward community relations. It involves either providing a program
directly or providing the financial, personnel or other resources the program requires.

Make sure there is a logical link between the activity being sponsored and the purpose or mission of your organization. For example, a science museum might sponsor a
trip to view a space-shuttle launch, a college might host a junior high school science fair
or a bookstore might support a literacy program.

Some sponsorships are based on existing marketing relationships. For example,
Lexus sponsors polo championships because polo enthusiasts reflect the luxury car's
customer base. So too with Budweiser and the Super Bowl. Other sponsorship programs
are designed to appeal to new publics. These programs often have a clear marketing
connection, paving the way for the company to obtain new customers.

Sponsorships can stretch a company's promotion dollars much farther than media advertising, at the same time creating more intensive relationships between the organization
and its publics. For example, during the 1994 Gay Games IV held in New York City, many
companies actively courted the gay and lesbian community, some for the first time. Miller
Brewing Company, AT&T and Naya Spring Water were corporate sponsors; Macy's and
Bloomingdale's had special promotions; Continental was the "official airline" for the
Olympic-style games. "The word is out there that there's a substantial gay and lesbian
market," explained Harold Levine, marketing director for the games. Organizers, sponsors
and consumers alike noted the value of the sponsorships, and many participants and fans
reported that they went out of their way to buy from the sponsors. Coca-Cola, Coors Brewing, David magazine and Southern Voice newspaper each contributed to Atlanta's bid to
host the 2006 Gay Games, which the city estimated would attract 1 million visitors and
bring $500 million to the local economy—twice as much as the SuperBowl brought to
Atlanta. Other companies are lining up to sponsor the games, all in an effort to create
stronger relationships with their key publics and/or potential customers.

Successful sponsor organizations find ways to attract continuing visibility and reputational benefits. This is the notion of *strategic philanthropy,* in which businesses seek
community relations gestures with an eye toward their employees and customers. For

Phase Two

Step
5

example, if a company that makes television sets wants to sponsor an educational program through the county library system, it could give $10,000 to the library for new books, earning a modest amount of visibility and appreciation. A better move, however, might be to donate $10,000 worth of television sets so the library can expand its use of educational and cultural videos. The TV sets would be a continuing reminder to library patrons of the company's donation to the community's quality of life.

A parallel principle of sponsorship is to give away something that you already own. A dollar given that generates only a dollar's worth of benefit is not a good sponsorship investment; a more strategic sponsorship is a donation with more value to the recipient than cost to the giver. This is the premise behind Operation Home Free (www.greyhound.com), begun in 1984 by Trailways Bus Lines and continued when Greyhound bought the company out. The program formed an alliance with the International Association of Chiefs of Police and the National Runaway Switchboard to help runaway youths. It ensures free bus rides to runaways returning home. The value? Tickets worth $120,000 in the first year alone. The actual cost? Virtually nothing to Greyhound, since its buses already were running, usually with some empty seats. The benefits? To runaways, a safe return home. To the police and runaway agencies, assistance in getting kids off the streets, into counseling and back home. To Greyhound, a boost in its reputation among employees, customers, police and other important publics. A real win-win-win situation!

Increasingly, national causes are going local with a coordinated series of events. One example of this is the Race for the Cure, which involved 1 million runners and walkers in 107 cities during 2000. The event, sponsored by the Susan G. Komen Breast Cancer Foundation (www.komen.org), has raised more than $240 million, making it the largest private funder of breast cancer research in the United States. Another coordinated fundraising activity is the Gus Macker 3-on-3 Basketball Tournament (www.macker.com), which attracted more than 200,000 players in 2001, raising $3.25 million for charities in 75 cities during the last five years.

Some sponsorship activities focus more on issues rather than on events. An example of this is the Rock the Vote campaign (www.rockthevote.org), which encourages young adults to register to vote. During the 2000 presidential campaign, Rock the Vote claimed to have led to a 20 percent increase in young-voter turnout, sparked by its promotions at malls, sporting events and college campuses, and through a 1-800 number promoted on television, particularly MTV. Working with L. L. Cool J's Camp Cool Foundation, Rock the Vote formed the Hip Hop Coalition for Political Change, extending its message into the inner city. It also has formed Radio Rocks the Vote, a partnership with urban, alternative and Top 40 stations.

Does all of this happen because MTV and the radio stations are civic-minded companies? Perhaps they are. But there's also an element of self-service, as there is with every good sponsorship. The purpose behind Rock the Vote, founded in 1990 by recording industry folks concerned about free-speech issues, is to motivate a core of supporters who can use the political process to the advantage of the music industry.

Finally, some sponsorships have involved a strong component of volunteerism. AT&T in 1996 gave each of its 127,000 employees worldwide a paid day off for volunteer work in community activities of their choice. The move cost the company

$20 million. Altruism isn't the only motivation. AT&T believes the move gave it a better standing in the community and potentially higher profits.

Activism. Another initiative planners can use is *activism,* a confrontational strategy focused mainly on persuasive communication and the advocacy model of public relations. A strong strategy to be used only after careful consideration of the pros and cons, activism offers many opportunities for organizations to present their messages and enhance their relationship with key publics, particularly their members and sympathizers.

Activism generally deals with causes or movements, such as social issues (crime, capital punishment or abortion, for example), environmental matters (pollution, suburban sprawl, nuclear waste), political concerns and so on. A distinction might be made between *advocates,* who essentially are vocal proponents for causes, and *activists,* who are more inclined to act out their support for the cause.

Consider some of the tactics associated with the strategy of activism: strikes, pickets, sit-ins, petitions, boycotts, marches, vigils, rallies and outright civil disobedience. Activists often make effective use of the news media because their tactics involve physical protests and thus are highly visible. Effective activism often has an element of the publicity stunt, a pseudoevent but nonetheless newsworthy action done as much for the television viewers as for any other public. For example, when death-penalty opponents marched past the Missouri governor's mansion in Jefferson City in 1999, they carried a cardboard coffin and paper tombstones. News photographers and television crews undoubtedly appreciated their visual creativity.

Sometimes activism involves *civil disobedience,* a nonviolent and nonlegal but generally visual undertaking. Often such protests are loaded with symbolism. Julia "Butterfly" Hill set the tree-sitting record in 1999, spending 738 days—more than two years—atop a 1,000-year-old redwood tree in Northern California protesting a logging project. The well-publicized protest was orchestrated by Earth First!, a radical environmental activist group waging a 12-year battle to save the trees. From her residence in the tree she called "Luna," Hill gave cell-phone interviews to reporters and talked with schoolchildren around the world.

This kind of activism often transforms itself into theater, particularly when protestors are courting TV coverage. During a presidential campaign debate in October 2000 in Boston, protestors dramatized what they saw as the candidates' contempt for the masses. Dressing as big-money contributors with top hats and three-piece suits, they chanted mockingly: "One-two-three-four. We are rich and you are poor." And the TV video crews were delighted!

The author's award for creative activist strategy goes to this well-orchestrated 1999 publicity stunt: Two dozen New York City community activists staged a sit-in on the marble floor of City Hall, singing "We Shall Overcome" accompanied by kazoos and wearing insect outfits and flowered hats. They were protesting Mayor Rudolph Giuliani's decision to auction off city-owned lots that neighborhood groups had turned into community gardens. Wait, there's more: Enter the New York Police Department in riot gear, and as the protestors went limp, the police had to carry them to a waiting police van. Now that's entertainment!

The Benefits of Employee Volunteer Programs

Employee volunteerism got high marks in a study cosponsored by the Conference Board (www.conference-board.org), a private business research group, and the Points of Light Foundation (www.pointsoflight.org), an organization that encourages community service (Wild, 1993). Based on responses by 454 companies representing all sectors of U.S. industry, the study reported the following findings:

- Employee volunteer programs offer bottom-line benefits to the company by boosting company productivity (agreed to by more than 60 percent of the executives), increasing employee productivity (about 75 percent) and furthering corporate strategic goals (nearly 80 percent).

- Such programs offer employee benefits, including building teamwork skills and improving morale (both more than 90 percent), as well as attracting better employees (almost 90 percent) and keeping valued employees (nearly 80 percent).

- These programs offer indirect community benefits by helping create "healthier" communities and improving corporate public image (more than 90 percent each) and improving relations with the community and with local government (nearly 85 percent).

But many protests are more serious. The Makah, a Native American tribe in Washington State, is the only whaling tribe in the lower 48 states. The tribal whaling commission declared its intention to return to its traditional ways and hold a whale hunt, its first in 70 years. In 1999, on live television, a successful hunt involved the ceremonial butchering of the captured whale. The media swarmed and whaling protestors gathered.

Activists sometimes stretch ethical boundaries, entering an area public relations practitioners should avoid. Pie throwing has become a tactic-of-choice for some activists, who found they could gain media attention and thus a platform for their messages by pulling their relatively benign stunts on famous people. Targets have included fashion designer Oscar de la Renta, who was pied because of his use of fur; Proctor & Gamble chairman John Pepper, over animal rights; Dutch finance minister Gerrit Zalm, over the new Euro currency; Renato Ruggiero, director-general of the World Trade Organization, over endangered sea turtles; and Microsoft chairman Bill Gates, just because. Usually the only consequence is media coverage, but in 1999 three activists who protested San Francisco Mayor Willie Brown's policies on the homeless by throwing tofu-cream and pumpkin pies in his face were sentenced to six months in prison.

If you are planning an activist strategy, keep a clear eye on all your publics. Certainly the news media are important. So too are the targets of your activism, whom you are attempting to persuade toward some kind of action or response. But perhaps most important is your internal public—generally volunteers, often with mixed motivations—who are being asked to give time and perhaps take risks on behalf of the cause. Activist strategy must provide for the "feeding" of these troops with continuing motivation, ongoing communication and, when possible, the attainment of milestone victories that can shore up their dedication.

Communication Strategies

While the previous proactive strategies focus on the action of the organization, another cluster of strategies deals more with communication. Two such strategies are newsworthy information and transparent communication.

Newsworthy Information.   Presenting newsworthy information is a must for any organization that hopes to use the news media to carry its message and capture the interest of its publics. For the communication strategist, news is one of the strongest proactive strategies because something truly newsworthy is almost guaranteed to gain the attention of the news media and, through them, the organization's other publics. Even if you are presenting a message through personal or organizational channels, keep in mind that your audiences will be more drawn to a newsworthy message.

What is news? The element of news deals with information that offers the audience a new idea or the latest development. From a journalistic perspective—which is the perspective every public relations practitioner needs to respect and adopt—news is information that involves action, adventure, change, conflict, consequence, contest, controversy, drama, effect, fame, importance, interest, personality, prominence, proximity and dozens of other attributes often listed in journalism textbooks.

For our purposes, we will define **news** as significant information relevant to the local area, presented with balance and objectivity and in a timely manner. The value of news is magnified by two more elements: unusualness and fame. Let's simplify things with the acronym **SiLoBaTi + UnFa.** This convenient way to remember the main ingredients of news is made up of the first two letters of each of the elements: *si*gnificance, *lo*calness, *ba*lance and *ti*meliness, plus *un*usualness and *fa*me.

First, news is information of *significance*. It has meaning to many people, even those beyond the organization; it is information of consequence and magnitude. News also deals with information relevant to the *local* area, as defined by the coverage area of the news medium featuring the information. News is information with *balance* and objectivity. While the public relations practitioner uses information to promote the organization or client, it should not be presented in a promotional manner; rather, it should be presented with an air of detachment and neutrality. The final key ingredient in news is that it is *timely,* being connected with current issues, especially those high on public and media agendas.

In addition to these four key elements, newsworthiness is magnified by two other factors. News interest is enhanced when the information deals with *unusual* situations. This is what writers call *human interest,* that hard-to-define quality involving rarity, novelty, uniqueness, milestones or slightly offbeat oddities. News interest also is enhanced when the information involves *fame.* "Names make news" isn't idle chatter. Well-known or important people can add interest to a newsworthy situation. Sometimes their involvement can take an otherwise routine event and elevate it to the status of news.

Exhibit 5.1   Relationship Between Organizational Activities/Messages, Media
Agenda and Interests of Key Public

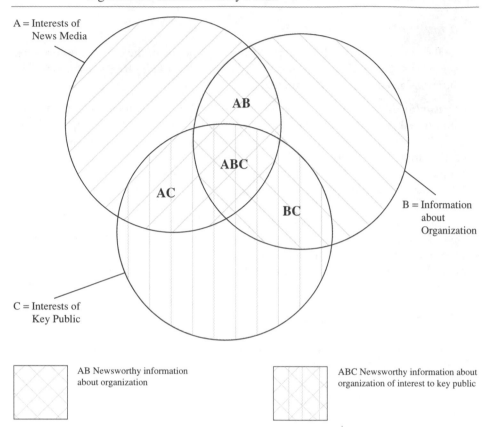

News judgment is relative. Public relations writers attempt to predict newsworthiness, but the decision to call something news is made only by the media **gatekeepers,** those people who control the flow of information in their various publications, newscasts or talk shows. Examples of media gatekeepers are editors, columnists, news directors, producers and webmasters.

As a public relations professional, part of your job is to analyze the relationship among three things to establish newsworthiness: (1) your organization's activities and messages, (2) the media agenda and (3) the interests of a key public. The Venn diagram in Exhibit 5.1 shows this relationship, with Circle A indicating the interests of the news media, Circle B information about the organization and Circle C the interests of a key public.

The AB area denotes newsworthy information about the organization. This involves activities and messages the organization potentially can publicize through the news media. The ABC area represents information about the organization that is of interest

Agenda-Setting Theory of the Media

How powerful are the news media? Can they make us care about an issue or act on it in a certain way just because they report it? Or are they simply information sources used at the discretion of their audiences?

Communication researchers and public relations practitioners believe there is a middle ground, explained by the *agenda-setting theory* associated with Maxwell McCombs and Donald Shaw (1972). The theory tries to explain the correlation between the media agenda (issues the media report on) and the public agenda (issues the public is interested in).

According to the agenda-setting theory, the news media raise up an issue that both they and their audiences consider legitimate areas of public interest. There is still a bit of a debate: Does an issue move into the public interest because the media report it? Or do the media report an issue because it already is a matter of public interest? Probably a bit of both.

For the public relations strategist, the important lesson from this theory is to link organizational information with the current news. Each day you should ask yourself: What is the news of the day and how does my organization fit into it?

Sometimes the link is obvious. During a high-profile trial in which child abuse is an issue, a local child-abuse agency would have a natural connection.

The agency easily could become a resource to reporters about the nature and extent of child abuse in the local community. Likewise, an insurance company could link to the issue of home safety during a string of house fires or a financial consultant could link to anticipation about new trends in the stock market.

Other times the public relations person must be creative in finding the links. In one situation, when control of Hong Kong was reverting from England to China, the local branch of a U.S. bank connected to the international story through its corporate genealogy: It was owned by a British company that also had a bank in Hong Kong. In another situation, a hospital linked to news about genocide in Rwanda because one of its doctors recently had returned from a stint as a medical volunteer in that war-torn country.

The media may turn to your organization if you already have built up a rapport, but it is often up to the public relations person to let reporters know that the organization is able and willing to provide information that will serve the news interests of the reporter. A word of caution: Don't turn this opportunity to serve as a news resource into a heavy-handed promotional message for your organization or you won't be invited back.

both to the news media and to the key publics. This represents information that is the primary focus of a media relations person, because it is newsworthy information that the public will look for or at least will be attentive to.

The BC area indicates non-newsworthy information that the organization will have to present to the public through organizational or advertising media, unless the public relations practitioner can reshape or enhance the information to make it of more interest to the news media.

The AC area indicates information not involving the organization that is of interest both to the media and to the key public, essentially information on the media and public agendas. Strategic communicators look to these agendas for opportunities to insert their organizations into the news of the day.

In some situations, Circle A could fully overlap Circle C, meaning that everything on the media agenda is of interest to the key public. In such a case, media relations would pay a major role in the organization's strategic communication program. In other

---

Ten Ways Organizations Can Generate News

1. Give an award to draw attention to values and issues.

2. Hold a contest to involve others in your values and issues.

3. Select personnel to head a new program or begin a new project.

4. Comment on a local need or problem.

5. Conduct research and issue a report about a local need or problem.

6. Launch a campaign to accomplish something.

7. Give a speech to a significant audience and tell the media about it.

8. Involve a celebrity to visit and/or address your organization on a topic of concern to you.

9. Tie into an issue already high on the public or media agenda or link your organization to the top news of the day.

10. Localize a general report.

Source: Smith, R. D. (In press). *Becoming a Public Relations Writer,* 2nd ed. Lincolnwood, ILNTC.

---

situations, Circle A might not intersect at all with Circle C, leaving the public relations person to develop alternatives to the news media to present the organization's message. It is up to the public relations professional to determine, both through research and through experience, the relationship among these three entities.

An interesting study by Kevin Barnhurst and Diana Mutz (1997) observed that newspaper journalism is moving away from simply reporting events to providing news analysis. They noted that in 1960, 90 percent of front-page election stories were about events; 32 years later, 80 percent of front-page stories were interpretive. Meanwhile, in broadcast reporting, the length of candidate sound bites decreased during the same time period as election coverage became more centered on journalist-commentators. "To qualify as news these days, an event also must fit into a larger body of interpretations and themes," reported Barnhurst and Mutz. The lesson for practitioners, then, is to build their events and frame their messages around the larger issues that blip on the media agenda screen.

Sometimes you will find that newsworthy activities are occurring within your organization, and your role becomes that of an in-house journalist reporting on the existing news events. But more often your role will be that of public relations counselor and strategist. Public relations people regularly create or orchestrate newsworthy events within their organizations to carry an important message to the key publics.

To attract the interest particularly of television reporters, the news must have a strong visual element. Stand-up commentators or talking heads don't make it on most television news reports, other than on occasional local-access cable programs that few people watch. Audiences have become sophisticated, some might say spoiled. Regardless, they demand active, even entertaining, visual presentation of their news. Reporters do their best to comply with the expectations of their audiences, so unless you are able to present newsworthy information with a visual dimension, you are unlikely to find the news media receptive vehicles for your message.

Opportunity Born of Tragedy

Suffering in silence may be a virtue, but public misfortune can make your cause hot.

Ever since First Lady Betty Ford put the topic of breast cancer on the public agenda in 1974, when she went public with her disease, the lesson for public relations practitioners in low-profile charitable organizations is to move quickly when injury or disease captures the nation's attention.

Often that attention surrounds celebrity. When track star Florence Griffith Joyner died in 1998 of a seizure, the Epilepsy Foundation mobilized quickly. Its medical expert told "Good Morning America" audiences about the disease that affects 2.5 million people. It sent news releases urging women to speak out about the discrimination that exists because of epilepsy, and it quickly sent a video news release to every TV station in America. Likewise, the National Parkinson Foundation found that public interest grew when actor Michael J. Fox revealed that he suffered from Parkinson's disease.

With media interest comes money. Donations doubled for the American Paralysis Association after actor Christopher Reeve was paralyzed in a horse-riding accident, and contributions to the Alzheimer's Association jumped after President Reagan was diagnosed with the disease.

Publicity about celebrities and their illnesses also can cause others to pay closer attention to their own health. When Dick Cheney was hospitalized in 2001 less than two months after becoming vice president, calls to health information lines increased from men concerned about their own cardiac health. In 2000, when Rudy Giuliani dropped out of a senate race against Hillary Clinton after being diagnosed with prostate cancer, demand for prostate screening nearly doubled.

Assisting the public relations efforts of some organizations, celebrities have helped turn the spotlight on illnesses and diseases afflicting themselves or their loved ones. In 2001, for example, model Christy Turlington became spokesperson for her own disease, emphysema, and for the lung cancer that killed her father. Other celebrities giving publicity to various maladies include cyclist Lance Armstrong and MTV host Tom Green for testicular cancer, talk-TV host Montel Williams for multiple sclerosis, soul singer Gladys Knight for diabetes, Backstreet Boy Kevin Richardson for colon cancer, basketball star Magic Johnson for HIV, R&B singer Tionne T-Boz Watkins for sickle cell disease, quarterback Doug Flutie for childhood autism, and ex-senator Bob Dole for prostate cancer.

Phase Two

Step
5

The quest for a strong visual element to news is an opportunity for creative minds, as noted in the previous section on the strategy of activism. Even in nonconfrontational situations, publicity stunts have their place—as long as they are vehicles for news and not simply hollow attention-getters. At one university, a student theater group called Casting Hall wanted to attract attention and new members, so its members went "fishing" in the student union on a very snowy January day. Students in waders carried fishing poles, casting and reeling in new members. It was a visual pun, appropriate for both the name and the theatrical nature of the organization. The gimmick drew attention, generated publicity, raised some interest and resulted in several new members.

What is the value of news reporting about your organization? Corporate executives sometimes believe there is a causal link between publicity and public support. It's not that easy, as we will see later in this section. But the underlying value of publicity is that it provides *third-party endorsement* for the organization's message. Audiences assume the news they obtain from television, radio and newspapers is more believable than information they obtain directly from the organization through vehicles such as advertising, Web sites, brochures and so on. That's because the information reported in the news media has passed the screen of the gatekeepers. Audiences know that not everything gets on the air or in the paper, so intuitively they recognize that the gatekeepers have made some choices as to what information to present as news. A reporter or editor considered what the organization had to say and decided it was accurate enough to pass along to their audiences.

Some media are more believable than others and thus deserve particular attention by the public relations strategist. Specialized newspapers and magazines—in one category, those dealing with business, industry and the professions; in another, those focused on a specific ethnic, political, religious, cultural or lifestyle group—have particular credibility with their audiences. Likewise certain commentators or talk-show hosts carry enormous influence among their steady listeners and readers.

Transparent Communication.   A relatively new concept, **transparent communication,** is an important idea in developing a proactive public relations communication strategy. It deals with the awareness objectives of increasing knowledge and understanding. Transparent communication simply means *making your case*. Many communication efforts have failed because the publics are aware of facts but not reasons behind those facts.

Too often, organizations exhibit a "just trust us" mentality by announcing plans without providing reasons why those plans are necessary, and today's publics aren't inclined to trust blindly. For example, within a four-month period in one mid-sized city, community opposition was strong in four different situations—a proposed relocation of the zoo, an announcement by an HMO to drop coverage for half the hospitals in the area, plans by a public radio station to suspend operations and the decision of a bridge authority to turn away millions of federal dollars for a high-profile "signature" bridge in favor of a less architecturally impressive bridge. In each situation, the organization in question drew criticism because it had failed to provide plausible reasons for its plans. Publics had been left confused and only partly informed; facts had been given, but there was no convincing rationale for the decisions and plans.

In an example of doing it right, the CIA's report of the crash of TWA flight 800 off Long Island not only detailed what the investigators found, but also included a thorough discussion of the investigation process that lead to the conclusion. "Report goes beyond being 'open,'" wrote Pat Jackson in *pr reporter* (1997). "Open implies something else is closed, which raises questions. CIA's report is transparent—everything is laid on the line. Its thoroughness leaves no questions."

When organizations engage in transparent communication, they provide the kind of communication that identifies the problem, gets people interested in it, airs the various options and otherwise creates a climate of understanding and involvement before plans are announced that affect the publics. If financial pressures are pushing your organization to curtail services, let your publics know about the financial problems and the various options before announcing a service cutback. Nobody likes bad surprises, especially when it is clear that the organization has been hiding information from key publics.

Reactive Public Relations Strategies

When accusations or other criticisms have been made, an organization is thrown into a reactive mode. In responding to outside forces, organizations should develop objectives such as gaining public understanding, maintaining and restoring reputation, and rebuilding trust and support. The field of *crisis communication management* is ripe with examples of response strategies that work.

The classical term for a communication response to negative situations is **apologia,** a formal defense that offers a compelling case for an organization's opinions, positions or actions. Don't confuse apologia with apology, which is an expression of fault and remorse. An apologia could include an apology, but it is much more. Through an apologia an organization explains its actions and positions with a clear eye toward convincing critics of its rightness. In an article applying the concept of apologia to corporate crises, Keith Michael Hearit (1994) noted that an apologia offers an organization a strategic opportunity to manage its reputation in the wake of accusations of wrongdoing. Hearit suggests a threefold approach: persuasive accounts offering (1) an explanation and if necessary a defense, (2) statements of regret and (3) disassociation tactics to separate the organization from the problem.

Another approach to public relations response strategy considers the *theory of accounts,* which refers to the use of communication to manage relationships in the wake of rebuke or criticism. Accounts can range from defensive to offensive. Some research

Phase Two

Step
5

When the Fur Flies

People for the Ethical Treatment of Animals (PETA) faced its own ethical problem when supermodel Naomi Campbell, a PETA volunteer who had pledged not to wear natural fur, was reported to be modeling in Europe wearing fur. After unsuccessful attempts to reach her, PETA took a public tack: With much fanfare, it fired Ms. Campbell as a spokesmodel.

The firing was a strategic design, a twist to several of the news-making tips, such as involving a celebrity, tying in to a public issue and appointing personnel as a way to highlight an issue. Instead, PETA un-appointed a volunteer—not coincidentally, a wayward one who also was a big celebrity.

PETA spokesman Michael McGraw described the activist group's plan: Once it got the media's attention by firing Ms. Campbell, PETA would turn the focus back to the issue of the suffering caused to animals in the name of fashion (Seideman, 1997).

"We were able to turn something quite negative into something quite positive," said McGraw, "because what it allowed us to do was get the message out that the fur industry hurts animals and kills them and tortures them."

(Cody & McLaughlin, 1985) found that the harsher the criticism, the more a strong offensive account is warranted. In *Accounts, Excuses, and Apologies,* William Benoit (1995) dealt with accounts and apologia, drawing on research from sociology, social psychology and communication. He presents a *theory of image restoration* based on the presumption that, in the face of criticism, both people and organizations seek to maintain or rebuild a positive reputation.

Organizations can use a range of verbal and behavioral reactions in managing their response to opposition and their recovery from criticism. The following typology of public relations responses is based on a reflection of contemporary research and consulting practices, as well as the work of the above-mentioned researchers.

Pre-emptive Action Strategy: Prebuttal

One type of strategy actually involves *pre-emptive action,* which is taken before the opposition launches its first charge against the organization. This strategy is called a *prebuttal.* The term itself is a play on the word *rebuttal,* but these are pre-emptive strikes when bad news is inevitable. The term was used, for example, to identify counterclaims by the Clinton White House of anticipated charges that begat impeachment even before those charges were made public.

A Typology of Public Relations Responses

Pre-emptive Action Strategy
  Prebuttal

Offensive Response Strategies
  Attack
  Embarrassment
  Threat

Defensive Response Strategies
  Denial
  Excuse
  Justification

Diversionary Response Strategies
  Concession
  Ingratiation
  Disassociation
  Relabeling

Vocal Commiseration Strategies
  Concern
  Condolence
  Regret
  Apology

Rectifying Behavior Strategies
  Investigation
  Corrective action
  Restitution
  Repentance

Strategic Inaction
  Silence

The concept of prebuttal is based on the observation that the first one to tell the story sets the tone, against which all alternative versions must compete. It's a lesson you may have learned in elementary school, when your sister or brother beat you home with a story of how you got into trouble on the playground. Following that account, your own version may have been not only second place but somehow second best. The first telling of the story becomes normative, and other versions are considered in light of the first account.

The same thing holds true for organizations. When something bad is about to happen, organizations can do more than merely brace for the aftershock. *Carpe diem!* as the Romans said. Seize the day!

Consider this real-life situation: A hospital had to deal with a pending report that would list it as having one of the highest patient-death rates in the state. Knowing that the report was only days away and that it was statistically accurate, the hospital held a news conference to announce the forthcoming report and to explain why the rate was high: This particular hospital accepted charity patients too poor to have regular health care, specialized in geriatrics and was the only hospital in the area treating AIDS patients at a time when the disease meant certain death. These were important reasons explaining the high death rate. Local reporters gave the hospital's announcement minimal coverage, and they entirely overlooked the state report a few days later.

Consider using the strategy of prebuttal when the public inevitably will hear the accusation or other bad news and when the organization can offer strong evidence to give its publics reasons to disregard the bad news or excuse the organization.

Attacking the news media is particularly risky, because they have the last word. But in 1999 Metabolife did so because it feared biased reporting from ABC News. "20/20" had spent four months in research and interviews, and Metabolife worried about how its popular but controversial herbal diet pill would be portrayed.

Combining the strategies of prebuttal and attack, Metabolife posted a Web site with its own videotape of ABC's 70-minute interview with its CEO, along with a full transcript and additional medical information. The company purchased full-page ads in the New York Times and the New York Post, gained coverage in the Wall Street Journal, and ran radio commercials across the country to draw hits to the Web site—all prior to the story's broadcast. Metabolife also placed a short ad during the program, asking viewers to visit its Web site.

The Web site received 1.1 million hits a day, and the company later claimed that its pre-emptive action caused the "20/20" story to be fairer than it otherwise would have been. ABC denied Metabolife's interpretation, calling the company's action "a not-so-subtle form of intimidation."

Offensive Response Strategies

Public relations planners sometimes use **offensive response strategies** such as attack, embarrassment or threat in response to criticism. These are based on the premise that the organization is operating from a position of strength in the face of opposition.

Attack.   An *attack* is an offensive response strategy of claiming that an accusation of wrongdoing is an attempt to impugn the organization's reputation by an accuser who is negligent or malicious. Often the objective behind this strategy is to encourage an opponent to retreat or at least to refrain from future criticism. Use this approach only when a strong case can be made that accusers have grossly overstated the organization's involvement in a problem. Let's look at two examples of the attack strategy—one that backfired, one that was successful.

Dow Corning used the attack strategy, to its own misfortune, in handling a lawsuit over its silicone-gel breast implants. Faced with reports filled with unfavorable scientific information, the company's first response was to attack the investigators. This and other strategic missteps led to a $7.3 million judgment against the company and class-action lawsuits of more than $4 billion that put the corporation into Chapter 11 bankruptcy, despite the fact that no reputable scientific evidence showed that implants caused disease or illness.

On the other hand, Itsy Bitsy Entertainment Company was successful in attacking criticism by the Rev. Jerry Falwell that its Tinky Winky Teletubby, seen by an estimated 16 million viewers, is a gay character. Company spokesman Steve Rice told reporters, "Falwell was attacking something sweet and innocent to further his conservative political agenda. To out a Teletubby in a preschool show is kind of sad on his part. I really find it absurd and kind of offensive."

Embarrassment.   A related offensive strategy deals with *embarrassment,* in which an organization tries to lessen an opponent's influence by using shame or humiliation. An example of this strategy was Butt Man, the character who dogged Senator Robert Dole during the 1996 presidential campaign as a constant reminder to voters that the Republican candidate had accepted money from tobacco companies. Be careful about using embarrassment, because it can backfire if the publics believe an organization is acting unfairly against its opponents.

Threat.   Making a *threat* is another offensive strategy, involving the promise that harm will come to the accuser or the purveyor of bad news. The threatened harm may be in the form of a lawsuit for defamation, for example. Use public threats only if the information cannot be disputed in some other way, and beware of the obvious ethical concerns about misusing this strategy.

Defensive Response Strategies

Another strategic communication response involves **defensive response strategies** such as denial, excuse or justification, all of which involve the organization reacting less aggressively to criticism.

Denial.   *Denial* is a defensive strategy in which the organization refuses to except blame, claiming that the reputed problem doesn't exist or didn't occur, or if it did, that it's not related to the organization. In the latter case, the claim generally is either one of *innocence* ("We didn't do it"), *mistaken identity* ("You have us confused with someone else") or *blame shifting* ("So-and-so did it").

A few years ago, a student at a public university was arrested for prostitution. She tried to justify her actions by claiming that she couldn't otherwise afford tuition because of a financial aid snafu. The university was quick to say "That's absurd!" and shifted responsibility back to the student.

But be careful in shifting blame, because the strategy can backfire if the organization was ultimately responsible. An executive who claims that an employee's inappropriate action was against company policy must be prepared for scrutiny of both the company's official policy and its way of doing business. After Denny's restaurant was criticized on various occasions in the mid-1990s for refusing to serve African-American and Asian-American customers, much attention was given to the company's training program. It is best to use the strategy of denial only when the case can be publicly supported and when it can be proven that neither the organization nor anyone associated with it was involved in the wrongdoing.

Excuse.   A commonly used defensive strategy is *excuse,* in which an organization tries to minimize its responsibility for the harm or wrongdoing. Excuse can take several forms, including provocation, lack of control, accident, victimization and mere association.

The organization may claim *provocation,* essentially saying that it had no choice. An example of this would be a police department that excuses its elimination of a popular mounted patrol by reporting that the police union insisted that seniority, not horse-riding ability, be the key factor in selecting officers for the patrol, thereby making the mounted patrol inefficient and even dangerous. A variation on the excuse theme is *lack of control,* in which the organization reports that its actions were forced upon it, such as the manager of a local manufacturing plant who blames local employee layoffs on decisions made at national corporate offices.

Another excuse is *accident,* in which the organization suggests that factors beyond anyone's control led to a problem. An example of this is a mayor who excuses his city's slow progress in snow removal on unusually heavy snowfall during a two-week period.

A related but even stronger excuse is *victimization,* in which the organization shows that it was the target of criminals. This was the excuse presented by Pepsi amid claims that syringes were found in its diet drink cans in 1993, an excuse so thoroughly accepted that consumers barely cut back on their consumption, then rebounded to give the company one of its best quarters ever in terms of sales.

A final type of excuse deals with mere *association,* in which the organization claims that it more-or-less inherited a problem. For example, a newly elected city administration might try to disassociate itself from a $2 million income shortfall by claiming that the financial loss was caused by careless planning by the previous administration.

Justification.   Another defensive strategy is *justification,* which admits the organization did the deed but did so for good reason. Like the excuse response, justification has several subcategories.

One type of justification is based on *good intention,* in which an organization attempts to soften the blow of bad results by claiming that it was trying to accomplish something positive. For example, a cab company may justify one of its drivers sideswiping a parked car by claiming the driver was trying to avoid hitting a pedestrian.

Another type of justification is *context,* in which the organization asks its publics to "look at it from our side." Robin Hood seen from the point of view of the sheriff of Nottingham looks much different than from the perspective of the Nottingham peasants. Likewise, investors and environmentalists each may view differently a company that violated technicalities of clean-air regulations.

Idealism is a type of justification based on an appeal to ethical, moral or spiritual values, such as leaders of a church protest against the death penalty who explain that their actions, though perhaps unpopular with some church members, are nevertheless in line with, even commanded by, their religious principles.

Another type of justification involves *mitigation,* with the admission that the problem occurred but that blame is lessened because of a factor such as impairment, illness, coercion, lack of training and so on. However, if the mitigating factor is the responsibility of the organization, the attempt at justification probably will fail, as the reported drunkenness of the *Valdez* captain did not allow Exxon to escape responsibility for the 1989 oil spill in the Alaskan waters of Prince William Sound.

Diversionary Response Strategies

Several **diversionary response strategies** also are open to communication planners. They include concessions, ingratiation, disassociation and relabeling, all of which are attempts to shift the gaze of the publics from the problem associated with the organization.

Concession.   *Concession* is a diversionary strategy by which the organization tries to rebuild its relationship with its publics by giving the public something it wants. The focus here should be on a concession that is mutually valued by both the organization and its public. For example, after objections to a car advertisement in 1998 parodying Leonardo Da Vinci's "The Last Supper" with the caption, "My friends, let us rejoice, because a new Golf is born," Volkswagen France and its advertising agency offered as a concession a major financial contribution to a religious charity whose work was supported by the protestors. The value of the donation by Volkswagen France was recognized by both the company and its offended public.

Use the strategy of concession only if the gift will be valued by your adversaries and if your organization will remain committed to the concession. Amid criticism of its marketing of infant formula in lesser-developed nations during the 1980s, Nestlé established the International Council on Infant Food Industries and a code of ethics, attempting to offer its critics concession. But the strategy provided only a temporary diversion for critics, who quickly saw evidence that the company was not abiding by its own code of ethics. Subsequent opposition to Nestlé grew in the face of what critics viewed as insincerity and hypocrisy.

Instead of providing gifts to involved publics, some concessions are aimed at generating favorable publicity for an organization under fire. An example of this is found in *Crisis Response: Inside Stories in Managing Image Under Siege* (Gottschalk, 1993), where crisis counselor James Lukaszewski revealed that he advised Exxon to charter aircraft to carry volunteers from major U.S. cities to Alaska in 1989 so they could help clean up some of the 11 million gallons of oil spilled in Prince William Sound. Exxon rejected the idea on grounds that the airlift would cost too much. The company eventually spent $2.2 billion in cleanup costs, another $1 billion to settle state and federal lawsuits and $300 million in lost wages to Alaskan fishermen. Exxon also has spent more than a decade fighting a $5.3 billion fine in punitive damages for criminal negligence in the oil spill. Certainly an environmental airlift would not have eliminated all of Exxon's expenses. But in hindsight it seems fair to conclude that an airlift would have helped the company's reputation, which in turn could have eased its legal battles as well as its strained relations with stockholders, consumers, government agencies and the media. In 1999, Business Week magazine commented that "Exxon could have emerged from the case with a far better image if it had taken a more conciliatory approach.... Instead, Exxon took a tough stand. And 10 years later, the furious debates, and the bitterness, continue." Showing the ramification of continuing anti-Exxon sentiment, a jury in 2000 ordered Exxon to pay $3.5 billion for defrauding the state of Alabama on royalties involving gas wells.

Ingratiation.   Another diversionary strategy, one of rather questionable ethical standing, is *ingratiation.* Essentially the organization attempts to manage the negative situation by charming its publics or "tossing a bone," giving something of relatively little significance to the organization in an attempt to turn the spotlight away from the accusations and criticisms. Ingratiation differs from concessions in that the latter involves something of real value to the public, while ingratiation is more cosmetic. Examples of ingratiation are seen in the case of state lawmakers who vote against long-term tax reform for homeowners while offering a token and temporary tax reduction.

Disassociation.   *Disassociation* is a diversionary strategy that attempts to distance an organization from the wrongdoing associated with it. This can be effective when a mishap occurred not because of organizational policy but because policy was not observed, especially when the organization was severing ties with the cause of the problem. Texaco accomplished disassociation when its corporate chairman quickly and publicly apologized for racist statements made by several top executives, suspended two of the officials, ordered sensitivity training and established a corporate hotline for reporting violations of company antidiscrimination policies.

Relabeling.   Another diversionary strategy, *relabeling,* tries to distance the organization from criticism. It involves offering an agreeable name in replacement of a negative label that has been applied by others. Lee Iacocca was doing this when, amid 1987 charges of odometer fraud, he claimed that Chrysler executives had merely driven new cars with disconnected odometers as part of a "quality test program" that was at worst a mistake in judgment. Chrysler was fined $7.6 million. But the judge said the test program, which he allowed may have been a good idea, went sour when Chrysler sold, as new vehicles, cars that had been in accidents.

The strategy of relabeling can backfire if an organization's publics conclude that the relabeling is deceptive or, worse, if it trivializes the problem. Relabeling is only a step away from *doublespeak,* which is deliberately misleading language and highly unethical practice. Don't go too far in your effort to put on the best face. Recall the widespread denunciation President Bill Clinton brought on himself by insisting even under oath that, according to his definition, he had not had sex with Monica Lewinsky.

Vocal Commiseration Strategies

Another family of strategies is **vocal commiseration strategies,** in which the organization expresses empathy and understanding about the misfortune suffered by its publics. These include concern, condolence, regret and apology.

Concern.   *Concern* is a type of vocal commiseration in which the organization expresses that it is not indifferent to a problem, without admitting guilt. The apparent lack of care and concern for women harmed by breast implants was a continuing public relations burden for Dow Corning, which seemed unable to balance lawyerly advice ("Admit nothing") with public expectation of compassion for people's suffering. The failure to respond aggravated the eventual legal judgments against the company, which climbed to $3.2 billion.

Condolence.   A more formal type of vocal commiseration is *condolence,* in which the organization expresses grief over someone's loss or misfortune, again without admitting guilt. A good example of this strategy is the response of ValuJet president Lewis Jordan to the 1996 crash of one of his airplanes in the Florida Everglades, which killed 110 people—a crash later attributed to a shipper who had illegally mislabeled canisters of highly flammable oxygen. "It's Mother's Day weekend—we know that," Jordan said in a news conference the day after the crash. "Words in the English language, at least the ones I know, are inadequate to express the amount of grief and sadness we feel." The company later put action behind its words, sponsoring a memorial service for 46 victims whose remains could not be identified.

Regret.   Another vocal strategy, *regret,* involves admitting sorrow and remorse for a situation. Like compassion, regret does not necessarily imply fault; in fact, statements of regret may specifically disclaim any liability. This is a very important perspective that public relations advisors bring in crisis situations. By expressing regret, public hostility can be tempered and the number and intensity of lawsuits may be contained. An example of the regret-without-apology strategy is shown by Canadian Prime Minister Jean Chretien, who in 1998 expressed regret over American and British bombing of Iraq, saying that he and visiting French Prime Minister Lionel Jospin regretted the air strikes but felt they were necessary. "We're not happy, but we had no choice," he said, "because Saddam Hussein asked for it." Chretien refused to apologize for his outspoken defense of the bombing.

Be aware, however, that regret without apology sometimes is not enough. Japan's Emperor Akihito learned that lesson when he visited England in 1998. The emperor spoke of his "deep sorrow and pain" over suffering during the Second World War. But former prisoners of war booed the emperor, and one protestor burned a Japanese flag in his presence. A spokesman for the veterans said, "The emperor's speech does not alter the position one jot as far as any expression of an apology to the POWs is concerned."

The reluctance of the Japanese government to officially apologize for wartime military atrocities has strained its relations with a number of countries.

Apology.   The vocal strategy focused most on the public's interests and least on the organization's is *apology*. Issuing an apology involves publicly accepting full responsibility and asking forgiveness. Use the strategy of apology when the organization is clearly at fault and when long-term rebuilding of relationships is more important than short-term stalling or legal posturing. Make sure the apology is straightforward, such as the statement by Frank Lorenzo, chairman of Continental Airlines, who said in a full-page newspaper ad: "We grew so fast that we made mistakes."

Like all strategies, apology must be considered in light of the particular public involved. Don't assume that the manner in which organizational managers or spokespersons might naturally frame an apology is the best way to do so. Ask yourself how the key public will respond to the apology. Naomi Sugimoto (1997) reported a study, for

---

Crisis Counsel: Public Relations v. Legal

Odwalla, Inc., a producer of juice products, faced a crisis in 1996 when its apple juice was found to be contaminated with E. coli. Several people became ill, and one child died.

When faced with media attention during the crisis, Odwalla used classic public relations techniques associated with Johnson & Johnson's handling of the Tylenol crisis, which put the public safety and the common good above the individual interests of the company. Odwalla initiated a voluntary recall in eight western states and a Canadian province. It sent representatives to meet with the family of the young victim, and it set up a Web page to update its customers.

Odwalla earned some praise by its response. A case study by Kathleen Martinelli and William Briggs (1998) noted that Odwalla relied on advice from both public relations and legal counselors, with strategists from each field taking a collaborative rather than an adversarial approach to the crisis. Nearly 47 percent of the company's statements reflected traditional public relations responses: explaining its policy, investigating allegations, expressing concern for victims, taking steps to prevent a recurrence of the problem. Meanwhile, only 12 percent reflected the common legal response of denying guilt, minimizing responsibility and shifting

blame to the plaintiffs. The remaining messages were mixed between legal and public relations approaches.

Kathy Fitzpatrick and Maureen Rubin (1995) pointed out that such collaboration between public relations and legal counsel usually results in more favorable media coverage and thus a more positive public response, serving the organization's long-term interests if the situation ends up in court.

In the Odwalla case, sales actually increased after the recall, a response similar to Pepsi's following its smooth handling of the syringe hoax.

Odwalla eventually was fined $1.5 million—a relatively mild sum, considering that juries have imposed much heavier fines in other cases, even those that didn't involve a death. Continuing its public relations approach, the company responded to the fine with grace. "We hope the visibility of [the size of the fine] will raise awareness and send a message to consumers about food safety," said a company spokesman.

Compare Odwalla's experience with that of a 1993 Jack-in-the-Box crisis, in which four people died from E. coli. The company's first response was from a legal standpoint: no comment, followed by attempts to shift blame to its supplier. Jack-in-the-Box eventually paid $58.5 million in fines.

example, that the Japanese are three times more likely than Americans are to ask for forgiveness as part of an apology, and the Japanese request is much more explicit ("Please forgive me") than is the typical American one ("I hope you will understand").

Apologies often are associated with relationship goals and with the symmetrical model of public relations that focuses on the long-term association of an organization with its publics. Cody and McLaughlin (1990) pointed out that apologies are more likely to occur when it is important to save face.

Strategic apologies often are opposed by lawyers who fear they will be used against an organization in a lawsuit. Such advice, presumably, was behind the reluctance of both Bill Clinton and George W. Bush during their political campaigns in not forthrightly admitting and apologizing for having used illegal drugs during their youths. Recall, also, the criticism each candidate received because of what was seen as dodging, hedging and other verbal exercises in evasion.

This concern is legitimate, but you also need to look at the opportunities an apology makes possible. An apology can prevent lawsuits or at least limit damages sought by claimants or assessed by judges or juries. Immediate apologies have short-circuited what could have been serious repercussions, such as when the Caldor department store in Norwalk, Conn., quickly apologized after 11 million copies of an advertising circular placed in 85 newspapers in 1989 had a picture of two smiling boys playing Scrabble on a board with the word "rape" spelled out. Instead of blaming its advertising agency, the company accepted responsibility and apologized. "Obviously, it's a mistake," said company spokeswoman Jennifer Belodeau in an Associated Press report. "It's not something that we would ever have done intentionally." It would be difficult to pursue legal or economic sanctions against a company that shows such integrity.

Conversely, lack of prompt apologies have been cited as the reason for lawsuits, such as a $400,000 claim against police in London, Ontario, by a man erroneously accused of drug trafficking; the man explained that he filed the lawsuit mainly because the police would not apologize.

Ford and Bridgestone/Firestone faced massive lawsuits after their products were linked to 148 rollover deaths. In January 2001, three Ford officials went to the bedside of a Texas woman who was paralyzed in one of the accidents. There they apologized, videotaping their action for broadcast on national television.

Defense attorneys often fear corporate apologies, but in personal-injury cases in particular, apologies can save the company money. Some attorneys point out that lawsuits often are brought by clients who seek an admission of corporate guilt, and a public apology can lessen the amount of money sought by an injured party or awarded by a sympathetic jury.

Easing the way for corporate apologies, California passed a law in 2000 stating that "apologies or benevolent gestures of sympathy connot be used or interpreted as admission of guilt or liability in California courts."

Communication strategists can take a lesson from etiquette columnist Judith Martin (1999), who advised in one of her Miss Manners columns that apologizing is a way to diffuse angry responses. A good apology should include an acknowledgment of having done something wrong, a sense of remorse, an attempt to repair the injustice if possible and a promise not to commit the offense again. Avoid pseudoapologies such as those by any number of politicians who have felt compelled to apologize "for anything I may have done that offended you" or stated "but it was only meant as a joke." Similarly, saying "I'm sorry that you took offense" is more critical than apologetic.

This strategy can be impacted by differing expectations about what an apology means. Americans received a culture lesson in 2001 when an American submarine surfaced quickly and collided with a small Japanese boat, killing nine fishermen and students.

In Japan, a person who injures others is expected to personally apologize, like the CEO of an airline company who visited the homes of 24 victim's families after the 1982 crash of one of his company's planes, or the milk company owner who, in 2000, called on each of his retail outlets to give his regrets after hundreds of people were poisoned by contaminated dairy products.

After the sea tragedy off Hawaii, the sub captain issued a statement through his lawyer expressing "sincere regret," but the Japanese rejected it as an apology. President Bush apologized, but the Japanese remained unsatisfied. Likewise apologies from the secretaries of state and defense and the American ambassador were found insufficient. Instead, the Japanese wanted to hear personally from the man who caused the accident, Commander Scott Waddle.

Three weeks later, Waddle hand wrote nine letters and asked that they be delivered to the families of the victims. Admiral William Fallon, the Navy's second in command, went to a small town in Japan to meet with the fathers of two of the dead students. Bowing deeply in a gesture of humility, he personally apologized and promised a full investigation.

A month after the accident, Waddle met personally—against his lawyers' advice—with family members who had been brought to Hawaii to observe the Navy investigation. He, too, bowed deeply and spoke with tears in his eyes about his remorse. And finally, the families accepted his apology.

Rectifying Behavior Strategies

A positive response to opposition and criticism involves **rectifying behavior strategies,** in which the organization does something to repair the damage done to its publics. These include investigation, corrective action, restitution and repentance.

Investigation.   *Investigation* is rectifying behavior in which the organization promises to examine the situation and then to act as the facts warrant. This is only a short-term strategy, a way of buying time—eventually the organization will have to respond with more substance. Use the investigation strategy only when the facts are uncertain enough to warrant a delay in other strategic response.

Corrective Action.   A stronger rectifying behavior is *corrective action,* which involves taking steps to contain a problem, repair the damage and/or prevent its recurrence. This is a strategy that can serve the mutual interests of both the organization and its public.

Take corrective action if the organization is in a position to fix a problem, especially if the organization was in some way unprepared or negligent. This was the case with

Texaco when, as noted previously, company executives made racist statements. Texaco responded aggressively with rectifying action that included sensitivity training and a procedure to weed out discrimination within the company.

Corrective action generally is expected when the organization has been at fault. But the response is even more powerful and positive when an organization willingly accepts responsibility for fixing a problem it did not cause. An example of this strategy is Johnson & Johnson's handling of the cyanide deaths associated with Tylenol. Though it was clear from the beginning that the company was not even negligently responsible for the product tampering, Johnson & Johnson nevertheless accepted the challenge to contain the damage and prevent any more. It recalled the product and then introduced a new triple-seal safety packaging that soon became the industry standard.

Restitution.   Another rectifying behavior, *restitution,* serves the mutual interests of the organization and its publics. It involves making amends by compensating victims or restoring a situation to its earlier condition. Such a response may be forced upon an organization through the legal process, but some organizations have found it beneficial to offer restitution before it is required.

Repentance.   The strongest type of rectifying behavior is *repentance,* which involves both a change of heart and a change in action. Repentance signals an organization's full atonement in the classic sense that it turns away from a former position and becomes an advocate for a new way of doing business. Many organizations, caught in a moral or legal embarrassment, promise repentance and a future of rightdoing, but few achieve such a turnaround.

One example of a repenting organization is Denny's restaurants, which faced accusations and lawsuits for racial discrimination at several of its 1,500 company and franchise restaurants. One of the most notorious cases involved 21 members of the Secret Service in 1994: while 15 white agents were served quickly, a waitress and manager delayed serving six black agents for 20 minutes as their food got cold. Publicity about that discriminatory act led to a series of lawsuits for similar acts of discrimination, and the company eventually paid $54 million in legal settlements.

Denny's also adopted an aggressive anti-discrimination policy that included hiring minority managers, increasing minority franchise owners from one in 1993 to 109 five years later, providing training for its employees and firing employees who discriminated against customers. "All of us at Denny's regret any mistakes made in the past," said CEO C. Ronald Petty when the legal settlement was ending. "But I want to emphasize that Denny's does not tolerate racial discrimination. Our company policy is clear and simple: If employees discriminate, they will be fired. If franchisees discriminate, they will lose their franchises."

Is the company living up to its promises? Situations may vary, of course, but one black college student tells of being cursed at by fellow customers when he and some friends were seated at a Denny's restaurant. The manager observed the situation, apologized profusely for the rude behavior by the customers and gave the group of black men free drinks.

Often an organization will use several strategies. An apology, for example, may also involve investigation, justification, restitution and concession. During the Tylenol crisis,

Johnson & Johnson used the strategies of investigation, compassion, excuse, relabeling and corrective action.

Strategic Inaction: Silence

The final category of public relations responses involves **strategic inaction,** the considered decision by an organization under siege to offer no substantive comment or to make no overt action. Occasionally strategic inaction—that is, *silence*—is an appropriate public relations response, a strategy of patience and composure. By not responding to criticism, an organization may be able to shorten the life span of a crisis situation. Strategic silence can work when publics accept that an organization is remaining silent not out of guilt or embarrassment but rather because it is motivated by higher intentions such as compassion for victims, respect for privacy or other noble considerations. In some circumstances, the law requires organizations to maintain silence, at least on particulars. If so, this requirement should be explained by the organization as the reason for its silence.

When considering strategic silence, however, remember that the response is likely to be accepted only by those publics that already trust the integrity of the organization; opponents will find plenty of ammunition in the lack of response. Silence also risks allowing negative statements to stand unchallenged, which could hurt the organization in the long run. Additionally, a policy of strategic silence may be difficult to maintain if a strong opponent is able to insist on a public response. Remember that silence can imply indifference not only to an opponent but also to the issue itself. This might be of real interest to some of an organization's key publics. By dismissing the issue, the organization also risks slighting anyone who feels the issue is worthy of response.

Strategic silence is not the same as "no comment." Such a statement invariably is interpreted as an acknowledgment of guilt, implying that the organization not only did something wrong but did it so ineptly or so blatantly that it can't think of any explanation that would be accepted by its publics. Avoid "no comment" responses and related disdainful statements such as "we won't dignify that accusation with a reply." If strategic silence is the chosen response, the organization nevertheless may need to make a public statement giving the reason it chooses not to address the issue further.

Strategic Planning Example: *Formulating Action and Response Strategies*

Upstate College will develop the following strategies:

Proactive Strategy
- Involve student public in celebrations and other special events focused on the academic expansion.
- Enhance alliances with other high schools based on new academic opportunities at the college.
- Take advantage of the many newsworthy activities associated with the expansion.

UPSTATE COLLEGE

Reactive Strategy

No responsive strategy is anticipated, because the expansion to a four-year program is unlikely to generate opposition or criticism.

■ ■ ■

Tiny Tykes will develop the following strategies:

Proactive Strategy

- Place a high priority on research and development as it relates to high-quality standards for toy products.
- Form alliances with customers and consumer advocates focused on the safety of children's toys.
- Initiate news activities focused on toy safety.
- Engage in transparent communication to allow employees and consumer advocates to observe the company's efforts to produce safe and high-quality toys.

Reactive Strategy

- Make a concession to customers and consumer advocates by sponsoring university research on the role of play in child psychological and educational development.
- If necessary, reiterate statement of regret issued prior to the toy recall.
- Display corporate repentance by publicly relaunching the product with a recommitment to quality and excellence.

Strategic Planning Exercise: *Formulating Action and Response Strategies*

Basic Planning Questions

1. What proactive strategies might you develop?
2. What reactive strategies might you develop?
3. How consistent are these strategies with past practices of your organization?

Expanded Planning Questions

A. Proactive Strategy

1. Is it appropriate to use any of the following approaches? If "yes," how?

   Action

   Organizational performance

   Audience participation

   Alliances

   Sponsorships

   Activism

Communication
> Newsworthy information
>
> Transparent communication

2. Summarize the proactive strategy of your organization.

B. Reactive Strategy

1. Is it appropriate to use any of the following approaches? If "yes," how?

Pre-emptive Response
> Prebuttal

Offensive Response
> Attack
>
> Embarrassment
>
> Threat

Defensive Response
> Denial
>
> Excuse
>
> Justification

Diversionary Response
> Concession
>
> Ingratiation
>
> Disassociation
>
> Relabeling

Vocal Commiseration
> Concern
>
> Condolence
>
> Regret
>
> Apology

Rectifying Behavior
> Investigation
>
> Corrective Action
>
> Restitution
>
> Repentance

Strategic Inaction
> Silence

2. Summarize the reactive strategy of your organization.

C. Action/Response Consistency

1. Is this action/response consistent with past verbal messages of this organization/ spokesperson? If "no," explain the inconsistency.

Phase Two

Step
5

2. Is the action/response consistent with past actions of this organization/spokesperson? If "no," explain the inconsistency.

3. Is the action/response consistent with the mission of this source? If "no," explain the inconsistency.

4. Is the action/response consistent with image of this source? If "no," explain the inconsistency.

5. Is the action/response ethical? If "no," develop a different response.

Consensus Check

Does agreement exist within your organization about the recommended strategies within this phase of the planning process?

   If "yes," proceed to the next section.

   If "no," consider the value and/or possibility of achieving consensus before proceeding.

Phase Two

Step
5

Using Effective Communication

Having identified your publics and established objectives for what is to be achieved, and having set into motion the way the organization is preparing to act to achieve those objectives, it is time to turn your attention to how best to communicate. Since strategic communication is carefully planned communication, this is an important step.

Remember what we said earlier about publics and audiences: Publics are groups of people in a relationship with your organization; audiences are people who receive messages. At this stage of the planning process, begin treating your publics as the audiences with whom you are communicating and consider the various elements of effective communication. Who should present the message? What appeals should be made in the message? How should the message be structured? What words should be used? What symbols?

Thousands of public relations and marketing messages bombard people each day—that's more than three different messages every minute of every waking hour—most of them trying to sell something or gain support. Amid all this noise, how can your organization's message stand out? It's not easy, but effective communication can help your message rise above the clamor.

Communication Processes

Several different approaches to communication are used in public relations and related fields. Three varieties are worth particular attention: information, persuasion and dialogue. These align loosely with the classic models of public relations. Informative communication plays out as press agentry and public information; persuasive communication is asymmetric, with a focus on advocacy and influence; dialogic communication is a symmetric approach that is rooted in relationships. Let's look more closely at each process of communication.

Information

Information focuses on the content and channels of communication. It involves a message sent by a source to a receiver, with ideas encoded and interpreted through symbols (words or images) that are transmitted person-to-person or through some technical connection. Harold Lasswell (1948) offered a simple verbal formula of

Exhibit 6.1   A Model of Information-Based Communication

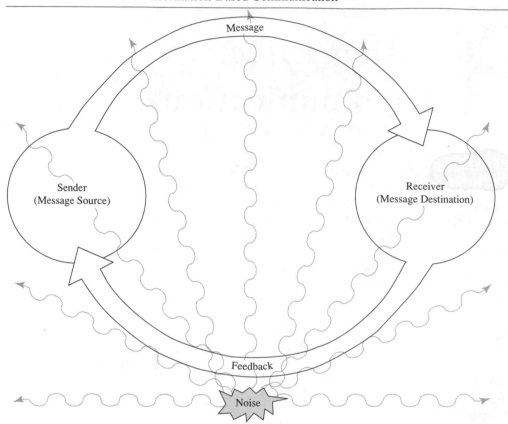

In this model of communication, a sender (which can be a person or an organization) *encodes* a message (using verbal and/or nonverbal symbols) that is sent through a particular *channel* (such as a speech, a brochure, a phone call, etc.) to a receiver, who *decodes* (or interprets) the message. The receiver in turn reacts and responds to the message by encoding feedback that is sent back to the original sender. Any communication context also involves *noise,* which is any interference that limits the ability of the channel to carry a message faithfully from sender to receiver. Such interference can be in the encoding or decoding of the message or in the channels used to transmit the message.

communication: "Who says what to whom with what effect." We might add "how" and perhaps even "why" to this formula.

Exhibit 6.1 provides a visual model of information-based communication. This model is based on the frequently cited work of Claude Shannon and Warren Weaver (1949) and Norbert Wiener (1954), echoed by David Berlo (1960) and Wilbur Schramm (1971). Shannon and Weaver, scientists with Bell Telephone Laboratories, developed a visual model of what they called the *mathematical theory of communication.* Their approach was linear, with virtually tangible data encoded and transmitted through a channel to a receiver. In essence, theirs was a model for monologue, with the source

---

Research Background on Persuasion

Several theories dealing with persuasion are relevant to much public relations and marketing activity. Here are a few of the most common theories.

The *balance theory,* articulated by psychologist Fritz Heider (1946, 1958), is the oldest consistency theory, observing that unbalanced mental stances create tension and force an individual to restore balance. Theodore Newcomb (1953) extended this to groups, calling it the *symmetry theory.* Charles E. Osgood and Percy Tannenbaum's *congruity theory* (1955) added some measurement in attitude. The lesson of these consistency theories for public relations practitioners is that attitude change can be stimulated by information that causes people to realize that two attitudes are in conflict and that the persuasiveness of the source is a major factor to accomplish this.

Social psychologist Leon Festinger's *cognitive dissonance theory* (1957) explained that the more people experience the psychological discomfort of having contradictory attitudes or beliefs, the more likely they will reduce the discomfort, usually by changing one of their attitudes or beliefs. An important element of this theory is the concept of *selective exposure,* which refers to seeking information that supports a currently held attitude while avoiding information that does not support it.

The *inoculation theory,* proposed by William McGuire and Demetrios Papageorgis (1961), suggested that unchallenged beliefs and attitudes can be swayed with persuasive information, while attitudes that have been tested are more resistant to change. This latter aspect is particularly useful to strategic communicators seeking to create resistance to potentially opposing arguments.

The *social judgment theory,* put forward by Muzafer Sherif and Carl I. Hovland (1961), observed that individuals accept or reject messages to the extent that they perceive the messages as corresponding to their internal anchors (attitudes and beliefs) and as being ego-involved (affecting the person's self-concept).

Phase Two

Step 6

---

person or organization talking at an audience. Wiener's *cybernetic model of communication* was more circular in design, involving feedback from the receiver to influence the sender. This model is a bit more focused on two-way communication.

Persuasion

Another process of communication, **persuasion,** consciously attempts to influence people, using ethical means that enhance a democratic society. Persuasion is an inherent part of social interaction, something people everywhere do. Persuasion is neither deception, which relies on miscommunication, nor is it coercion, which relies on force rather than on communication. Nor is it propaganda, which is associated with half-truths and hidden agendas.

Persuasion is particularly associated with the advocacy or asymmetric approach to strategic communication, in which an organization presents its point of view in an attempt to convince its publics to give their agreement and support.

The practice of persuasion is widespread and popular. In marketing, for example, most companies try to convince potential consumers to buy the company's products or services. In public relations, organizations try to convince publics to agree with this concept, support that candidate, or follow certain procedures. In public health and safety campaigns, agencies try to persuade young people to stop smoking, motorists to start wearing seatbelts and middle-aged people to get more exercise. In international relations, governments try to convince counterparts in other countries to adopt democratic practices, and nongovernmental organizations try to influence governments to respect human rights or to eliminate gender, religious or racial discrimination.

Dialogue

Dialogue involves the deeply conscious interaction of two parties in communication. It involves a sincere and competent attempt at mutual understanding, the kind of communication described by existentialist philosopher Martin Buber (1947). It is what Sieberg (1976) called "confirming communication," which seeks to heal and strengthen relationships: "Confirmation, like existential dialogue, is a mutual experience involving sharing at several levels—sharing of talking, sharing of self, sharing of respect, sharing of trust."
Dialogue involves four goals useful to public relations:

1. To provide for an information exchange between individuals or groups
2. To help communication partners make responsible and personally acceptable decisions
3. To help revive the original vitality of a relationship
4. To foster a deep relationship that continues to unite communication partners ever more closely

Dialogue also generates two management practices: consensus building and conflict resolution. **Consensus building** is a process of identifying and then preventing or overcoming barriers between people and/or organizations. The related concept of **conflict resolution** involves making peace and restoring harmony, often with communication as the primary tool. Both concepts are based on dialogue, which helps parties consider issues in light of their mutual needs and arrive at solutions that enhance their relationship.
Carl Botan (1997) observed the relationship between dialogue and ethics. He noted that dialogic communication is characterized by a relationship in which both parties genuinely care about each other rather than merely seek to fulfill their own needs. This kind of relationship is embodied in the symmetrical model of public relations, in which organizations try to adapt and harmonize with their publics. It elevates publics to an equal footing with the organization itself, allowing either party in the interchange to take the initiative. An example of this would be an equal relationship between corporate management and either an external public such as an activist group or an internal public such as an employee union, in which either side could call meetings, propose agenda topics, conduct research, launch a communication program and so on. Botan also noted that advances in communication technology have made it easier for organizations to engage with their publics in a two-way dialogue.
In the practice of strategic communication, there is a role for each type of communication model: information, persuasion and dialogue. Information approaches to communication often focus on the message sender, while persuasive communication

deals with the content of the message. Dialogue, in turn, emphasizes the relationship between the parties in the communication process. Each of these elements is important to public relations, which necessarily deals with the actors in the communication process, the messages shared between them, and their relationship.

Rhetorical Tradition

The use of communication to influence ideas and actions and to strengthen relationships is a basic element of human society. History has handed down to us some ancient examples of the art of effective communication. Much of it comes from the dawn of Western civilization in the lands encircling the Mediterranean Sea. Two of the oldest-known pieces of literature, the *Iliad* and the *Odyssey,* both ascribed to the Greek poet Homer about 2,800 years ago, feature several examples of effective persuasive speeches, such as Odysseus' discussion with the Cyclops about why the monster should not eat him.

About 300 years later, Corax of Syracuse wrote a handbook on **rhetoric**—persuasive communication—in which he noted the relationship between certainty and probability: while physical evidence can prove something true and thus beyond argument, verbal evidence can show only greater or lesser probabilities that something is true. In Athens, Socrates and his student Plato criticized rhetoric as verbal maneuvering that could make right seem wrong and important appear unimportant. They called for a grounding in truth and taught some of the skills associated with ethical communication, such as logical organization of ideas.

The first person to study persuasive communication systematically was one of Plato's students, Aristotle, who became the court educator to Alexander the Great. Twenty-five centuries ago, Aristotle identified three central elements of rhetoric that today remain as cornerstones of persuasive communication: ethos, logos and pathos. Following the principle of "don't mess with success," *Strategic Planning for Public Relations* uses these elements as the framework for developing a strategic and effective public relations and marketing communication message. Each will be discussed in detail shortly.

From the Greek foundation, the study of communication passed over to classical Rome, where Cicero organized rhetoric into five principles (roughly argumentation, organization, style, delivery and memorization). Quintillian wrote on the education of communicators, advising that they were about more than simply persuasion; they also were in the business of informing, motivating and inspiring.

During the Middle Ages, the Saxon theologian Alcuin, teacher and advisor to the Emperor Charlemagne, reinterpreted Roman rhetoric and applied it to practical areas such as public policy, legal and judicial proceedings, and the placement of blame or praise.

Rhetoric also influenced the field of religion and vice versa. Augustine of Hippo, a bishop in Roman Africa, became one of the most influential figures in persuasive communication with his study, teaching and personal examples dealing with preaching. Later the Italian philosopher-monk Thomas Aquinas applied Aristotelian principles of ethos, logos and pathos to the understanding and explanation of religious belief.

Phase Two

Step
6

More contemporary figures in the evolution of our understanding of communication include the English philosopher Francis Bacon, credited with formulating the scientific method; American language theorist Kenneth Burke, who studied the nature and power of symbols in human interaction; language critic Richard Weaver, who dealt with the cultural role of persuasion; and Belgian philosopher Chaim Perelman, who analyzed how communicators can gain "the adherence of minds."

Ethos: Convincing Communicators

Ethos is communication effectiveness based on the character of the speaker and on the common ground shared by speakers and audiences. Years of research by social scientists have produced a snapshot of an effective **message source.** This is a person or an organization perceived by an audience as being credible, having charisma and exercising some kind of control—what we might call the "Three C's" of an effective communicator. These are presented visually in Exhibit 6.2. Individually, each of these perceptions is a powerful tool for the practitioner; in combination, they create a compelling factor in effective communication.

It is important to note that each of these elements is based on the audience's perception of the speaker. Aristotle observed that reputation precedes the speaker,

Exhibit 6.2   The Three C's of Effective Communication

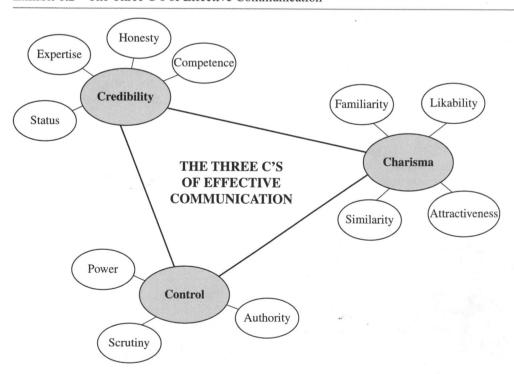

setting the stage for the audience to accept or reject the speaker's message. Even before the speaker presents a message, the audience makes a judgment based on the speaker's prestige and prominence. Precisely because reputation has such a direct and predictable impact on their ability to influence their publics, organizations pay much attention to what people know and think about them.

Let's look at the Three C's in detail.

Credibility

A source who has **credibility**—the power to inspire belief—is one who demonstrates the qualities of expertise, status, competence and honesty. The most important factor in making a message source effective is *expertise,* which means that the source knows what he or she is talking about. *Status* is related to expertise but rests more with the audience's deference to the social position or prestige of a message source. Another related concept is *competence,* the ability to remain calm under pressure and to be clear and dynamic in presenting the message to others, especially those who may not share the same knowledge or loyalties. Finally, *honesty* means that the source is willing to provide full and accurate information, is operating without bias, and thus is worthy of trust.

Credibility is tremendously important to persuasion. Though we might wish it were different, being a good speaker or writer is more effective than having good physical evidence. Sources perceived as being highly credible are believed on their own merits and whatever evidence they present has little added value. Even audiences that don't understand the issues will accept their messages, just because the sources are believable.

Highly credible sources also can appeal to fear and use intense or opinionated language that would be counterproductive coming from sources with lesser credibility. For example, it was his high credibility that allowed President Ronald Reagan to call the Soviet Union "an evil empire" and be effective in such extreme speech.

As part of the process of strategic planning, you can enhance source credibility by reinforcing each of these characteristics. Remember that perception is the key: The source's expertise and honesty must be apparent to the audience. Some campaigns have faltered because the audience didn't realize the source was an expert or because the source didn't appear trustworthy.

Perceived expertise can be intensified by using a message source who has experience, knowledge, intelligence, occupational or professional background or the wisdom that comes with age. Likewise, *perceived status* is enhanced by the use of message sources who have social status and prestige. Of course, both of these must be relevant to the topic being addressed—a physician may be very credible on the issue of health but not particularly so on a political topic. Expertise and status can be borrowed from recognized experts by quoting them.

Communication competence is obviously a matter of perception. The audience perceives (or not) that the speaker is calm, clear and able to communicate. *Perceived competence* can be enhanced by two elements associated with effective presentations. One element is physical stature, which includes being tall, sitting or standing erect, maintaining eye contact and having facial composure. The other element that

---

Credibility and News Sources

A survey of 545 Americans by Burson-Marsteller Public Relations (1998) probed the relative credibility of different types of news sources on an environmental issue, specifically global warming. The researchers identified several hypothetical news sources and asked respondents to rate the credibility of each. Here are the credibility levels reported:

53%   Professor of atmospheric science at a well-known university

43%   Government scientists from the National Oceanographic and Atmospheric Administration

29%   Spokesperson for an environmental group

11%   Spokesperson for an oil or natural gas company

10%   Hollywood celebrity active on environmental issues

What's the lesson to be learned from this research? It deals with expertise. Recognized experts without apparent self-interest are the most credible message sources. The public may admire celebrities and may even pay attention to them without being persuaded by the messages they present.

---

enhances competence is vocal quality, which involves enunciating clearly, initiating communication, speaking with conviction and authority, exuding energy and enthusiasm, and avoiding language fillers such as "um" and "uh." Two kinds of skill builders—coaching in public speaking and training for media interviews—can help a speaker strategically develop vocal emphasis, convincing gestures and other aspects of communication competence.

Like the other characteristics of credibility, *perceived honesty* can be enhanced to help a source appear more trustworthy by emphasizing the objectivity, integrity and neutrality with which the source approaches the subject. Message sources who advocate positions contrary to their personal interests or who take an unexpected position have a special credibility. For example, a physician who recommends herbal medicine will be particularly believable because the health-care establishment traditionally has ignored, even scorned, the medicinal value of herbs. Honesty also is enhanced when the message source shows a consistency between past and present and between words and deeds.

As a side note, if you are presenting a position that differs from one taken by your organization in the past, signal the change and carefully explain not only the new posture but also the reason for the change. Try not to allow yourself to be labeled as inconsistent or as contradictory of past statements. Certainly you can change your mind, but make sure you let your audience know the reason for such a change.

Charisma

The magnetic appeal or personal charm that some message sources enjoy over an audience is called **charisma,** another important element of persuasion. Like credibility, charisma is a matter of perception, and it varies greatly from one person to another and from one public to another.

Charisma has several specific characteristics: familiarity, likability, similarity and attractiveness. One important aspect of charisma is *familiarity,* the extent to which the audience already knows (or thinks it knows) the message source. Charisma also involves *likability,* the extent to which the audience admires what it knows about the source or what it sees and hears when the source begins to communicate. This generally means that the message source is neutral on divisive social and political issues and not associated with controversy or partisanship—unless the audience itself is particularly partisan. The principle of likability may suggest that, for a general and mixed audience, you would avoid using a message source who is closely associated with a particular cultural, ethnic or religious group, because the audience may not like someone closely identified with alien characteristics.

Charisma also involves *similarity,* the extent to which the source resembles the audience (or the way in which audience members would like to see themselves). This may be a reflection of audience demographics in terms of age, gender, occupation, ethnicity, religion, culture, shared values or sociopolitical perspectives. Thus the principle of similarity offers a parallel guideline to that of familiarity. You might consider using a message source closely associated with a particular cultural, ethnic or religious group when the audience also is associated with that group. Similarity is particularly important when a communicator is seeking long-term persuasion, less so for short-term objectives. It also is a major factor in enhancing dialogic communication.

Finally, charisma is affected by the *attractiveness* of the source, which involves the source's physical looks, demeanor, poise and presence, as well as both the clothing worn and the setting in which the source is presented. Note, however, that physical attractiveness and beauty are significantly less important than credibility and other aspects of charisma. Despite the Hollywood emphasis on plenty of sex appeal and glamour, average-looking people can be highly effective message sources. Indeed, speakers who are very good-looking, especially if they flaunt their looks, may have difficulty being perceived as much more than pretty faces and beautiful bodies.

Control

The third component of an effective message source is **control,** which is rooted in a message source's command over the audience and on the perceived willingness to exercise that power. One of the most important aspects of control is *power,* the raw and recognized ability to dominate and to reward or punish. Guilt appeals (which we will discuss later) often are associated with powerful message sources. Control also may be based on a message source's *authority,* which is the right to rule over or direct the actions of another. Authority implies that the audience more or less willingly has granted the right of control and thus will give obedience. Authority often involves a legal or social prerogative. It also can involve moral leverage, such as by summoning the audience to its stated values or calling it to its accepted duty. Both guilt appeals and virtue appeals (which we will discuss later) may be associated with authority figures. Finally, the persuasive element of control suggests *scrutiny,* the ability to examine. Someone who is able to investigate you also is able to pronounce your blame, proclaim your innocence and perhaps grant forgiveness.

As with the previous characteristics of an effective source, control must be perceived by the receiver. Keep in mind that perceptions change. The so-called **halo effect** demonstrates that a source perceived as credible, charismatic and/or in control can rely on this reputation. Think of the many situations in which a politician—you supply the name, from either side of the aisle—can do no wrong in the eyes of his supporters but can do nothing right in the eyes of those who despise him. The same can be said about some athletes and entertainers who evoke passionate responses of either adoration or condemnation. The halo effect is very useful for the communicator. But halos slip and stars fall, so be careful about where you shine your spotlight.

Identifying Organizational Spokespeople

The elements of credibility, charisma and control can be maximized as part of strategic planning, for example, by selecting an appropriate spokesperson who is likely to appeal to an organization's publics.

Celebrity Spokespersons.   Celebrities often are used because they are charismatic and familiar. Entertainers and sports figures frequently are spokespersons for companies and social causes. Politicians are used less so, because they often have as many foes as they have supporters. Several ex-politicians, however, have found second careers as organizational representatives, such as former New York City Mayor Ed Koch (Weight Watchers) and former senator and presidential candidate Bob Dole (MasterCard and Pfizer Pharmaceutical). Sometimes spokespersons actually are likable "spokescharacters," such as Morris the Cat, Officer McGruff or Budweiser's frogs.

Discretion is needed in identifying celebrity spokespersons. Their fame draws attention to your cause or company, but celebrities aren't yours alone, and endorsements can bring unwanted attention. A drug-education agency understood this and took great care in selecting a professional sports figure as a spokesperson and board member. After rejecting several athletes, the agency signed a football player who had a consistent reputation and a clean record not only on alcohol but also with respect to both recreational and performance-enhancing drugs.

Some organizations, however, have been humiliated by celebrity spokespersons. Hertz endured great embarrassment during the murder trial of O. J. Simpson, its spokesperson of many years. Pepsi cancelled million-dollar advertising commitments involving Madonna, Michael Jackson and Mike Tyson after embarrassing personal publicity about each. Seagram's dropped Bruce Willis after reports that he had a drinking problem, and the Beef Industry Council dropped Cybill Shepherd after she told a national magazine that one of her beauty secrets is avoiding red meats. When the then-world's fastest runner, Canadian Olympic athlete Ben Johnson, was stripped of his gold medal for using steroids, he also was dropped as spokesperson for companies in the United States, Canada, Japan, Finland and Italy. And the Florida Citrus Commission had a sting of negative publicity over its spokespersons: Anita Bryant, who began a crusade against gay rights; Burt Reynolds, who became embroiled in a bitter divorce; and controversial political commentator Rush Limbaugh, who lasted just one year. After that, the commission kept a lower profile.

Public relations and marketing people selecting celebrity spokespersons generally look for a connection with their key publics. It's not accidental, for example, that Hurley Hayward is the spokesperson for Porsche. Ninety percent of Porsche's customers are men, and most of them are racing fans. Hayward is one of the world's best race-car drivers, the multiple winner of LeMans, Sebring and Daytona. Likewise, it makes sense for people like tennis great John McEnroe and basketball player Karl Malone to be the pitchmen for Rogaine Extra Strength in an ongoing promotional campaign using sports figures who have had positive results with the hair-growth formula. And after newsman Mike Wallace went public with his struggle against depression, the Colorado Behavioral Healthcare Council felt he would be just the famous face to participate in its public service campaign on suicide and depression prevention.

Researchers Alan Miciak and William Shanklin (1994) reported that advertisers look for five characteristics when selecting spokespersons: They must be trustworthy, readily recognizable, affordable, at little risk for negative publicity and appropriately matched with intended audiences. In some cases, the selection of celebrity spokespersons is made easier by scientific research. For example, Performer Q Scores, compiled by Marketing Evaluations, Inc., uses consumer panels to calculate the familiarity and likability of about 1,500 famous personalities each year.

Company Spokespeople.   In identifying organizational spokespersons, don't confine yourself to a single individual if more than one would better serve your communication needs with various publics. Your organization must speak with a *single voice,* but this may be accomplished effectively with two or more speakers presenting coordinated and complementary messages. The important thing is to make sure that a single, consistent message is being presented in the name of your organization.

Also, give careful thought to who from your organization might be selected as a spokesperson for a particular issue. Don't presume that the CEO is the best person in every case. There are three good reasons not to use the CEO as organizational spokesperson. First, you don't want to overexpose the boss; save him or her for the big issues. Second, the CEO may not know the level of detail necessary for a news conference or interview; perhaps a project planner, department manager or another hands-on person would be more knowledgeable and credible. Third, the CEO may not have the personality to exhibit in public or especially on camera the calm, credibility, charisma or other characteristics of an effective spokesperson.

Some organizations buffer the CEO by appointing another spokesperson for negative news, saving the CEO for the more positive public and media encounters. In a news conference, the CEO could be put on the spot and expected to indicate what the organization's activity or response might be; another organizational spokesperson could more easily deflect such forecasts and avoid inappropriate speculation.

Don't presume that the public relations director should automatically become the spokesperson, either. Especially in confrontational or other crisis situations, the director may be busy behind the scenes advising on strategy and message delivery. Also, the media often don't recognize the public relations director as a high-ranking organizational official; instead they see him or her as a mere mouthpiece for the people they really wish to interview. Most organizations use their public relations directors as preliminary media contacts, conduits for factual information that doesn't require attribution, or sources for other media background information.

Spokespeople and Ethos.   Celebrity or not, speakers should strive to identify with their audiences. One way is to emphasize similar backgrounds, especially when such common ground may not be evident to the audience. For example, a university professor before a group of entering freshmen may recall her first months in college or an affluent politician may explain to a group of inner-city residents his experience of growing up amid poverty, albeit of a rural variety.

Another way for speakers to emphasize similarity is to avoid language that separates them from their audience. A white speaker couldn't use the phrase "you people" before a black audience without emphasizing his differentness and insulting his listeners. Recall the flap when an aide to the mayor of Washington, D.C., used the term *niggardly* correctly but inappropriately for his listener, who assumed the obscure word was a racial slur. Remember that words properly used may not be words properly understood, especially if they are not part of the shared experiences of both the speaker and the audience.

Strategic Planning Example: Identifying Message Sources

In its current efforts to expand enrollment and retention, financial contributions and community support, Upstate will use the following three spokespeople:

Dr. Alexandra Jolin, president of Upstate College

Dr. Jolin will be perceived by most audiences as highly credible because of her position. She is a dynamic speaker who projects an enthusiasm and friendliness that most people appreciate. In addition, she holds various leadership positions not only with the college but within the local community and within the state's higher education establishment.

Michael McMillan, chair of the Upstate College Board of Trustees, Upstate alumnus and prominent business leader in Upstate City

Mr. McMillan will be perceived as a credible source, especially by residents of Upstate City. He has received media training and is articulate and competent in media and other public presentations. He is in a position of leadership.

Inez SantaElana, president of the UC Student Government

Because of her leadership position with the student government, Ms. SantaElana will be perceived as a credible source, especially with current and potential students. She also is a regional celebrity among area high-school students who has developed much poise and confidence as a result of her athletic achievements, including state records in speed skating.

■ ■ ■

In its campaign to increase consumer confidence, Tiny Tykes will use the following two spokespeople:

Michael Beaucheforte, senior vice president for consumer affairs

Mr. Beauchefort will be perceived as credible because of his expertise within the company and because he was hired specifically to address consumer issues. He is a persuasive speaker with a friendliness that exudes trust and disarms skeptics. (Note that company president Theodore Frankelberger should not be used as a spokesperson in media situations because he becomes very nervous when speaking in public; this nervousness is often perceived as insincerity and evasiveness.)

Mary Margaret O'Sullivan, Tiny Tykes Consumer Advisory Council member

Ms. O'Sullivan is a consumer whose child was stained by the defective toy. She now sits on the Consumer Advisory Council that helped relaunch the product. Because of her personal involvement, Ms. O'Sullivan will be perceived as a trustworthy and expert spokesperson. She is not an accomplished public speaker, but her uneasiness adds to her credibility and charisma.

Strategic Planning Exercise: *Identifying Message Sources*

Basic Planning Questions
1. Identify several possible spokespersons who could present your message.
2. What is the level of credibility for each possible spokesperson?
3. What is the level of charisma for each?
4. What is the level of control for each?

Expanded Planning Questions
Answer the following items for each possible message source. Then compare your responses to determine the sources best suited for this communication task. An effective message source will have mainly high and positive rankings in each item.

Credibility
1. How expert on this topic is the message source?
2. How well known are his/her credentials to the audience?
   If expertise is high, should the audience be reminded of this?
   If expertise is not known, can the audience be made informed of this?
3. Does the message source enunciate clearly?
4. Does the source speak with dynamism and authority?
5. Does the source speak calmly and reassuringly on this topic?
6. How trustworthy will the source be perceived as being?
7. Can the source speak truthfully and independently about the topic?
8. Does the source have any associations that compete with the organization?

Phase Two

Step
6

9. Does the source have any associations that are inconsistent with the organization's image?

10. Is the source available to your organization?

Charisma

1. How similar is the source to the audience?
2. How familiar is the audience with the source?
3. How attractive is the source to the audience?
4. Can the source be presented in an attractive setting?

Control

1. Does the source have any moral leverage with this audience?
2. Does the source have any power over this audience?
3. Does the source have the willingness to use this power?
4. Does the source have the ability to investigate this audience?
5. Does the source have the authority to reward or punish this audience?
6. Does the source have the authority to blame or forgive this audience?

Logos: Appealing to Reason

Communication effectiveness based on the rational appeal of the message was known to the ancient Greeks as **logos.** The conscious attempt to persuade by appealing to logos— logic and reason—is an obvious place to start planning your strategic message. Distill your message and resist the temptation to bombard your audience with every bit of information available to you. Clarify and simplify.

The ancient art of rhetoric is kept current with an expanding research base (see Larson, 2000; Benjamin, 1997; Infante, et al., 1996; Johnston, 1994; and Ross, 1994). Following is a summary of recommendations and conclusions from many different research studies into effective communication and persuasion.

Proposition

The primary idea in a speech, editorial, advertisement, television program or some other communication vehicle is called a **proposition** or a **claim.** Only one proposition should be presented at time; more than one can confuse the audience and lessen the impact of the message. There are four kinds of propositions: factual, conjecture, value and policy.

- A *factual proposition* states that something exists, based on provable (usually physical) evidence. For example, proof of an increase in urban air pollution may be environmental tests. Factual claims often are linked with communication objectives focused on awareness, which seek to increase attention or build greater understanding.

- A *conjecture proposition* states that something probably exists, based on reasoned conclusion drawn from physical evidence, and asks audiences to agree with the conclusion. An example of this is a conclusion for or against the continuation of affirmative action regulations, in which the conclusion flows logically from the facts as they are presented. Conjecture propositions often relate to communication objectives dealing with acceptance, fostering supportive attitudes.

- A *value proposition* identifies the virtue of something, such as the merits (or folly) of health-care reform. Value claims also relate to objectives dealing with acceptance, which try to increase interest or build positive attitudes.

- A *policy proposition* identifies a new course of action and encourages its adoption, such as advocacy for changing the legal drinking age or for beginning a school dress code. Policy claims often reflect objectives associated with opinion and action.

Whatever the type of proposition, it should be supported with strong arguments and clear proof. Such proof varies from person to person, and group to group. To some, an intelligent argument with understandable data and logical conclusions may prove a point; to others, only the strongest and most consistent of physical data may be considered as proof.

Verbal Evidence

About 2,500 years ago, Corax of Syracuse taught that disputes are settled easily when clear physical evidence shows inarguably the truth or falsity of a claim. That remains true today. Most of the time, however, we are not lucky enough to have such unchallenged hard evidence, so we have to rely on other forms of proof. This verbal evidence can take several different forms, including analogies, comparisons, examples, statistics and testimonials. Here's a brief look at each.

Analogies.   As a type of persuasion technique, *analogies* use similar situations and allusions to help your audience understand new ideas, specifically by making a comparison between two things that are essentially different but nevertheless strikingly alike in an important aspect. For example, cars double-parked on a congested city street can be analogous to the effect of cholesterol in clogging arteries. Analogies usually are presented as similes and metaphors.

Comparisons.   By highlighting the characteristics or values related to an issue, *comparisons* can liken it to something else the audience might understand. Make positive comparisons to things the audience already acknowledges and admires, and make negative comparisons to things the audience holds in low esteem. Make comparisons that are easy to understand, such as by showing how one issue, product or theme relates to another. For example, show how a particular tax-reform proposal is more economically feasible than an alternative proposal.

Examples.   *Examples* provide conclusions drawn from related instances. Such illustrations can be effective, particularly if the case is recent, reliable and relevant to the

Phase Two

Step
6

situation at hand. Be careful not to argue from far-fetched examples that are easy to dismiss as being not only irrelevant but also deceitful.

Statistics.　The use of *statistics* can provide clear and hard-to-dispute facts to make the best case. For example, it is easy to argue the superiority of a particular automobile with statistics dealing with safety, cost and other easily understood data. But be careful, because statistics can be misinterpreted and manipulated, and many people have learned through hard personal experience that comparative statistics are not always as neat and clean as they appear to be.

Testimonies and Endorsements.　Comments by witnesses and people who have used your organization's product or service or who espouse an idea your organization supports can provide effective verbal evidence. Such *testimonies* can take the form of letters or other statements of support from satisfied customers. Similarly, *endorsements* and recommendations from celebrities can be persuasive, especially if the celebrity is known to have used the product (such as Bob Dole and Viagra), participated in the service or program (Sarah Ferguson and Weight Watchers) or espoused the idea being presented (Charlton Heston and firearm training).

Avoiding Errors of Logic

As you are preparing your rational message, try to avoid errors in logic. Some common errors result from *unfounded presumptions*. For example, don't overgeneralize the argument or leap to an *unwarranted conclusion* that is not supported by evidence. Make sure your facts are indisputable and understood by your audience; building on incorrect or uncertain data will create a case that is easy to refute. Also, be careful not to make a *false assumption* the audience may not accept, such as by arguing that U.S. schools should adopt a Japanese school calendar on the untested presumption that the audience agrees that the intensity of Japanese education produces better graduates.

Other errors in logic deal with ignoring the issue and instead *attacking* the person or reacting with an air of pity or disdain. Finally, remember that any *appeal to authority or tradition* will be effective only if the audience already respects and accepts that authority or tradition.

Visual Supporting Evidence

Strong visual presentation can enhance the effectiveness of these writing techniques. Use photographs, charts, graphs and diagrams as visual aids in presenting statistical and technical information. Also think about ways to include demonstrations and performances in your presentation. Consider too the role that computer-based presentations can make.

Pathos: Appealing to Sentiment

Of course, human beings are not mere thinking machines. We see in Mr. Spock of the original "Star Trek" series examples of inappropriate responses that are so "logical" they are absurd. As humans, we rely heavily on our feelings, and effective

Appealing to Hearts and Minds

Research tells us it is also tremendously important to provide messages that appeal to both the mind and the heart. Three areas of study—two from psychology, one from physiology—shed some light on the question of how we can best frame messages to our audiences.

- **Psychological Type.**   The concept of *psychological type* is based on the work of Carl Jung and the application of his theories by the mother-daughter team of Isabel Myers and Catharine Briggs (Myers & Myers, 1980; Myers, 1987) and a host of their disciples. This approach observed that people have different natural preferences in how they gather information, make decisions and act on those decisions. Some people, labeled "thinkers" in Myers-Briggs terminology, tend to rely mainly on logic and data in making decision. "Feelers," on the other hand, base their decisions more on sentiment and emotion. Seldom will your publics and audiences be so like-minded as to uniformly prefer one type of message appeal over the other. Thus good strategy calls for the use of both types of messages.

  Note that this may not be a natural response for many practitioners, because many of the artistic or creative disciplines—writing, journalism, design, advertising and public relations—tend to attract people who themselves are feelers rather than thinkers. The disciplines more associated with management, such as research and marketing, attract a higher-than-average percentage of thinkers. In either case, it is undependable to rely simply on your personal preferences.

- **Temperament.**   The concept of *temperament* is an approach related to personality and natural disposition, associated with psychologists David Keirsey and Marilyn Bates (1984) and their followers. From them we learn of four specific temperaments with different innate preferences regarding organization and creativity.

- **Left Brain/Right Brain Differences.**   The working of the human brain and in particular the relationship between the two hemispheres of the brain were explored by Roger Sperry (1985) of the California Institute of Technology. He received a Nobel Prize in 1981 for his pioneering work on the field. Evidence suggests that the left side of the brain is responsible for logical and analytical thought, while the right side controls creativity and imagination. Like psychological type and temperament, hemispheric brain studies suggest that most individuals are stronger in one function and weaker in the other.

These three fields have many common bonds. That's not surprising for the first two, because Keirsey-Bates is a conscious reworking of the psychological insights of Myers-Briggs. Sperry took a different path that led him through physiology, but he arrived at surprisingly similar patterns. By comparing and blending this research, evidence suggests that some people are innately more deliberate or logical, while others are more spontaneous and imaginative.

[Source: Adapted from Smith, R. D. (1993). Psychological type and public relations: Theory, research, and applications. *Journal of Public Relations Research.*]

Phase Two

Step
6

communicators take this into consideration. An important part of the strategy of public relations and marketing communication is to link the message to an emotional appeal, either positive or negative.

Positive Emotional Appeals

Many persuasive appeals seek to generate responses based on a variety of positive emotions. Here is a brief look at positive appeals to love, virtue, humor and sex.

Love.   Love appeals can vary—bittersweet poignancy, family togetherness, nostalgia, pity and compassion, sensitivity, sympathy or any of the many other sides of love. Pleasant images lead consumers not only to remember the persuasive message but also to be more likely to act on the message. For years, Michelin has built a successful advertising campaign around warm images of cute babies sitting in tires, and the verbal cue "so much is riding on. . . ." Maxwell House coffee and Hallmark cards also have been successful with this "warm and fuzzy" approach. Fundraising appeals frequently evoke images of compassion and sympathy.

Virtue.   Appeals based on virtue can evoke any of the various values that society or individuals hold in esteem. These are qualities that most people treasure. Recall how patriotic appeals inspired record levels of volunteerism, blood donations, and financial contributions to relief agencies in the wake of the attacks on the World Trade Center and the Pentagon.

- Justice appeals deal with fairness, human or civil rights, and with issues of right or wrong.
- Altruism appeals focus on generosity, charity, kindness and unselfishness.
- Loyalty appeals focus on patriotism and fidelity.
- Bravery appeals evoke images of boldness, endurance and courage.
- Piety appeals focus on religious faith, spirituality and prayer.
- Discretion appeals relate to restraint, moderation, wisdom and self-control.
- Improvement appeals focus on progress, social advancement and making the world a better place.
- Esteem appeals focus on self-respect, pride, vanity and self-worth.
- Social acceptance appeals focus on the importance of peer support—the "everybody's doing it" theme.

Humor.   Appeals based on humor can be very powerful because comedy and amusement are strong human instincts. Humor is useful in reinforcing existing attitudes and behaviors, but it generally is not very effective in changing them.

Humor can make the speaker more liked by the audience, but seldom does it make the speaker seem more credible. However, the use of humor can reduce the speaker's likability when audiences perceive the humor as excessive or inappropriate. Additionally, humor tends to get old fast, so its use in public relations and advertising limits the effectiveness of the otherwise valuable practice of repeating messages. Finally, if audiences evaluate the message from an entertainment perspective, they can fail to take it as a serious persuasive message. With these cautions in mind, here are some guidelines on using humor in persuasive communication:

- The humor should complement a clear and consistent message about the organization or the product/service/concept. It should never be used as a substitute for an understandable message.

- The humor should be relevant to the issue and appropriate for the organization. For instance, it is unlikely that a funeral home could effectively use humor in its brochures.

- The humor should be tasteful. The "South Park" phenomenon aside, bathroom and bedroom humor generally are counterproductive for most audiences, as is disparaging humor directed against others, particularly groups of people. Self-deprecating humor can be effective in causing an audience to like a speaker.

- The humor should be funny. This is difficult to achieve, because what is humorous to one person may be droll, too cute, ludicrous or simply unfunny to others. Make sure the humor does not insult people's intelligence by becoming absurd or pointless. Also, given the choice, prefer the lighthearted and amusing touch over an attempt to present uproarious farce.

- Humor is more effective with dull topics (which need sparking up) than with topics the audience already finds interesting. With interesting topics, humor can detract from the message.

Sex.   Appeals based on sex range from nudity to double entendres to outright shock. These sexual messages can be effective in commanding attention, though audience demographics affect how that attention is received. But the very pulling power of sex appeals has a built-in problem. Tests show that audiences often remember the sexual content of an advertisement but fail to associate it with the brand being promoted or the issue being discussed.

Likewise, what one demographic group may find appropriate and positive, another may judge unnecessary and negative. For example, men respond to sex appeals more than women do, and younger people more than older audiences.

An even bigger problem with sex-appeal messages is that, for all their high ability to gain attention, they are notoriously weak in leading receivers toward desired action.

One consistent finding from persuasion research is that sex appeal should not be used simply for shock value. It is far more effective when the sexual theme has a legitimate association with the product (such as lingerie, perfume or condoms) or with the cause (such as birth control or responsible sexual behavior).

Negative Emotional Appeals

Some messages invoke responses based on negative emotions, fear and guilt being the most common. A third type of negative appeal, to hatred, has no ethical use for public relations and thus is not worth considering here.

Fear.   Fear appeals, which deal with one of the strongest human emotions, are intended to arouse anxiety or worry among receivers, such as advertising that focuses on

Phase Two

Step
6

the fear of body odor or political messages centered on the alleged disasters that await the public if the opposing candidate is elected.

The key to using fear appeals effectively is to accompany them with an easy, reasonable and immediate solution. Fear appeals to persuade audiences to obtain a one-time vaccination, for example, are more effective than those designed to persuade audience to floss over a lifetime in the name of dental hygiene.

Moderate fear appeals can be effective, but too much fearful content can make people either avoid the message or take a defiant stance against it. Appeals that present harsh consequences may cause audiences to cope with their fear simply by refusing to consider the message or even by denying the underlying issue.

Another problem with fear appeals is that the balance point between effective and ineffective shifts according to various demographic factors such as age, education and gender. Younger people, for example, have higher point of tolerance for fear appeals, and some research suggests that the effectiveness of stronger fear appeals increases when audience members have high self-esteem and feel immune to pending doom.

Fear appeals sometimes increase levels of awareness without resulting in the desired action. For example, strong fear appeals used in a seat-belt campaign may leave audiences with an awareness of the consequences of not wearing seat belts—perhaps even with the intention of wearing them—without actually changing the likelihood that they will, indeed, buckle up.

There is a way to make fear appeals more effective: Include in the message a strong how-to approach. For example, don't just deal with the dangers associated with poor nutrition; give several clear and simple examples of how to prepare or order more nutritional meals.

Source and significance of also play a role in the effective use of fear appeals. For example, fear appeals are more effective when they come from highly credible sources who are dissimilar to the audience. Often this dissimilarity can be reinforced by symbols, such as clothing a doctor in a lab coat as she presents moderate fear-based information about disease prevention or using someone in a military uniform to speak about threats to national interests and preparation for war. Fear appeals also can be effective when the issue is significant or important to the audience. In a study related to environmental threats—specifically plutonium contamination from a nuclear-weapons plant—Connie Roser and Margaret Thompson (1995) observed that fear appeals can motivate even latent publics to become active, especially to take action against the fear-producing organization.

Guilt.   Appeals to a personal sense of guilt or shame comprise another negative message strategy, one that is the flip side of the virtue appeal. Consider the "Buy American" theme. Only a fine line separates a positive appeal to patriotism from one that tries to make people feel guilty. With a positive approach, the message focuses on the common economic good, shared values among citizens and a healthy pride in the quality of American products. With a negative approach, however, the same appeal can elicit a sense of guilt for having bought foreign-made products. Since nobody wants to feel guilty, a typical reaction against guilt appeals is to justify our actions ("Foreign cars are made better") and to lament the alternative ("American cars just don't last as long").

Like fear appeals, the use of guilt strategy can be effective in moderation. In a fundraising message, for example, a guilt message might try to make readers feel a bit uneasy or apologetic in their relative comfort amid so much misery elsewhere. But try to move guilt appeals away from the negative emotion and toward a positive sentiment such as compassion and justice. If guilt appeals are to be effective, their messages must make people feel part of the solution. "Will you help? Or will you turn the page?" is the kind of modest guilt appeal that can be quite effective. Like the fear appeal, guilt appeals should feature solutions to the problem of conscience that they raise.

Regardless of the type of emotional appeal being made, consider the ethical ramifications. Ask yourself: Is this appeal ethical? Is it the right way to communicate about this issue? Is it fair? Will the organization gain respect by using this approach?

Strategic Planning Example: Determining Message Appeals

Upstate College will combine rational and emotional message appeals in its message.

UPSTATE COLLEGE

Rational Appeal
Upstate College will present several appeals:

- A factual proposition based on advantages to students, including current and future academic programs, accreditation, financial aid and alumni and community commitments for internships and mentoring
- A value proposition asserting that this expansion is in the best interests of students and this region of the state

These messages will include statistics, personal endorsements and specific examples of hypothetical students in various academic and economic situations. They also will include visual elements such as photographs, charts and graphs.

Emotional Appeal
UC will present appeals to positive emotions, particularly the virtues of self-improvement and the realization of personal potential. For fundraising purposes, it will appeal to the virtue of altruism and sharing with students who need an assist in obtaining a college education.

■ ■ ■

Tiny Tykes will present both rational and emotional message appeals.

Rational Appeal
Tiny Tykes will present several rational propositions:

- A factual proposition based on information about the product redesign
- A value proposition stating a renewed commitment to consumer safety
- A policy proposition asserting the rightness of continuing to use Tiny Tykes products, which have a long history of being responsive to customer concerns

Phase Two

Step
6

These messages will include physical evidence from outside testing agencies about the safety of Tiny Tykes products, a comparison with similar products by competitors and testimony by consumers and consumer advocacy groups.

Emotional Appeal
Tiny Tykes will present several types of emotional appeals:

- To positive emotions such as child development and family fun
- To negative emotions such as a mild level of fear appeal about using toys not tested and approved by independent agencies

---

Strategic Planning Exercise: *Determining Message Appeals*

Basic Planning Questions

1. What is the key message that forms the basis of this public relations or marketing communication program?
2. How does this message use a rational appeal?
3. How does this message use an emotional appeal?

Expanded Planning Questions

1. Does your message include a rational appeal and/or an emotional appeal? (Note: Most persuasive messages provide both kinds of appeals.)

Rational Appeal
1. How does your message make a rational appeal?
2. Does the message feature a factual proposition, a value proposition or a policy proposition?
3. Which of the following provide arguments for your claims: physical evidence, analogy, audience interest, comparison, context, examples, statistics, testimony and endorsements, and/or visual presentation?

Emotional Appeal
1. How does your message make an emotional appeal?
2. Does the message feature an appeal to positive emotions or negative emotions?
3. What is the emotion?
   Love Appeal
       What kind of love?
   Virtue Appeal
       What virtue?
   Humor Appeal (If you answer "yes" to these questions, the humorous message may be effective.)
       Will the use of humor make the source more persuasive?
       Is the humor relevant to the issue?

Is the humor funny?

Is the humor appropriate for the audience?

It the humor appropriate for the organization?

Will the humor enhance the message?

Will the humor help meet the objectives?

Sex Appeal (If you answer "yes" to these questions, the sexual message may be effective.)

Will the use of sex appeal make the source more persuasive?

Is the sex relevant to the issue?

Is the sex appropriate for the audience?

Is the sex appropriate for the organization?

Will the sex help enhance the message?

Will the sex help meet the objectives?

Fear Appeal (If you answer "yes" to these questions, the fearful message may be effective.)

Will the use of fear appeal make the source more persuasive?

Is the fear relevant to the issue?

Is the fear appropriate for the audience?

Is the fear appropriate for the organization?

Does the message include a solution to overcome the fear?

Will the fear enhance the message?

Will the fear help meet the objectives?

Guilt Appeal (If you answer "yes" to these questions, the guilt appeal may be effective.)

Will the use of guilt appeal make the source more persuasive?

Is the guilt relevant to the issue?

Is the guilt appropriate for the audience?

Is the guilt appropriate for the organization?

Does the message include a solution to overcome the guilt?

Will the guilt enhance the message?

Will the guilt help meet the objectives?

Phase Two

Step 6

Verbal and Nonverbal Communication

Logical and emotional appeals can be communicated either verbally or nonverbally. Let's look at both verbal and nonverbal communication as they apply to public relations, marketing and related disciplines.

Verbal Communication

Verbal communication occurs through written and spoken words. The right words—and the right use of those words—can effectively present your organization's message to its publics. Several verbal factors combine to create an effective message, among them structure, clarity, power words and ethical language.

Message Structure.   The structure of the message and the relationship between the arrangement of the message and its effectiveness have been subjects of much research. Several particular elements have been researched: giving one side or two sides of an argument, the order of presentation and the value of drawing conclusions or making recommendations.

Should you present only your point of view, or should you address the opposition's argument? The research suggests that it depends upon the audience and the circumstances.

One-sided arguments present the organization's or speaker's point of view but not the opposing views. This kind of argument is useful in reinforcing opinions, because one-sided arguments don't confuse the audience with alternatives, but one-sided arguments are less effective in changing opinions. Four conditions warrant the use of one-sided arguments: (1) The audience is friendly and already agrees with your position, (2) its members have low educational levels, (3) your position will be the only one presented, or (4) the objective is immediate opinion change. Presenting only one side of an argument can cause a temporary attitudinal change, but this is likely to be eliminated if the audience later hears a convincing argument from the other side.

Two-sided arguments present both the pros and the cons of an issue, though not necessarily objectively. They usually criticize the opposition's position. Two-sided arguments are necessary with better-educated audiences, with audiences that are undecided on an issue, and with audiences aware that another side of the issue exists. Such arguments can improve your ability to persuade these audiences because you will be perceived as being more honest and more respectful of the audience's intelligence. If you present both sides of the argument, you have a better chance of achieving a greater attitude change that will remain high when the audience hears the opposing argument from another source.

Order of presentation refers to the way the argument unfolds. Should you present arguments in order of least to most important or vice versa? It generally doesn't seem to matter, as long as you are consistent. However, in developing your persuasive message, you may have reason to choose one form over the other. For example, do you think your audience will be more attentive at the beginning of the message? If so, then use your strongest arguments there.

The *final word* is also very important, and plenty of research points out that the last-made point is the one best remembered. This is especially true with less sophisticated audiences, as well as for audiences that are less knowledgeable or less personally involved in the issue. Comic Paula Poundstone said it well in a stand-up routine referring to a political campaign that dealt with the economy: "I don't know anything about the economy. I tend to agree with the last guy who spoke."

In your two-sided arguments, *sandwich the information.* That is, first present your side—the first argument often is perceived as the strongest. Then present and refute the opposing arguments. Finally restate your position, because of the power of the last word.

Drawing conclusions, and understanding whether this is a good idea or not, also have been the subject of much research. To date, most of the findings suggest that making a recommendation or drawing a conclusion usually is more effective than leaving it

Barriers to Effective Communication

Several factors can limit the effectiveness of communication. Each of these is a type of "noise" within the communication process. By knowing what they are, communication planners may be able to eliminate these noise types or at least minimize their impact. Here are some of the common barriers:

- *Physical noise,* such as ineffective communication channels that do not transmit the message from sender to receiver or distracting sounds within the communication process that interfere with the receiver's reception of the message
- *Psychological noise,* such as emotional distractions by the receiver
- *Semantic noise,* such as the use of jargon that is not understood by the receiver or other language that carries different meaning for the sender and the receiver, often because of different backgrounds and experiences
- *Demographic noise,* such as differences between sender and receiver in terms of age, ethnicity, social status and so on

With all the barriers that can interfere with effective communication, it's a wonder people and organizations are able to communicate at all. But the noise can be turned down and the barriers overcome. Senders who understand the potential communication pitfalls can find ways to avoid them; receivers can be particularly attentive to the message and engage in active listening to overcome communication noise.

Phase Two

Step
6

to the audience to draw its own conclusion. However, some evidence suggests that if audience members, especially educated ones, do draw their own conclusion, both the conclusion and the attitude on which it rests are more resistant to change than if the conclusion is presented by the source. Some studies have indicated that, when the purpose of a message is to reduce criticism or opposition, it may be better not to draw conclusions for the audience. However, can you risk not having the audience draw the "right" conclusion?

Reiteration is the final area to consider for effective message structure. Reiteration refers to internal repetition of the main ideas within a persuasive message. This is not the kind of redundancy that involves superfluous words, such as "puppy dog," "totally destroyed" or "small village." Rather, reiteration means presenting the same message in different forms, with different words and different examples, each reinforcing the other. For example, an effective fundraising letter will ask for a donation frequently throughout the letter, each time making the request with different words and phrases and perhaps based on different types of appeals. Such internal repetition can make messages more memorable and, over time, more acceptable.

Reiteration often means using synonyms, different words with similar meanings, as a way of restating the main point. Another technique is to develop parallel structure within sentences and paragraphs to make your information easier to recognize and remember. For example, use a B list—"Be alert. Be prepared. Be resourceful." Alliteration, using words that have the same beginning sounds, is another memory enhancer.

Persuasive Arguments

A classic pattern for persuasive arguments comes from Hugh Rank (1976), a researcher with the National Council of Teachers of English who outlined a model that considered both positive and negative arguments. In what has become known as *Rank's model of persuasion,* he observed that persuaders generally choose between two different strategies when comparing their own and their opponent's positions. One approach is to magnify both their own good points and their opponents' bad points. The other is to downplay their own bad points as well as their opponents' good points.

Rank believes that message receivers can make themselves resistant to persuasive manipulation by recognizing the intensifying/downplaying strategies of advertisers and other would-be persuaders and then by downplaying the messages the persuader emphasized and intensifying those that were minimized. Rank's model also can give strategic communicators insight into how they can more effectively present a persuasive argument.

Clarity.   Clarity helps the audience quickly and easily understand your message. To accomplish this, use words precisely, with an eye to their exact and commonly understood meaning. Use simple language—*try* instead of *endeavor, use* rather than *utilize, say* instead of *articulate.* Avoid jargon unless the language is shared by your listeners, readers or viewers. In all cases, use a vocabulary appropriate to your audience. Consider the differences in language fitting for teens, senior citizens or business executives. Consider also the setting for your verbal message, such as the differences in language appropriate for boardrooms, locker rooms and dining rooms.

The *Fog Index* (also called the *Gunning Readability Formula*) is an easy-to-use tool that helps writers measure the level of reading difficulty for any piece of writing and then adjust the writing according to the skills of their audience. Some computer programs also can calculate grade-level readability measures. In addition to clear writing, communication strategists should ensure that their messages use correct and simple English, avoid redundancies, generally use active voice and observe the other guidelines for good writing. Consult a good textbook on public relations writing to brush up on your writing skills.

Power Words.   Power words play a significant role in communication effectiveness. Edward Bernays, the public relations pioneer who rooted the profession in social psychology, said he had achieved "semantic tyranny" with his name for the anniversary campaign to commemorate Thomas Edison's invention of the electric light. Light's Golden Jubilee was the title Bernays devised, linking three words that he believed guaranteed interest and support.

Bernays' advice to choose words carefully is particularly valid today, when media are overflowing with messages that compete for attention and interest. *Power words* is the name for terminology and definitions that are so influential that they often can determine public relations success for a movement or campaign. Descriptions such as "low-fat," "environment-friendly" and "Bible-believing," and labels such as "family values," "Vietnam veteran," "right to bear arms" and "tax-and-spend liberal" are terms

How to Use the Fog Index

1. Select a 100-word passage of writing.
2. Count the number of sentences. If the passage ends within a sentence, estimate a percentage of the final sentence. Round this to a single decimal space.
3. Determine the average sentence length by dividing 100 by the number of sentences in the passage.
4. Count the number of long words in the passage. Long words are those with three or more

syllables. But don't count words in which *es*, *er* or *ed* form the third and final syllable, hyphenated words such as *state-of-the-art* or compound words such as *newspaper*.

5. Add the average sentence length and the number of long words (totals from steps 3 and 4).
6. Multiply this total by 0.4. The resulting number indicates the approximate grade level of the passage.

that have been carefully orchestrated to present a particular emotional connotation. The same gunmen who robbed, raped and mutilated villagers in Central America were called "freedom fighters" by their political supporters and "terrorists" by opponents. Instead of referring to "political prisoners," Amnesty International uses a more convincing expression, "prisoners of conscience."

Rhetorical warfare is associated with some of society's most divisive issues. For example, "pro-choice" activists generally disavow the label "pro-abortion" foisted upon them by the other side (which calls itself "pro-life," and which in turn is called "anti-choice" by opponents). One side speaks of a "fetus," the other side of an "unborn baby"— a differentiation in terminology on which hinges the entire controversy. When obstetrician-gynecologist Barnett Slepian was killed by a sniper in 1998, most initial news reports called him an "abortion doctor," rhetorically bolstering abortion opponents and ignoring the bulk of his medical practice. News media first called the Watergate break-in a "caper," a minimizing and rather frolicsome term that might have saved President Richard Nixon's job had the media not switched to a more momentous term, "scandal."

Rhetorical peacemaking can lead to more beneficial relationships when organizations and their publics engage in shared language, and the path of consensus building and conflict resolution is made smoother by sensitivity to the words used to communicate.

Product names receive much attention in commercial enterprises. Thus we find luxury automobiles with names such as Imperial, Coupe de Ville and Continental, while sport utility vehicles are named Explorer, Blazer and Pathfinder. If you aren't convinced of the power of names, try thinking up a promotional campaign for the all-wheel-drive Chevrolet Petunia, the luxury Ford Cockroach or the sporty GM Aardvark.

The naming game can be a lucrative and mutually beneficial endeavor, with sports serving as the primary stage. From the Virginia Slims Legends Tour for professional women's tennis to the Federal Express Orange Bowl to San Francisco's 3COM (formerly Candlestick) Park, companies are spending millions of dollars to keep their names on the tongues of their publics.

Program names in the nonprofit sector traditionally receive less attention than product names. Organizations sometimes attempt to devise memorable acronyms, though these often end up being somewhat less effective than hoped. In the same locality, the acronym CASA might stand for Central American Scientific Association, Council on Alcoholism and Substance Abuse, Christian Associates in South America, Catholic Appeal for Saint Anthony, Center for the Advancement of Saudi Arabia and Coalition to Annex South Alexandria. A title like CASA might look nice on the letterhead, but it doesn't communicate much about an organization.

Be careful that the program name does not deliberately mislead people; serious ethical issues arise from names of front organizations or programs that fail to reflect their partisan or sectarian sponsors.

Slogans can be quite effective, especially during the awareness phase of a strategic communication campaign. But make sure the slogan is relevant. In 1995, Los Angeles County launched the slogan "Together, We're the Best. Los Angeles." But this slogan begs the questions: Who is together? Best at what? On the other hand, state tourism slogans such as "Virginia is for Lovers" and "I ♥ New York" have been quite effective because they are both clear and open to having various interpretations laid upon them. Many effective slogans are associated with social movements or organizations. Consider these: "Guns don't kill people; people kill people." "Only you can prevent forest fires." "A mind is a terrible thing to waste."

Service marks are closely related to slogans. Service marks are words and phrases which marketing and public relations people develop to be closely associated with organizations. Examples are the Army's "Be all you can be," Budweiser's "This Bud's for you" and Nike's "Just Do It." These service marks often are registered, much as trademarks are, and corporate lawyers go to great lengths to protect them. Burger King is the only restaurant that can claim to be the "Home of the Whopper" and the New York Times is the only paper that can claim to have "All the news that's fit to print."

Memorable and meaty quotes are also an important aspect of verbal communication. Public relations writers should use strong quotes in their news releases, news conference statements, interviews and other occasions for interacting with the media.

Here is an example of a real pithy quote. In 1998 Oliver Stone directed a television special that promoted the theory that TWA Flight 800, which had exploded two years earlier killing all 230 passengers and crew, was downed by a missile. FBI investigators had specifically ruled out that possibility. Consider the passion in this response by James Kallstrom, who headed the FBI investigation: "The real facts are glossed over by the likes of Mr. Stone and others who spend their life bottom-feeding in those small, dark crevices of doubt and hypocrisy."

Wow! That is so much better than a dreary bureaucratic statement such as, "The FBI stands by its original report" or "We disagree with Mr. Stone's missile theory." This is a quote with attitude. It both sings and stings.

Another way to be memorable is to use colorful language. Consider this statement by attorney Johnny Cochran who, during O. J. Simpson's criminal trial, rhymed a key message meant not only for the jury but also for the viewing public: "If the glove doesn't fit, you must acquit."

Setting.   The setting or environment also has strong symbolic value, and much meaning can be created by putting a speaker in, say, a cemetery, laboratory or library.

This concludes the Strategy phase of the planning process for public relations and marketing communication. Having completed these steps, which have built on those of the Formative Research phase, you now should have a clear sense of direction for your program. Before going any farther, present your planning thus far to the decision makers, such as your client or boss. Gain the buy-in from the key decision makers in your organization, who must agree with the direction you suggest, with the objectives and with the resulting strategy recommendations.

In the next phase of planning, you will turn your attention to preparing and implementing specific communication tools to carry the strategic message you have just devised.

Strategic Planning Example: *Planning Verbal/Nonverbal Communication*

Verbal Communication

- One point of view will be presented: expansion is beneficial for students, the community and the college.
- Conclusion will be drawn: students should consider Upstate College.
- Message clarity will be enhanced by a Fog Index level of tenth grade.
- Messages will include power words such as "benefit to community" and "quality education."
- Messages will avoid any exaggeration.
- Messages will rely on facts and documentation rather than empty claims.

Nonverbal Communication

- College logo will be featured in messages.
- Upbeat music popular with teens and young adults will be featured in messages.
- College mascot, salamander "Upstate Eddie," will be featured.

■ ■ ■

Verbal Communication

- Opposing points of view will be included in messages: Tiny Tykes is committed to toy safety; the company had a problem in the past but has learned from mistakes and now is recommitted to toy safety.
- Conclusion will be drawn: The company now makes high-quality, safe toys and deserves consumer support.
- Message clarity will be enhanced by a Fog Index level of ninth grade.
- Messages will include power words such as "commitment to excellence" and "baby safe."

Ethical Language.   Using ethical language is a must for every public relations practitioner. In considering the verbal formulation of your message, pay attention to the implication of language. Certainly you will want to use language with pizzazz. Power words can lead audiences to perceive an image instantly and to take on an immediate mood—"beautiful people," "cutting edge," "right wing," "workaholic." But be careful with the stereotypes on which power words are built and make sure that reality underlies these images.

Pretentious language is words or phrases that imply more than is warranted. Avoid them, because they can mislead readers. Examples of pretentious language are "experienced vehicles" for used cars or "follicly impaired" for bald. Such words can have a backlash if they are perceived as either silly or too crafty. Sometimes pretentious language raises confusing questions. For example, if pets are "companion animals," then should pet owners be called "human associates of companion animals"?

Doublespeak is outright dishonest language meant to obscure the real meaning behind the words. Don't use such language. Besides being unethical, it invites the obvious criticism that the organization is trying to hide the facts. Examples of doublespeak include military terms such as calling civilian wartime deaths "collateral damage" or genocide "ethnic cleansing" and business references to employee layoffs as "downsizing," "rightsizing," "employee repositioning," "workforce readjustment" or "retirement for personal reasons." Bureaucratic reports have called drunkenness a "non-sober condition" and suicide on a train track "pedestrian involvement."

Unfortunately, many examples of doublespeak are associated with governmental agencies and officials who, through such language, betray an appalling lack of commitment to the honest communication necessary in a democratic society. Business and other organizational leaders, too, have demonstrated far too much creativity in concocting language that clouds rather than illuminates.

The task for practitioners of strategic communication is to avoid dishonest language for themselves and to counsel their organizations and clients to avoid it as well, not only for ethical reasons but for the practical benefit that honest and clear language provides the best means to communicate effectively and thus to generate understanding and continuing support.

Defamation is a legal condition to be avoided at all costs. Defamatory language meets a five-fold test: It is (1) false information, (2) published or communicated to a third party, (3) that identifies a person (4) and holds that person up to public hatred, contempt or ridicule (5) while involving some measure of negligence and/or malice on the part of the communicator. Defamation is classified either as *libel,* which is written or broadcast defamation, or *slander,* which is spoken defamation.

A related area of problematic language is information that intrudes on someone's *privacy.* These language indiscretions generally can be avoided if you pay attention to ethical principles, such as those found in the professional conduct codes of such organizations as the Public Relations Society of America and the Canadian Public Relations Society. Such codes call upon practitioners to adhere to high standards of accuracy, honesty, fairness, truth and concern for the public interest. (See Appendix B: Ethical Standards.)

Nonverbal Communication

Nonverbal communication occurs through actions and cues other than words that carry meaning. Images and ambiance create the most powerful and enduring aspects of communication. For example, when the words say "I'm happy to be here" but the facial expression shows boredom, we tend to believe our eyes. Likewise, corporate spokespersons who use facial or other body language associated with hedging and lying limit their effectiveness in gaining audience trust.

Most communication relies not on mere words but rather on the images, symbols, setting, mood, music, clothing and so on that carry messages. Here is an overview of some of the most common types of nonverbal communication.

Symbols.   As visual representations of realities beyond themselves, symbols are among the most effective ways to communicate. Good symbols have a complex and rich psychological impact on people who see and use them. Baby harp seals and red AIDS ribbons have generated widespread public acceptance for the causes associated with them; armbands associated with the Holocaust or classic news photos of the Vietnam War and anti-war protests evoke emotions decades after those events; and personal keepsakes from weddings, proms and special vacations summon up emotions over a lifetime.

Some of the most enduring symbols are rooted in religion (such as the crescent, cross, Star of David and the Madonna figure) and country (for Americans, for example, the Capitol dome, the Statue of Liberty and especially the flag). A nation's flag is more than a piece of cloth; to many people it is the symbol of family, country, patriotism, duty and honor, which many have been willing both to die for or kill for. As such, it has the power to inspire both devotion and disrespect, and much energy has been spent in nations around the world on the issue of the appropriate role the national flag plays in both patriotism and social protest.

Logos.   Corporate logos are special kinds of symbols, which visually identify businesses, nonprofit organizations and other groups. Contemporary or traditional? Elegant or casual? Much attention goes into the development of a corporate logo, which needs to present the right image and send the proper message. Consider the promotional value and enduring impact of the Nike swoosh or the Dodge star. For an organizational symbol to be effective, it must be both memorable and appropriate for the organization. It also must be unique to the organization, one reason that much legal energy is spent protecting registered trademarks.

Music.   Music has a special symbolic vlue. Songs such as "Auld Lang Syne," "God Bless America" and "Pomp and Circumstance" have special meanings related to New Year's Eve, patriotic holidays and graduation, respectively. The next time you go to the movies, pay attention to the power of the background music in setting the right mood of romance, happiness, pending doom and so on.

Passions were stirred when Japan's parliament in 1999 approved a law making the traditional "Kimigayo" the official national anthem. The vote over the imperial hymn, Japan's unofficial anthem since before the Second World War, revived bitter memories and renewed the controversy over nationalism and war guilt. Much of the debate centered on schools, particularly on how children should be educated about the war and on the role of national symbols such as the anthem and the flag in school ceremonies.

Language.   In some contexts, language itself can be symbolic. Consider the cultural symbolism of Hebrew, Latin, Arabic, Hindi and other languages associated with religious traditions. Consider also how some of the "in" language used by groups of teenagers, for example, has a symbolism for its users that is neither appreciated nor understood—nor meant to be—by outsiders.

Physical Artifacts.   Symbolic value is sometimes attached to physical artifacts, such as the gavel used by a presiding judge or the badge worn by a police officer. Over the years, cigarettes have been presented as symbols of independence, youth, rebellion, ruggedness and adventure. Automobiles are presented as symbolic mirrors of the people who drive them. And it was the symbolic power of the Pentagon and the World Trade Center as icons of America that led terrorists to target those buildings.

Clothing.   A particular type of physical artifact, clothing, often takes on symbolic proportions. This is why much attention often is paid to military uniforms, academic attire, religious vestments, ethnic apparel or royal garb, where each design element often has a special meaning. Mini-controversies sometimes arise over the symbolism of clothing, such as the appropriate dress for nurses. Attention is also given to less formal but nonetheless powerful symbols such as designer clothing or trendy brand-name eyeglasses. For persuasive purposes, a spokesperson might wear clothing related to a particular profession or occupation as a way of suggesting expertise.

People.   Even people can function as symbols, especially royalty such as a king or queen, religious figures such as the Dalai Lama or the Pope, and other important and well-known characters. As symbols, they stand as more than human beings; they represent the dignity of the office they hold. Recent media attention given to scandals involving princes, presidents and prime ministers, however, has weakened the symbolic value of such figures.

Mascots and Promotional Characters.   Another kind of symbol is the mascot. From Smokey Bear to the San Diego Chicken, mascots embody much of the spirit of an organization. Meanwhile many companies and organizations use promotional characters. Ronald McDonald is an example of this.

The symbolic significance of such fictional personifications can change. Betty Crocker and Aunt Jemima have gotten younger and more professional looking each decade as their company's customers have changed. Sports teams are under increasing pressure to retire their Native American mascots.

Colors.   Colors also can be symbolic or emblematic—green for environmental issues, pink for Owens-Corning fiberglass insulation and so on. But the symbolic value of colors is socially defined, and the Western identification of white for happy occasions such as weddings and black for funerals is not universally shared, something that communicators in international or multicultural settings need to consider.

- Messages will avoid any exaggeration.
- Messages will rely on facts and documentation rather than empty claims.

Nonverbal Communication
- Messages will be enhanced by happy music.
- Corporate spokespersons will be shown wearing research and professional clothing, reinforcing the message of research and high standards.
- Clinical settings will be used for presentations by corporate spokespersons, reinforcing the message of research and high standards.

Strategic Planning Exercise: *Planning Verbal and Nonverbal Communication*

Basic Planning Questions

1. How does your message use verbal communication?
2. How does your message use nonverbal communication?
3. How can either be made stronger?

Expanded Planning Questions

A. Verbal Communication

Message Structure
1. Does your message present only one point of view or more than one (opposing) point of view? If more than one point of view is presented, is your message sandwiched (stating your argument, noting the opposing argument and finally restating your argument and refuting the opposing argument)?
2. Does your message present a conclusion?
3. Does your message reiterate its main idea?

Clarity
1. Will your publics find your message clear, simple and understandable?
2. What is the education level of your target public?
3. How does this compare with the Fog Index for your written message?

Power Words
1. Have you used powerful language in your message?
2. Does your product/program have a descriptive and memorable name?
3. Does your product/program have a descriptive and memorable slogan?

Ethical Language
1. Does your message use pretentious or exaggerated language?
2. Does your message use dishonest or misleading language?
3. Does your message use defamatory language?
4. How could any of these verbal elements be made stronger?

B. Nonverbal Communication

1. Does the presentation of your message include a symbol, a logo, music, symbolic language, symbolic physical artifacts, symbolic clothing, symbolic people, a mascot, symbolic use of color and/or a symbolic setting?

2. How could any of these nonverbal elements be made stronger?

Consensus Check

Does agreement exist within your organization about the recommended strategies within this phase of the planning process?

   If "yes," proceed to the next section.

   If "no," consider the value and/or possibility of achieving consensus before proceeding.

Phase Two

Step
6

Citations and Recommended Readings

Barnhurst, K. G. & Mutz, D. (1997). American journalism and the decline in event-centered reporting. *Journal of Communication, 47 (4),* 27–53.

Benjamin, J. (1997). *Principles, elements, and types of persuasion.* Fort Worth, TX: Harcourt Brace.

Benoit, W. L. (1995). *Accounts, excuses, and apologies: A theory of image restoration strategies* (SUNY Series in Speech Communication). Albany, NY: SUNY Press.

Berlo, D. (1960). *The process of communication: An introduction to theory and practice.* San Francisco: Rinehart.

Botan, C. (1997). Ethics in strategic communication campaigns: The case for a new approach to public relations. *Journal of Business Communication, 34 (2),* 188–202.

Buber, M. (1947). *Between man and man.* London: Routledge & Kegan Paul. Reprinted in F. W. Matson & A. Montagu (Eds.). (1967). *The human dialogue: Perspectives on communication.* New York: Free Press.

Burson-Marsteller Public Relations (1998). Market Facts Omnibus—May 1998. In *Knowledge Works on-line newsletter.* www.bm.com.

Christians, C. G., Fackler, M. & Rotzoll, K. B. (1997). *Media ethics: Cases and moral reasoning* (5th ed.). New York: Longman.

Cody, M. J. & McLaughlin, M. L. (1985). Models for the sequential construction of accounting episodes: Situational and interactional constraints on message selection and evaluation. In R. L. Street & L. Capella (Eds.). *Sequence and pattern in communication behavior* (pp. 50–69). London: Edward Arnold.

Cody, M. J. & McLaughlin, M. L. (1990). Interpersonal accounting. In H. Giles & W. P. Robinson (Eds.). *Handbook of language and social psychology* (pp. 227–255). Chichester: John Wiley.

Fearn-Banks, K. (1996). *Crisis communications: A casebook approach.* Mahwah, NJ: Lawrence Erlbaum.

Festinger, L. (1957). *A theory of cognitive dissonance.* Stanford, CA: Stanford University.

Fitzpatrick, K. R. & Rubin, M. S. (1995). Public relations vs. legal strategies in organizational crisis decisions. *Public Relations Review, (Spring),* 21–33.

Gottschalk, J. A. (Ed.). (1993). *Crisis response: Inside stories in managing image under siege.* Detroit: Gale Research.

Hearit, K. M. (1994). Apologies and public relations crises at Chrysler, Toshiba, and Volvo. *Public Relations Review, 20 (2),* 113–125.

Heath, R. L. (1997). *Strategic issues management: Organizations and public policy challenges.* Thousand Oaks, CA: Sage.

Heider, F. (1946). Attitudes and cognitive organization. *Psychological Review, 51,* 358–374.

Heider, F. (1958). *The psychology of interpersonal relations.* New York: Wiley.

Infante, D. A., Rancer, A. S. & Womack, D. F. (1996). *Building communication theory* (3rd ed.). Prospect Heights, IL: Waveland.

Jackson, P. (Ed.). (1997). Items of importance to practitioners. *pr reporter, 40 (46),* 3.

Johnston, D. D. (1994). *The art and science of persuasion*. Boston: McGraw-Hill.

Kowalski, R. M. & Erickson, J. R. (1997). Complaints and complaining: Functions, antecedents and consequences," *Psychological Bulletin, 119(2),* 179–96.

Keirsey, D. & Bates, M. (1984). *Please understand me*. Del Mar, CA: Prometheus Nemesis.

Larson, C. U. (2000). *Persuasion: Reception and responsibility* (9th ed.). Belmont, CA: Wadsworth.

Lasswell, H. D. (1948). The structure and function of communication in society. In L. Bryson (Ed.). *The communication of ideas*. New York: Harper.

Lipstein, B. (1985). An historical retrospective of copy research. *Journal of Advertising Research, 24 (6),* 11–14.

The Lives We Touch. (1992). In J. A. Hendrix. *Public relations cases* (2nd ed.). Belmont, CA: Wadsworth.

Macdaid, G. P., McCaulley, M. H. & Kainz, R. I. (1986). *MBTI Atlas of Type Tables* (2 vols.). Gainesville, FL: Center for Applications in Psychological Type.

Marconi, J. (1996). *Image marketing: Using public perceptions to attain business objectives*. Lincolnwood, IL: NTC/Business.

Martin, J. (1999). Miss Manners [column]. (May 10).

Martinelli, K. A. & Briggs, W. (1998). Integrating public relations and legal responses during a crisis: The case of Odwalla, Inc. *Public Relations Review, 20 (Winter),* 443–460.

McCombs, M. E. & Shaw, D. L. (1972). The agenda-setting function of mass media. *Public Opinion Quarterly, 36,* 176–187.

McGuire, W. J. & Papageorgis, D. (1961). The relative efficacy of various types of prior belief-defense in producing immunity against persuasion. *Journal of Abnormal and Social Psychology, 62,* 327–337.

Miciak, A. R. & Shanklin, W. L. (1994). Choosing celebrity endorsers: The risks are real, but sports and entertainment spokespersons still burnish corporate images and sell brands. *Advertising Management, 3 (3),* 51+.

Myers, I. B. (1987). *Introduction to type*. (A. L. Hammer, Rev.). Gainesville, FL: Center for Applications of Psychological Type.

Myers, I. B. & Myers, P. B. (1980). *Gifts differing*. Palo Alto, CA: Consulting Psychologists Press.

Nager, N. R. & Allen, T. H. (1984). *Public relations management by objectives*. Lanham, MD: University Press of America. (Originally published by Longman.)

Newcomb, T. M. (1953). An approach to the study of communicative acts. *Psychological Review, 60,* 393–404.

Nyer, P. U. (2000). An investigation into whether complaining can cause increased consumer satisfaction. *Journal of Consumer marketing, 17(1),* 9–19.

Nyer, P. U. 1999). Cathartic complaining as a means of reducing consumer dissatisfaction, *Journal of Consumer Satisfaction, dissatisfaction and Complaining Behavior, 12.*

Osgood, C. E. & Tannenbaum, P. H. (1955). The principle of congruity in the prediction of attitude change. *Psychological Review, 62,* 42–55.

Pfau, M. & Parrott, R. (2001). *Persuasive communication campaigns*. Boston: Pearson.

Rank, H. (1976). Teaching about public persuasion. In D. Dieterich (Ed.). *Teaching and doublespeak*. Urbana, IL: NCTE.

Ray, M. (1973). Marketing communication and the hierarchy of effects. In E. Clarke (Ed.). *New models for communication research*. Newbury Park, CA: Sage.

Ries, A. & Trout, J. (1987). *Positioning: The battle for your mind*. New York: McGraw-Hill.

Rogers, E. (1995). *The diffusion of innovations* (4th ed.). New York: Free Press.

Ross, R. S. (1994). *Understanding persuasion* (4th ed.). Englewood Cliffs, NJ: Prentice Hall.

Roser, C. & Thompson, M. (1995). Fear appeals and the formation of active publics. *Journal of Communication, 45 (1),* 103–119.

Schramm, W. (1971). The nature of communication between humans. In W. Schramm & D. F. Roberts (Eds.). *The process and effects of mass communication*. Urbana, IL: University of Illinois Press.

Schreiber, A. L. (1994). *Lifestyle and event marketing: Building the new customer partnership*. New York: McGraw-Hill.

Seideman, T. (1997). Nonprofit prophets. *Reputation Management, (May/June),* 46–53.

Shannon, C. E. & Weaver, W. (1949). *The mathematical theory of communication*. Urbana, IL: University of Illinois Press.

Sherif, M. & Hovland, C. I. (1961). *Social judgment*. New Haven: Yale University.

Sieberg, E. (1976). Confirming and disconfirming organizational communication. In J. L. Owen, P. A. Page & G. I. Zimmerman (Eds.). *Communication in organizations*. St. Paul, MN: West.

Simons, H. W., Morreale, J. & Gronbeck, B. (2001). *Persuasion and society*. Thousand Oaks, CA: Sage.

Smith, R. D. (1993). Psychological type and public relations: Theory, research, and applications. *Journal of Public Relations Research, 5 (3),* 177–199.

Smith, R. D. (in press). *Becoming a public relations writer* (2nd ed.). Mahwah, NJ; Lawrance Erlbaum.

Sperry, R. W. (1985). Consciousness, personal identity and the divided brain. In D. F. Benson & E. Zaidel (Eds.). *The dual brain: Hemispheric specialization in humans* (UCLA Forum in Medical Sciences, No. 26). New York: Guilford.

Stewart, C. J., Smith, C. A. & Denton, R. E. (2001). *Persuasion and social movements* (4th ed.). Prospect Heights, IL: Waveland.

Sugimoto, N. (1997). A Japan-U.S. comparison of apology styles [Special issue: Cultural variability in communication]. *Communication Research, 24 (4),* 349–370.

Wiener, N. (1954). *The human use of human beings: Cybernetics and society* (2nd ed.). Boston: Houghton Mifflin.

Wild, C. (1993). *Corporate volunteer programs: Benefits to businesses*. Report 1029, The Conference Board, 845 Third Avenue, New York, NY.

Young, D. (1996). *Building your company's good name: How to create and protect the reputation your organization wants and deserves*. New York: American Management Association.

Phase Two

Phase Three

TACTICS

If the strategy phase of the planning process provided the skeleton and muscles for your communication programming, Phase Three is the flesh. This section deals specifically with communication tactics, which are the things we see—the visible elements of a public relations or marketing communication plan.

In the Introduction to *Strategic Planning for Public Relations,* you encountered the concept of integrated communication, the conscious blending of the instruments of both public relations and marketing communication. Integrated communication creates a comprehensive and cohesive program aimed at implementing the best possible mix of communication tools. It is here, in Phase Three, that this integrated approach will become most visible, as you consider the various communication tactics that can be used to achieve your objectives. The menu of tactics outlined in this section will feature communication vehicles drawn from the full range of disciplines and specialties. For

Step 7
Choosing
Communication Tactics

Step 8
Implementing the
Strategic Plan

example, you will consider interpersonal communication opportunities that involve speeches and special events, and organizational media such as newsletters and Web sites. Also on the menu will be a full plate of tactics involving the journalistic side of the news media, as well as tactics associated with advertising and promotion appropriate for issues and situations associated with strategic communication.

The activities in Phase Three also will lead you to select an effective mix of tactics, packaging your creative and strategic ideas into a comprehensive program. To accomplish this, you will need to tap your creative side. Your goal here is to boost your plan well above the level of a mere laundry list of tactics. Instead, you will attempt to create a compelling and resourceful action plan that can help your client organization achieve its goals and objectives.

You also will deal with the administrative details of budgeting and scheduling that are so important for the smooth implementation of your plan.

This tactics phase calls for the twin skills of creativity and attention to detail. All aspects of implementation involve many components, and the person who can manage simultaneous tasks skillfully should find success in the field of strategic communication.

The need for micromanagement might seem overwhelming, but by remaining focused on your plan you will avoid unnecessary side trips that sap your time and resources without advancing you toward your goal.

At the same time, effective tactics call for a measure of creativity and innovation—that certain spark that separates the ordinary from the unusual, replacing the commonplace with the memorable or exceptional.

Choosing
Communication Tactics

Communication tactics are the visible elements of a strategic plan. They are what people see and do—web sites and news releases, tours and billboards, and so much more. Tactics are also the elements of the plan that can carry a hefty price tag, so planning and coordination are particularly important.

The range of communication tactics is extensive, and it is continually growing because of technological advances. Step 7 offers you a convenient menu of the various tactics. These tactics should be considered in light of your goals and objectives, evaluated in relationship to each other, matched to the taste of the organization and the publics, and chosen with an eye toward time and budget constraints. At a restaurant, you wouldn't order every item on the menu. Likewise, don't try every tactic you can think of. Instead, review this menu of public relations tactics carefully, then select a full plate of items appropriate to the situation you are addressing.

Before we review the menu, let's look at some of the conventional categories of communications tactics, along with a description of the distinctions this book uses.

Conventional Communication Categories

Media and media tactics are often divided into categories based on distinguishing features. Here are several frequently used pairs that describe types of media: controlled versus uncontrolled, internal versus external, mass versus targeted, popular versus trade, public versus nonpublic, and print versus electronic.

The first category of media is based on the organization's ability to control the content of its messages. **Controlled media** allow the organization to determine various attributes of the message—most importantly its content, but also its timing, presentation, packaging, tone and distribution. Examples of controlled media are newsletters, brochures and corporate videos. Conversely, **uncontrolled media** are those in which someone unrelated to the organization, such as a media gatekeeper, determines those message attributes. Examples of uncontrolled media tactics include news conferences and interviews.

The second category of media describes the relationship of the media to the organization. **Internal media** exist within the organization and thus parallel the previous definition of controlled media. **External media,** which exist outside the organization, may be controlled (such as advertising media) or uncontrolled (such as news media). Specific examples include billboards, newspapers and television news broadcasts.

Another category is defined by the size and breadth of the intended audience. **Mass media** are those that are accessible to most people; thus they are media that enjoy vast audiences, such as television networks and the mainstream daily newspaper establishment. On the other hand, targeted media have not only much narrower but also more homogeneous audiences. Examples of **targeted media** are special-interest publications (such as a magazine for people who live aboard sailboats) and broadcast programs that appeal to a particular narrow audience (such as a program on retirement finances).

The next category of media is also defined by its audience, and it is largely made up of publications such as newsletters, newspapers and magazines, although it also includes some broadcast programs. **Popular media** focus on information of interest to people in their personal lives, including fashion, grooming, relationships, hobbies and self-help, as well as news and current events. These are the publications found at the supermarket or the book store. Examples of popular media include *Runner's World, Vegetarian Times* and top-of-the-hour radio news broadcasts. **Trade media,** on the other hand, generally are distributed via subscription and are read for professional or business purposes. They are a main focus for many public relations writers. Examples of trade media include *Auto Glass Journal* and *Wine Business Monthly*.

Another categorization defined by the audience, mainly in terms of availability and access, is public/nonpublic media. **Public media** generally are accessible to everybody. Examples of public media are local newspapers and both commercial and public radio and television stations. **Nonpublic media** are more restricted in their coverage and their availability. They often choose to limit access and circulation to audiences drawn from specific occupations, professions or associations. Examples of nonpublic media are company newsletters, e-mail news groups, and magazines and other trade publications that circulate mainly to members of a particular industry or profession.

The final categorization of media is based on the technical production methods of the medium. **Print media** are those that involve the printed word, such as newsletters, newspapers and magazines. **Electronic media** are based on newer technologies. Examples of electronic media include television (both broadcast and cable), radio, and computer-based media such as e-mail and Web sites.

Strategic Communication Categories

Don't look for any single categorization style to suit every purpose. For one thing, there is a significant amount of overlap in these styles. For another, no single classification is necessarily superior to the others. Rather, use these various categories to help you analyze the pros and cons of each communication tool you might consider as you put together your tactical plan.

Strategic Planning for Public Relations looks at the various media and communication tactics in their complexity. In doing so, this book tries not to be overly simplistic, so you won't find media grouped according to any of the conventional categories described in the section above.

A better way to categorize communication media and tactics is to consider their distinctiveness as they relate to the organization using them. Thus, this book presents a menu of communication tactics in four categories:

1. **Interpersonal communication** offers face-to-face opportunities for personal involvement and interaction.
2. **Organizational media** are published or produced by the organization, which controls the message content as well as its timing, packaging and distribution.
3. **News media** provide opportunities for the credible presentation of organizational messages to large audiences.
4. **Advertising and promotional media** are controlled media, generally external to the organization, that also offer access to large audiences.

Together, these four categories offer hundreds of different communication tactics. Each can be used by organizations to communicate with their publics, though not every tool is appropriate for each issue. Remember to be selective in choosing your communication tools.

These four categories of communication tactics complement each other. In Exhibit 7.1, notice how they fit within a reversed pyramid pattern that reflects the relationship between the size of the audience each type of media can reach and the impact it can have on that audience. Interpersonal tactics may reach only a few people, but they have a stronger impact on their audiences than any other form of communication. The reverse is true of advertising and promotional media: They can reach people in great numbers, but with less impact. Don't forget that impact often is the bottom line

Exhibit 7.1   The Relationship Between Audience Reach and Persuasive Impact

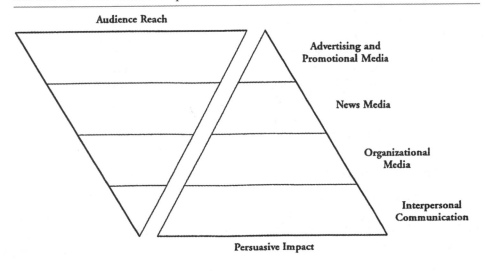

Phase Three

Step
7

for a strategic communication program, whether it uses the persuasion or the dialogue model of communication.

With insight into the strengths and limitations of various kinds of media, communication planners try to create a tactical mix, using several types of communication activities to engage key publics in different ways that, blended together, will effectively achieve the organization's public relations or marketing objectives.

Technological advancements are offering ever more tools for communicators, but the new technology isn't squeezing out the old. In a 1998 study of 480 marketing and communication executives (Corder et al., 1999), Ketchum Public Relations (www.ketchum.com) found that the use of Internet home pages is on the rise. Eighty-eight percent of respondents reported having a home page, compared with 65 percent a year earlier. More significantly, 84 percent expected to increase their Internet activities within the next three to five years. Meanwhile, 95 percent reported using news releases and 40 percent of those expected to increase use of this tactic. Likewise, trade shows and special events were expected to be up 25 percent, direct mail up 48 percent and brochures up 31 percent. Clearly the traditional tools are going to be around for a long time, even as new media are added to the mix.

Let's look first at interpersonal communication tactics.

Interpersonal Communication Techniques

In the disciplines of public relations and marketing communication, both the academic experts who are proficient in concepts and theories and the professional experts with applied training and practical experience agree on a crucial point: Interpersonal communication is the most persuasive and engaging of all the communication tactics.

Don't think this statement demeans other forms of communication. To the contrary, newspaper and television news reports can extend an organization's message to vast audiences. Direct mail can be a cost-effective way to reach great numbers of the key public. Advertising can present messages to large numbers of people with great precision. But in terms of influential communication, the effectiveness of other types of communication pales beside the vigor of direct, face-to-face, interpersonal communication.

Interpersonal communication channels can serve the needs of both businesses and nonprofit organizations. In your consideration of the various tools of communication, then, interpersonal methods should get your first attention. Let's consider the strategy of using interpersonal tactics and then we'll look at the various types of face-to-face communication that can be used for public relations purposes: personal involvement, information exchange and special events.

The Strategy of Interpersonal Communication Tactics

Interpersonal communication tactics offer several strategic advantages to organizations. For one thing, they are controlled tactics through which the organization can oversee its message and the way that message is delivered. Remember, however, that audience response to the message can't be controlled.

Like all public relations tactics, interpersonal ones can be misused if they are applied too generally. But with careful planning, they can be tailored for specific publics, both internal and external.

In terms of organizational resources, interpersonal tactics generally are inexpensive or cost only a moderate amount, though some types of special events can become quite expensive projects if the budget permits. However, interpersonal tactics as a group will claim more staff time to plan and implement than some of the other categories of tactics that we will consider.

Interpersonal tactics can work with either internal or external publics, but the organization should have some relationship with the publics for these tactics to be successful. Interpersonal tactics have the potential to make a strong impact. They are particularly useful in achieving acceptance objectives, which is the most difficult category of objective to reach. Through interpersonal tactics, the organization can communicate with its publics in ways that can have a major effect not only on what they know but especially on how they feel about that information. Thus interpersonal tactics are useful for both the persuasion and dialogue models of communication.

Similarly, interpersonal tactics generally involve information-seeking publics—people who have gone somewhat out of their way to interact with the organization. These people presumably are already interested in the issue, perhaps have some knowledge of the relevant facts and are at least open to (perhaps even leaning toward) the organization's message.

The downside? Interpersonal tactics reach only a small number of people, compared to tactics in other categories. So if numbers are important, these tactics won't be heavy producers.

Like all the categories of tactics presented in this book, interpersonal ones should never be considered in isolation from those in other categories. These are the first ones to consider precisely because they can make such an impact, but they are not necessarily the first ones that will be used chronologically.

Personal Involvement

Personal involvement is a powerful element of communication, whether for purposes of information, education, persuasion or dialogue. When the organization actively involves its publics and creates an environment rooted in two-way communication, the mutual interests of both the organization and its publics are likely to be addressed. This category of tactics includes organizational-site involvement and audience-site involvement.

Organizational-Site Involvement.   A growing number of audience-involvement activities are bringing members of the audience to the organization, as more and more organizations realize the importance of public interaction. "Keep Out" signs are being replaced by welcome mats.

Examples of this type of audience interaction include *plant tours* and *open houses*. For example, Hershey Foods Corporation (www.hersheys.com) sponsors Chocolate World, a free plant tour that feels like a theme park. Such tactics offer for-profit and nonprofit organizations alike an opportunity to "show off" for the various publics of the organization: employees and volunteers, both current and prospective; current and would-be customers; investors, donors and other funding sources; community or governmental supporters.

Some interpersonal tactics involve more hands-on activities. Auto dealers, for example, routinely give *test drives*. Fitness clubs, dance studios and other activity centers may offer *trial memberships* to allow potential members to personally experience the facility and its atmosphere. Likewise, educational activities such as martial-arts programs and cooking schools may offer a limited number of *free classes* to give potential recruits a sample of their offerings.

Private schools have *shadow programs* in which potential students are invited to spend a day accompanying a current student on the daily round of classes. Police, fire and emergency crews offer *ride-alongs* so local residents can see first hand how various situations are handled. *Sneak previews* and *premiere performances* of movies and plays also are effective in generating future audiences.

Audience-Site Involvement.   Sometimes the organization goes to its publics, a real convenience for the audience. For example, door-to-door canvassing offers an opportunity for organizations with a political, social or religious cause to take their message or charitable solicitation directly to people who might be interested. Petition drives seek to get signatures of voters and other constituents. Meanwhile, in-home demonstrations can help people to see how various products or services will work and personally evaluate their effectiveness.

Information Exchange

Another significant category of interpersonal communication tactics, **information exchange,** centers on opportunities for organizations and their publics to meet face-to-face and thus to exchange information, ask questions and clarify understandings. This category includes educational gatherings, product exhibitions, meetings, demonstrations and speeches.

Educational Gatherings.   Various types of meetings provide an opportunity for both commercial and nonprofit organizations to educate large numbers of information-seeking people. *Conventions* are gatherings that generally involve the transaction of organizational business such as the election of officers. Many conventions also have a component of education or professional development. Likewise, *councils* are meetings with a policy-setting agenda. *Convocations, synods* and *conclaves* are formal conventions, often with a religious or academic purpose. *Conferences* are similar to conventions, though the term transfers the focus away from organizational business and toward professional development and education.

Seminars are educational meetings, often ones that bring together peers who discuss issues among themselves. *Symposiums* also are educational meetings in which specialists deliver short papers, whereas *colloquiums* are educational meetings in which specialists deliver formal addresses and then conduct a public discussion of the topic.

Workshops and *training sessions* have a more practical, applied focus, often with an interactive presentation style.

Product Exhibitions.   Companies often seek opportunities to display their products to sales people and potential customers. The special feature of these *trade shows* is that they bring together information-seeking publics—often people who attend trade shows specifically to find out about new products—as well as companies and their competitors. Because competitors are displaying their wares at the same show, each company is challenged to provide a bigger and better presentation than others with a similar product line. For this reason, trade shows generally feature elaborate displays and state-of-the-art interactive technology, often with colorful and attention-getting entertainment and refreshments.

Trade shows often are held as part of conferences and conventions that bring together potential customers. Indeed one of the reasons people attend conferences is to view the latest products associated with their industry or profession. When the National Rifle Association scaled down its 1999 annual convention in Denver just days following the massacre at a high school in suburban Littleton, the absence of the usual trade show featuring the latest in weapons disappointed many conventioneers.

Meetings.   Meetings provide an excellent opportunity for organizations to set up positive information interchanges with their publics. Some of these settings are formal occasions. For example, *annual stockholder meetings* are required of companies that issue stock. While many such meetings are pretty dull, a growing number of companies are turning the required annual event into a sort of internal trade show with elaborate luncheons, refreshments and colorful displays about the company's current and future products, as well as its financial success.

Often, meetings are business-like occasions that involve fewer participants. *Lobbying exchanges* and *public affairs meetings,* for example, may involve just one or two representatives of an organization and a few staff members to an elected official.

Demonstrations.   Some activities focus on advocacy or opposition. *Rallies* can bring together hundreds, even thousands, of people in support of a particular cause, often with speakers. Similarly, *marches* are public processions, often for the purpose of making a political or social statement. Consider, for example, the numerous rallies for social or political causes that are staged in Washington, D.C., or in state capitals.

Other public gatherings are negative in nature. *Demonstrations,* for example, with an element of protest, are opportunities for information exchange, often through speakers as well as by the distribution of printed literature. *Pickets* are demonstrations against an organization, often by trying to prevent people from doing businesses with the organization, and usually with vocal and visual messages criticizing the organization. *Boycotts,* meanwhile, are public protests, sometimes accompanied by picketing, in which customers refrain from using the products or services of the organization being opposed, often accompanied by public education endeavors.

Such demonstrations also tend to generate news coverage, which we will discuss later. Additionally, they can galvanize existing support.

Speeches.   *Speeches* are public discourses in which the speaker controls the presentation and intends to impact the awareness, acceptance or action of an audience. As such, speeches are excellent vehicles for face-to-face communication, especially when *question-answer* sessions are part of the speech presentation.

Consider the different opportunities for giving speeches. *Orations* are very formal and dignified presentations with a high and eloquent rhetorical style. *Talks,* on the other hand, are informal, off-the-cuff speeches, usually on a professional subject. *Lectures* are carefully prepared speeches, often read, associated with classrooms and the presentation of academic information; *guest lectures* are often more practical educational presentations given by an expert in a particular area. *Addresses* are formal speeches that require significant preparation, and *keynote speeches* are major addresses at conferences and other meetings. Two kinds of speeches are associated with the field of religion: *sermons,* morals exhortations based on religious teaching, and *homilies,* explanations of the practical application of a scriptural passage.

In other speech-like situations, the speaker gives up much of the control of the communication. Consider, for example, *panels,* in which a moderator guides the discussion of several speakers. Panels often involve a short, formal opening statement followed by questions offered by the moderator or by other panelists. *Debates* are formal, adversarial speaking occasions, in which one side (an individual or a team) argues with an opponent, using a set of formal rules. *Forums* and *town meetings* are speeches with questions and generally lively discussion, usually on topics of civic or public interest.

Speaker's bureaus are programs within organizations to promote the availability of knowledgeable and trained employees or volunteers to give presentations, usually free, to organizations within the community on topics related to the organization's interests. For example, a fuel-gas company may make speakers available to community associations, tenants groups and homeowners clubs, as well as to business and professional organizations that often have the ear of various opinion leaders. Topics for such a company might include energy saving, high-efficiency heating and cooling equipment, and energy-tax matters.

Special Events

The most common category of interpersonal communication tactics is **special events,** activities that are created by an organization mainly to interact with members of its publics. The list of special events is bounded only by the imagination of the planners, but some of the more common types of special events are civic events, sporting events, contests, holiday events, progress-oriented events, historic commemorations, social events, artistic events and fundraising events.

Civic Events.   Public activities can bring a community together in celebration and fun. Some of the popular civic activities are *fairs,* which feature food and entertainment, and *festivals,* which sometimes offer games and are often organized around a theme, such as ethnic heritage, flowers or music. *Carnivals,* with an atmosphere of public merriment, and *circuses,* with animals, can also be important civic events.

Parades are another form of popular civic celebration, as are *theme events,* such as those associated with community history.

Sporting Events.   Many special events are created around a sports theme. *Tournaments* often are associated with activities such as skiing, fishing and golf that have several levels of difficulty and thus can attract a wide range of participants. *Marathon* races of all sorts and *triathlon events* are increasingly popular athletic events, as are *outdoor spectator events,* such as rodeos, lumberjack roundups and Highland games. Other athletic activities, such as *track meets* and *field days,* provide opportunities to turn sporting events into larger community activities. Other sporting events are designed more as spectator activities.

Contests.   Competitive engagements offer another type of special event, allowing participants to display their knowledge, skills or other assets. By their nature, contests create winners, which also leads to increased visibility because of the built-in news value. *Science fairs, spelling bees* and other types of academically oriented contests are popular contests, as are those that mimic various television quiz shows. Such contests can attract wide audiences, as can *beauty pageants* and *talent contests,* which attract both participants and spectators.

Often grand openings and similar events feature purely fun contests—pizza tossing, pie eating, dancing and so on—in which every participant is a winner.

Holiday Events.   Some special events are based on popular and widespread observances. Many of these are civic celebrations, such as Memorial Day, Independence Day, Labor Day and Thanksgiving. Some holiday activities are rooted within a particular cultural group, such as the Kwanzaa and Juneteenth celebrations in the African American community or Chinese New Year. Some of the most popular holidays, such as Hanukkah and Easter, have religious roots; others are hybrids of popular religion and cultural celebrations, such as St. Patrick's Day, observed by the Irish and Irish-at-heart, or the pre-Lenten Mardi Gras and Carnaval festivities.

Progress-Oriented Events.   Several different kinds of events celebrate the growth and development of an organization or community. Ships and boats traditionally are launched by smashing a champagne bottle on the ship's bow, or by the more environmentally friendly pouring of champagne over the bow. Progress-oriented events often are marked by musical entertainment, fireworks and other celebratory activities.

When a school or religious congregation moves into a new nearby building, the transition often is marked by a *procession* from the old building to the new, such as when students carry symbols such as textbooks, globes and other artifacts of school life. Similarly, a *motorcade* might be arranged to inaugurate the opening of a new bridge.

A single project might lend itself to several progress-oriented special event. Consider, for example, the building of a new community center. You might schedule a *ground-breaking ceremony* for the turning of the first shovel-full of dirt, a *cornerstone ceremony* when construction begins, and a *dedication ceremony* including a *ribboncutting* to mark the completion of the center. Follow these with *tours* and *grand opening events.*

Phase Three

Step
7

Historic Commemorations.   The history of an organization or community provides the background for another kind of special event. Towns observe *founders' days;* companies mark the *anniversary* of their incorporation. Sometimes historic events are observed by recreating the sights and sounds of an earlier era, such as a *centennial celebration* that features costumes, buggies or antique cars, and music and food of the bygone era.

Some historic commemorations include *plays,* dramatic re-enactments of historical events, and *pageants,* and historical plays with a certain amount of music and pomp. Additionally, *caravans* re-enact historic travels.

Social Events.   Social events comprise a major type of special event. *Luncheons* and *dinners* are events sponsored by all kinds of organizations. These social events involve entertainment activities. Receptions with beverages and hors d'oeuvres or snacks are a similar kind of events. Among the various special types of ceremonial meals are *tributes,* which honor people or organizations, and *banquets,* which offer more sumptuous menus and entertainment. *Roasts* use sometimes sarcastic humor to recognize a person's achievements and contributions.

Many social events are aimed at employees and volunteers, and their purpose is to thank or recognize members of an important public. The purpose of *awards dinners* and *recognition lunches* is to enhance the camaraderie among people who work together, a potential boost to worker productivity. In other cases, luncheons and banquets often may have educational or fund-raising objectives and involve a variety of publics.

Social events often occur at elegant or unusual locations, including cruise ships, museums and private mansions. Budget limitations can be offset by an extra dash of creativity, and many social events have been successful because they have had an interesting theme, such as a Caribbean island getaway complete with appropriate music, food and dancing, or historical themes related to the Old West, medieval knights, the flapper era or the antebellum South. Futuristic themes also can be popular.

Other social events include *fashion shows* and *teas.*

Artistic Events.   Another area of special events deals with art and culture. Consider events such *concerts* or *concert tours, recitals, plays, film festivals, arts shows, photo exhibits* and related activities.

Fundraising Events.   Activities in which nonprofit organizations interact with their key publics, especially individual donors, for the purpose of generating support can be important public relations opportunities. Americans donated more than $203 billion to charitable organizations in 2000 ("Giving USA, 2001"). Nearly 78 percent of this amount was given by individuals, the remainder by foundations and corporations. Religious organizations received more than a third of the total, followed by education, health charities, human-service organizations, arts organizations, public benefit groups, and environmental causes (in that order).

The variety of fundraising events is limitless. Consider the following ideas: antique shows, auctions, haunted houses, pony rides, murder mystery dinner theater, fashion shows, house or garden tours, tasting parties (see Amos, 1995; Williams, 1994). All of these require careful planning and an eye for detail.

The Donor Bill of Rights

Philanthropy is based on voluntary action for the common good. It is a tradition of giving and sharing that is primary to the quality of life. To assure that philanthropy merits the respect and trust of the general public, and that donors and prospective donors can have full confidence in the not-for-profit organizations and causes they are asked to support, we declare that all donors have these rights:

1. To be informed of the organization's mission, of the way the organization intends to use donated resources and of its capacity to use donations effectively and for their intended purposes.

2. To be informed of the identity of those serving on the organization's governing board, and to expect the board to exercise prudent judgment in its stewardship responsibilities.

3. To have access to the organization's most recent financial statements.

4. To be assured that their gifts will be used for the purposes for which they were given.

5. To receive appropriate acknowledgment and recognition.

6. To be assured to the information about their donations is handled with respect and with confidentiality to the extent provided by law.

7. To expect that all relationships with individuals representing organizations of interest to the donor will be professional in nature.

8. To be informed whether those seeking donations are volunteers, employees of the organization or hired solicitors.

9. To have the opportunity for their names to be deleted from mailing lists that an organization may intend to share.

10. To feel free to ask questions when making a donation and to receive prompt, truthful and forthright answers.

This statement was developed by the American Association of Fundraising Counsel (www.aafrc.org), the Association for Healthcare Philanthropy (www.goahp.org), the Council for the Advancement and Support of Education (www.case.org) and the Association of Fundraising Executives (www.nsfre.org), formerly the National Society of Fund Raising Executives.

It also has been officially endorsed by the Independent Sector (www.indepsec.org), the National Catholic Development Conference (www.amm.org/ncdc), the National Committee on Planned Giving (www.ncpg.org), the Council for Resource Development (www.ppcc.cccoes.edu/crd) and United Way of America (www.unitedway.org).

Phase Three

Step
7

The ethics of both public relations and fund-raising require honest and forthright disclosure of organizational information to donors and to the media.

Special events and most of the other tactics noted in this section require a tremendous amount of careful planning; attention to detail is a must during the preparation stages. Organizations sometimes handle these details internally; other times, they hire events-management companies to help plan and execute the activities. Either way, consider some of the following practical questions that can arise around a special event.

- Is the date appropriate for everyone? Does it conflict with holidays (particularly cultural or religious holidays that may not be familiar to the planners)? Does it conflict with other major happenings, such as sporting or social activities—not only local events but larger events such as the Kentucky Derby, the Super Bowl or the opening of fishing season? Any such competition can limit attendance at your event.

- What is the appropriate length of an event? If it is too long, participants will become bored or restless or may leave early. If it is too short, they may decide it's not worth attending in the first place.

- Is the theme appropriate? Will it offend anyone, or will anyone feel excluded because of it?

- Is the site appropriate and accessible? Is climate a factor? If it is an outdoor event, is there an indoor location to serve as a backup in the event of bad weather? Does the location of a conference or meeting offer too many pleasant diversions that might tempt participants away from the conference itself?

- Are speakers and entertainers appropriate to the participants of the special event or meeting?

- Is planning assistance available through a convention and visitors' bureau in the host city of a meeting? If so, the agency may be able to simplify local contacts.

All special events call for careful planning, staffing and financing, and they need creative promotion. Use the planning process presented throughout this book to identify and analyze key publics, establish objectives, and develop a strategy for the special event or other type of interpersonal communication tactic. Also make sure you evaluate its effectiveness, showing in measurable terms how well the activity achieved its objectives.

Strategic Planning Example: *Choosing Interpersonal Communication Tactics*

Upstate College will develop interpersonal communication tactics to publicize its expanded program:

Tactic	Characteristics
Open house for recruiting	Key publics, hands-on, low cost, audience feedback
Rededication ceremony	Low cost, news value, reaffirming existing support
Academic convocation	Existing event, little additional cost, news value, power of ritualization
Musical events	Key student publics, moderate cost, serving acceptance objectives
Picnic	Key student publics, low cost, serving acceptance objectives
Festival	Key student publics, high visibility, moderate cost
Banquet	Key publics (community leaders, donors), high cost, high impact

■ ■ ■

Tiny Tykes will develop the following interpersonal communication tactics for an employee-oriented public relations program:

Tactic	Characteristics
Customer satisfaction workshops	Key external publics, high impact
Work-group meeting	Key internal public, interaction and feedback
Product safety and quality session	Key publics, direct benefit to employees and training management, indirect benefits to customers
Motivational speech by CEO about safety and quality	Key employee public, low cost, moderate impact
Samples of reintroduced products	Maintain credibility with employees (and family/friends of employees) as customers, moderate cost

---

Strategic Planning Exercise: *Choosing Interpersonal Communication Tactics*

Basic Planning Questions

1. What interpersonal communications tactics will you use?
2. How will these tactics help the organization achieve its objectives?
3. What resources will these tactics require?

Expanded Planning Questions

A. Selection of Tactics
From the following categories of interpersonal tactics, identify several that you would consider using:

Personal Involvement
- Organizational-site involvement

  Plant tour, open house, test drive, trial membership, free class, sample, shadow program, ride-along, premiere
- Audience-side involvement

  Door-to-door canvassing, in-home demonstration, petition drive

Information Exchange
- Educational Gathering

  Convention, council, convocation, synod, conclave, conference, seminar, symposium, colloquium, workshop, training session
- Product Exhibition

  Trade show
- Meeting

  Annual stockholder meeting, lobbying exchange, public affairs meeting

Phase Three

Step
7

- Demonstration

  Rally, march, demonstration, picket, boycott
- Speech

  Question-answer session, oration, talk, lecture, guest lecture, address, keynote, sermon, homily, panel, debate, speaker's bureau, forum, town meeting
- Special Event

  Civic event: fair, festival, carnival, circus, parade, theme event

  Sporting event: tournament, marathon, triathlon, outdoor spectator event, meet, field day

  Contest: science fair, spelling bee, beauty pageant, talent contest

  Holiday event: civic, cultural, religious

  Progress-oriented event: procession, motorcade, grand opening, groundbreaking, cornerstone, dedication, ribbon cutting

  Historic event: founders' day, anniversary, centennial, play, pageant, caravan

  Social event: luncheon, dinner, reception, tribute, banquet, roast, awards, recognition, fashion show, tea

  Artistic event: concert, concert tour, recital, play, film festival, art show, photo exhibit

  Fundraising event

B. Strategic Implications

For each item identified, answer the following questions:

1. Will this tactic help the organization to interact with the appropriate public?
2. What level of impact will this tactic make on the key public?
3. Will this tactic advance the organization toward its awareness objectives?
4. Will this tactic advance the organization toward its acceptance objectives?
5. Will this tactic advance the organization toward its action objectives?
6. What is the main advantage of this tactic?
7. What advantages does this tactic offer that other tactics do not?
8. Are there any disadvantages with this tactic? If so, what are they?

C. Implementation Items

For each item identified, answer the following questions:

1. How much will it cost to implement this tactic? Is the cost justified? Is the cost practical, based on the organization's resources?
2. How much staff time will it take to implement this tactic? Is the time practical, based on the organization's resources?
3. What level of skill, equipment and expertise is needed to implement this tactic? Is the needed level available within the organization? Is the needed level available from outside sources?

Organizational Media Tactics

A host of communication vehicles are managed by the organization and are used at its discretion. These media generally are controlled, internal, nonpublic media that can be classified in four categories: general publications, direct mail, miscellaneous print media and audiovisual media. Let's consider the overall strategy and then look at each category of organizational media.

The Strategy of Organizational Media Tactics

When should you select organizational media tactics? When your publics are too wide-spread or too large to interact with on a more personal level, or when you want to keep control of the content of your organization's message, as well as its timing and distribution.

When would you not use organizational media? When the audience is too small to warrant it, or so scattered that dissemination would be next to impossible. Or when you need the higher credibility associated with other categories of tactics.

One of the benefits of organizational media tactics is that they provide a middle ground between high-impact, small-audience interpersonal tactics and lower-impact, large-audience news and advertising tactics. Organizational media can reasonably be addressed to both internal and external publics that fall in the mid-size range. Because tactics in this category can be tailored to specific publics, they are more likely than news or advertising tactics to achieve success with acceptance and action objectives.

Another significant benefit of organizational media is that they are likely to be used by information-seeking publics, those who are actively searching for information on a particular topic. These are the people who will access a Web site, read a brochure or watch a video.

Organizational media can be expensive to use, but because they can be targeted to specific publics and individuals, they usually are very cost-effective. For example, the tactic of direct mail can involve high postage costs. But the impact of direct mail—if it is done properly—is higher than most other media, and thus the results are greater.

Remember that organizational media are only one set of tools for public relations and marketing communication. Consider them carefully, but always with the intention of combining them with other kinds of communication tactics.

General Publications

General publications include a variety of materials published and printed by an organization. Their distribution generally is handled by the organization as well. This category includes serial publications, stand-alone publications, reprints, progress reports, user kits and research reports.

Serial Publications.   Most organizations make heavy use of serial publications, which may be issued weekly, monthly or quarterly.

The most common serial publication is a *newsletter,* which combines the informative approach of newspapers and magazines with the relationship-building features of mail. It's hard to tell just how many organizational newsletters exist. Guesses range from 100,000 to more than a million. But some figures are available. For example, more than 50,000 in-house corporate newsletters in the United States have a combined readership of about 500 million. *Newsletters in Print* lists about 11,500 newsletters in the United States and Canada that are national or regional in their outlook and are available to the public. Additionally, there are untold numbers of private publications and *house organs,* which are newsletters published by companies and organizations, with distribution to members, employees and other specific individuals.

Whatever the total, an estimated two-thirds of newsletters are *internal publications* directed toward employees and volunteers. The remaining third are *external publications*. External publications include *advocacy newsletters,* aimed at persuading readers, such as that published by a waste management company as part of a campaign to minimize opposition among local residents, and *special-interest newsletters,* which deal with a particular industry, profession or pursuit (such as financial investments, stamp collecting or white-water canoeing), or with a particular group of people (such as economists, breast-cancer survivors or former nuns). Another type of external newsletter is the *subscription newsletter,* which is often a high-cost publication providing insider information on a particular profession or industry; two such newsletters popular with public relations and marketing practitioners are *pr reporter* (www.prpublishing.com) and *Communication Briefings* (www.briefings.com/cb/editors).

Many public relations and marketing communication campaigns publish one or more newsletters as a convenient way to communicate with an organization's publics. If you plan to use the tactic of newsletters, having an appropriate mailing list is a must. When writing newsletters, follow the principles of newsworthiness and audience self-interest. Make sure the articles provide information of interest to the readers, rather than simply data the organization wishes to present to the readers.

Bulletins, meanwhile, are a different kind of serial publication. Typographically, bulletins often feature only headlines and body text, with little or no graphic content. They generally include official organizational information and are most often circulated to internal audiences.

Stand-Alone Publications.   Another common tactic used in public relations is the stand-alone publication, which differs from a newsletter or bulletin in that it usually is issued only once rather than periodically. This category of publications includes brochures and flyers.

A *brochure* is a common stand-alone piece, dealing with a particular topic or issue. *Organizational brochures* focus on recruiting, product/service lines, membership services, organizational history or some other aspect of a particular organization. *Advocacy brochures* attempt to educate or generate support on a particular issue important to the sponsoring organization. Additionally, some brochures are action-oriented publications with a definite sales pitch, though these are more likely to be associated with marketing efforts than with public relations activities.

A *flyer* is similar to a brochure in that it is a stand-alone piece. But whereas a brochure is meant to be read in panels, a flyer is meant to be read as a single unit.

Brochures and flyers are commonly accepted terms for stand-alone organizational publications, but other names also may be used. Some names deal with the size of the publication. In addition to flyer, other terms for single-sheet publications include *leaflets* or *folders*. In addition to *brochure*, other terms for multi-page publications are called *pamphlets* or *booklets*. Other name distinctions grow out of the purpose of the publication. Persuasive brochures called *tracts* deal with political or religious topics, and marketing-oriented stand-alone publications often are called *circulars*.

A *fact sheet* that presents information in bullet form is another common stand-alone piece, as is an *FAQ sheet*, a presentation of frequently asked questions about a particular issue or organization.

Reprints.   Copies of published articles about an organization or an issue significant to it can be quite useful in meeting public relations objectives. *Reprints* are articles previously published in newspapers, magazines or newsletters. By issuing a reprint, the organization is able to extend the reach and impact of the original publication, particularly by giving it to the organization's publics, who may not have had access to the original article.

A similar tactic is to reprint speeches, especially formal presentations such as keynote addresses or testimony before state, provincial or federal legislative bodies. These often are shared with key publics, such as boards of directors, major donors or stockholders, community and civic leaders and other opinion leaders.

Related to reprints is the distribution of *news releases* to internal audiences. News releases will be discussed more in the section under News Media. While releases are meant primarily for distribution to journalists, some public relations practitioners also selectively send them to key internal publics, such as senior executives, major donors and stockholders.

Progress Reports.   Several different types of *progress reports* focus on the continuing development of an organization, particularly its activity within a recent period of time.

The *annual report* is a special kind of progress report. Annual reports are required by the federal Securities and Exchange Commission (SEC) for American companies that issue stock. These can be simple statements with required information, such as the identification of corporate officials, salaries and benefits of the top executives, financial statements and the auditor's certification of accuracy. Often, however, they feature much more. Many annual reports are glossy, magazine-like publications designed not only to provide required information but to affirm investors' loyalty to the company, attract new investors and enhance the company's reputation with financial analysts and the financial media.

Some companies also produce *quarterly reports*, though these are not required by the SEC. Quarterly reports usually are not as elaborate as annual reports.

Though private companies and nonprofit organizations are not required to issue annual reports, many do so. These often provide financial and organizational information of interest to donors and other supporters. Businesses often find that annual and quarterly reports are convenient vehicles for attracting new customers by demonstrating the work they have previously done.

User Kits.   Several print tactics, generically called *user kits,* are associated with the people who use a product or service. These kits or manuals often include background and how-to information, as well as implementation ideas. For example, *teacher kits* provide a variety of information and materials that can be used in the classroom; these often include sample lesson plans, suggestions for activities, posters, student handouts, even test items. To produce these, the public relations person often would team up with teachers so the information is most useful to the intended public.

Research Reports.   Sometimes, when organizations conduct or sponsor formal research on an issue related to their interests, they consider the information proprietary, that is, private and confidential. After all, they paid for the research, and they may not want to share it with competitors.

Other times, however, they may choose to share the research findings, and they would prepare a *research report.* In such a report, the organization has an ethical requirement to be clear as to its involvement in the research study. The report also needs to include background information, a description of the research methods and how any samples were drawn, presentation and analysis of the research findings, a discussion of the significance of the findings and sometimes some recommendations based on the findings. The report may be distributed like other organizational media—to organizational managers, employees, stockholders or donors, regulators and others.

The report also may be shared with the news media. It is never a good idea to conduct research simply so it can be used for publicity. That would be more like a publicity stunt, and it raises ethical questions about the appropriate use of research and thus about the organization's professionalism. But if the organization believes that a legitimate research report contains some positive news, it may decide to publicize its findings. Often this would involve providing reporters with the research report as well as a news release. In the release, emphasize the validity and objectivity of the study while acknowledging the organization's involvement. Don't use the organization's name too many times in the release.

Direct Mail

Direct mail is a category of organizational print media which, though perhaps general in nature, can be addressed to individual recipients. Direct mail pieces can include memos, letters, postcards, invitations and catalogs.

Memos.   A *memorandum,* or *memo,* is a brief written message addressed to an individual or to a group of people. Memos generally are internal messages; when issued externally, they usually are directed to persons known to the sender. Memos begin with a format that clearly identifies the sender, recipient, date and subject. In writing style, memos are informal, crisp and usually action-oriented. Memos are a good public relations vehicle when you are writing to colleagues, media gatekeepers, or members of key publics, such as when you attach a memo to a reprint you are sending to a major benefactor or stockholder.

Letters.   In the category of direct mail, the most common vehicle is the business let-ter, which generally is a form letter addressed to individuals. Often these will carry the actual name of the reader, such as "Dear Mary Jones," or "Dear Ms. Jones." Sometimes for very large mailings the letters will be addressed more generically, such as "Dear Friend of the Environment" or "Dear Fellow Stamp Collector." *Appeal letters* are direct-mail pieces sent to potential donors by nonprofit organization engaged in fundraising campaigns. *Marketing letters* are direct-mail pieces sent by businesses for advertising purposes.

With both types of direct-mail letters, response rates generally are very low, often less than one percent. But the response rate increases considerably when the letters are sent to people who in the past have made contributions or done business with the sending organization. The best advice regarding direct mail, as with every other form of public relations or marketing communication, is to target the mail to each public and address the reader's self-interest.

Direct-mail packages generally contain more than a marketing or appeal letter. They often also include a brochure about the company or organization, a *response de-vice,* such as a donor card or order form, and a *return device,* such as a payment envelope, usually with return-postage paid.

Postcards.   Similar to letters, *postcards* generally are addressed to individuals, usually by name. Postcards, which include brief messages, are not placed in envelopes, thus their content should never be of a personal or confidential nature. Postcards often are used as announcements or reminders, and they often complement messages pre-sented through news or advertising media. In some cases, postcards may replace other such tactics, especially when it is possible to obtain a mailing list of members of the key public.

Invitations.   Organizations sponsoring events, whether public or private, often send formal, personalized *invitations* to prospective participants.

Catalogs.   Catalogs are books or brochures aimed at consumer publics, generally with an inventory of items available for purchase, though nonprofit organizations can use the catalog approach to list available services or programs. Several types of catalogs can be developed. *Retail catalogs,* with merchandise available in the sponsors' stores, seeks to generate in-store consumer traffic. *Full-line catalogs* feature the entire range of items in a department store. *Specialty catalogs* feature products of very narrow consumer interest, such as a catalog of weaving supplies. *Business-to-business catalogs* contain information on products of interest to businesses.

In recent years, some companies have developed catalogs along the lines of lifestyle-oriented magazines, turning a traditional marketing tool into a public relations vehicle as well. For example, the Patagonia Company (www.patagonia.com) enhances its clothing catalog with pictures by award-winning outdoor photographers, commen-taries on the environment, and field reports about outdoor activities around the world. Abercrombie & Fitch (www.abercrombie.com) sparked calls for a boycott of the cloth-ing store over what critics called racy photos and soft porn in its catalog. The company

Phase Three

Step
7

defended its quarterly publication as being not only a sales tool but also a magazine aimed at the college market.

Miscellaneous Print Media

A whole range of other tactics offer several opportunities for the public relations planner. Consider the following tactics. *Posters* are visual materials, often approximately 3 by 5 feet, that can be displayed prominently. Companies often use *window displays* to give visibility to their products or services; nonprofit organizations sometimes use commercial storefront space made available to them, often during a vacancy in a store in a mall or on a downtown street.

Employees and customers alike can benefit from well-maintained *bulletin boards,* and *suggestion boxes* are excellent opportunities for organizations to solicit feedback and input from their publics. Other traditional tactics that still have value are *pay stuffers* or *bill inserts,* which are messages placed within pay envelopes or bills, respectively. *Door hangers* that advocate a cause or promote a product or service also can be useful.

Business cards remain another effective tactic for organizations to keep their names before potential customers and associates.

Some miscellaneous tactics involve recognition programs. For example, *certificates* are used to acknowledge achievement or participation. Formal *proclamations* are issued by governmental and sometimes by organizational leaders to draw public attention to a particular cause or theme.

Audiovisual Media

Modern technology has added new choices to the menu of tactics that can be used for public relations and marketing communication. Most of these technologies in some way enhance the audio and/or visual aspects of communication. This category includes audio media, video media and computer-based media.

Audio Media. An expanding inventory of audio media are available to public relations planners. *Telephone media* involve new opportunities for information-on-demand, such as *dial-a-message* tactics that allow people to obtain information on topics such as weather or sports scores or to access self-help information and advice on a variety of categories. Dial-a-message services also offer prayers, jokes and so on. Telephone media also can involve the use of *recorded information* or persuasive messages to help people wile away the time spent waiting on a telephone. Some organizations add a public relations dimension to their *voice mail,* such as a community college where the president has recorded a brief welcome message as part of the routing of all incoming phone calls.

Additionally, organizations make frequent use of *toll-free lines* that give customers and other publics free telephone access to the organization; similar *900 lines,* in which callers are charged for the phone call, can generate income for organizations.

Some organizations also have found that *demo tapes* or *demo CDs* can be useful audio tools.

Video Media.   Video media offer opportunities in *nonbroadcast video* that use television technology to produce programs which are then disseminated through organizational rather than public channels. For example, organizations may use nonbroadcast video in conjunction with a stockholders' meeting, open house or some other type of interpersonal tactic. A survey of American business communicators conducted by *Communication World* (Stenson, 1993) indicated that 84 percent of respondents said their companies used some form of nonbroadcast video, also called *corporate video* or *internal video*. Here is a breakdown of the nonbroadcast uses of video technology: training, 51 percent; fund-raising, 47 percent; employee information, 40 percent; product information for brokers, distributors or customers, 36 percent. Other uses of video as an organizational medium included annual meetings, education and internal marketing.

A particular use of nonbroadcast video is as *direct-mail video* to promote both products and causes. *Advertising Age* has reported the effectiveness of direct-mail video (Kim, 1995). For example, in 1994, 60 million tapes were distributed by various organizations. In one case, 94 percent of people viewed the video they received from a gubernatorial candidate in New Jersey. In another study, a direct-mail video that inaugurated a campaign to encourage landowners in the Connecticut River Tidelands region to develop long-term conservation plans was evaluated as being both educational and persuasive, with increases in six key indicators of environmental behavior (Tyson & Snyder, 1999).

Nonbroadcast video sometimes is live, such as *videoconferences,* also called *teleconferences.* Videoconferences use television technology to produce live informational or educational programs for remote audiences. These events are made interactive through the use of satellite or fiber-optic video transmission, sometimes with long-distance telephone connections to link the remote sites to the originating studio.

However, it is more common that nonbroadcast video is taped. Many organizations use *videotapes* (also called *videocassettes*) to present information of interest to donors and stockholders as well as potential customers. Videotapes also have much value for employee training.

Slide shows are informational or educational presentations using 35mm photographic slides. Newer technologies enhance this tactic by making possible interactive multiple-slide presentations.

Computer-Based Media.   The growing field of computer-based media provide even newer strategic communication opportunities. For example, versatile *presentations software* such as PowerPoint often are used instead of the more traditional slide presentations or overhead transparencies.

A mushrooming group of these tactics is associated with the Internet. *Electronic mail,* or *e-mail,* has become an accessible means of instantaneous communication between two persons or with large groups. Using electronic mailing lists called *listservs,* public relations practitioners can communicate with information-seeking publics. Meanwhile, electronic *news groups* bring together people interested in discussing a particular topic.

The Internet also has made it possible for virtually every organization and many individuals to develop *homepages* on the World Wide Web, an interactive network with growing capabilities, such as the use of *Web-based television* and *Web radio*.

Phase Three

Step
7

Web sites are becoming standard fare for organizations of every kind. From corporations to colleges, social advocates to political groups, it seems that almost everyone is using an Internet homepage to provide communicate with people who are actively seeking their information. For example, as the Makah tribe was planning to revive a dormant practice of hunting whales in the Pacific Northwest, the tribe used a Web site (www.makah.com) to provide a detailed question-answer page about its controversial plan. Animal-rights protestors retaliated with a counterfeit rogue site (www.makah.org) that mocked the tribal site.

Additionally, *touch-sensitive computers* make it possible to apply an information-on-demand approach to several situations in which customer can use the computer to interact with the organization, both gaining and giving information.

Strategic Planning Example: *Choosing Organizational Media Tactics*

Upstate College will develop the following tactics using organizational media to publicize its expanded program:

Tactic	Characteristics
College viewbook	Key publics, high visual impact
Transfer brochure	Key publics, high impact, low cost
Letter to former applicants	Targeted, low cost
Poster	Moderate cost, high visual impact
Video	Target key publics, high cost
Homepage at www.upstate.edu for potential transfer students	Information seeking publics, low cost, interactive

■ ■ ■

Tiny Tykes will develop the following tactics using organizational media for an employee-oriented public relations program:

Tactic	Characteristics
Newsletter articles in employee publication about safety, quality and customer satisfaction	Target key publics, low cost
Memo about product reintroduction	Target key public, low cost
Employee bulletin with updates on customer response to product reintroduction (pro and con)	Target key public, low cost
Brochures about safety, quality and customer satisfaction	Moderate cost

Letter to families of employees thanking them for supporting employees and company during difficult reintroduction period	Target key public, low cost
Suggestion box soliciting employee input about safety and quality, with feedback via employee newsletter	Low cost, interactive

Strategic Planning Exercise: *Choosing Organizational Media Tactics*

Basic Planning Questions

1. What organizational media tactics will you use?
2. How will these tactics help the organization achieve its objectives?
3. What resources will these tactics require?

Expanded Planning Questions

A. Selection of Tactics

From the following categories of organizational media tactics, identify several that you would consider using:

General Publications
- Serial publication: newsletter, house organ, bulletin
- Stand-alone publication: brochure, leaflet, folder, pamphlet, booklet, tract, circular
- Reprint, internal news release
- Progress report: annual report, quarterly report
- User kit, teacher kit
- Research report

Direct Mail
- Memo, appeal letter, marketing letter, postcard, invitation, catalog

Miscellaneous Print Media
- Poster, window display, bulletin board, suggestion box, pay stuffer, bill insert, door hanger, business card, certificate, proclamation

Audiovisual Media
- Audio: Telephone, dial-a-message, recorded information, demo tape, demo CD
- Video: Nonbroadcast video, corporate video, internal video, video conference, teleconference, slide show
- Computer-based media: e-mail, listserv, news group, Web site, homepage, Web TV, Web radio, touch-sensitive computer

Phase Three

Step
7

B. Strategic Implications

For each item identified, answer the following questions:

1. Will this tactic help the organization to interact with the appropriate public?
2. What level of impact will this tactic make on the key public?
3. Will this tactic advance the organization toward its awareness objectives?
4. Will this tactic advance the organization toward its acceptance objectives?
5. Will this tactic advance the organization toward its action objectives?
6. What is the main advantage of this tactic?
7. What advantages does this tactic offer that other tactics do not?
8. Are there any disadvantages with this tactic? If so, what are they?

C. Implementation Items

For each item identified, answer the following questions:

1. How much will it cost to implement this tactic? Is the cost justified? Is the cost practical, based on the organization's resources?
2. How much staff time will it take to implement this tactic? Is the time practical, based on the organization's resources?
3. What level of skill, equipment and expertise is needed to implement this tactic? Is the needed level available within the organization? Is the needed level available from outside sources?

News Media Tactics

The news media are communication vehicles that exist primarily to present newsworthy information to various audiences. There is much variety within among news media. Consider the possibilities: print news media, such as newspapers and magazines; broadcast news media, including radio and television; and interactive news media, including interviews and conferences. Though all of these media are focused on news, each provides a somewhat different opportunity for public relations and marketing communication.

The Strategy of News Media Tactics

The news media offer public relations and marketing practitioners several benefits not usually associated with tactics in the other categories.

First, the news media generally reach large audiences—certainly larger than most audiences associated with interpersonal communication tactics, and usually larger than those for organizational media. News media audiences may encompass most residents of a particular community, most members of a certain profession or most people who are seriously interested in a given topic. Thus news media tactics can further an organization's pursuit of awareness objectives.

Second, the publicity that can be generated through these media is free. Unlike the built-in cost of organizational media and the fees associated with advertising, no price tag is associated with publicity. Obviously the organization will have overhead costs, such as staff or agency time in researching and writing materials such as news releases, as well as the cost associated with printing and distributing such releases, but these are internal administrative costs and incidental expenses.

The news media are considered uncontrolled media, which creates the environment for the third, and perhaps most important, benefit they offer: The news media can add much credibility to an organization's message. They have the power of what's called *third-party endorsement,* meaning that someone outside the organization preparing the message—in this case reporters, editors and news directors—is in some way attesting to

---

Media Directories

Media directories are useful resource documents that provide much valuable information about newspapers and magazines, radio and television stations, broadcast networks, and related information. Here are some of the widely used directories.

- *Bacon's Directories* (www.baconsinfo.com): Newspaper directory for daily and weekly publications, news services, syndicates, publishers, columnists, Sunday supplements, ethnic publications; magazine directory with market classifications; radio/television directory with stations, broadcast and cable networks, satellite systems, syndicates.
- *Bowden Media Directory* (www.bowden.com): Directories of Canadian media and related services.
- *Burrelle's Media Directory* (www.burrelles.com): State-by-state listings for more than 40,000 media outlets including daily and nondaily newspapers, news services, syndicates, magazines (trade, professional and consumer), newsletters, radio and television stations, cable services and networks.
- *Cable & Station Coverage Atlas* (www.warrennews.com): Directory with coverage maps.
- *Editor and Publisher International Yearbook* (www.editorandpublisher.com): One-volume directory of daily U.S. and Canadian newspa-

pers; weekly, ethnic, special interest papers; foreign newspapers; and news syndicates.
- *Gale Directory of Publications and Broadcast Media* (www.gale.com): State-by-state listings for 63,000 daily, weekly, special interest newspapers; periodicals; radio; television; cable; networks and news syndicates.
- *Gebbie Press All-in-One Directory* (www.gebbieinc.com): One-volume directory of business, trade, financial, and consumer publications; news syndicates and daily and weekly newspapers; ethnic newspapers; television networks; television and radio stations. Available in print or CD-ROM.
- *Matthews Media Directories* (www.matthews.ca): Directories specializing in Canadian print and electronic media.
- *Newsletters in Print* (www.gale.com): Newsletters in United States and Canada.
- *Television and Cable Factbook* (www.warrennews.com): Commercial and public television stations, cable systems, instructional systems, low-power stations, foreign-language programming, media organizations, networks, satellite services, communication attorneys and engineers in the United States, Canada, Mexico and international markets.
- *Writer's Market* (www.writersdigest.com): Freelance-oriented information on consumer, trade and professional magazines.

Phase Three

Step
7

the significance and validity of the information being presented. Unlike a newsletter, Web site or advertisement, in which the organization can say pretty much anything it likes, the news media demand a certain level of accuracy. Reporters can evaluate the accuracy of information presented and can check the claims being made before the story is presented to readers, listeners or viewers. This added credibility can go a long way toward achieving the acceptance objectives of the organization.

Despite a steady erosion of credibility, the news media still maintain an impressive respect from their audiences. Frank Newport, editor of *The Gallup Poll,* and managing editor Lydia Saad (1998) indicated that Americans report a high level of trust and preferences for television news reporting. Most trusted are, in order, CNN, public television news, local television newscasts and prime time TV newsmagazines. Network news is somewhat less credible, followed by local and national newspapers and then weekly news magazines. At the bottom of the credibility list are radio and television talk shows and Internet news.

Whereas interpersonal tactics and organizational media generally involve information-seeking publics, the news media more often carry the organization's message to people who are not actively seeking it. True, readers intend to catch up on the day's events when they sit down in the evening with the newspaper, but they aren't especially looking for information about a particular organization. They more-or-less stumble over it and, if it seems to suit their interests and needs, they will read the information and perhaps act on it.

The impact of messages presented by the news media can be looked at from two perspectives. On the one hand, there is the added credibility associated with news reporting. On the other hand, individual news reports seldom affect people who were not previously interested in the topic or in the organization associated with the story. The lesson for public relations: Strive for good publicity, but don't expect it to work miracles. Remember that the news media offer only one set of items on the menu of communication tactics.

Newspapers

Newspapers are publications that boast of up-to-date printed information—reports of what happened the previous day or even earlier on the day of their distribution. They may be published daily or nondaily (usually weekly, some with more or less frequency). Media directories list more than 12,000 newspapers in the United States and Canada—1,600 daily newspapers, 900 Sunday papers, 700 bi- or tri-weekly, 8,000 weekly and 1,100 less often than weekly.

Circulation for daily newspapers sometimes is very high. In the United States, the *Wall Street Journal* is the largest newspaper, circulating more than 1.7 million copies every day; internationally, the *Yomiuri Shimbun* in Tokyo circulates 14.5 million copies daily, according to Editor & Publisher's *International Yearbook 1999* (Maddux, 1998). At the other end of the spectrum, the yearbook notes that two-thirds of daily newspapers in North America circulate in towns and cities of less than 50,000 residents. Many weekly newspapers circulate only a few hundred copies.

Exhibit 7.2 The Competitive Media Index

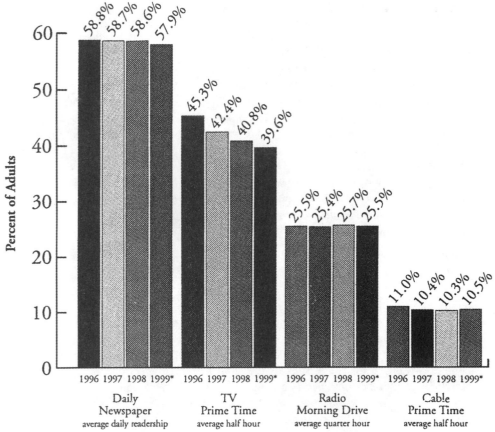

Top 50 Market Media Trends

Source: Scarborough Research Top 50 Market Report. Prepared by NAA Market & Business Analysis Dept.
* CMI Spring 1999—Scarbrough Research, 1998 Release 2

The number of newspapers has been declining in recent decades as the cost of publishing, corporate mergers and the pressures of competition have forced financially weaker publications out of business. Simultaneously, the newspaper audience is declining: Audiences are getting older, and younger information consumers are more likely to get their news from radio or television than from newspapers. Nevertheless, most opinion leaders—business people, educators, politicians, clergy and others in positions of influence—are staunch newspaper readers, and many "average citizens" make newspaper reading a part of their daily information-gathering habit.

As Exhibit 7.2 shows, daily newspapers still dominate the media market for adults. The Newspaper Association of America (1999) reported that, in both the United States

Phase Three

Step
7

and Canada, daily newspaper readership remains close to 60 percent and Sunday readership almost 70 percent among all adults. But in a trend that could affect the future practice of public relations, the association (www.naa.org) reports that young adults aged 18 to 34 show significantly lower readership—45 percent for daily papers and 58 percent for Sunday newspapers.

General-Interest Newspapers.   *General-interest newspapers* are the most common types of newspapers, appealing to the diverse interests of a wide spectrum of readers. Most of these are local newspapers published for the residents of a particular town, city or metropolitan area. They cover topics such as current events, including crimes, accidents, births and deaths; political and business news; sports and entertainment reports and reviews; information about leisure pursuits such as cooking and gardening; announcements of upcoming meetings and activities; and specialized information relating to issues such as education and health. Most local newspapers also include opinion sections with editorials and letters from readers.

The category of general-interest newspapers can be further divided into *national newspapers* such as *USA Today, city* or *metropolitan newspapers* such as the *Atlanta Constitution,* and *community newspapers* such as the weekly *Idaho Enterprise* (circulation 1,500) in rural Malad City, Idaho.

Trade Newspapers.   Newspapers that are focused on a particular industry or profession are called *trade newspapers.* Unlike organizational newspapers that are published by a particular company or nonprofit organization, trade newspapers are usually published by professional organizations or trade associations that serve the needs of several different companies and nonprofit groups linked to a particular industry or profession. Some trade newspapers are independently published, such as *Overdrive,* a biweekly newspaper for truckers. Others are published by industry associations for people working in that field, such as *Carolina Cattle Connection,* the newspaper for members of both the combined North and South Carolina Cattlemen's Associations, or *Panthers' Plus,* a newspaper published for members of the Canadian Grey Panthers senior citizen's advocacy organization.

Special-Interest Newspapers.   *Special-interest newspapers* are devoted to issues such as the arts, business, sports or entertainment. Though the topic for each publication is narrow, information in such newspapers is intended for a wide audience. *The Hockey News* and *Advertising Age* are examples of special-interest newspapers.

Special-Audience Newspapers.   *Special-audience newspapers* are similar to the special-interest newspapers, but they are written for particular audiences, such as gay and lesbian, military, black, Jewish or Hispanic, as well as about 40 other ethnic or special-interest groups, according to media directories such as Editor & Publisher's *International Yearbook* (www.editorandpublisher.com) and the *Gale Directory of Publications and Broadcast Media* (www.gale.com). Information in these newspapers often is diverse, though the appeal is clearly linked to the audience. Often such newspapers are printed in languages other than English.

Organizational Newspapers.   *Organizational newspapers,* also called *house organs,* are published by political, ethnic, religious, educational and other groups. Information in them generally deals with those organizations and their members. *Public Relations Tactics* is an example of an organizational newspaper, published for members of the Public Relations Society of America. As a category, this sometimes overlaps special-interest and special-audience papers. For example, the *Navajo Times* is the official newspaper of the Navajo Nation that is read, not surprisingly, mainly by Navajos (special audience) and by others who are particularly interested in the Navajo people (special interest).

Magazines

Magazines are publications with less frequency and less immediacy than newspapers; prepublication time may include several days, even several weeks, from when a story is written until when the magazine is distributed to readers. Some magazines are local or regional and thus focused on a particular geographic area, but most are of more general interest and their content is more feature-based than most newspapers.

Like newspapers, magazines based in the United States and Canada are published in many different languages—about 50 languages in all. These include the three most common languages in North America—English, French and Spanish—as well as less-common languages such as Welsh, Urdu, Latin, Icelandic and several Native American or Native Canadian languages.

Writer's Market, a comprehensive annual listing of magazines published in North America, lists thousands of *popular* or *consumer magazines,* the kind found on newsstands and through subscription services. These are published in several different categories—general circulation, college, health, foreign language, ethnic, music, men's interest, women's interest, sports and so on.

Additionally, there are an untold number of *house organs,* which are magazines produced within a particular company or organization. These usually focus on organizational issues and are intended for employees, volunteers, stockholders, donors and other interested audiences. Examples of house organs are *Women Police,* a quarterly magazine published by the International Association of Women Police, and *Handball,* the official magazine of the U.S. Handball Association.

Sometimes the categories can overlap. Some magazines are published for special audiences, such as *Essence* for black women, *Seventeen* for teenage girls and *Sisters Today* for nuns. Meanwhile, *trade magazines* are published by and/or for particular businesses, professions and industries. Some of these are published by organizations, such as the *Canadian Guernsey Journal* published by the Canadian Guernsey Association. Others are independently published, such as *Sheep!,* a magazine for sheep farmers.

Especially in the trade press, distinctions often blur among newspapers, magazines and newsletters, because the distinguishing features related to physical format are offset by a similar content and readership. Consider the financial media, for example. It includes daily business-oriented newspapers such as the *Wall Street Journal,* weekly newspapers such as the *Business Journal of Central New York,* regional magazines such as *Colorado Business,* the business sections of most metropolitan daily newspapers, business magazines such as *Barron's* and *Business Week,* consumer magazines such as *Money* and *Fortune,* financial newsletters such as *The Kiplinger Report,* company newsletters published by brokerage firms and investment companies, and financial columnists such as Jane Bryant Quinn. And that's just the print media.

The actual number of magazines is impossible to calculate accurately, but it is vast. In just the area of religion, for example, *Religious Periodicals of the United States: Academic and Scholarly Journals* (Lippy, 1986) estimated that there are about 2,500 religious magazines, many of them associated with a particular denomination, diocese or religious order.

E-zines, e-mail based magazines, are a new addition to the publishing field. The trend toward e-zines began in the mid 1990s, when magazine publishers began placing editorial content, stories and photographs at their magazine Web sites. Now many online magazines also feature interactive opportunities for readers, much of this involving catalog sections of the magazines where readers can order products from a variety of companies.

Radio

Radio provides opportunities in both the AM and FM formats (generally AM is more oriented toward news, sports or talk, whereas FM often includes more all-music formats). Radio stations may be commercial or public. The United States and Canada together have about 9,000 radio stations, about 4,000 AM stations and 5,000 FM stations, according to the Gale Directory. Most of these are commercial stations; about 1,260 are public. Many radio news opportunities exist at the local level, others through about 115 national networks. These include large networks such as ABC Radio or the UPI Radio Network, and smaller, specialized networks such as the Beethoven Satellite Network of classical music, Tobacco Radio Network with agricultural information and Kidwaves Radio Network with children's programming.

Radio is found virtually everywhere, and 19 out of 20 people listen to radio at some time during a typical week. Radio is very mobile—a positive quality in that it can travel with people, but also a negative one, because people listen passively to radio while doing other things (such as driving, working and reading).

Many people who turn on radios can hardly be called listeners—they use radio mainly to overcome silence, without really listening to it. Because of this, research shows that audience recall of radio commercials is less than that for television; however, the relatively low cost of radio advertising allows for heavier repetition than many organizations generally can afford via television. On the other hand, radio generally attracts individuals alone (unlike television, which often is watched by people in groups). So when do radio audiences do listen, they can focus on what is being said.

Because radio formats are specific, audiences tend to be very different from one station to another. National Public Radio, for example, is popular with people who are identified as opinion leaders in many different environments. Classic rock stations, meanwhile, find that two-thirds of their listeners are between the ages of 18 and 34; they are particularly strong with young men under age 25, with many listeners apparently

Lead Time

The amount of time it takes reporters and other media professionals to gather and present their news is called *lead time*. This varies with both the type of medium and the kind of presentation that will be given.

The best way to know the lead time required by various media is to ask. Contact the city editor of a newspaper, the news director or assignment editor of a radio or television station, or the acquisitions editor or news editor of a magazine. Or ask an individual reporter or columnist.

Here is an outline of typical lead times needed for various news media tactics.

- *Daily newspapers:* Give about a week's notice for routine information, a day or several hours for important news, and less than an hour for major on-deadline news. Information for special sections such as travel, food and social events may have a longer lead time. News releases can be submitted at any time, but Sunday and Monday often find less competition for space because weekends traditionally are slow news days, are lightly staffed by most newspapers, and have more pages because of increased advertising.

- *Nondaily newspapers:* Plan to provide information three publication dates before the relevant date of the information. For example, three weeks for a weekly newspaper, or a week-and-a-half for a twice-weekly newspaper.

- *Magazines:* Most monthly magazines require at least a two-month lead time for information to be published. Weekly news magazine have a much shorter lead time but seldom take information from public relations sources.

- *Radio:* Give about a week's notice for routine information and for upcoming events that reporters might cover, with important news being handled up to news time. Breaking news may be covered live. Other live coverage may be planned with a lead time of a week or longer. Talk shows and other programs with guests may require several weeks to schedule.

- *Television:* Provide up to a week's notice for routine information and for events that reporters might cover, with important news being handled up to news time. Breaking news may be covered live. Talk shows and programs with guests may require several weeks to schedule.

Phase Three

Step
7

nostalgic for an era they never personally experienced, according to Simmons Market Research Bureau (1993). Simmons also found that news and talk stations draw an audience heavy with men and women 55 and older (though 22 percent of the audience is aged 18 to 34), with the total audience better educated than Americans in general. It also found that stations focused on contemporary hits attract women under 30 and teens. Thus it is important to know your key publics before making decisions about particular stations.

What are the strategic implications of all this? Let's say you are operating a restaurant or a retail store. If you want to attract younger customers, pipe classic rock or progressive rock over the sound system. On the other hand, if you want more senior citizens, use easy listening (favored by 51 percent of radio listeners aged 50 or older) or nostalgia music (72 percent of listeners), according to Simmons. Want to appeal to women customers more? Simmons reports that country music listeners tend to be women aged 25 to 54, with lower incomes than women in the Top 40 audience. This kind of demographic information has implications for public relations strategists—for example, in the kind of music-related events they might sponsor or possible topics for articles in a newsletter or Web site for consumer or employee publics.

Television

Like radio, television may be commercial or public, with opportunities to reach audiences through both local stations and national or regional networks. Other television opportunities include cable programming, both through national networks and local production facilities.

Nearly 1,400 television stations operate throughout the United States and Canada. Most stations are affiliated with a major network. In the United States, the largest commercial networks are ABC, NBC, CBS and Fox, with PBS as the public network; in Canada, CBC and CTV are nationwide English-language television networks, and Radio-Canada is the French-language public TV network. Nearly 50 broadcast television networks operate in the United States and Canada, including many specialized networks such as Inuit Television of Canada, Newfoundland Television (NTV), Univision Spanish-language network, and several state-based PBS affiliates such as Pennsylvania Public Television Network.

Additionally, about 115 cable television networks are in business, including CNBC, Discovery Channel, MTV and Nickelodeon.

When public relations is able to gain the attention of television reporters, organizations find themselves facing potentially vast audiences. Obviously, however, not every public relations activity is newsworthy, nor should it be. To help you determine what is or is not newsworthy, review the definition of news and the characteristics of newsworthiness in the Strategy section of this book.

Serving Media Information Needs

The relationship between a public relations practitioner and a journalist is *symbiotic;* that is, it is a relationship in which each side needs the other and benefits from the other. Public relations people need journalists, who can provide a vehicle to present the organization's messages. Reporters need public relations practitioners to help them identify newsworthy stories and report on them.

Most newspapers are private commercial enterprises. About 70 percent of their income is derived from advertising and 30 percent from circulation; news and commentary are the products these companies are selling. As businesses protected by the First Amendment of the U.S. Constitution, American newspapers are not required to publish any particular material, including news releases and other information originating from public relations practitioners. Not even government agencies can command news coverage. Television and radio stations generally are private businesses as well. While they must meet certain government regulations (because they have, in effect, a franchise to operate on a particular channel frequency), they nevertheless have much discretion over what news to cover.

However, editors and news directors usually are receptive to public relations information when they believe it will satisfy the interests of their readers. An estimated half to two-thirds of the information in daily newspapers originates from public

Public Relations Helps Write the News

The news media owe a lot to public relations. Estimates vary on how much information carried in the news media comes from public relations practitioners—half, two-third, three-fourths. Whatever the actual number, it's evident that most editors and reporters get a lot of their information from public relations sources.

A classic 1981 study by the *Columbia Journalism Review* counted 45 percent of the 188 news stories in one edition of the *Wall Street Journal* as originating with public relations practitioners. A press secretary to a former New York City mayor estimated that public relations generates 50 percent of stories in that city's newspapers (Wilcox et al., 2000). An academic journal reported that 78 percent of journalists surveyed said they use news releases, at least to spark story ideas, more than half of the time (Curtain, 1999). In that survey, many said they have strict guidelines for using public relations materials, such as

using only those from nonprofit organizations promoting social causes but not from businesses seeking economic gain.

The term for such assistance is *information subsidies,* information from public relations sources that increasingly short-staffed editors use to help underwrite the costs of gathering news. In his book *Market-Driven Journalism: Let the Citizen Beware?,* John McManus (1994) predicted that newsrooms will turn more frequently to low-cost public relations information subsidies.

That could be good for public relations practitioners. But there is a down side to the trend. If the media lower their journalistic standards to the point that they lose credibility with their audiences, public relations people will find less value in news media coverage. So despite easier entree to the news columns and broadcasts, media coverage will be worth less. Something to think about.

relations practitioners, either through vehicles initiated by practitioners, such as news releases, news conferences and media alerts, or because practitioners have responded to journalists with interviews or background information. The rate for radio and television news broadcasts is slightly less, because these media proportionally give more coverage to accidents, crime and other breaking news. As rising corporate costs lead to news-gathering teams becoming smaller at many publications and broadcast stations, news-oriented public relations practitioners can be of increasing assistance to the remaining reporters, and thus more effective in service to their organizations.

The most common way for public relations practitioners to provide news people with information is to give it to them in writing. News releases and other written information traditionally has been distributed through the mail, sometimes though news wires; increasingly, fax and e-mail are become accepted distribution tools, and some organizations service reporters through Web sites. For breaking news and sometimes for story ideas, some public relations practitioners make telephone contact with reporters.

Virtually all journalists now use the Internet. The Survey of Media in the Wired World (Middleberg & Ross, 2001) reported that 98 percent of journalists go online at least daily to check for e-mail. Other findings in this seventh national survey: 92 percent use the Internet to research their articles, 76 percent of reporters use the Internet to find news sources and experts, 73 percent look for news releases online, and 53 receive story

Phase Three

Step
7

pitches via e-mail. Digital photography is gaining support, with 46 percent of magazine journalists and 61 percent of newspaper reporters preferring digital photography for receiving images, as compared to slides and prints. The study also found that e-mail matches the telephone as the preferred methods for interviewing news sources.

Let's look at some of the ways in which public relations practitioners can provide the news media with newsworthy information and thus disseminate their messages to the vast media audiences. There are four general ways to present information through the news media: direct news material, indirect news material, opinion material and interactive news opportunities.

Direct News Material

One of the most frequently used categories of news media tactics is **direct news material**—information that is presented to the media more-or-less ready for use. These tactics include news fact sheets, event listings, interview notes, news releases, feature releases, actualities, audio news releases, video B-rolls, video news releases, photos and captions, and media kits.

News Fact Sheets.   Brief, generally one-page outlines of information about a newsworthy event or activity are called *news fact sheets*. These often are presented as bulleted items; the format makes it easy for reporters in both print and electronic media to use the information as they write their own stories. Fact sheets also can be used by people other than reporters, such as speech writers, tour guides, employees and customers.

Fact sheets are easy to prepare. Simply gather the relevant information and present it along the traditional journalistic lines of who, what, when, where, why and how. It also may be useful to add sections on background, history, significance and benefits. Additionally, it may be appropriate to include a brief direct quote.

Event Listings.   *Event listings* are another information format for print media. Also called *community calendars,* these are simple notices that most newspapers and many magazines print about upcoming activities such as benefits, meetings, entertainment events, public lectures and so on.

Interview Notes.   *Interview notes* are verbatim transcripts presented in a question-answer format, based on an interview that a public relations writer has done with an organizational news source. For example, a university news bureau might interview a geology professor about breakthrough work involving earthquake prediction, then provide the transcript of that interview for science writers. Interview notes usually begin with a brief narrative paragraph to set the stage. They often include a biographical sketch of the person being interviewed.

Interview notes allow reporters to build their stories as they see fit. Even if they decide to do their own interviews, the interview notes can save them time and give them information to build on.

News Releases.   Most organizations find that *news releases* are a mainstay of media relations. These are news stories written by public relations practitioners and given to

---

Wire Services

Here is a brief overview of the most commonly used news wire services, along with their Internet addresses:

- *Associated Press* (www.ap.org) has bureaus in 144 U.S. cities and 93 international bureaus, serving 1,700 U.S. newspapers, 6,000 radio or television outlets and 8,500 international subscribers.
- *Canadian Press* (www.canpress.ca) has 16 offices, including ones in London and Washington.
- *Reuters* (www.reuters.com) operates bureaus in 21 U.S. and five Canadian cities.
- *United Press International* (www.upi.com) has bureaus in 15 U.S. cities, one each in Canada and Mexico, and eight other international bureaus.

Many smaller and more specialized wire services serve the particular needs of their client newspaper and broadcast stations. Examples of these include Cox News (www.cox.com), Environmental News Service (www.ens-news.com) and Catholic News Service (www.catholicnews.com).

Additionally, there are several public relations and business wire services. Most carry news releases, photos, media alerts and audio or video transmissions and offer broadcast fax and fax-on-demand services:

- *PR Newswire* (www.prnewswire.com) has offices in 19 U.S. cities and serves more than 1,500 cities throughout the United States.
- *Canada NewsWire* (www.newswire.ca), an affiliate of PR Newswire with seven offices across the country.
- *Business Wire* (www.businesswire.com) has offices in 21 cities.
- *Bloomberg News* (www.bloomberg.com) handles business and financial news and columns.
- *Dow Jones News Service* (www.dowjones.com) also handles business and financial news.

Relatively current information about wire services can be found in most media directories, which are updated annually.

Phase Three

Step
7

media gatekeepers for use in their news publications and programs. Submit them to newspaper city editors or to editors or beat reporters of special-interest sections such as sports, business and entertainment. Special-interest magazines also may use news releases, especially for brief items.

For broadcast media, submit news releases to news directors or assignment editors. Also, consider taking the time to rewrite the standard (that is, print-oriented) releases when you intend to send them to radio or television stations.

Traditionally, news releases were distributed through the mail or were hand-delivered, either by the public relations practitioners or by a courier. Some practitioners still try to maintain the face-to-face interaction with reporters by delivering their releases. And most media outlets report that the majority of their news releases continue to arrive through the mail or via fax.

Increasingly, however, organizations are disseminating news releases via e-mail to individual journalists, or they are posting releases on Web sites where reporters can retrieve the information. Some practitioners notify reporters via an e-mail distribution list when they post news releases on their Web sites.

News releases also may be submitted to wire services such as the Associated Press, though most wire-service stories are obtained from local bureaus and member newspapers. Radio stations often obtain information from specialized radio wire services such as North American Network and News/Broadcast Network.

In addition to submitting information directly to broadcast stations, some organizations provide frequently updated recorded news releases and sound bites that reporters can dial up on a telephone system or download from a Web site and record for their broadcast news reports. Additionally, news releases can be disseminated through commercial public relations wire services.

If you are considering preparing a news release, note that there are several different kinds. *Announcement releases,* for example, often are subcategorized as dealing with events, personnel, progress, bad news, programs or products. *Response releases* deal with new or updated information, comments, public interest tie-ins and speeches. *Hometowner releases* are sent to newspapers serving the permanent residential areas of employees, students, members of the military and so on.

News briefs involve only a two- or three-paragraph story that provides the basic information of the summary lead as well as a clear indication of the benefit. Some public relations writers try to write each news release so the first couple of paragraphs can be pulled out to serve as a news brief.

Note that the news media is not obligated to use news releases. In fact, most releases are rejected, usually because they are either more self-promoting than news-reporting or because they are weak in local interest.

Feature Releases.   In addition to releases that present solid news, other releases focus on some kind of background on the news. Known as *feature releases,* they fall into several categories.

Biographies, for example, provide the personal background on news makers and other people significant to an organization. They can be written in chronological style or as personality profiles. *Histories,* meanwhile, provide a similar focus on the organization itself, usually providing a chronological narrative or an outline of the development of the organization since its founding. Histories generally deal not only with milestones but also with issues facing the organization. Both histories and biographies are written so they can be updated easily when new developments warrant.

Narrative articles providing objective information on an issue are called *backgrounders*. They usually deal with the cause of the problem or issue, a chronological history of how the issue has progressed, its current status and perhaps clear projections of its direction and likely future. Backgrounders also provide information on the significance or impact of the issue. The key element for a backgrounder is that it should remain neutral—objective and free of opinion or unsupported speculation; indeed, all sides in an issue should be able to agree on the facts within a backgrounder.

Other categories of feature articles are based on the writing format used in the release. Some releases are presented as a *question-answer piece* (also called a *Q&A*). Others are written in the step-by-step format of a *service article,* or *how-to piece,* which provides readers with an instructional approach to solving a problem.

Actualities.   When public relations writers want to quote someone in a news release going to print journalists, they include a sentence or phrase in quotation marks. When they want to provide radio reports with similar quoted material, they use an *actuality* (sometimes called a *sound bite*), because radio stations prefer to present quoted information in the voice of the news source. An actuality is a recording—sometimes on cassette, sometimes digitized and made accessible by computer. It involves a couple of highlight quotes from a speech or statement by an organizational spokesperson.

Audio News Releases.   *Audio news releases (ANRs)* are edited story packages that public relations writers offer to radio journalists. ANRs are news stories complete with announcer and sound bite. About 84 percent of United States radio stations use audio news releases, according to a study by Medialink ("Survey Shows Radio Use Patterns," 1996). Most of those stations said they prefer ANRs with a local angle. Another study showed that radio stations use ANRs most often as a 60-second spot plugged into a station's morning drive-time news reports.

Video B-Rolls.   Quoted statements and other visual information can be made available to television stations through *video B-rolls,* which are tapes providing a series of unedited video shots and sound bites related to the news story. A written news release or other background material often accompanies B-rolls to give television reporters an idea of what the story is all about.

Video News Releases.   *Video news releases (VNRs)* are edited story packages given to television journalists by public relations people. VNRs are usually 30 to 90 seconds long, complete with narration, interviews and background video, even names titled at the bottom of the screen. B-rolls are sometimes used with VNRs to provide for easier editing of newsworthy material.

Television stations use about 5,000 VNRs each year. One survey (West Glen, 1997) found that 90 percent of television stations in the United States use outside-produced video for newscasts, and the trend seems to be increasing. Morning and early evening are the two news slots when VNRs and B-rolls are most likely to be used. However, many VNRs are not used because television news directors judge them to be lacking in local news value or some other important news criterion. Another reason some VNRs are rejected is that they are overly commercial, lacking what the reporters consider strong news judgment. But when they are used, the impact can be huge. For example, Pepsi-Cola reached an estimated 365 million viewers with four VNRs during the syringe hoax.

Because of the production costs involved, most video news releases are developed by organizations with widespread publics rather than for single-market use. VNRs and B-rolls may be distributed nationally or regionally. National distribution can cost from $25,000 to more than $100,000. Local or regional distribution, especially of B-rolls, can involve only a nominal expense for an organization that has its own video production setup or the assistance of a video production studio.

Photos and Captions.   Photographs and written captions that explain the people and action in the photos also are of interest to newspaper and magazine editors. *Stand-alone captions* are complete stories based on a news-related event, written instead of a news

Phase Three

Step
7

release with an accompanying photo. For most newspapers, photos are provided in black-and-white formats, though increasingly newspapers are using color slides, especially in feature sections such as those devoted to travel, entertainment, gardening, decorating and similar pursuits. Most magazines use only color slides.

Media Kits.   Most of the above-described direct news materials can be gathered together in a *media kit,* sometimes called a *press packet.* These are presented to the journalists who attend news conferences and often are delivered to invited reporters who fail to attend. Media kits generally include one or more news releases along with fact sheets, feature releases, photos and other graphics.

Indirect News Material

In addition to the direct materials noted above, public relations practitioners also can use several **indirect news materials** to communicate with reporters, editors and news directors. These are messages that are not meant to be published but rather are intended to interest or inform media gatekeepers. Consider the following in your tactical program: media advisories, story idea memos and query letters.

Media Advisories.   Brief notes given to media gatekeepers are called *media advisories* or *media alerts.* These memos inform the gatekeepers of upcoming news opportunities. For example, a public relations practitioner might use a media advisory to announce a news conference, to invite photographers to a newsworthy event or to inform editors and news directors about a newsworthy activity involving the organization. Media advisories differ from news releases in that the advisory is not meant to be published but rather is intended as useful information for a journalist.

Story Idea Memos.   *Story idea memos* or *tip sheets* are informal idea memos submitted to the gatekeepers of newspapers, magazines and electronic news media. The intention is to spark a reporter's interest in developing a feature article. The public relations practitioners suggest available interview subjects or topics for articles that can be developed by the publication's own writers.

Query Letters.   *Query letters* are written to editors or broadcasters proposing a story and inquiring about their interest in it. These are more commonly used by freelance writers than by public relations practitioners, though some practitioners find it useful to write queries to magazines and then prepare feature articles if an editor expresses interest. Additionally, some practitioners work with freelance writers who prepare stories on assignment for magazines.

Opinion Material

Another category of tactics rooted in the news media involves several opportunities for using newspapers, magazines and radio and television stations to present an organization's opinion rather than simply the factual information that is the focus of most of the preceding news tactics. Both in proactive situations in which the organization wishes to advocate for a particular position, or when it reactively seeks to explain or defend its position, an organization often realizes several benefits by producing this **opinion material.**

Consider the following vehicles through which organizations can present their formal opinions about various issues: position statements, letters to the editor and guest editorials.

Position Statements.   Going a step beyond backgrounders (which were discussed above in the section on Direct News Material), *position statements* add an organization's official and carefully considered opinion on an issue. Position statements can be used in a variety of ways, not only as materials for journalists but also as the basis for editorials in organizational publications, source material for speeches and organizational letters, and documents to be provided directly to employees, donors or stockholders, supporters, legislators and other influential publics. Position statements often are published as stand-alone organizational publications.

Position statements can vary in their depth and intensity. A *position paper,* sometimes called a *white paper,* may be a detailed and lengthy discussion of a major issue of long-term significance. A *position paragraph* is a much shorter statement, often providing an organization's comments on a local or short-lived issue. A *contingency statement* or *standby statement* is a prepared comment written so an organization may express its voice in various potential situations. For example, a company nearing the resolution of a lawsuit may prepare several contingency statements to cover the possible outcomes— winning the case, losing it, being convicted of lesser charges, having the charge dismissed and so on. Obviously, contingency statements should be kept in strict confidence until one of them is needed.

Letters to the Editor.   Opinion letters written to newspapers and magazines offer many opportunities for public relations practitioners to communicate through the news media even when the gatekeepers have overlooked the organization. Use *letters to the editor* as publicity vehicles to announce things that don't make it into the news columns. Also, use letters to advocate a cause that likewise hasn't caught the attention of journalists. Occasionally letters can be used to correct errors, though most organizations find it better to ignore all but the most serious factual misstatements in published reports.

Guest Editorials.   *Guest editorials* generally are placed opposite the editorial page of a newspaper, hence their alternative name, *op-ed pieces*. A guest editorial is a grander version of a letter to the editor. It is a signed essay that, because of its length and placement, has higher prestige and credibility than a letter. Usually it's necessary to contact the publication before submitting an essay to be considered as a guest editorial. In many cases, guest editorials are written by public relations people but carry the signature of an organizational executive, thereby giving the piece additional credibility because of a high-ranking message source.

Interactive News Opportunities

A final category of news activities is **interactive news opportunities**—that is, those communication opportunities in which public relations practitioners and journalists interact with each other. These include news interviews, news conferences, studio interviews, satellite media tours and editorial conferences.

News Interviews.   Sessions in which journalists ask questions and public relations practitioners or organizational spokespersons respond are a mainstay of the interaction between an organization and the news media.

News interviews usually are one-on-one question-answer sessions. Public relations practitioners prepare for interviews by anticipating questions reporters will ask and gathering relevant information to answer the questions. They also help organizational spokespersons frame appropriate responses to reporters' questions. Often this coaching includes mock interviews prior to the actual encounter between the spokesperson and the reporters.

Most interviews are face-to-face encounters. Sometimes, however, when a reporter is seeking mainly factual information, especially from a news source the reporter has worked with in the past, the interview may take place over the telephone or via e-mail.

News Conferences.   Essentially group interviews, a *news conference* is a contrived media happening in which an organizational spokesperson makes a newsworthy statement or reads a prepared news statement; this generally is followed by a question-answer session with reporters.

Journalists do not like news conferences because the format puts them in the awkward position of doing their newsgathering—always a highly competitive endeavor—in the presence of their competitors. Only a few circumstances justify holding a news conference: (1) to announce news or give a response of major importance (in the eyes of the media, not simply the hopes of the organization), such as a new product or policy initiative, response to an attack, update in a crisis situation, or comment on a breaking news story; (2) to serve the media's interests when a prominent spokesperson or news maker is available for only a short period of time, such as the whirlwind visit or sandwiched-in interview of a celebrity, official, candidate or some other important person; and (3) to avoid accusations of playing favorites among reporters, such as by disseminating information to one medium ahead of another.

As an alternative to a news conference, consider making the announcement through a news release, or invite reporters to a coordinated series of interviews with an organizational spokesperson. Another option is to invite reporters to a participatory activity, such as a media preview of the opening of a new roller coaster by an amusement park.

If you do judge it appropriate to invite reporters to a news conference, consider the following guidelines:

- Invite all media that may be interested, even those you don't like. Notify the wire services, which in turn may announce the news conference as part of their advisories to member media.
- In a major market with a variety of media outlets, schedule the news conference mid- to late morning, if possible. Because normal business is slow on weekends, also consider Sunday or early Monday news conferences. In a smaller market with few print reporters and television reporters from stations miles away, you'll have to accommodate the schedule of the reporters. In either case, ask key reporters about convenient times and conflicting news events.

- Hold the news conference in a meeting room rather than in an office. Or if possible, hold the conference at an appropriate on-site location relevant to the information. For example, if you are announcing a new public housing project, hold the news conference at the building site.

Studio Interviews.   *Studio interviews* are a kind of hybrid between regular interviews and news conferences. Like regular interviews, they involve a reporter/questioner and generally a single interviewee. Sometimes they are set up as a questioner moderating an interview panel. Like a news conference, they often are televised, so everything is presented in "real time" with all the spontaneity of a live interview (even if it is taped for later broadcasting). The growth in popularity of talk radio and, to a lesser extent, talk television offers many new opportunities to public relations and marketing people promoting new ideas, products, books and so on. At-home interviews generally include feature or personality profiles for celebrities and other news makers. They can be useful in helping to humanize organizational leaders.

Satellite Media Tour.   A related development in interviewing style is the *satellite media tour (SMT),* a kind of in-studio interview or news conference with a widely dispersed audience. The unique feature of the SMT is that a news source is interviewed by reporters who are in different locations, linked via special television signal transmitted through satellite technology from the interviewee's location to many reporters throughout the nation, even around the world. Usually these are individual one-on-one interviews, packaged in segments of five minutes or less. SMTs are increasingly being used both in political campaigning and in crisis communications.

Editorial Conferences.   *Editorial conferences* are meetings with editors and editorial boards of newspapers to present them with background information on important issues. Generally such conferences are arranged on the invitation of the editors, though public relations people often try to solicit such invitations. Such conferences may generate news reports, feature stories and editorial comment on the issue.

Strategic Planning Example: *Choosing News Media Tactics*

Upstate College will develop the following news media tactics to publicize its expanded program:

UPSTATE COLLEGE

Tactic	Characteristic
News release	Low cost, accessible, target to potential students, parents, donors and community leaders
Fact sheet for media	Low cost, target to media publics
Fact sheet for students	Low cost, target to potential students
Media alert	Low cost
Photo and caption of preparation for ceremony	Low cost, interest community about expanded program

Letter to the editor	Low cost, target to key publics (parents, donors, community leaders)
Editorial conference	Low cost, interactive with media, potential to generate support for recruitment and fundraising
News interview with reporters	Low cost, high visibility

■ ■ ■

Tiny Tykes will develop the following news media tactics to publicize its dedication to consumer safety and demonstrate its improved crib toy:

Tactic	Characteristics
Letters to the editor	Low cost, target key publics
Story idea memo to reporters	Low cost, possible high visibility
News release	Low cost, accessible, target key publics
Video news release	High cost, possible high visibility

Strategic Planning Exercise: *Choosing News Media Tactics*

Basic Planning Questions
1. What news media tactics will you use?
2. How will these tactics help the organization achieve its objectives?
3. What resources will these tactics require?

Expanded Planning Questions

A. Selection of Tactics
From the following categories of news media tactics, identify several that you would consider using:

Direct News Material
-   News fact sheet, event listing, community calendar, interview notes, news release, feature release, actuality, video B-roll, video news release, photo and caption, media kit

Indirect News Material
-   Media advisory, story idea memo, query letter

Opinion Material
-   Position statement, white paper, contingency statement, standby statement, letter to the editor, guest editorial, op-ed piece

Interactive News Opportunity
-   Interview, news conference, studio interview, satellite media tour, editorial conference

B. Strategic Implications

For each item identified, answer the following questions:

1.   Will this tactic help the organization to interact with the appropriate public?

2.   What level of impact will this tactic make on the key public?

3.   Will this tactic advance the organization toward its awareness objectives?

4.   Will this tactic advance the organization toward its acceptance objectives?

5.   Will this tactic advance the organization toward its action objectives?

6.   What is the main advantage of this tactic?

7.   What advantages does this tactic offer that other tactics do not?

8.   Are there any disadvantages with this tactic?

C. Implementation Items

For each item identified, answer the following questions:

1.   How much will it cost to implement this tactic? Is the cost justified? Is the cost practical, based on the organization's resources?

2.   How much staff time will it take to implement this tactic? Is the time practical, based on the organization's resources?

3.   What level of skill, equipment and expertise is needed to implement this tactic? Is the needed level available within the organization? Is the needed level available from outside sources?   ■

Advertising and Promotional Media Tactics

The final category of communication tactics involves media associated with advertising and promotion. The list in this category includes four major sections: print advertising media, electronic advertising media, out-of-home advertising media and promotional items.

The Strategy of Advertising and Promotional Media Tactics

Most advertising is used for marketing purposes, to sell a particular product or service or to position a particular brand in the minds of its customers. But as noted earlier, the tools and techniques of advertising can serve the public relations goals of an organization as well.

Advertising can combine the strengths of two other important categories of tactics: organizational media and news media. Like organizational media, advertising is a form of controlled media that provides another opportunity for the organization to oversee all the details of its messages: content, tone, presentation style and timing. Advertising also can reach vast audiences, a characteristic shared with the news media.

At the same time, advertising has the combined weaknesses of these tactics. Like organizational media, advertising lacks the credibility of third-party endorsement found in the news media. And like the news media, advertising tends not to be able to address itself to information-seeking publics but instead can simply be available when people stumble upon the message, such as while they are reading a magazine or watching television.

Advertising is more of a public medium than a personal one, and it is used most often with external publics, mainly because many forms of interpersonal and organizational are better suited for internal publics.

At one time, advertising was thought of only as a mass medium, but increasingly it is able to target its audiences. This is so largely because advertising can piggyback on more and better targeted media, both print and electronic.

A major negative for advertising is the cost. It is the most expensive of all the categories of communication tactics discussed so far. A mid-sized daily newspaper, for example, might charge $185 per column inch (PCI) for an ad, meaning that one full-page ad (PCI cost times 157 column inches) would cost more than $29,000. National magazines may charge $150,000 per page. One 30-second spot on the local TV evening news might cost $5,000 in a mid-sized market. Compare this with the cost of other tactics, and it is easy to see why advertising often is used as a tactic of last resort.

Print Advertising Media

Because print advertising can reach both local and more widespread audiences, and because it is less expensive than broadcasting alternatives, print advertising is used by many organizations. There are various opportunities available in the category of print advertising: magazine advertising, newspaper advertising, directory advertising and house ads.

Magazine Advertising.   Ads in magazines tend to focus on national brands rather than local retail outlets and individual products, because of the diverse and widespread readership of most magazines and because of the high advertising cost.

Magazine advertising generally is sold on the basis of full or partial pages.

Most advertising is placed as *run of book (ROB),* which means the ad can be placed anywhere within the magazine. Trade magazines sometimes place ads with an eye toward the articles that are on the same or facing pages.

Special placements usually entail extra costs, with the highest costs going to advertising on the inside or outside covers. Extra costs also are charged for *bleed ads,* which eliminate the white border and carry the advertising image to the edge of the page, and for *center spreads,* which feature two facing pages. Some magazines also feature *inserts,* such as coupons or postcards. Occasionally magazines will publish an *advertising section,* sometimes called an *advertisorial,* a series of consecutive pages dealing with a single theme or product/service line.

Increasingly, advertisers can place *breakout ads* in national publications for distribution to particular groups of readers. Geographic editions are those copies of a magazine that are distributed within a particular region, perhaps a metropolitan area or a single state. Magazines also offer demographic editions aimed at subscribers with particular interests or backgrounds. For example, *Sports Illustrated* has special advertising packages for editions that are distributed to golf enthusiasts, homeowners, residents of particular

Pushing the Envelope a Bit Too Far

Imagine you are a public relations director for a company or nonprofit organization, and you receive the following offer via fax and a follow-up phone call from a local television station:

> We plan to produce a series of news segments highlighting prominent businesses in the area, and we want you to be part of this series. Specifically we will produce three news segments in one week about your organization, along with several promotional spots. Remember that our newscast is the most credible programming for the image of your company. This will cost you $15,000.

That's the offer made in 1999 by WDSI Fox-61 television in Chattanooga, Tenn.

The offer surprised and shocked several area public relations practitioners, who criticized the TV station for "putting a price on its newscast." One called it "grossly unethical." Another said his organization wanted "to earn any good publicity we receive."

The TV station quickly backed away from its controversial offer, saying it had been considered but should not have been made. The offer was attributed to the naive but nevertheless good intentions of the advertising department.

Let's consider the ethical questions raised:

- Is it ever appropriate for a television news team to offer (or appear to be offering) favorable news coverage for a price?

- Is it ever appropriate for a public relations or marketing communication practitioner to accept such an offer?

- Is this offer substantively different from the practice of some television stations in which advertising sales people try to solicit ads from companies that, independent of the advertising department, are being featured in news stories?

- Is it substantively different from the common practice among newspapers of publishing topical advertising sections or progress editions in which stories and photos from the advertisers are prominently featured?

- Is it substantively different from the common practice within the trade press of linking advertisements with news or feature stories?

regions and residents of high-income ZIP code areas. *Newsweek* has an advertising package that can be directed to high income and/or managerial subscribers.

Information on advertising rates is published in most media directories. A particularly comprehensive information source is the *Standard Rate & Data Service* (www.srds.com).

Newspaper Advertising.   Newspaper ads offer several different opportunities for promoting goods, services and ideas. The two different kinds of *newspaper advertising* are display ads and classified ads.

Display ads are located anywhere throughout the newspaper except the front pages of various sections and the editorial pages. Display ads feature illustrations, headlines and copy blocks. Most are marketing-oriented ads placed by local retailers selling various products and promoting sales.

Some display ads, however, are placed for public relations purposes, such as to promote events, support political candidates or present position statements on public issues. For example, a hospital that has come under public scrutiny because of

---

Television Dayparts

Here are the standard time periods within a typical broadcast day for television stations. Times reflect Eastern Standard Time; there may be some variations with network programs in other time zones.

Prime access	7 p.m. to 8 p.m.
Prime time	8 p.m. to 11 p.m.
Late news time	11 p.m. to 11:30 p.m.
Late night	11:30 p.m. to 1 a.m.
Overnight	1 a.m. to 6 a.m.
Weekend morning	8 a.m. to 1 p.m.
Weekend afternoon	1 p.m. to 7 p.m.

Early morning	6 a.m. to 9 a.m.
Daytime	9 a.m. to 4:30 p.m.
Early fringe	4:30 p.m. to 7 p.m.

---

accusations of sexual or racial discrimination may choose to address those charges in a full-page newspaper ad where it can control the entire message—its content, packaging and timing. Likewise, a health maintenance organization that feels reporters have not adequately explained its new coverage policy may use a full-page ad; the HMO may use such an ad even if it likes what reporters have written, simply as a way to increase awareness of its new policy.

Most newspaper advertising is purchased to run any place in the newspaper, called *ROP (run of press),* as compared to special placement on a particular page as in a specific section.

Classified ads are brief, all-text messages. In most newspapers, the three largest categories of classified ads deal with employment, real estate and automotive, but they also are used to find roommates, sell used vacuum cleaners, find homes for puppies, promote social causes and so on. Classified ads may be used for some public relations purposes, such as to invite participants to job-training programs, college courses and similar activities.

Directory Advertising.   *Directory advertising* uses Yellow Pages and professional directories to place business promotional announcements. Some organizational directories, like *Public Relations Tactics Green Book,* published by the Public Relations Society of America, are focused on particular professions and industries. Others are more geographic, such as the telephone Yellow Pages directories, published both by the utility companies themselves and by independent publishers who may target a particular public, such as business-to-business markets. Increasingly, directories are putting both their information listings and their advertising onto CD-ROM and on the Internet.

House Ads.   Some organizations place *house ads* or *program advertising*—honorary or congratulatory announcements in the organization's name that are placed in programs and publications associated with special events or in publications such as school yearbooks and member directories. Opportunities for this type of advertising include a variety of programs for sporting events, banquets, anniversaries, graduations and other occasions. This kind of advertising may involve full-page or partial-page display ads similar to those used in newspapers and directories, or they may be business-card ads.

Radio Dayparts

Here are the standard time periods within a typical broadcast day for radio stations. Times are for Eastern Standard Time; there may be some variations with network programs in other time zones.	Morning drive time	6 a.m. to 10 a.m.
	Midday or daytime	10 a.m. to 3 p.m.
	Afternoon drive time	3 p.m. to 7 p.m.
	Evening	7 p.m. to midnight
	Late night	midnight to 6 a.m.

Electronic Media Advertising

Advertising on radio, television and related media is a high-cost promotional expense that also can generate vast audiences. Consider the following possibilities: television commercials, cable television advertising, radio commercials and computer media.

Television Commercials.   Commercial and public relations advertising messages are placed on television in one of two ways. First, *network placement* puts the advertisement on all of the stations affiliated with the network. For some of the largest of the 115 television networks in North America, that could mean hundreds of different local stations. Alternatively, organizations can use *spot advertising* to place messages on individual local stations.

Most television commercials are 30 seconds long, though stations are opening up shorter slots for 10-, 15-, and 20-second advertisements. Less-competitive time slots sometimes carry 60-second advertisements. In addition to regular commercials, most stations provide times of 30 minutes or more for *infomercials,* program-length advertisements that often are packaged as interviews, talk shows, game shows or educational programs, sometimes masking their identity as paid advertisements. Certainly there is nothing wrong with combining promotion and entertainment, but an organization raises serious ethical questions if it hides behind pseudo-news or entertainment programs when in reality it is presenting a sales pitch.

When placing television advertising, consider the specific time of day the ad will run. Television programming is broken into several *dayparts,* time periods that reflect different viewing patterns and thus have different costs associated with buying advertising and different opportunities for the public relations or marketing communications practitioner.

Local advertising tends to focus on specific stores or venues for purchasing products (for example, the Uptown Dodge dealership on North Main Street). National television advertising is more associated with marketing of companies (the Dodge brand) or specific company products (the Dodge Dakota pickup truck).

Television advertising also provides some public relations opportunities. One such opportunity is associated with campaigns aimed at building awareness, acceptance and supportive action toward an organization or an industry group (such as the "Got Milk?"

campaign for the National Fluid Milk Processor Promotion Board). Additionally, public service advertising takes on even more public relations functions when it becomes an advocate, such as television spots encouraging the use of seat belts or early detection of breast cancer, or discouraging drug abuse.

Nonprofit organizations sometimes find that limited budgets require them to be creative, but this also can produce some very effective campaigns. Additionally, many spots for nonprofit organizations are based on contributed services through the Advertising Council, a cooperative venture of the American Association of Advertising Agencies, the Association of National Advertisers and various media. The Ad Council estimates that its annual campaigns are worth $1.1 billion of donated media. It has produced many memorable campaigns, such as a series for the United Negro College Fund showcasing poet Maya Angelou.

Because of the appeal of many nonprofit causes, some high-profile organizations are able to attract top talent. For example, when the Navy fell 7,000 recruits short of its goal in 1998, it turned to the BBDO advertising agency, which hired director Spike Lee to produce a series of recruiting commercials. He used a documentary style that focused on Navy SEALS, travel opportunities, sailors in a rock band and related high-interest topics. The Navy ended 1999 with more recruits than expected, while the Air Force, Army and Marines fell short of their goals, despite an increase in marketing budgets for all the services. Similarly, after New York City budgeted $10 million for an advertising campaign to help recruit minorities for its police department and to enhance the overall reputation of the department, Arnell Group Brand Consulting volunteered to develop the campaign, freeing the budget for the purchase of newspaper ads, TV commercials and subway and bus posters.

Cable Television Advertising.   Cable networks offer much the same opportunities for advertising as do broadcast networks and local television stations. Additionally, cable television also offers the opportunity to feature *cable crawls,* messages that scroll out across the bottom of the TV screen, often on channels focused on weather, news or television program listings.

In many areas, advertising contacts with cable companies are handled not by the individual cable system but by a cable broker that places advertising on a variety of cable systems.

Radio Commercials.   In placing commercials with radio stations, consider the audience you are aiming for and the time of day the spot will run. Media buyers and radio sales people can provide information on several aspects of a radio audience that you can use in comparing stations to make the proper placement choices.

Radio advertising spots generally run for 10, 30 or 60 seconds. Like television advertising placement, radio placement can be made through *network radio,* which includes about 115 national or regional networks providing advertising to perhaps several hundred network-affiliated stations, or as *spot radio,* which means placement on individual local radio stations. Radio commercials can be designated for a specific *daypart,* or they can be given to the station for use at any time, called *run of station (ROS)* placement.

Computer Media.   The newest communication channel for electronic advertising is in the rapidly expanding field of *computer-based media*. Internet Web sites offer a growing number of advertising and promotional opportunities.

A lot of creativity goes into Internet promotion. For example, check some beer sites on the Internet. They don't simply advertise beer, they have games and contests so the sites can reinforce one of the perceived benefits of the beverage: fun and excitement. Likewise, Web sites for investment companies feature interactive financial and retirement planning. Provide the asked-for data about your income, lifestyle, work plans and financial obligations, and the program will tell you how much money to invest for the eventual savings you desire.

Several new forms of computer-based advertising have potential for public relations messages. Some Web sites feature *pop-ups* or *interstitial ads* that insinuate themselves onto the screen as a person is using the Internet. At other times while the user is waiting for a linked connection, pages called *superstitial ads* can appear to fill in the time. Meanwhile, in a blend of computer and television technology, some companies are using *virtual ads* such as product billboards that appear the background during a televised sporting event—except that the signs don't really exist on the field; they are digitally inserted for the TV audience.

Electronic catalogs are not merely electronic versions of printed catalogs. Instead they are interactive versions designed to engage the customers. For example, a Web-based clothing catalog can let users select among a range of fabric, styles and colors and then see the result of this custom design.

Out-of-Home Advertising

Out-of-home advertising focuses on several different opportunities to take a persuasive message to a public that is on the move, making it possible to reach people subtly. Sometimes the advertising itself can become an attractive diversion. For example, people waiting for a bus, riding on the subway or sitting in the stands often pay much attention to outside advertising.

This kind of advertising offers several advantages over print and electronic advertising. For example, outdoor ads have 24-hour-a-day visibility to a wide variety of people. They also offer repeat exposure to the advertising message. On the down side, out-of-home advertisements are expensive, and they are limited to short, simple messages.

Categories of out-of-home advertising include outdoor posters, arena posters, signage, out-of-home videos, transit advertising, aerial advertising and inflatables.

Outdoor Posters.   *Poster* is a generic name for several different kinds of outdoor stationary advertisements—billboards, paints and spectaculars.

Billboards are huge signs placed along highways or on the sides of buildings, where they most often are intended to be seen by motorists. Sheets of paper or vinyl are glued onto the billboards, usually for one-month periods. Many billboards are lighted so they can be easily seen day or night. Advertisers have found ways to enhance the basic posters, often with the help of computer-produced images. Some advertisers add *snipes* to their billboards—strips pasted over part of an existing billboard so its message can be updated without the poster being completely changed.

Painted bulletins, or *paints,* are another type of outdoor sign. They are larger than posters, usually 14 by 48 feet, and because they actually are painted signs they generally are more permanent than billboard posters. Most paints are sold on an annual basis. *Permanent paints* are displayed in a single location, most often along highways, where they advertise motels, restaurants and tourist attractions. *Rotary paints* can be physically moved from one location to another.

Spectaculars are another type of outdoor poster involving some kind of extra elements, creatively called *extras,* to the basic flat rectangular surface of the poster. For example, some billboards feature 3-D elements, such as one for an auto dealer with blinking "headlights" or another for a golf course featuring a giant 3-D golf ball. On one billboard, Mothers Against Drunk Drivers (MADD) hung the actual wreck of a car in which a family had been killed. Extras also may be sections added on a poster to alter its basic rectangular shape. Some spectaculars use computers to add a continuously changing message to billboards, such as a state lottery billboard with the amount of the current week's payout.

Another outdoor venue is *wall murals* or *wallscapes,* the painted exterior of buildings leased for advertising purposes.

Arena Posters.   Billboard-like advertisements placed on walls and fences of arenas such as sports stadiums and ball parks are called *arena posters.* Smaller posters are located inside arenas, often hanging in front of the various levels of seating. Some of these posters are computer generated, allowing for message crawls. Some computer-generated posters are rotated every few minutes to provide a sequence of showing during a single public event.

Signage.   Visible and appropriate signs can be important aspects in an organization's promotional program. *Signage* includes a variety of stationary outdoor signs, including signs enhanced by a variety of lighting techniques.

Out-of-Home Video.   The category of *out-of-home video advertising* is one of the newest additions to the inventory of promotional vehicles. Out-of-home video includes the giant video screens on which some sports arenas and concert halls present poster-like or full-video images. Another example of this tactic is the *video wall* that features an ever-moving series of computer-generated images.

Advertisements in movie theaters that precede the showing of feature films also fall into this category. Because of the variety in films, these are easy to target to specific audience demographics.

Transit Advertising.   *Transit advertising* includes ads placed on and inside of public commuter vehicles such as buses and trains, as well as stationary ads located on bus shelters and at locations such as subways and air terminals.

Bus signs are available in several common sizes for different areas of busses—street-side, curb-side, front or back. Each can target different audiences. *Car cards* are signs placed above the windows inside buses and trains. *Station posters* or *dioramas* often are small vertical panels located in subway, train and bus stations, as well as in airport terminals. *Shelter posters* are located in bus shelters.

An advantage of transit advertising is that it can be very specific, focusing on local organizations and addressed to people who live in a particular neighborhood. In large cities, for example, shelter and subway signs may be in a language other than English that is used by a majority of the residents, or they may feature highly specific ethnic images or cultural symbols.

The category of transit advertising also includes *mobile billboards,* the painted sides of tractor-trailer or delivery trucks that increasingly are being rented out as advertising venues.

Aerial Advertising.   Aerial advertising includes various vehicles—*blimps* with signs or computer-generated scroll messages, *airplane tows* featuring planes pulling banners over beaches and ballparks, and *skywriting airplanes* that trail smoke and write messages in the sky. These techniques can be particularly effective if a large number of your target audience is assembled in a single location.

Inflatables.   Air-filled objects called *inflatables* are sometimes used as attention-getters. Inflatables range from giant outdoor balloons with a corporate logo to air-filled promotional items such as an ice-cream cone for the grand opening of a dairy bar. Some rooftop inflatables are 20 feet high or larger.

Promotional Items

Many organizations augment their advertising program with promotional items—give-aways for customers that the organization hopes will be a continuing reminder of its cause, product or service.

Promotional clothing includes designer labels such as Tommy Hilfiger or the Gap, which, because they are trendy, are particularly sought out by young people. Most advertisers, however, are not lucky enough to find that their logo is a popular status symbol. On the contrary, it is the advertiser that pays to place the logo on T-shirts, athletic and leisure clothing and other garments.

Costumes are another type of promotional clothing, such as the flamboyant chicken suits worn by promoters for the opening of a new fried-chicken restaurant. *Uniforms* for sports teams and individual athletes often carry the name and logo of the corporate sponsor. Likewise, companies increasingly are applying their name, with strong visual reminders, to everything from sports cars and golf tournaments to sports arenas and hospital waiting rooms.

Some organizations place promotional logos or messages on *office accessories* such as calendars, pens and note pads. Others promote themselves through *home accessories,* household items such as coffee mugs, bottle openers, matches, napkins, and related goods.

Direct-mail gimmicks are another type of promotional item. Small or miniaturized samples of company product, for example, can be mailed to potential clients. Symbolic items also can be quite effective.

Phase Three

Step
7

Be very careful, however, about what you send through the mail. When one California law firm wanted to let potential clients know that it had the ammunition to fight their legal battles, it mailed out hundreds of fake hand grenades. But the come-ons looked so real that some recipients evacuated buildings and called the bomb squads and postal inspectors. In another case, a dot-com company wanted to warn prospects not to be unprepared for computer viruses. Its message strategy: Don't shoot yourself in the foot. So the company mailed out empty bullet shells on a postcard without a return address—just to build suspense—asking. "Who's been shooting [your] readers?" Again, police and FBI were called in.

Strategic Planning Example: **Choosing Advertising and Promotional Tactics**

UPSTATE COLLEGE

Upstate College will develop the following advertising and promotional tactics to publicize its expanded program:

Tactic	Characteristic
Display ad in local newspaper	Moderate-to-high cost, target to key publics
Display ad in campus newspapers at other colleges	Low cost, highly targeted to transfer students
Cable TV crawl	Low cost, low impact
Radio commercial	Moderate-to-high cost, target to potential students
Promotional T-shirt	Moderate cost

(Note: No television advertising because of the expense involved.)

■ ■ ■

Tiny Tykes will develop the following tactics for an employee-oriented public relations program:

Tactic	Characteristics
T-shirts with safety logo	Low cost
Display ads in trade magazine featuring employees with theme of customer safety	Moderate cost, target to industry leaders
Display ads in consumer magazines featuring employees with theme of customer safety	High cost, target to parents
Sponsorship of public television series about raising infants and toddlers	Moderate-to-high cost, target to parents

Strategic Planning Exercise: **Choosing Advertising and Promotional Tactics**

Basic Planning Questions

1. What advertising media and promotional tactics will you use?
2. How will these tactics help the organization achieve its objectives?
3. What resources will these tactics require?

Expanded Planning Questions

A. Selection of Tactics
From the following categories of advertising and promotional tactics, identify several that you would consider using:

Print Advertising Media
- Magazine advertising, advertisorial
- Newspaper advertising: display, classified, personal classified
- Directory advertising
- House ads
- Program advertising

Electronic Advertising Media
- Television: commercial, spot, infomercial
- Radio: commercial, network radio, spot radio
- Cable television: advertising, cable crawl
- Computer media: e-zine, electronic catalog

Out-of-Home Advertising
- Outdoor poster: billboard, paint, spectacular, wall mural
- Arena poster
- Signage
- Out-of-home video, video wall
- Transit advertising: bus sign, car card, station poster, diorama, shelter poster, mobile billboard
- Aerial advertising: blimp, airplane tows, skywriting, inflatable Promotional Item
- Clothing, costume, office accessory, home accessory

B. Strategic Implications
For each item identified, answer the following questions:

1. Will this tactic help the organization to interact with the appropriate public?
2. What level of impact will this tactic make on the key public?
3. Will this tactic advance the organization toward its awareness objectives?

Phase Three

Step
7

4. Will this tactic advance the organization toward its acceptance objectives?

5. Will this tactic advance the organization toward its action objectives?

6. What is the main advantage of this tactic?

7. What advantages does this tactic offer that other tactics do not?

8. Are there any disadvantages to this tactic?

C. Implementation Items

For each item identified, answer the following questions:

1. How much will it cost to implement this tactic? Is the cost justified? Is the cost practical, based on the organization's resources?

2. How much staff time will it take to implement this tactic? Is the time practical, based on the organization's resources?

3. What level of skill, equipment and expertise is needed to implement this tactic? Is the needed level available within the organization? Is the needed level available from outside sources?

Packaging the Communication Tactics

The various communication tactics have been likened to items on a menu, so let's take the analogy a step further. Menu items can be grouped into categories: appetizers, salads, main courses, desserts, beverages and so on. When you order a meal, you'll probably cover the whole range of menu categories. Additionally, when you review the restaurant menu, you often make your selections based on a particular culinary focus—Japanese, Tex-Mex, Southern, and so on. It's unlikely you would start with raw tuna sashimi as appetizer, add a dollop of cole slaw on a bed of lettuce, feature jalapeña chili as main course with sides of grits and ravioli, and end with a flaming cherries jubilee for dessert. Rather, you'd probably develop a culinary theme, creatively packaging your choices to concoct a special dining experience appropriate to the occasion and suitable to your resources, needs and interests.

The same is true with strategic planning for communication. Now that you have considered items in each of the menu categories, you need to package them into an effective set of tactics to help you achieve your objectives. This should be much more than a "to do" list. Consider how various tactics can be woven together; group some around the themes associated with your strategic planning from Steps 5 and 6.

Remember: You don't need to be tied into a chronological implementation scheme just because you selected interpersonal items before those in the other categories. Let the natural relationship among tactics determine how they fit into your plan. Consider what you learned in Phase Two: Strategy. For example, the diffusion of innovations theory tells us that information presented through the news media can pave the way for personal interaction between opinion leaders and the ultimate public. Or think about the example of some companies which have preceded an advertising schedule with a publicity program, thus allowing for a smaller advertising budget with higher-than-usual results.

Thinking Creatively

What's the best way to present your plan? You decide. Look for the simplest and most logical way to present the tactics that grow out of your planning. Later on we'll look at some suggestions to help you get started, but first let's consider the importance of creative thinking. As you decide how to package your tactics, try to leap ahead of the crowd with an innovative approach to the problem or opportunity you are dealing with.

For example, if you have a new organizational logo to unveil, consider making it a real unveiling, perhaps with a ceremonial removal of a sequined cloth. Or maybe you could have the logo painted large on the outside of the company's building, temporarily draped. One nonprofit organization introduced a new logo by involving five local political and media celebrities who each gave a short testimonial about the organization and then, one by one, placed cut-out pieces on a giant jigsaw puzzle of the new logo.

Consider another scenario. Your organization has an announcement to make— usually a routine matter, but you want to have it stand out. One corporation engineered an interactive announcement in two cities at different ends of the state, with a teleconference hook-up. The president of the corporation was in one city, a congressman who actively supported the organization in the other city. The two together announced a significant multimillion-dollar project that the corporation was developing. And just in case the technology failed, the public relations planner had prepared a script and a videotape that could be used at each location.

An Indiana group used a symbolic protest as part of its announcement strategy. Hogs Opposed to Government Waste and Silly Highways (HOGWASH) in 1999 sent Arnold the Pig to deliver a ham to the governor's press secretary, announcing its opposition to the extension of Highway I-69 through southern Indiana. The protesters said the road project was an example of pork-barrel politics, so it was only fitting for Arnold to be their spokespig.

Some organizations have specially designed vehicles used for promotion and other public relations objectives. For example, Rural/Metro Ambulance Service has a three-foot high talking, winking, lighted ambulance called Amby that EMTs take into classrooms during safety presentations. United Parcel Service has a miniature delivery truck that it uses in athletic arenas to deliver a coin for the ceremonial coin toss at the start of football games. Notice that each of these vehicles relate to the primary mission of the organization.

Putting the Program Together

When the time comes to begin putting your public relations or marketing communication program together, first review the information gathered during the research phase of the program (Steps 1, 2 and 3). Reconsider the issue and review pertinent information about the organization, its environment and perceptions about it. Next examine the various publics and your analysis of them.

Following this review, consider several different ways to package the tactics you have chosen. No particular format is best for every issue, so let common sense be your guide. Consider the most distinctive element of your program. Your purpose is to select

Phase Three

Step
7

the format that most readily allows you to present your analysis and recommendations to your colleagues, boss or client.

Among the various ways of packaging your tactics is by tactical category, public, goal, objective and department. Look at each of these with an open mind; perhaps you'll be able to devise a better way to package the tactical recommendations in your program.

Packaging by Tactical Category.   Using this approach, you move from the research phase to an overview of the goals, objectives and strategy associated with Steps 4, 5 and 6. Next, list each tactic according to the outline of media categories provided in the Step 7 inventory. That is, list each tactic in order of interpersonal communication, organizational media, news media and advertising media. With each public, indicate the relevant publics and objectives.

This presentation by media type can guide you to draw tactics from each category, though the presentation can appear a bit disjointed because it may overlook a more logical grouping of tactics. Nevertheless, it is a good starting point, or at least an effective preliminary checklist before using one of the following presentation formats. The presentation by tactics is followed by evaluation methods (Step 9), which will be discussed shortly.

Packaging by Public.   The research phase moves to an outline of each key public and, for each, an overview of the relevant goals and objectives (Step 4), then the strategy phase focuses on interacting and communicating with each public (Step 5 and 6). - Tactics associated with each strategy (Step 7) and evaluation methods (Step 9) are included for each tactic.

Use this format if the internal cohesion of your plan centers on the differences among several publics. For example, if you are planning a program that identifies three categories of publics—customers, employees and community—you may decide that you can present your analysis and ideas best by focusing separately on each public.

Packaging by Goal.   Using this approach, the plan begins with the common research phase and provides an overview of goals associated with the issue. It then identifies a series of initiatives based on each goal and focuses the rest of the plan serially on each initiative. In your presentation of each initiative, identify relevant research and background information, key publics (Step 3), objectives (Step 4), strategy with key messages (Steps 5 and 6), tactics (Step 7) and evaluation methods (Step 9).

Use this format when goals are sufficiently distinct to allow you to treat each one independently. For example, a public relations and marketing communication program for a university might identify several goal-based initiatives, such as enhancing its reputation among students in high school and community colleges, increasing support from the business and civic community, recruiting more students to professional development programs, and enhancing knowledge and pride among students, faculty, staff and alumni.

Packaging by Objective.   Presentation by objective begins, like the previous approach, with the common research phase of Steps 1, 2 and 3 and provides an overview of the goals and objectives from Step 4. Then it selects each objective as the focus for the remainder of the presentation, identifying key publics (Step 3), strategy with key messages (Steps 5 and 6), tactics (Step 7) and evaluation methods (Step 9) for each objective.

Use this approach when it is the objectives rather than the goals or publics that are the most significant distinction within the plan. For example, a plan that has only a single goal might be presented according to the objectives associated with awareness, acceptance and action.

Packaging by Department.   Similar to presentation by goals or objectives, presentation by department acknowledges that the distinctive segments of the strategic communication plan parallel existing organizational structures, such as departments, divisions and programs.

Use this approach when the structure of the client's organization coincides with program areas in your strategic plan.

Strategic Planning Example: *Packaging the Communication Tactics*

The following initiative is packaged according to one of the four task goals identified in Strategic Planning Example: Establishing Goals and Objectives.

UPSTATE COLLEGE

Initiative on Transfer Students
(Transcribe research, goal, key public, objectives and strategy information.)

Upstate College will sponsor a weekend-long *Celebration! UC* (Friday evening, Saturday afternoon and evening and Sunday afternoon), celebrating the expansion of UC to a four-year institution.

Entertainment during this event will include a picnic with two bands, a formal banquet and strolling entertainers. The event will include:

- a rededication ceremony with public officials, leaders of neighboring colleges and universities and UC students, faculty and alumni
- a fall festival for current students and alumni
- an open house for prospective transfer students

Support materials for the festival will include a revision of the college viewbook, a new transfer brochure and a poster, as well as production of a video. A special page will be added to the Web site homepage.

Students who applied to UC within the last two years and were accepted but did not attend will be sent a letter inviting them to them festival events, along with a fact sheet about Upstate College.

More generally, the festival will be promoted with media fact sheets and news releases, a photo with caption and a cable TV crawl. Students attending the event will be given a UC T-shirt designed by UC art students. A media advisory will be sent to the news media, inviting them to cover the event, and news interviews will be offered with the UC president, provost and student government president. Additionally, the media relations office will seek out an editorial conference with the local newspaper to elicit editorial support for the expansion; failing that, a letter to the editor will be sent by a UC official noting the benefits of the program expansion for the community.

The festival also will be promoted with a newspaper advertisement in campus newspapers at other colleges and with radio commercials. Additionally, a display ad

Phase Three

Step
7

in the local newspaper will be aimed at parents as well as community leaders, alumni and donors.

(Note that each of the other goals would be developed in a similar manner.)

■ ■ ■

The following initiative is packaged according to the four key publics identified in Strategic Planning Example: Identifying Key Publics.

Public Relations Program for Tiny Tykes Employees
(Transcribe research, goal, objectives and strategy information.)

The internal component of a training program for employees will include workshops on customer satisfaction as well as a training session on product safety and quality; brochures about safety and quality issues will be available. Several work-group meetings will be held, at least one involving a motivational speech by the CEO. Similar motivational themes will be presented in newsletter articles and in the employee bulletin.

The program will have an external component to provide employee support. Elements of this component will include letters sent to families of employees, letters to the editor of local newspapers about employee dedication to customer safety and print advertisements in trade magazines and in the local newspaper. A news release will announce the new safety and quality initiatives, and a story idea memo will be given to reporters about employee dedication to customer safety.

(Note that each of the other publics would be developed in a similar manner.)

Strategic Planning Exercise: *Packaging Communication Tactics*

Basic Planning Questions

1. What specific initiatives or sections make up this plan?
2. What tactics are associated with this plan?
3. What public and objective does each tactic serve?

Expanded Planning Questions

A. Selecting the Approach

1. From the following categories, indicate which one offers the greatest likelihood of a package of program tactics that is cohesive and logical: by public, by goal, by objective, by department or by tactic.
2. List specific initiatives or sections in your plan

B. Strategic Implications

1. Will this approach help the organization to interact with the appropriate public?
2. What is the main advantage of this approach?
3. What advantages does this approach offer that other approaches do not?
4. Are there any disadvantages to this approach?

Step 8

Implementing the Strategic Plan

Now that you have put together a full plate of ways to present your message, turn your attention to implementing these tactics. In this step you will consider some of the specifics of implementation, especially turning your inventory of tactics into a logical and cohesive program. You also will deal with specific topics dealing with scheduling and budgeting for the program.

The Written Plan

The campaign plan book, or more simply, the program plan, is the formal written presentation of your research findings and program recommendations for strategy, tactics and evaluation. This report should be concise in writing, professional in style and confident in tone. Here are some of the elements the plan book should include:

- *Title page* with a program name as well as the names of the client organization, consultant or team members, and date.
- *Executive summary,* a one-page synopsis of the plan written as an overview for busy executives and for readers who are not directly involved in the program.
- *Table of contents* outlining the major segments of the program.
- *Statement of principles* or *philosophy statement* (optional) laying out the planner's approach to strategic communication campaigns (particularly whether it is rooted in public relations, marketing communication or integrated communication). Also included are definitions of key concepts used in the book.
- *Situation analysis* outlining your research and synthesis of the issue (Step 1), organization (Step 2) and publics (Step 3). Some program plans present the research data and summaries on paper of a different color from the rest of the report.
- *Presentation of recommendations* for goals and objectives, strategy and tactics. Present these by public, goal, objective, program or tactic (in the format most appropriate to the issue).
- *Schedule* outlining the time and calendar considerations for implementing the various tactics.

Four Patterns of Message Repetition

An insight drawn from advertising is that the pattern of communication can be of crucial importance. If you know that a one-time message is inappropriate, the question becomes when and how you should plan for repetition of the message. Consider the following concepts:

- *Continuity* is an approach to scheduling that presents a message at a consistent level throughout a particular period of time. This may mean integrating several tactics such as direct mail, publicity and advertising for external audiences; for internal audiences, the tactics also could include posters, meetings and brochures.

- *Flighting* (also called *bursting*) refers to the presentation of messages in waves, with periods of intense communication interspersed with periods of communication inactivity. A variety of media can be used during the peak communication periods.

- *Pulsing* is a combination of the two approaches, with a continuous base augmented by intermittent bursts of communication activity.

- *Massing* is the bunching of various presentations of a message into a short period of time.

- *Budget* outlining resources needed for the program. Include in this figure the cost of personnel time, money and equipment, as well as any income to be generated.
- *Evaluation plan* with information on the methods to be used to measure the program's effectiveness.
- *Consultant background* (optional) should indicate the resources the consultant or agency can office. This element of the plan is especially useful in competitive situations in which more than one consultant or agency prepares program recommendations.

A complete strategic campaign is located in Appendix C.

Sometimes you may decide not to use a particular tactic, perhaps not even a particular category of communication tactics. For example, an employee relations project may not lend itself to involving the news media, or an investor relations project may not include advertising. When you deliberately choose not to use what might seem to be an obvious tactic, offer your reasoning in your plan. Especially if you are developing a proposal on competitive-bid basis, it is good to let the potential client know why you recommend against using what others might suggest.

Regardless of the way you package your tactics, it is important to show the internal logic within your planning program. Make it clear to your client or boss how the various elements work together for a common purpose.

A good way to show this internal harmony is to note for each tactic the specific public, goal and objective to which it is linked. In this way, planners can make sure that each public is adequately served by the various tactics. Likewise, planners can be certain that each goal and objective is played out through a variety of tactics.

Consider how the following section of a program proposal for a new graduate program shows the internal linkage between a specific tactic; previously identified publics, objectives and strategy; administrative details such as budgeting; and subsequent evaluation methods.

Tactic: Open house

- Public: Professional architects (specifically a minimum of 45 practicing architects within a three-county area)
- Objective: To increase the understanding of professional architects about the new program (50% of the professional community prior to beginning the academic program)
- Strategy: Attract attention of the professional community and create a core of opinion leaders; give specific attention to leading architects, particularly those who have received recognition from the Midstate Association of Professional Architects
- Budget $1,500
- Evaluation Methods: Attendance figures; follow-up mini-survey conducted as part of a telephone thank-you for attending

In a complete proposal, each tactic would receive similar treatment. Even individual tactics might have multiple components. For example, the open house noted above might have additional publics, perhaps donors or potential students. Each of these would require its own statement of objectives and strategies, though the budget and evaluation methods may remain constant.

Another useful element within the tactical plan is to note the name of the person or department charged with implementing the tactic. Sometimes this is a moot point, because one person will handle the entire project. But for more complex programs and campaigns, several different people may be involved, each managing different tactics. Either within the plan itself, or in an implementation guide to be worked out later, be clear about who is responsible for each tactic.

The Schedule

You already addressed one aspect of scheduling when you built into your objectives in Step 4 an indication of when you planned to achieve each. This provided the deadline upon which you will measure your effectiveness in reaching the objectives.

Now that Step 7 has generated an outline of tactics, you can establish specific time requirements. This involves two considerations: (1) the pattern and frequency of your communication tactics and (2) the actual timeline of tasks to be accomplished as the tactics are implemented.

Frequency of Tactics

As noted in Step 6, the average person is exposed to thousands of public relations and marketing messages each day, yet most fall on deaf ears. Clearly, mere exposure to a message is insufficient to move someone to action. However, the frequency of exposure is an important factor in whether the message takes root in a person's consciousness. Repetition increases awareness and leads to greater acceptance.

Research has been done both on **message frequency**—the number and pattern of messages presented to a particular public in a given period of time—and on **message reach**—the number of different people who are exposed to a single message. Most of the research on frequency has been focused either on advertising or on the learning process. However, it is possible to generalize a bit about applications for public relations. It is known, for example, that one exposure to a message has little or no effect unless the audience is particularly attentive. Rather, a minimum of three exposures seems to be needed to make an impact. Much more than this, and effectiveness wanes. This concept has enjoyed general support within the advertising trade since it was articulated by ad manager and theoretician Herbert Krugman (1972). Gerard Tellis (1998) has noted that studies in laboratory settings confirmed Krugman's three-exposure formula, although in natural settings in which consumers are distracted by competing messages, three exposures may not be enough.

The lessons for the public relations manager? Don't rely on just one presentation of your message to key publics. Don't think that even three exposures guarantee success. Find ways to repeat your message, especially through various media; this not only will increase retention among your key publics, but it also will add to the credibility of the message because it will have the third-party endorsement of several different media gatekeepers.

Another lesson gleaned from research is the value of repetition over a period of time. For example, most audiences remember a message they have seen daily for several days more than one presented several times in a single day. Too-frequent presentation of the message seems unnecessarily redundant and can lead to wear-out, which, by the way, comes faster with a humorous message than with a neutral or serious one.

But a message presented may not be a message heard, and there is no specific number for how many repetitions is best. Sometimes, even your best efforts won't gain complete success, especially with audiences who are not particularly interested in the issue. For example, for several years one of the most successful television advertising campaigns featured a pink rabbit beating the drum for a battery company. Yet 40 percent of viewers in a national survey identified the wrong company as the sponsor of the ad, despite the company's best effort to promote the Energizer Bunny.

Bruce Vanden Bergh and Helen Katz (1999) pointed out that most organizations with limited budgets must find a balance between reach and frequency. A basic guideline for advertising seems to hold true for other aspects of marketing communication and public relations: Rather than trying to reach a greater number of people, try instead to reach a targeted number of key people more frequently.

Timelines of Tasks

At this point in your planning, you know three things about your tactics: (1) which ones you want to use, (2) how you will package them and (3) how often to run them. Now turn your attention to carefully considering each significant task needed for these tactics.

One of the easiest ways to schedule tasks is to work backwards from the final tactic date. For example, if you want a brochure to be received in the readers' homes by May 15, work backward to develop the following hypothetical schedule:

May 12	Deliver to the post office
May 11	Attach address labels
May 10	Receive from printer
May 5	Deliver to printer
April 28	Finalize copy and design, and obtain approvals
April 21	Complete draft, including copy, artwork and layout
April 14	Begin writing, develop artwork
April 7	Assign writer and designer
April 6	Obtain approval for objectives, determine budget
April 2	Begin planning for brochure.

Total time required: 41 days

This plan is your *timeline,* or implementation schedule. Timelines are essential when you are dealing with a variety of tactics and managing different programs at the same time. Having a written plan makes it easier to train others and delegate responsibilities. Additionally, having a written timeline makes it easier to keep work records that may be needed for billing purposes.

A good way to manage the scheduling process is to chart out each of the tasks you have identified. You could use a large calendar or a timetable narrative with sections for time periods and bulleted task items to be accomplished during each time period.

However, flow charts are particularly helpful in tracking public relations tactics because they provide a visual representation of the tasks to be completed.

A common type of flow chart is the *Gantt chart,* developed by engineer Henry Gantt during the First World War to track shipbuilding projects. The Gantt chart lists each tactic and the various associated tasks, then indicates the time needed for each task. Times can be indicated in days, weeks or months, depending on the type of project. The advantage of the Gantt chart is that it provides a map of the work that needs to be done. These charts can be kept on computer, written on paper charts, or displayed as wall charts. Exhibit 8.1 shows a Gantt chart for an activity that has not yet been implemented. As the various tasks are completed, underline the X's or replace them with solid lines.

Because the Gantt chart shows every task associated with the various tactics, planners can spread out activity according to a convenient schedule. For example, under normal conditions preparation of a brochure may take about six weeks. But the Gantt chart may show that several other important and time-consuming activities will be taking place within the same six-week period. Thus you may need to begin work on the brochure earlier.

Another commonly used flow chart is the *PERT chart* (Program Evaluation and Review Technique), a process first developed for the Polaris missile system in the 1950s. This chart, shown in Exhibit 8.2, lists tasks within circles, with arrows indicating how one task flows into another. PERT charts generally include dates and assignment to particular individuals, though they lack the calendaring aspect of the Gantt chart.

Exhibit 8.1   Gantt Chart for Brochure

	April																May							
	2	4	6	8	10	12	14	16	18	20	22	24	26	28	30	2	4	6	8	10	12	14

Brochure

Planning (myself)   xxxxxxx
Objectives (supervisor)   x
Assign writer (myself)   x
Writing (freelancer)   xxxxxxxxxx
Complete Draft (freelancer)   x
Final copy (myself)   xxxxxx
To printer (myself)   x
From printer (printer)   x
Labels (staff)   x
To Post Office (staff)   x
Deliver (Post Office)   xxx

Exhibit 8.2   PERT Chart for Brochure

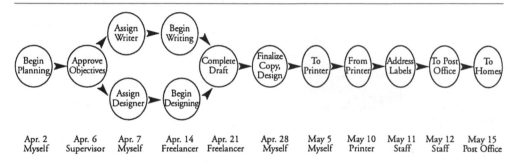

An effective implementation schedule of public relations tactics generally includes more than dates. Include the name of the person or group responsible for the task. In addition to the deadline date, some charts indicate the latest date by which the tactic can be implemented and still remain useful.

The Budget

Budgeting, the development of resources needed to achieve objectives, is a topic that has been "on the table" since the beginning of this planning process.

In Step 1 you considered the importance of the issue and its potential impact on the bottom line of the organization. In Step 2 you analyzed the organization itself, with some consideration going to the level of resources available to address various aspects of public relations and marketing communications. These resources included personnel, equipment, time and budgeted money. Throughout the strategic development in Steps 4, 5 and 6, you were advised to be realistic in setting forth on a course of action appropriate to the organization. One measure of propriety is based on the organization's resources.

At every turn in a planning process, you must be practical. Consider budget constraints and limitations—and no organization is free of these—so your recommendations will be realistic, practical and doable.

Budget Item Categories

Remember that budgeting is about more than money. It deals with all the needed resources to implement a tactic. Thus budgets for public relations and marketing communications should consider five elements: personnel, material, media costs, equipment and facilities, and administrative costs.

Personnel.   Personnel items in a budget include the number of people and the amount of time needed to achieve the results expected of the tactic. This may include both organizational personnel and outside people, such as consultants, agency staff, subcontracted specialists and freelance workers. Specifically, personnel costs may be associated with research, analysis, planning, writing, editing, design, photography, events management and so on. Personnel costs can be expressed either in terms of time (hours or days) needed to complete the task or in labor dollars. In some billing situations, public relations agencies present personnel items in the form of billable hours. Some agencies have a general and average hourly rate; others make distinctions among strategic planning, research, account management, and administrative and support activities.

Material.   Material items in a budget include the "things" associated with the tactics: paper for brochures, banners for an open house, media kits for a news conference, uniforms for the softball team your company is sponsoring and so on. Additionally, material items may be associated with research activities, such as the cost of questionnaires or materials for focus groups. Each of these items carries a price tag, and it is very important to know exactly the cost of each recommended tactic. If you simply guess or work from old figures, you may find that you cannot implement the tactic for the amount that has been budgeted.

Media Costs.   Money generally is needed for communication activities, particularly the purchase of time and space associated with advertising tactics. Budgets often identify commissionable media—advertising in newspapers and magazines or commercials on radio and television. When working with an advertising agency, you may find that a *commission* or *agency fee* of about 15 percent has been added as a surcharge to the cost of final art, production charges for audio and video and talent or model fees, as well as the cost of buying advertising time or space. Meanwhile, public relations agencies sometimes bill all out-of-pocket expenses (perhaps with the exception of travel expenses) at cost plus 15 percent. However, in the face of growing competition among agencies, commissions increasingly are being replaced with flat fees.

Equipment and Facilities.   This category includes the capital cost of equipment that must be purchased to implement a tactic, such as a computer, scanner, printer or desktop publishing software needed to publish a newsletter. Also included here are the capital costs of obtaining a needed facility, such as modifying a storage area into an in-house

Phase Three

Step
8

television studio. Note that items in this category often are one-time expenditures, though a forward-looking budget process would amortize such expenses over the expected life of the equipment or facility and would be prepared for the time when replacements would be needed.

Administrative Items.   A budget also should include the cost of telephone charges, delivery costs, photocopying and other office activities, as well as travel costs associated with the project. Some organizations assess a surcharge, often 15 percent, to offset the cost of overhead expenses such as rent, maintenance, utilities, taxes and so on.

Approaches to Budgeting

A recurring problem with public relations budgeting is that public relations often is not seen as strategic management but rather as the mere production and distribution of messages. Additionally, public relations often may be thought to deal with hard-to-measure intangibles such as good will or visibility. Because of this mindset, public relations budgets sometimes are set according to a formula based on last year's budget, or worse, as an arbitrary percentage of the wider administration or marketing program of an organization.

If you have followed the guidelines in *Strategic Planning for Public Relations,* you should find that you can overcome these difficulties. You have learned to conduct public relations and marketing communication as a management activity, and you have learned to work with precise objectives that bring an element of measurement to concepts such as goodwill and support.

Still, the question often comes up: How much should an organization spend on public relations and marketing communications? People asking this often are looking for a simple, accepted formula. But there is no simple answer to that question, because so much depends on variables—the nature of the issue being addressed, the objectives sought, the tactics employed and so on. Some nonprofit organizations can operate impressive and successful campaigns for only a few hundred dollars. On the other hand, some major motion pictures, which easily run into the tens of millions of dollars to produce, may spend even more on promotions, most of that for paid advertising. Every organization and every issue is different. Each requires careful attention and insightful management.

Establishing an appropriate budget can be a difficult task. Often you will find that a client simply has no notion what the appropriate budget should be. Every organization wants to prevent unnecessary spending, but most also are willing to spend the necessary amount to get the job done. Let's consider some of the many different ways to approach budgeting: competitive parity, same-as-before, percentage-of-sales, unit-of-sales, all-you-can-afford, cost-benefit analysis, what-if-not-funded, zero-based, stage-of-lifestyle and objectives-based.

Competitive Parity.   The *competitive parity approach* bases an organization's budget for various activities on the level of similar activity by major competitors. For example, University A may base its budget for recruiting new students on the apparent budget of University B, its biggest competitor. A drawback of this approach is that University A will have to guess what University B is spending, and much of what University B is doing may not be apparent. Additionally, the two universities may have significantly different situations, such as the amount of informal recruiting being done by alumni, the reputation of the two institutions and the amount of their financial endowment.

Same-as-Before Budgeting.   *The same-as-before approach* looks as how much the organization spent on a similar recent project and allows the same budget for this project. But such an approach presumes that two projects are sufficiently similar that one can serve as a benchmark for the other; it also presumes that the first project was successful and deserves to be imitated. A related approach is *same-as-before-but-more* budgeting, which adds an inflationary increase to a same-as-before budget.

Percentage-of-Sales Budgeting.   The *percentage-of-sales approach* is drawn from the field of marketing, where some companies base their advertising budget on the previous year's profits. This approach may give a generous marketing budget following a good year but only a meager budget after a lean year—perhaps just the opposite of what is needed to overcome a sales slump. In the university recruiting scenario above, the budget for public relations might be based on the amount of money obtained through tuition fees. For example, 2 percent of each tuition payment may be earmarked for the recruiting public relations program. However, because much public relations activity is difficult to quantify on a short-term basis, the percentage-of-sales method generally is a weak approach in this field.

Unit-of-Sales Budgeting.   The *unit-of-sales approach,* similar to percentage-of-sales budgeting, is based not on dollars but rather on prior outcomes. In the university recruiting situation, the budget might be pegged to the number of students who register as students. For example, for every student recruited, the university might earmark $75 for the public relations program. This approach has a similar drawback to the percentage-of-sales approach in that it pegs future budgets on past prosperity rather than current needs.

All-You-Can-Afford Budgeting.   The *all-you-can-afford approach* works better in good times than in bad. It provides for public relations funding when the organization's financial condition is sound, but limits funding during lean times. While this is not a good approach, in reality it is the way too many organizations approach public relations, as an optional luxury that can be dispensed with when money is tight. Actually, the hard times are when even more public relations activity may be needed.

Cost-Benefit Analysis.   The *cost-benefit analysis approach* to budgeting identifies the cost of implementing a tactic, then compares this cost to the estimated value of the expected results. Ideally, the cost will be significantly less than the probable benefit. For example, the cost of holding an open house for a day-care center for seniors with Alzheimer's might be $1,500, while the benefit of this tactic, if the projected registration goal is met, might be $10,000 from new participants in the program.

What-If-Not-Funded Analysis.   *What-if-not-funded budgets* deal with the consequences of inaction and their effect on the organization's mission. This approach forces a planner to consider expected outcomes. For example, the what-if-not-funded scenario for the tactic of producing a video would have you indicate the expenses necessary to achieve the objective without the video. This might mean more workshops involving additional time from the CEO, or perhaps more brochures with fewer benefits than with the video. Implicitly or explicitly, the recommended tactic is compared with the alternatives.

Zero-Based Budgeting.   *Zero-based budgeting* is a technique based on current needs rather than past expenditures. It is common for ongoing organizational budgets, such as those associated with annual community relations or investor relations programs; however, the zero-based approach can work with one-time campaigns as well. In this approach, various tactics are ranked according to their importance (see the Worksheet for Setting Priorities in Step 3). The cumulative cost of each tactic is then calculated. The "cut-off line" of the predetermined budget indicates in effect when the client has run out of money and therefore must reject the remaining tactics. This is not really an effective method for public relations planning, because it allows a financial formula and a calculator to determine what tactics will be implemented.

Stage-of-Lifecycle Budgeting.   *The stage-of-lifestyle approach* looks closely at the phase of development of the issue, knowing that start-up programs generally require more financial resources than maintenance programs. Consider, for example, the needs of a university communication department in transition. Let's say the university is well known for its "academic" approach to communication, with a focus on research, theory and critical analysis. Let's further presume that the university decides to extend itself into more applied communication areas such as public relations, advertising and electronic journalism. The financial resources needed to recruit students for the new program will be greater than what is needed to maintain applications to the current program focus.

Objective-Based Budgeting.   *Objective-based budgeting* is a more enlightened approach to budgeting because it focuses on objectives, which are aligned with needs and goals. The underlying premise of this approach is that the organization will provide the resources necessary to achieve its objectives, which already have been approved by organizational decision makers. The consensus check that concludes Step 4 is perhaps the most important part of this approach to budgeting, as it is at this point that agreement is reached on what must be accomplished. The tactics simply provide ways to achieve what already has been adopted as the objective.

Even with the objective-based approach to budgeting, however, financial reality and common sense must rule. The wise strategic planner will develop tactics that are within the reach of the organization. The ability to create effective programs suitable to almost any budget is one of the real advantages of an integrated approach to public relations and marketing communication.

Fee Structures for Public Relations Agencies

Three different approaches to billing are common with public relations consultants and agencies, as well as with the growing number of public relations departments that are being reorganized into an in-house agency model within organizations.

- *Hourly rates plus expenses* are based on the actual amount of time spent on a project, plus the amount of money spent on materials, production costs and media. Some agencies lower the hourly rate as the actual number of hours increases. Examples of hourly rates are $45 an hour for copyediting, $150 an hour for research analysis or $200 an hour for account supervision.

- *Project fees* or *fixed fees* are flat charges for projects, such as $250 for a news release or $1,000 for preparing a brochure for printing.

- *Retainer fees* are fixed monthly base charges paid in advance for a predetermined level of agency availability. The benefit to the agency is that a minimum income is guaranteed; the client benefit is that the retaining charge is calculated lower than regular hourly rates.

Managing the Budget

In Step 8, you are developing the actual budget for your public relations program. The best way to do this is to list each of the tactics you recommended in Step 7, then indicate the various costs associated with each tactic.

For example, if you have recommended the creation of a brochure, indicate the various costs associated with this tactic. Include one-time costs such as copywriting, artwork and design. Include costs based on the number of brochures needed, such as paper, printing, folding and mailing. Add in the value of personnel time, such as hourly figures based on annual salaries of organizational employees or the hourly fees for outside consultants, agency personnel or freelance workers. Then add these various costs to obtain a total for the brochure tactic. Notice how each of these budget elements is included in Exhibit 8.3.

By breaking out each of the various costs associated with the tactic, you are able to more precisely predict the total cost associated with the program. Additionally, this breakout allows you to adjust the total budget more easily. Say, for example, that all of your recommended tactics add up to $12,500, but your overall budget is supposed to be only $11,000. You need to shave $1,500 from your recommendations.

One way would be to find a tactic that costs $1,500 and eliminate it, but then you probably would have a hole in your plan—after all, the tactic was recommended to achieve a particular objective. However, by knowing the cost of each aspect of every tactic, you can make minor revisions in several areas. Perhaps you could use spot color rather than four-color printing and save a few hundred dollars on the brochure, or perhaps mail fewer brochures and find an alternative distribution method that would cost less. By modifying enough tactics but not eliminating any of them, you can keep your original plan intact and still meet the budget.

How closely should you stick with the overall budget that your boss or client originally indicated? That probably depends on the boss or client, and how you read their

Phase Three

Step
8

Exhibit 8.3   Fixed Budget for Brochure

Administrative Costs (in house) ....$ 125
      Hourly Rate: $25
      # hours: 5

Setup Costs (outsourced) ....$ 900
      Copywriting 500
      Artwork 200
      Design 200

Production Costs x 2,500 Copies ....$ 775
      Paper 125
      Printing (2-color @ $.24) 600
      Folding 50

Distribution Costs ....$ 500

TOTAL $2,300

budget projection. If you think the budget was meant merely as a guideline, then going a bit over probably won't hurt. If you know them to be the type of manager who routinely cuts a percentage of every budget request, then you may be tempted to pad your budget request a bit, knowing that it will be cut back to the point where you really want it to be. But if you sense that the budget figure was firm, you should make sure your recommendations fall within the projected budget.

One way to deal with a budget that doesn't seem to stretch quite far enough for your ideas is to offer the client a range of costs—low-end and high-end tactics, perhaps with a preferred or optimal level of funding. Take another look at the brochure budget. As Exhibit 8.4 shows, a variable budget could be presented. The $2,300 total for brochure costs is based on printing with spot color. But the final cost actually could range from a low of $1,675 by printing in one color only and not using the mail for distribution, to a high of $2,900 for four-color printing and mail distribution.

Another way to stretch a budget is to provide a basic set of recommendations that fit within the projected budget, then offer an add-on list of optional tactics that the client may wish to fund because of the added expected benefit.

Budgets also have a way of inching upward. Perhaps a supplier charges a bit more than when you first called for an estimate. Or some of your expense items were based on a similar project six months ago, but those items now have increased in price. Most organizations are aware that budget creep can occur, and agencies or consultants often build into their contracts provisions for such changes. A common technique is to assure the client that, for any increase of more than 10 percent, the cost overrun will be submitted for the client's prior approval.

Once the budget has been approved, it should be used as a tool to help manage the implementation of the project. The budget can offer guidance in scheduling activities, monitoring their progress and assessing their results.

Exhibit 8.4 Variable Budget for Brochure

Administrative Costs (in house) .... **$ 125**
    Hourly Rate: $25
    # hours: 5

Setup Costs (outsourced) .... **$ 900**
    Copywriting 500
    Artwork 200
    Design 200

Production Costs x 2,500 Copies .... **$ 550-1,375**
    Paper 125
    Printing (1-color @$.15; 2-color @$.24; 4-color @$.48) 375-1,200
    Folding 50

Distribution Costs .... **$ 100-500**
    Non-mail/bulk-mail distribution 100
    Mail distribution (optional) 0-500

TOTAL **$1,675-2,900**

Additionally, the budget should be treated as part of a living document. The strategic plan is not set in stone once it is approved. Rather, it must have the flexibility to respond to a changing environment and differing organizational needs.

Full-Cost Budgets

In presenting the budget to your boss or client, include the full cost of all the tactics in the program. Some tactics may not have a specific price tag, but if they are of value to the organization they should be noted, along with equivalent costs if the tactics were to be purchased.

Note the value of donated or contributed services. In particular, include the value of volunteer time as you calculate the full cost of the budget items. For example, a human-services agency might get help from a college public relations class in developing a brochure for new clients. The students may not charge for their services, but the project budget should include a dollar estimate of what those services would cost if the agency had to hire professionals such as a freelance copywriter or a design firm.

Communication plans usually don't feature income items, but don't overlook implicit revenues. For example, corporate sponsorship may have a specific dollar value, which should be presented in the budget as an offset to expenses. It also is appropriate to include projected revenues if you have built a fund-raising tactic into your program recommendations.

Likewise, it may be appropriate to include both the actual expense and real value of that expense item. For example, the full value of discounted consulting fees or free airtime for a public service advertisement can be listed to show the difference between the

Phase Three

Step
8

total value and the actual cost to the organization. A word of caution: Don't be tempted to set a dollar value on publicity by calculating how much the same space would cost for advertising. This will be discussed in more detail in Step 9; for now let's just agree that publicity should not be confused with advertising.

By including all of this information, you are presenting a full view of the real value of the campaign, even though the organization's actual cost may be considerably less.

How Much Success Is Necessary?

It sometimes can be useful to determine how much success is necessary. This *break-even point* is the level of achievement needed simply to cover the cost of the program.

Calculate the break-even point (BEP) in three steps: Identify the total project cost (c); determine the outcome value (v), the dollar value for each unit of the desired outcome, especially those associated with the action objectives; then divide the total project cost by the value of the desired outcome. Thus the formula BEP = c/v, cost divided by value.

Let's say a private college will spend $100,000 in recruiting costs this year to develop brochures and booklets, produce and distribute an informational video, and place paid radio commercials and billboards. Let's add another $80,000 in salaries associated with this particular project. Add another $10,000 for expenses such as postage, travel and phone calls. That's $190,000 in all, the total project cost. Now let's presume that tuition at this college is $10,000. Apply the formula: cost $190,000 divided by outcome value $10,000 equals 19. That's the break-even point, the number of students who must be recruited before the communication program has paid for itself. (Note that this is an over-simplified example that doesn't take into account that the real cost of education is borne not only by tuition but also by donations, endowments and state aid.)

Another useful budgetary calculation is the *per-capita cost,* the cost associated with the number of people needed to cover the cost. Calculate the per-capita cost (PCC) by dividing the total project cost (c) by the number of people (p) who perform the desired outcome. The formula: PCC = v/p.

Returning to the college scenario, divide the cost by the number of new recruits (let's say that's 1,800). Apply the formula: $190,000 divided by 1,800, which equals $105.56. This is how much the college is spending to recruit each new student. In percentage terms, that is about 1.05 percent of tuition income, or about a penny for every dollar paid in tuition.

Break-even points and per-capita costs also can be calculated for other public relations objectives, as long as the objectives themselves have been stated in precise and measurable terms.

Strategic Planning Example: *Implementing the Strategic Plan*

The following schedule shows one of several events within the four initiatives of the plan to publicize Upstate's expanding program. It shows the event and its component tactics, along with a cost, assigned manager and start date for each tactic.

Rededication Ceremony

Event	Cost	Manager	Begin Work
Printed materials		Publications Office	12 weeks
Print & mail 1,000 invitations	$ 800	Publications Office	10 weeks
Print 500 programs	0*	Publications Office	3 weeks
Program Planning		Rededication Committee	12 weeks
Keynote speaker honorarium	$1,000	President's Office	10 weeks
Musicians	$ 200	Music Dept. Chair	
Academic procession/ritual	$ 200	Provost's Office	
Video about UC expansion		Video Task Force	20 weeks
Production	$4,000	Broadcasting Division	18 weeks
Viewing equipment	$ 300	Facilities Office	4 weeks
Plaque engraving	$ 400	Facilities Office	4 weeks

*The cost of printing programs was offset by advertising.

■ ■ ■

The following schedule shows one of the several events outlined for the employee publics of the strategic communication plan focusing on consumer confidence.

Tactic

Newsletter articles in employee publication about safety, quality and customer satisfaction.

Implementation Schedule

With publication slated for the first Wednesday of each month, relevant articles will be written for each publication date, according to the following schedule:

Safety Issues

- January: Industry-wide safety standards and government safety regulations.
- April: Product-safety record of Tiny Tykes Toys for the last 15 years.
- July: External/marketing consequences of product safety.
- October: Internal/employee consequences of product safety.

Quality Issues

- February: Industry-wide quality issues in the toy industry.
- May: Quality comparison between Tiny Tykes Toys and major competitors.
- August: Quality-control and quality-goal programs at Tiny Tykes Toys.
- November: Involvement of employees in quality issues at Tiny Tykes Toys.

Customer Satisfaction Issues

- March: Industry-wide importance of customer satisfaction to company's bottom line.

- June: Importance of customer satisfaction to Tiny Tykes Toys' reputation.
- September: Empowering employees to achieve customer satisfaction.
- December: Employee training/motivation for customer satisfaction.

Staffing

The Communication Director in the public relations office will notify appropriate interviewees two months prior to publication date. A Communication Specialist will arrange interviews three to four weeks prior to publication and will give completed article to the Communication Director two weeks prior to publication date.

Budget

There is no significant operating cost to research or write articles. Staff time is already provided, but approximately five hours will be allocated for each article for preparation, research, interviewing and writing.

Strategic Planning Exercise: *Implementing the Strategic Plan*

Basic Planning Questions

1. What is the schedule for this project?
2. What is the budget for this project?
3. Who is responsible for this project?

Expanded Planning Questions

Scheduling

- Message repetition
- Frequency
- Scheduling pattern (optional): continuous, flighting, pulsing or massing?

Timeline for each tactic?

Assigned manager for each tactic?

Budget

Budget line items:

- Personnel
- Materials
- Media costs
- Equipment and facilities
- Administrative items

Full-cost budget?

Break-even point?

Per-capita cost?

Citations and Recommended Readings

Amos, J. S. (1995). *Fundraising ideas: Over 225 money making events for community groups, with a resource directory.* Jefferson, NC: McFarland.

Braun, G. (Ed.). (2001). *Gale directory of publications and broadcast media* (135th ed.). Detroit, MI: Gale Research.

Cameron, G. T. (1994). Does publicity outperform advertising? An experimental test of the third-party endorsement. *Journal of Public Relations Research, 6 (3),* 185–207.

Corder L., Deasy, M., & Thompson, J. (Spring 1999). PR is to experience what marketing is to expectations. *Public Relations Quarterly, 44 (1),* 23–26. See also (May 1999). Answering the age-old marketing question: What have you done for me lately? *Public Relations Tactics,* 12.

Curtain, P. A. (1999). Reevaluating public relations information subsidies: Market-driven journalism and agenda-building theory and practice. *Journal of Public Relations Research, 11 (1),* 53–90.

Gagne, L. (Ed.). (2001). *Newsletters in print.* (14th ed.). Detroit, MI: Gale Research.

Giving USA, 2001 (2000). AAFRC Trust for Philanthropy.

Holm, K. (Ed.). (1998). *1999 Writer's market.* Cincinnati, OH: Writer's Digest Books.

Kim, J. B. (1995). The cassette is in the mail. *Advertising Age, 68 (May 22),* 51.

Krugman, H. E. (1972). Why three exposures may be enough. *Journal of Advertising Research, 12 (Dec.),* 11–28.

Lang, K. & Lang, G. E. (1983). *The battle for public opinion:* The president, the press, and the polls during Watergate. New York: Columbia University Press.

Lippy, C. H. (Ed). (1986). *Religious periodicals of the United States: Academic and scholarly journals.* New York: Greenwood.

Maddux, D. (1999). *International yearbook* (79th ed.). New York: Editor & Publisher.

McManus, J. (1994). *Market-driven journalism: Let the citizen beware?* Thousand Oaks, CA: Sage.

Middleberg, D. & Ross, S.S. (2001). *The Middleberg/Ross survey of media in the wired world, 2000.* New York: Middleberg Euro.

Newport, F. & Saad, L. (1998). A matter of trust: News sources Americans prefer. *American Journalism Review, 20 (6),* 30–33.

Newspaper Association of America (1999). *Competitive Media Index.* Vienna, VA: NAA.

Simmons Market Research Bureau (1993). The study of media and markets. Cited in *American Demographics (1994), 16 (5),* 40–46.

Stenson, P. (1993). How (and why) corporate communicators use video. *Communication World, 10 (10),* 14–15.

Survey Shows Radio Use Patterns (1996). *PR News, 52 (15).*

Tellis, G. J. (1998). *Advertising and sales promotion strategy.* Reading, MA: Addison-Wesley.

Tyson, C. B. & Snyder, L. B. (1999). The impact of direct mail video. *Public Relations Quarterly, 44 (1),* 28–32.

Phase Three

227

Vanden Bergh, B. G. & Katz, H. (1999). *Advertising principles: Choice, challenge, change.* Lincolnwood, IL: NTC Business.

West Glen Communications (1997). *The 1997 survey of newsrooms on the use of outside-produced video.* New York: West Glen Communications.

Wilcox, D. L., Ault, P. H., Agee, W. K. & Cameron, G. T. (2000). *Public relations: Strategies and tactics* (6th ed.). New York: Longman.

Williams. W. (1994). *User friendly fund raising: A step-by-step guide to profitable special events.* Alexander, NC: WorldComm.

EVALUATIVE RESEARCH

The strategic planning that began with research in Phase One comes full circle in this final phase of the process. Here you turn once again to research techniques, preparing to evaluate the effectiveness of your tactics in achieving your objectives once those tactics are set into motion.

Perform well in this phase and you may be able to soar above the competition, because public relations practitioners too often are weak in evaluative research. And they're the first to concede this fault. Professional workshops in evaluation and measurement always seem to draw large audiences. Surveys of public relations practitioners in all kinds of settings—agencies, for-profit corporations and nonprofit organizations—indicate that, while they may talk a lot about doing evaluative research, often their actions don't quite match their words.

Step 9
Evaluating the
Strategic Plan

A good baseline for considering the prevalence of evaluative research may be a study by Ketchum Public Relations ("Evaluation Research on the Rise," 1994). When he was Ketchum research director, Walter K. Lindenmann found that 48 percent of public relations practitioners wanted a systematic and scientific assessment of the impact of their programs on awareness, attitudes, opinions and behaviors. You might consider that a low percentage—less than half the practitioners. Still, that figure had increased from 30 percent in a previous study.

Similarly, Rick Fischer (1995) of Memphis State University noted that only a minority of the Silver Anvil winners (somewhere between 30 and 48 percent) measured how well the campaign met predetermined goals. The Silver Anvil awards are sponsored by the Public Relations Society of America, presumably the best of the best in terms of public relations programs and projects.

In a more recent corporate survey by Edelman Public Relations, Opinion Research Corporation, and Northwestern University ("Planning, Goals and Measurement," 1997), 75 percent of respondents agreed that measurement of communication efforts on the achievement of corporate goals is an important trend. Yet only 27 percent said their own communication programs actually have evaluation components.

Meanwhile, even marketing executives—who are generally more comfortable with quantifiable evaluation criteria than are public relations executives—give "greater focus on doing the marketing than on proving it works" (Corder et al., 1999).

So much talk, but so little action. Why? Several reasons. For one, it is sometimes difficult to know just what to evaluate and how to do so. Research is a specialty many practitioners have not mastered, perhaps not even studied. Another reason is that public relations measures may not be as precise as those used in areas such as finance, operations and safety. Still another difficulty in measuring public relations is that everything is in motion, clouding the possibility of an accurate count; it's like going into a tropical fish store and trying to count the number of neons in a tank. Additionally, some public relations measures are negatives—to what extent did something bad not happen? How many negative opinions were minimized? Finally, research takes time, money and creative energy, three things public relations practitioners guard as precious commodities to be used in only the most important situations.

So perhaps after all the explanations and excuses, it comes down to this: Evaluation is infrequent because public relations practitioners—or their bosses or clients—simply don't recognize its importance. But as you will discover in this section, good evaluative research does not have to be costly or time consuming, nor is it beyond the means of an adequately prepared practitioner. Properly built into the overall strategic plan, evaluative research can increase the effectiveness of public relations and marketing communication. That's an advantage that should appeal to bosses and clients everywhere.

Additionally, proper evaluation can enhance the prestige and role of public relations within an organization. And that's an even bigger advantage—one that every practitioner surely can recognize.

Evaluating
the Strategic Plan

Program evaluation is the systematic measurement of the outcomes of a project, program or campaign, based on the extent to which stated objectives were achieved. As part of the strategic planning process, establishing appropriate and practical evaluation methods wraps up all the previous plans, ideas and recommendations.

Research Design: What to Evaluate

You've heard the phrase "starting off on the right foot." In precision marching, the first step is the most important, because it sets up the pattern for the rest of the cadence. The same is true in putting together an effective research program. Starting off on the right foot means setting out to answer the appropriate questions.

The plan for program evaluation is called the **research design.** It outlines the criteria for judging what is effective. The research design considers several issues: the criteria to be used to gauge success, timing of the evaluation and specific ways to measure each of the levels of objectives (awareness, acceptance and action). The research design may prescribe the various evaluation tools, and it should also indicate how the evaluation will be used.

Note that this planning happens before any tactics are implemented. Although the design of evaluative research focuses on the results of the program, it is developed as part of the initial planning. It points to how evaluation will be conducted at the appropriate times.

Design Questions

As you design an effective program for evaluation research, ask yourself the following questions:

- On what criteria should the program be judged?
- What information is needed?
- What standards of accuracy and reliability are needed for this information?

Next, focus some attention on the source of the information needed:

- Who has this information?
- How can this information be obtained from them?

A Ray of Hope?

Through a series of interviews with public relations practitioners and corporate executives, one researcher has identified what may be a hopeful trend in public relations evaluation research. Linda Childers Hon (1998) reported several interesting findings:

- Practitioners seem to be moving toward more systematic public relations programming.
- Both practitioners and CEOs have long-range plans to build more formal evaluation into their public relations efforts.
- Practitioners are trying to educate CEOs and others in their organizations of the importance of public relations measurement.

- Understanding is growing among both practitioners and executives of how public relations feeds into the strategic goals of organizations.
- Junior practitioners, who are relatively new to the field of public relations, are more likely than veteran practitioners to be integrating evaluation into their public relations programming.

Is this the beginning of a trend? It's too early to make the call. So far the research has been based only on small samples. But it may signal a time to come when evaluation research routinely plays a more prominent role in the public relations planning and programming.

Finally, consider how the information will be used:

- Who will receive the final evaluation, and what will they do with the information?
- How willing and able are decision makers to receive less-than-fully-positive evaluations?
- Besides decision makers, who else would have an interest in the evaluation?

Remember that research design is always a trade-off between the perfect and the practical. Strategic planners must make choices about the importance of the program, the accuracy and reliability of the information to be received, and the needed resources (time, personnel, financial and so on).

Evaluation Criteria

Before you develop specific evaluation techniques, consider first the criteria on which you will judge something to be effective. What yardsticks should you use? The appropriate standards vary with the objectives and the tactics, but here are a few general guidelines. Evaluation criteria should be (1) useful to the organization by being clearly linked with the established objectives; (2) realistic, feasible and appropriate as to cost, time or other resources; (3) ethical and socially responsible; (4) credible, with accurate data; and (5) presented in a timely manner.

As an example, consider the following possible criteria for an organization to judge the effectiveness of its Web site:

- Ability to navigate easily throughout the site (a measure of awareness objectives)
- Breadth of content (awareness objectives)
- Ability to convey key messages (awareness objectives)
- Number and tenor of questions and comments by site visitors (acceptance objectives)
- Interactivity (action objectives)
- Number of visitor names that are captured for organizational response or follow up (action objectives)

Notice that measures of message production and exposure are not included as significant. For example, what matters is not so much the number of hits but rather the number and content of comments by visitors to the site and the number of retrievable names so the organization can engage the visitor in two-way communication. With appropriate evaluation criteria in mind, the public relations strategist can turn to the task of developing evaluation measures that can rate the Web site on those criteria.

Notice, too, that all of the criteria should be developed before any implementation of the Web site, because the particular criteria you identify as necessary will determine some of what you do in putting the web site together.

Linda Childers Hon (1997) compared a study by MediaLink (Weiner, 1995) with a survey conducted by the Detroit chapter of PRSA. MediaLink found that 98 percent of public relations practitioners felt that the number of positive stories in the media was most important; less than 60 percent measured awareness or attitudes. The Detroit survey, however, found that most CEOs felt awareness and attitude were most important, and they rated media clippings as the least important indicators of effectiveness. So the question is worth asking: Just what should we be measuring?

Ken Gofton (1999) noted the difference between advertising and public relations measurement. He observed that advertising often focuses evaluative research on audience exposure. Public relations evaluation, meanwhile, may measure exposure, but it goes further: profiling audiences, tracking attitude change and assessing impact in terms of behavioral outcomes.

Timing: When to Evaluate

There are three stages in the process or program evaluation: implementation reports, progress reports and final evaluation. Each is different; each is important.

Implementation Report

The first level of evaluation is to track the implementation of each tactic, making sure that it is proceeding according to plan. This *implementation report* documents how the

Twelve Reminders About Evaluative Research

Here are a dozen suggestions for planning and implementing an effective evaluative research program. Most of these tips are based on common-sense principles that you probably already know. But reminders are meant to be remembered, so review these tips and consider them as you prepare your evaluation program.

1. **Don't wait for the program's completion before you evaluate.**   Evaluation begins with the planning process, before you actually "do" anything. Effective planning means you determine in advance what you will evaluate and how you will measure a program, both during and at its conclusion.

2. **Guesses aren't good enough.**   Evaluation must rely on facts, not estimates or approximations. Hunches and gut feelings can point the way, but hard facts are needed to accurately assess the impact of a project or program.

3. **Friends may be telling you what they think you want to hear.**   Get beyond the limitations of information volunteered by people who already look kindly on your organization. Also, be cautious of relying too heavily on information solicited from friends and acquaintances in interpersonal situations that don't encourage candor.

4. **Employees have a vested interest in the program's success.**   Realize that they may be seeing what they want to see, for the programs they evaluate affect their own job security and economic future, as well as their day-to-day social relationships on the job. Employees usually are not able to be totally objective about projects in which they were involved.

5. **Samples must reflect the population.** Formal evaluative research draws on a sample that represents the publics addressed in the public relations activity. This kind of research is likely to generate information that

is accurate, neither unduly positive nor negative.

6. **Hard work and cost aren't measures of effectiveness.**   Be careful not to equate activity with achievement. Your campaign may have been expensive, and it may have claimed a lot of resources in time, energy and budgets. But these are not the measure of program effectiveness.

7. **Neither is creativity a gauge of effectiveness.**   "Everybody thinks it's a neat idea" may indicate innovation, and an award from your public relations association may attest to your ingenuity. But neither is the mark of a successful program (unless creativity is the sole objective).

8. **Dissemination doesn't equal communication.**   A mainstay principle of public relations is that distribution of a message does not guarantee that real communication is achieved. Every piece of unopened junk mail, every commercial zapped through on a home VCR, every half-time show missed by spectators heading for the rest room is an example of failed communication. The message was disseminated, but the audience simply wasn't paying attention.

9. **Knowledge doesn't always lead to acceptance.**   The press agentry and public information models of public relations presume that information is the key. Better informed publics are more supportive ones, says the common wisdom. Not necessarily. Knowledge is an important aspect of the road to support, but this road has an off-ramp as well. Sometimes the more people know about an organization or the issues it faces, the less supportive they may be of the organization.

10. **Behavior is the ultimate measure.** Awareness and acceptance objectives are important, and many public relations activities

seek to increase knowledge, generate favorable attitudes or foster supportive opinions. But knowledge that doesn't lead to action is pretty weak, and attitudes or opinions that don't have an outcome in behavior are like books sitting unread on the shelf. Missed opportunities. Unrealized potential.

11. **Evaluation doesn't have to be expensive or time consuming.**   A concern of many public relations people is that evaluation takes so much time and costs so much that it simply can't be done except in unusual situations of affluence. Not so! Like other aspects

of public relations planning, evaluation research—done appropriately—is linked to the organization's resources. Proper evaluation requires insight and creative thinking, not necessarily a lot of time or money.

12. **Evaluative research enables action.**   It allows organizations to do something with the information they obtain through the evaluation. They may modify programs that are still in process, or they may use the evaluation research to analyze and justify the current program or to make decisions about similar future programs.

program tactics were carried out. In it, include a schedule of progress to date toward implementing each tactic, as well as any work remaining. Identify any gaps, defects or potential delays that could hurt the plan. Note any difficulties encountered and how they were (or might be) resolved. Discuss the efficiency with which the tactics were set in motion.

Additionally, note the name of the person or group responsible for each tactic, as well as other personnel resources such as staff, freelancers, consultants and so on. It

What Should Be Measured?

Knowing what to measure is sometimes the key to effective evaluation research. The answer often can be found in the objectives. But sometimes the objectives themselves are in conflict, with one of them measuring positively and another barely moving the dial.

That was the case with the "Got Milk?" campaign by the National Fluid Milk Processor Promotion Board, which presumably sought the range of objectives: awareness, acceptance and action.

The advertising series featured Annie Liebovitz's popular photos of celebrities with milk mustaches. Visibility was high, and everybody seemed to be familiar with the campaign and the ads. Acceptance also ran high. The ads became collector items and earned praise from creative designers. They found appeal with

a diverse audience largely because of their use of many different celebrities: Dennis Rodman, Kristie Yamaguchi, Pete Sampras, Christie Brinkley, Bart and Lisa Simpson, Kermit the Frog, Conan O'Brien, Neve Campbell—the list goes on and on.

There's just one problem: $110 million a year, and no evidence the campaign increased milk consumption. Oops! Milk sales dropped. The board's research showed that attitudes toward milk have improved, but the Agriculture Department's inspector general said milk usage was up 0.85 percent one year, down 0.42 percent the next.

So the question is posed: How effective is a campaign that improved attitudes but doesn't effect action?

Phase Four

Step
9

might also be useful to include budgetary information, such as how much money has been spent or committed thus far.

Progress Report

It is important to monitor progress at various key points as the tactics are being implemented. *Progress reports* are preliminary evaluations, on which planners can make strategic modifications as they further implement the program. Such mid-course corrections can keep the project functioning at peak efficiency. In this way, the plan is used as a written guideline rather than a rigid rulebook.

Consider, for example, an interactive computer travel map for a cross-country road trip. This mapping program receives hourly weather updates and daily progress reports on highway construction projects. It also monitors traffic jams around congested urban areas and newspaper reports of tourism-related events. Before you leave on the road trip, you map out a tentative plan, indicating your goal (traveling cross country) and your objectives (the various points of interest along the way to the destination). A rigid use of your plan would be to follow the map with no deviation—after all, you've planned this trip for a long time, and you shouldn't be distracted by unscheduled changes. However, a more effective use of the map would allow the computerized mapping program to alert you to an interesting community festival only a few miles off the scheduled route or to travel delays resulting from snow buildup on a mountain pass.

The mapping program demonstrates the value of feedback: You can use information gathered during the course of the project to update strategy and tactics. This type of in-process evaluation is important for both public relations and marketing communication programs. After a pilot project and following each significant phase within a program, evaluate whether the program is unfolding as it was planned to do. Ask questions: Are the messages being disseminated as expected? Are they being understood? Are people responding as expected? If the answers turn out to be no, there is still time to make adjustments before the rest of the program is implemented.

This kind of evaluation allows a public relations plan to be a living document that enhances the atmosphere of open communication. It allows the planning organization to be impacted by its environment and by its publics.

Final Evaluation

Final reports, sometimes called *summative reports,* review the whole of the program. They measure impact and outcome for the various tactics. The final evaluation gauges how well the tactics achieved what they set out to achieve, namely the various objectives.

Research Design

The question of when to evaluate leads to a related aspect of research design: How to structure the evaluation in relation to the measurement standards. There are several possibilities, the most common being after-only studies and various types of before-after studies.

Cybernetics and Public Relations

Norbert Wiener's cybernetic model of communication (1954) was noted in the Strategy section of this book. Cybernetics deals with the feedback mechanisms of goal-seeking systems, in which goals are established, action and output is monitored and feedback mechanisms implement corrective action to keep the system on the target of its goal. Furnace thermostats, heat-seeking missiles and cruise-control devices on cars are examples of cybernetics.

In public relations and marketing communication, examples of cybernetics include crisis planning and issues management that feature a radar-like early warning system of monitoring the environment in which the organization operates. An example is the kind of in-process evaluative research being presented in this book.

Cybernetics in public relations operates most effectively in an open-systems approach. In this approach, public relations functions as the liaison between the organization and its publics, with responsibilities to each and to the mutual benefits of both. Two-way communication between the organization and the environment keeps the organization moving toward its goal, with this approach continuously adjusted through the feedback provided by the publics.

After-Only Study.   An *after-only study* is common in public relations evaluation projects because it is simple to conduct. Implement a tactic, measure its impact and presume that the tactic caused the impact. This approach can be appropriate for action objectives that measure audience response, such as attendance, contributions, purchase and other easily measured reactions. For example, a political candidate running for office would need no preliminary baseline. She simply would be interested in the numbers of votes received in an election.

The after-only approach is not appropriate for every situation, however. Its weakness is that it does not prove that the tactic caused the observed level of awareness or acceptance. Perhaps the levels were there all along but simply not noticed.

Before-After Study.   Another format for evaluation research is the *before-after study,* also called a *pre-test/post-test study.* These involve an initial observation before any public relations programming is implemented. This initial observation provides a benchmark or baseline for comparing studies that will be conducted later.

For example, if the candidate noted above wanted to gauge the effectiveness of a new type of campaign message, she would need to measure her support before the message was presented and measure it again following the presentation. The difference would indicate the change—positive or negative—created by the new campaign message. In another example, a public transit system might compare ridership figures before and after a promotional campaign. Note that a before-after study is integrated into both the formative research phase and the evaluative research phase of the planning process.

The simplest before-after study involves three stages: (1) observe and measure a public, (2) expose the public to a public relations tactic and (3) measure the public again. Any change in the public's awareness, acceptance or action can likely be attributed to the tactic.

Remember that public relations activities generally don't take place in a vacuum or in a pure environment. Be aware of extraneous factors. Not every change in your key public may appropriately be linked, cause-effect fashion, to your programming. One of the challenges for evaluative research is to sort out the effective public relations tactics from unrelated outside forces.

Controlled Before–After Study.   A more sophisticated type of evaluative research is a *controlled before-after study,* which involves two samples drawn from the same key public. One sample is the group to receive the message; the other is a control group that does not receive the message. Here is how the process works: (1) observe and measure each group; (2) expose one group to a tactic, but do not expose the control group; (3) measure each group again; and (4) compare the results of each group. The control group is likely to have remained unchanged, while any change noted in the exposed group can be presumed to be linked to the public relations tactic. For example, the transit system noted above might also compare before-and-after ridership figures with those of a transit system in a similar city in another state (the control group), where riders were not exposed to the promotional campaign.

Remember also that research design is always a trade-off. Strategic planners must make choices that consider the importance of the program, the accuracy and reliability of the information to be received, and the needed resources (time, personnel, financial and so on). They also should look at the whole picture, focusing not on each tactic in isolation but rather on how the various tactics together have achieved their objectives.

Also be aware of extraneous factors that can mask your evaluation efforts. Not every change in a public's awareness, acceptance or action may be caused by your public relations programming. Try to account for other activities and influences that the publics have been exposed to. Let's return to the example of the transit system. If a few days after the ridership campaign begins, an international crisis sends oil prices up 30 percent, you probably would notice a lot more riders on the trains and buses. But you couldn't really attribute this to your public relations campaign. It's more likely motorists are reacting to the higher cost of gasoline at the pumps, and your research report must note this.

A benefit of most evaluative research is that it is unobtrusive—the research subjects do not know they are being observed, at least not until after the fact, when their awareness of being observed can't affect what they have already done. An exception to this is the before-after study. When conducting a before-after study, be aware of the *Hawthorne effect,* also called the *placebo effect.* For example, in the 1930s researchers were trying to find out how the intensity of lighting affected factory workers. It was discovered that any change in lighting, brighter or dimmer, increased worker productivity. Researchers concluded that the increase was simply because the subjects knew they were being observed and knew that the company was concerned about worker productivity.

Methodology: How to Evaluate

A question was posed at the beginning of Step 9: What information is needed in order to evaluate a program's effectiveness? Answer this question wisely, and you'll have a

---

Methods of Evaluative Research

Like formative research, evaluative research involves techniques that can be either quantitative or qualitative.

Quantitative methods that are used frequently for evaluation include surveys, content analyses, cost-effectiveness studies, readership studies, head counts and tracking of feedback, as well as direct observation and monitoring of specific results.

Qualitative techniques commonly used for evaluation include interviews, focus groups and case studies.

Don't let the availability of so many different research methods hide the fact that direct observation of outcomes can be the simplest way to evaluate the effectiveness of public relations programs. For more information on research techniques, see Appendix A: Applied Research Techniques.

---

strong final phase to your strategic planning. Answer blindly, and you could end up measuring the wrong thing. In this section we will discuss five levels of evaluation: judgmental assessments; evaluation of communication outputs; and evaluation of awareness, acceptance and action, respectively.

Judgmental Assessments

Judgmental assessments are evaluations made on hunches and experience. This type of informal feedback is common in public relations and marketing communication. It is the kind of research that everybody seems to do, because it comes naturally. Judgmental assessment relies on personal and subjective observations such as the following: "The boss liked it"; "The client asked us to continue the project"; "Everybody said this was a success"; "The customers seem happy"; "Hey, we won an award for this project."

Judgmental assessments are based on personal observations, and that can be both their strength and their limitation. Some judgmental evaluations, though informal, can be very helpful to an organization. For example, the assessment by outside experts, perhaps a public relations colleague in another organization, might offer an excellent analysis of the program. So too with judgmental assessments based on a formal review of an organization's program by a panel of outside experts. An example of the latter is an evaluation based on a program that received an award through a competition sponsored by a professional organization, such as the Silver Anvils sponsored by the Public Relations Society of America, the Gold Quill Award sponsored by the International Association of Business Communicators, or local professional competitions. Additionally, senior practitioners often draw on their experience to make informal judgments about program effectiveness.

However, such informal research has its limitations. For one thing, the informal assessments often are made by program managers who are never disinterested and seldom impartial. For another, their personal observations often are imprecise and arbitrary, and sometimes downright fickle. Granted, the anecdotes on which this feedback is based can provide a lot of insight into the success or failure of a program, but because informal

Outputs and Outcomes

It is important to make a clear distinction between outputs and outcomes.

James Bissland (1990) identified communication outputs as the work done in a public relations activity. He likened this work to the who-says-what-in-which-channel part of Lasswell's classic verbal formula for communication.

The Institute for Public Relations Research and Education (Lindenmann, 1997) went on to describe outputs as short-term, immediate results of a public relations program Examples of outputs are the number of times a company official is quoted, the number of people who participated in a special event and the number of placements that appear in the media.

Outcomes, meanwhile, are far more important. Bissland called them "terminal goals"—what this book has defined not as general goals but as more specific and measurable action objectives. Examples of outcomes are the number of new recruits, the amount of money raised or the passage of desired legislation.

The Institute said outcomes "measure whether target audience groups actually received the messages directed at them . . . paid attention to them . . . understood the messages . . . and retained those messages in any shape or form. Outcomes also measure whether the communications materials and messages which were disseminated have resulted in any opinion, attitude and/or behavior changes on the part of those targeted audiences to whom the messages were directed."

So measure outputs if you wish. They can provide useful assessment of what has been done. But don't stop there. Far more important is to measure program outcomes, specifically as they relate to your objectives.

---

research and gut feelings don't involve representative samples and standard measures, they can't confirm the effectiveness of a public relations activity.

Another problem with judgmental assessment is that it often gives undue emphasis to apparent creativity and to the expenditure of energy and resources. Throughout this entire planning process, you have put in a great deal of effort and energy. In doing so, you have articulated a strategy and produced a range of tactics. These of course are important, but they are not what you should be measuring. Rather, the evaluation phase should focus on your objectives at each of their three levels: awareness, acceptance and action. Just like objectives, evaluation research should deal with the impact your program has made on your various publics.

Judgmental assessment also can lull you into taking for granted what you should be analyzing. Consider tax-free shopping weeks. Increasingly, state lawmakers are waiving sales tax to encourage spending and help consumers save money. One popular time is the back-to-school shopping time in late August. It's oh-so-obvious that consumers win; they save money when buying clothing and school supplies. Politicians benefit from the gratitude of their constituents. And merchants like it because buyers flock into their stores. On the surface, tax-free shopping weeks are both popular and successful. But is popularity a valid standard? Stores that used to discount merchandise 15 or 20 percent no longer have sales because they know the consumers will flock in to save what? Six percent? Meanwhile, states lose important tax revenues, threatening services or leading to other kinds of taxes. So customer satisfaction, if it is based on whim rather than fact, isn't a useful measure. The lesson is this: Effective evelution requires careful analysis. Don't rely on the obvious—because what obviously is true sometimes isn't.

Let's look at how an approach to evaluation based on each type of objective can provide more reliable information than judgmental assessments alone can provide.

Evaluation of Communication Outputs

Outputs evaluation is a measure of communication products and their distribution. It focuses on the development and presentation of a message, specifically its production and dissemination and the calculation of its cost and advertising equivalency. These may be necessary tasks to do, but they really are not effective measurement tools. Let's look at each.

Message Production.   Several techniques of evaluation research deal simply with whether the message is produced. For example, count the number of news releases written, brochures printed or pages formatted for a Web site. Or note the creation of special message vehicles, such as a company float for the Fourth of July parade. Measurement of message production simply quantifies the work output of a public relations office. While it may be useful for a measure of individual job performance, don't be deluded into thinking that it is a measure of program effectiveness.

Message Distribution.   Another approach to awareness evaluation focuses not merely on the production of messages but rather on their distribution. In this category, the evaluator focuses on media contacts and asks how many of the news releases written were actually mailed or faxed, or how many new pages were uploaded to the Web site. Measuring message dissemination tells what an organization did to spread the message, but it doesn't measure its effectiveness or its impact.

Message Cost.   Another type of measurement deals with the cost of messages. This approach analyzes how much money an organization spent to present its message. For paid media such as brochures or advertisements, the organization simply divides the cost of the communication vehicle by the number of times the message was reproduced. For example, if it costs $150 to produce 2,500 copies of a flier, then each piece costs 6 cents.

When dealing with electronic media, the common standard is *cost per thousand,* identified as CPM (from the Latin word *mille,* meaning "thousand"). For example, if a radio station with 75,000 listeners during a particular time period charges $150 for a 30-second commercial, it would cost $2 for each thousand listeners—a mere one-fifth of a penny per listener.

Cost per thousand is an effective way to compare costs among various media, even print vehicles. Consider the following:

- A national magazine with a regional edition circulating 17,000 copies charges $9,000 for a full-page color ad. CPM = $529 (nearly 53 cents per each local subscriber).
- A city newspaper with a circulation of 338,000 charges $22,000 for a full-page ad. CPM = $65 (about 6-1/2 cents per reader).

- A local radio station with an estimated 10,000 listeners charges $35 for a 30-second commercial. CPM = $3.50.

- A transit system of bus and light rail service in a metropolitan area charges $290 for each transit poster, with 40 needed to saturate coverage in what is called "100 showing" (100 percent of the audience—3 million—is likely to see the poster within a 30-day period). The cost for 40 posters is $11,600. CPM = $3.87.

- A cable advertising service charges $150 for a 30-second commercial on a cable network carried on a system with 520,000 subscriber households and 25 cable channels available to them (thus an average per/channel subscriber base of 20,800). CPM = $7.21.

When comparing media costs, however, remember that the elements you are comparing may not be similar. The impact of various media and the amount of repeat presentation for messages to have an impact must be considered, as well as how closely a particular media audience resembles an organization's key public.

Consider this example of a newspaper ad and a brochure. A 50,000-circulation newspaper charges $5,500 for a half-page ad. CPM = $110. A printer charges $600 for 10,000 copies of a direct-mail letter. CPM = $60. Additionally, it will cost $1,900 to distribute the letters. Now the CPM cost to the organization is $250. Purely on the basis of production and distribution costs, the newspaper ad is a better deal. But most newspaper readers skip over the ads because they are not particularly interested in the topic. Chances are you don't need to communicate with 50,000 newspaper readers because most of them are not even in the key public you identified in your planning. Meanwhile, people who receive brochures often are more likely to read them, especially if the organization did a good job identifying its public and designed the brochure to be of obvious interest to the readers. So the $2,500 brochure could well be the more cost-effective way to communicate with members of the key publics: less total expense and—more important—more effective message delivery. On the other hand, if your public is widespread and difficult to reach individually, then the newspaper cost would be the better way to communicate with them.

Advertising Equivalency.   A common but generally inappropriate evaluation technique is related to the message cost. *Advertising equivalency* means treating a non-advertising item as if it were an ad. For example, a news report about your organization is published in a local newspaper, involving a space totaling 21 column inches including headline, story and photo. How can you evaluate this report? Using the advertising equivalency method, you would look up the advertising cost for a 21-inch ad in that newspaper. At $165 per column inch, for example, that story would have cost $3,465 if it were an advertisement.

That's a neat way to put a dollar figure on a news story, costing it out as if it were an ad. But that "as if" causes a big problem. A news story isn't an advertisement, so the dollar figure is meaningless. Why? Audiences know the difference between news and advertising, and they treat the two information vehicles differently. Generally news stories are far more credible than are advertisements. So how much extra should you add for credibility? On the other hand, news stories don't necessarily have only positive information about an organization. How much should you deduct because the news report wasn't glowingly positive? But wait. People read news stories more than they do ads. Perhaps you should add value because of higher audience attention? Back and forth it goes, and in the end any dollar value you give to the news story is simply a fiction, worse than worthless because it gives a false impression that a meaningful assessment has been made.

Despite the obvious misconception that underlies advertising equivalency, it's a myth that doesn't want to go away. Some public relations agencies even have devised formulas to impress their clients. For example, they calculate the value of publicity as being four times the cost of advertising. Or 10 times. Such arbitrary weighting schemes are all smoke and mirrors.

Evaluation of Awareness Objectives

The methods associated with outputs evaluation focus on documenting communication activity. But it is even more important to demonstrate the value that communication tactics offer an organization, specifically their effectiveness in achieving awareness, attitude and action objectives.

The first level of public relations objectives, awareness, provides an important category of evaluation research. *Awareness evaluation* focuses on the content of the message. It considers how many people were exposed to the message, how easy the message is to understand and how much of the message is remembered. Here are some of the common measures for awareness evaluation.

Message Exposure.   Measurement of message exposure, which focuses on the number of people in key publics who were exposed to the message, is a bit more sophisticated than the previous evaluation methodologies. That's because these measures look more closely at communication tactics, evaluating not only distribution but also audience attention.

For example, the evaluator may ask how many hits were registered at a Web site or the actual number of people in the audience who heard a speech or saw a performance. Instead of counting the number of news releases distributed, the evaluator would ask how many newspaper stories or broadcast reports resulted from the release, or more importantly, how many people actually read those stories or heard the broadcast reports. This is a more difficult number to obtain. Some public relations offices track this on their own; others hire *clipping services,* companies that track publications and/or broadcasts on a regional, national or even international basis.

Some measures of message exposure count actual audiences, such as the number of people who attended an open house or some other public relations event. Unfortunately, some other measures deal with inferred or potential audiences, weakening the value of this measure by linking it to mere estimates.

Some concepts associated with message exposure are drawn from advertising practice, which often considers *media impressions:* the potential total audience of people who could have been exposed to the message presented in various media, from interpersonal settings to viewers of a television newscast to motorists who pass by a billboard. Sometimes these calculations can be quite impressive, even seductive, such as the 1.1 billion impressions counted by MasterCard for its sponsorship of the 1994 World Cup Soccer Championship through public relations tactics such as news conferences, news releases, interviews and bylined columns.

Remember, however, that media impressions and other counts of message exposure may simply estimate audience size. Even if the count is an actual one, such measures indicate only how many people saw or heard the message. They don't indicate whether the audiences understood it, accepted it or acted on it in any way.

Still, despite little evidence that impression counts are an effective evaluation tool, many respectable public relations and marketing executives continue to use them. The Ketchum study (Corder et al., 1999) reported that 53 percent of respondents, all business-to-business marketing executives, track media impressions as their main approach to evaluation, though only 11 percent said they are happy with this.

Message Content.   An important type of evaluation focuses on the content of the message. Was it positive, or did it provide erroneous data? Unwarranted conclusions? Outdated information? It is far more important to analyze the content of a message than merely to count the number of newspaper clippings. Appendix A: Applied Research Techniques provides specific information on how to conduct a content analysis. For now, don't forget to include it prominently in your evaluation program.

Readability Measures.   Another way to evaluate awareness deals with comprehension—how easy a message is to understand. One of the first steps in developing a public relations plan is to identify and analyze the publics to be addressed. Part of that

Real-World Research Practices

Ketchum Public Relations surveyed 480 marketing executives (Corder et al., 1999) to learn how they evaluated their communication activities. Here are some highlights from this study:

Research Method	Percent Using this Method
Increase in sales volume	61
Number of news releases, direct mail and other tactics distributed	59
Number of impressions generated	53
Content analysis of key messages in reported stories	45
Advertising equivalency	37
Opinion change based on before-after surveys	33

More complete information can be found at the Ketchum Web site (www.ketchum.com).

analysis involves an assessment of their reading level, usually translated into the level of education they have achieved.

For example, most newspapers are written at about a ninth-grade reading level so everybody with that level of education or more—the vast majority of readers—should be able to understand the articles, columns and editorials. If you are preparing a news release or guest editorial for such a publication, plan on writing for readers with a ninth-grade reading ability. On the other hand, if you are writing a fundraising letter aimed at health-care professionals, it would be safe to presume that all your readers will have completed some level of higher education. Whatever you estimate to be the appropriate reading level, test your writing against that estimate.

Robert Gunning's Fog Index, which measures reading ease or difficulty, is one of the easiest readability measures to use; review the directions in the discussion of verbal communication in the Strategy section of this book. You should also be familiar with other commonly used readability instruments: Rudolf Flesch's Readability Score, which is more complicated than the Fog Index but which measures human interest; Edward Fry's Readability Graph, which relies on a chart to calculate reading ease; the Dale-Chall Formula, based on sentence length and the number of infrequently used words; the Cloze Procedure, which measures comprehension of spoken and visual messages; and Irving Fang's Easy Listening Formula, which provides a comparable way to calculate the comprehension of broadcast copy. Many computer word-processing programs feature one or more of these readership aids in the program's tools section.

Message Recall.   This approach involves techniques drawn from advertising research, where day-after recall studies are commonplace. Using this method, participants in interviews, surveys or focus groups are exposed to a news story, television program and so on. Then they are interviewed to determine what they remember from the message. A staple of research drawn from advertising is the Starch Readership Reports. These indicate three levels of reader study: "noted" readers, who remember having previously seen an advertisement; "associated" readers, who can link the advertisement with a particular brand or advertiser; and "read most" readers, who were able to describe most of the written material in the ad.

Here are two examples of how to measure awareness objectives.

> *Awareness objective:* To increase clients' understanding of changes in insurance policy coverage.
>
> *Possible evaluation technique:* Note exposure patterns; do content analysis to gauge how consistent the messages are with the facts; ask a focus group to discuss message recall.
>
> *Awareness objective:* To increase awareness of a new consumer product being manufactured by a client.
>
> *Possible evaluation technique:* Track dissemination of messages, noting the size of the potential audience; analyze the message content, noting its accuracy and the use of the client's telephone number and/or Web site address; survey customers in the company data base regarding message recall.

Evaluation of Acceptance Objectives

A major shortcoming of all the message-based evaluation techniques noted above is that they do not address the consequence of the public relations tactics. Instead, they simply gauge the existence of the tactics. At best, message-based evaluation techniques can deal with the level of awareness surrounding a public relations message.

A more effective area of evaluation, however, is based on levels of acceptance and action. Objectives in the Strategy phase note the desired impact on interest and attitudes (acceptance) and on opinion and behavior (action). Take steps now to evaluate how well each of those objectives has been achieved.

Audience Feedback.   Some evaluation measures count and analyze the voluntary reaction of the audience, such as the number of hits on a Web page, the number of telephone calls and letters, or the number of requests for additional information. This can be an effective measure of the level of the audience's information and interest.

Benchmark Studies.   *Benchmark studies* (also called *baseline studies*) provide a basis for comparing program outcomes against a standard. Actually, benchmark studies can be based on any of several different standards: the starting levels of interest or positive attitudes, outcomes of similar programs by other organizations, outcomes of the same program during a previous year or cycle, outcomes of industry or professional models, or the hypothetical outcomes of an "ideal" program.

Here are a couple of examples of how to evaluate acceptance-level objectives.

> *Acceptance objective: To enhance favorable employee attitudes toward a client's company.*
>
> *Possible evaluation techniques: Compare retention figures from before and after the tactic was implemented; record oral and written comments given to the human resource department of the company; solicit anecdotal input from managers and supervisors; survey employees about their attitudes and try to learn what they have been telling family and friends about working for the company.*

> *Acceptance objective: To increase employee affirmation of the company's need to change employee benefits.*
>
> *Possible evaluation techniques: Record immediate anecdotal feedback after the announcement is made; conduct a survey within two days of the announcement; after two weeks, invite employee feedback through response cards provided in pay envelopes.*

Evaluation of Action Objectives

The ultimate objectives for most public relations activities should focus on bottom-line issues for an organization, primarily the action sought from the key publics. In this evaluation phase of the planning process, careful consideration should be given to ways to measure these action objectives.

Audience Participation.   Figures on the number of people who actively responded to the message generally are easy to obtain. Attendance figures are effective measures when attendance itself is the desired objective, as may be the case with concerts and exhibitions, athletic competitions, benefit fund-raising events and so on. Implicit in these attendance figures also is a measure of the effectiveness of publicity and promotion that preceded the events.

However, attendance figures can be misused if the presumption is made that attendance at some information-sharing session necessarily equates with action impact. For example, attendance at an event in which a political candidate gives a major speech can't be used as a reliable indicator of either audience acceptance or action. People heard the speech and the message was presented, but desired action is not guaranteed. Therefore, be careful how attendance figures are interpreted and what value is placed on them.

Direct Observation.   Sometimes the simplest way to measure the effectiveness of action objectives is to look around. Let's say the objective sought an outcome of enough voter support to win an election. If your candidate won, your objective was achieved. If you sought financial contributions of $2.2 million, count the number of donations and pledges; anything above the target amount means you were that much more successful than planned. Other easy-to-quantify objectives deal with capacity attendance for sporting and artistic events, sales figures, academic scores, membership expectations and so on.

In some instances, the action objective deals with the general outcome rather than with any quantification. For example, passage (or defeat) of a particular piece of legislation may fully satisfy an action objective.

Some evaluation research calls for strategic and creative thinking. Individual behaviors that may not be easily observable are more difficult to measure than the preceding examples. Here are two examples of how to deal with difficult-to-evaluate action objectives.

> **Action objective:** *To increase the use of seat belts.*
>
> **Possible evaluation technique:** *Place observers in highway toll booths, and have them record the number of drivers and driver-side passengers wearing seatbelts as they pass through the booths.*
>
> **Action objective:** *To have elementary, secondary and college teachers become more active in lobbying state government for increased support of education.*
> **Possible evaluation techniques:** *In a tactic encouraging sending e-mail letters to state officials, attach instructions for sending a copy to your organization. Then simply count the number of copies received. To take this to a higher level of sophistication, work with several sympathetic state legislators; compare the number of e-mail messages sent to their office with the number of copies you received. From the difference, extrapolate the number of messages sent by teachers to all legislators.*

Some of the benchmark techniques for evaluating acceptance objectives, noted above, can be equally useful for evaluating action objectives.

Phase Four

Step
9

How to Measure Publicity Effects

Measuring the effects of media relations takes a bit of creativity, but it's not impossible. Consider the following possibilities:

- Set clear objectives in advance and establish the criteria that will form the basis for success.
- Use a pre-test, such as an awareness survey, to identify the beginning point. Follow this with a parallel post-test to measure changes in awareness.
- Use a focus group to probe the relationship between awareness, acceptance and action.

- Track media placement with clippings and logs. Evaluate these not only in terms of distribution and use and other measures of audience exposure, but also conduct some form of content analysis to evaluate the effectiveness of the message itself.
- Build in some kind of measurement of action, such as noting changes in attendance, traffic, purchase, or other behaviors associated with the campaign.

Data Analysis

Having gathered the data through a variety of means, it is now time to analyze it carefully. Match the observed and reported results with the expectations outlined in your statement of objectives. If the program failed to meet its objectives, do some further analysis. Try to learn if the shortfall was because of a flawed strategy that undergirded the program or because the tactics were not implemented as effectively as they might have been. Consider also if there might be a flaw in the evaluation techniques used to gather the data.

If evaluation of the program is particularly important, ask an outside auditor to review the data. For some formal presentations of research findings, in order to enhance credibility, an organization may ask an outside expert or a panel of stakeholders to attest to the validity of the tools used in the evaluation research.

Evaluation Reports

After the evaluation is completed and the information gathered and analyzed, make sure it is presented in a form that is understandable and accessible to decision makers within the organization. They usually are busy executives and managers with global but not necessarily specific understandings of the issue. They may not have a high level of insight or information about the program, so be careful not to obscure evaluation findings in the final report. Instead, be very clear, draw obvious conclusions and highlight the most important data.

If the decision makers have been involved in establishing the objectives of the program, they probably will be disposed to using the evaluation findings. Another way to increase the likelihood that the evaluation will be used is to concentrate on elements that can be changed in subsequent programs.

Evaluative Research: Who Uses What?

The various types of evaluative research used in this book loosely parallel the categories that D. M. Dozier (1984) identified:

- Seat-of-the-pants evaluation (what this book calls judgmental assessment)
- Scientific dissemination (evaluation of awareness objectives)
- Scientific impact (evaluation of acceptance and action objectives)

Dozier studied public relations practitioners and noted the kind of research they used to evaluate programs and projects. He found that most practitioners he identified as communication technicians (that is, practitioners generally in entry-level jobs with little decision-making responsibilities) showed no patterns as to the type of research they did. The exception to this was media relations specialists, who favored the scientific dissemination type that measured awareness objectives, such as distribution, placement, media impressions and readability.

He also found that communication managers supplemented the seat-of-the-pants evaluation that relied heavily on their professional experience with scientific impact type of evaluation, the kind of evaluation that used quantitative research methods to measure the more advanced objectives, such as those dealing with acceptance and action.

Structure of the Evaluation Report

There is much variety within evaluation reports, which can be of several types. These may be presented separately or merged into a single report. The report itself can take the form of a formal document, an oral presentation or a meeting agenda item.

Whether written or presented orally, evaluation reports should be carefully crafted to clearly link the expectations outlined in the objectives with the outcomes. Here are several elements to include. Note how these outcomes were measured, discuss the degree to which they achieved the objectives, and note the significance of this achievement (or lack of it). Finally, make clear recommendations closely linked with the data. For reports of major significance, visual elements such as photographs, tables and charts can enhance the understanding of readers and listeners.

Evaluation reports sometimes become the basis of a news release or even a news conference if the topic under review is one that is particularly newsworthy. For example, the final evaluation of public relations programs on popular and highly visible social issues such as campaigns to reduce drug abuse or teen pregnancy may warrant a news report.

Any evaluation report longer than five pages should be preceded by an executive summary that provides an overview of the findings and a simplified set of recommendations. An executive summary serves the needs of those decision makers, sometimes the most important ones, who may not have the time to digest the longer document.

The Ultimate Evaluation: Value-Added Public Relations

Most evaluation of public relations and other strategic communication programs focus on objectives and tactics: What did we do? What did we accomplish by doing it? And how did this achieve what we set out to do? These questions are very important. But there is another, equally important, question to be asked and answered: What did public relations do for the organization as a whole?

Once again a reminder: The premise underlying *Strategic Planning for Public Relations* is that strategic communication is about more than tactics and mere activities. Rather, it deals with the overall planned program of both proactive and reactive communication that enhances the relationship between an organization and its various publics, a relationship that needs to be linked to the bottom-line concerns of the organization. You might call it value-added public relations, the notion that public relations adds value and benefit to the organization as a whole.

Based on qualitative interview research with both public relations practitioners and their CEOs, Linda Childers Hon (1997) reported six such values that effective public relations brings to organizations or to the clients of a consultant or agency. Keep these in mind as you complete your evaluation and present it to your client or organization.

1. Effective public relations helps organizations survive, by reversing negative opinions, promoting awareness of organizational benefits to the community and effecting balanced media coverage.

2. Effective public relations helps organizations make money, by generating publicity about products and services as well as the organization's plans and accomplishments; attracting new customers, volunteers, donors and stockholders; and improving employee performance and productivity.

3. Effective public relations helps other organizational functions make money, by creating an environment of understanding and goodwill, influencing supportive legislation and enhancing fundraising efforts.

4. Effective public relations helps organizations save money, by inducing favorable legislation, retaining members and minimizing negative publicity during crisis incidents.

5. Effective public relations helps organization weaken opposition, by generating favorable public opinion and obtaining cooperation from governmental and other organizations.

6. Effective public relations helps organizations save lives, through social goals such as advancing highway safety, medical care and research, and so on.

Strategic Planning Example: **Evaluating the Strategic Plan**

Upstate College will evaluate its Initiative on Transfer Students according to the following plan:

1. Placement report tracking distribution and media use of news releases and other materials disseminated by the public relations department.

Evaluation Schedule

1. Timeline for implementation report
2. Timeline for progress report
3. Timeline for final evaluation

Evaluation Program Checklist

Is this evaluation program

✓ Useful to the organization?

✓ Clearly linked to established objectives?

✓ Appropriate as to cost?

✓ Appropriate as to time?

✓ Appropriate as to other resources?

✓ Ethical and socially responsible?

✓ Credible, with accurate data?

✓ Doable?   ∎

Phase Four

Step
9

Citations and Recommended Readings

Bissland, J. H. (1990). Accountability gap: Evaluation practices show improvement. *Public Relations Review, 16 (2)*, 25–35.

Broom, G., & Dozier, D. (1990). *Using research in public relations: Applications to program management*. Englewood Cliffs, NJ: Prentice Hall.

Corder L., Deasy, M., & Thompson, J. (1999). Answering the age-old marketing question: What have you done for me lately? *Public Relations Tactics, (May)*, 12.

Dozier, D. M. (1984). Program evaluation and the roles of practitioners. *Public Relations Review, 10 (2)*, 13–21.

Evaluation research on the rise, study finds. (1994). In P. Jackson (Ed.), P*ractical, actionable research for public relations purposes*. Exeter, NH: PR Publishing.

Fischer, R. (1995). Control construct design in evaluating campaigns. *Public Relations Review, 21 (1)*, 45–58.

Gofton, K. (1999). The measure of PR: Measurement and evaluation of public relations campaigns. *Campaign, (April 2)*, S13 (1).

Hon, L. C. (1998). Demonstrating effectiveness in public relations: Goals, objectives, and evaluation. *Journal of Public Relations Research, 10 (2)*, 103–135.

Hon, L. C. (1997). What have you done for me lately? Exploring effectiveness in public relations. *Journal of Public Relations Research, 9 (1)*, 1–30.

Lindenmann, W. K. (1997). *Guidelines and standards for measuring and evaluating PR effectiveness*. www.instituteforpr.com. Also see Lindenmann, W. K. (1997). Setting minimum standards for measuring public relations effectiveness. *Public Relations Review, 213 (1)*, 391–408.

Planning, goals and measurement (Corporate Communications Benchmark 1997, Section III). Cited in Written PR plans now common—but many not integrated. (1997) *PR Reporter, (Aug. 25)*, 3–4.

Rossi, P. H., & Freeman, H. E. (1993). *Evaluation: A systematic approach*. Newbury Park, CA: Sage.

Weiner, M. (1995). Put client "values" ahead of newsclips when measuring *PR. PR Services, (March)*, 48.

Wiener, N. (1954). *The human use of human beings: Cybernetics and society* (2nd ed.). Boston: Houghton Mifflin.

Appendix A

Applied Research Techniques

Academic Research and Applied Research

As a student, you already should be familiar with academic research from journals and textbooks. **Academic research** generates theory, explores new interests and focuses on universal knowledge. This is knowledge for its own sake, also called *theoretical research, basic research* or *pure research*.

In your professional life beyond the classroom, however, you are more likely to deal in **applied research** (sometimes called *market research* or *administrative research*), which delves into the practical problems faced by an organization and guides effective resolution of those problems. Your bosses and clients will ask you to get information as quickly and inexpensively as possible to help solve their very real problems. Your applied research may contribute to the theory base of your profession, but that is a side benefit; its primary role is to deal with practical matters for your client.

This appendix gives you a how-to guide to several techniques for doing applied research. In addition to discussing the ethics of research, we'll also look at sampling techniques, secondary research, interviews, focus groups, case studies, surveys and content analysis.

Each research technique in this section takes you through a four-phase process of (1) defining the research problem, (2) designing a way to obtain information, (3) actually gathering the information and (4) analyzing your findings and applying them.

Appropriate Research Topics

Applied research is especially important when program planning brings together a specialist (you) working for an expert (your boss or client), because the research can help prevent problems by putting both the specialists and the experts more in touch with their publics.

Take, for example, the experience of a senior campaigns class in which university students developed a comprehensive public relations and advertising program for a new space exhibit at a science museum. The museum had a wealth of marketing research, but as part of the course assignment the four student teams tried out several different strategic concepts on a sampling of their target public: school children and their parents. This research paid off.

Academic Versus Applied Research Topics

Most of the studies published in the *Journal of Public Relations Research* deal with academic research, which by its nature is public and meant to be shared, challenged and continuously developed. Here are some topics from the last few years: attribution theory and crisis communication, contingency theory of accommodation, rhetorical-organizational approach to organizational identity, knowledge predictors, integrated symmetrical model of crisis communication, self-efficacy theory, image and symbolic leadership, and information processing and situational theory. Several other journals also publish academic research focused on public relations.

Applied research more often than not remains unpublished because it is proprietary, meaning that it is conducted for and owned by a particular client. A review of the Web sites of several major public relations agencies indicates they have conducted the following research topics for specific clients and companies: Media content analysis, survey of residents to identify a location for a chemical plant, monitoring legislation and conducting legislative research, corporate reputation, impact of public relations and advertising programs, Internet monitoring, audience surveys, surveys of the impact of congressional hearings, and audience analysis of sports organizations to increase both fan and corporate support.

One team considered three different themes: a digitized close-up of a man in a spacesuit with the slogan "Put Your Face in Space"; a rocket being fired from its launch pad with the slogan "Blast Off! Explore the infinite possibilities"; and a close-up of a footprint on the moon with the slogan "Space. Touch it!" When they presented the three possible approaches to the museum CEO and his marketing and public relations directors, the clients were enthusiastic and unanimous. They really liked the footprint, because it so poignantly reflected the Apollo 11 lunar landing. But the students cautioned: "Don't jump to conclusions. Our research supports the second option; it shows that the children you want to attract like the action of the space launch much more. For them, the footprint from the first moon landing is part of history, not something that excites their imagination." Applied research prevented a false start with a misguided theme.

Do-It-Yourself Research

Many research experts offer a simple warning: Don't try this at home! Research methodologies can be incredibly complex, and many pitfalls exist for the novice who plunges headlong into research using inappropriate techniques that result in inaccurate data and unwarranted conclusions. Clearly some issues are so critical and the needed research so important that you really should get professional research assistance.

Nevertheless, the research techniques explained here are not impossible for the do-it-yourselfer. The key is knowing when you should do it yourself and when to call in an expert.

Consider the following generalization: You might do your own research when you have the time, interest, patience and self-confidence; when you don't need highly accurate statistics and other data; when the decisions riding on the study are relatively minor in terms of your organization's overall mission; or when your budget is such that the choice is between doing your own research or doing none at all.

Should You Do Your Own Research?

1. Do you need objective data?
2. Can you be objective in your study even though it involves your own organization?
3. Do you have the ability to conduct the study?
4. Do you have the time and other resources to conduct the study?
5. Does your organization, boss or client have enough confidence in you to respect and use your findings?

6. Can you tolerate less-precise statistics than a professional researcher might generate?

If you answered "yes" to each question, you probably can conduct your own research project. If you answered "no" to any question, find a professional researcher.

Research Ethics

Ethics deals with the rightness or wrongness of behavior, especially professional or organizational behavior (as compared with personal morality). Social science research involves several areas that can pose ethical risks and temptations.

Most colleges and universities have clearly defined policies related to research ethics. So do many companies and public relations counseling agencies. Specific standards may vary, but some common ground can be found in many ethical guidelines. Broadly speaking, the areas of common ground deal with the treatment of the people involved in the research study and the use of information.

Ethical Treatment of People

Below are eight guidelines for dealing ethically with people involved in research programs or projects. These principles apply to the kind of applied research that is common in public relations and marketing research, such as interviews, focus groups and surveys. These principles do not apply to content analysis, because no active participants are involved in that kind of research.

1. *Respect the dignity of participants* in every study. This is the umbrella that covers all the other principles. It is rooted in common sense and decent interaction with people. Most colleges and universities, as well as other research organizations, have formal requirements for research involving human subjects, so make sure your research is in compliance with these regulations.

2. *Respect the privacy of participants.* Abide fully by any privacy commitments that are made. Note the difference between anonymity and confidentiality. *Anonymity* means the participant's identity will not be known to anybody, including the researcher, and cannot be linked to his or her particular response. *Confidentiality* means the researcher will not disclose the participant's identity nor allow it to be linked to his or her particular responses. Anonymity is

difficult for most public relations research: interviews and focus groups obviously can't be anonymous, and it is difficult to maintain anonymity for surveys that require more than one mailing. Confidentiality is the more likely protection for participants. Remember that any privacy guarantees extend beyond the time of the research study; questionnaires and notes should be stored in a non-public place and should be discarded when they are no longer needed.

3. *Seek only voluntary participation by respondents.* Would-be participants in interviews, focus groups and surveys should be told explicitly that they may choose not to participate. They must be allowed to decline at the beginning of the research activity or to end their participation at any point. The voluntariness of participation is less of an issue with mail or phone surveys, where respondents can easily ignore the questionnaire or hang up on the researcher.

4. *Obtain informed consent.* Participants should be told enough about the research project so they clearly know what they are being asked to do. When a person agrees to participate in an interview, survey or focus group, informed consent can logically be presumed, and asking participants to sign consent statements could negate a guarantee of anonymity that might be part of the project. Increasingly, however, researchers are asking participants in studies involving sensitive matters to sign a consent form; the confidentiality issue can be handled by having the consent form separate from any questionnaire that is part of the research tool. Consent forms are generally used for experiments, and they are becoming more common with other types of public relations or marketing research. Informed consent extends to practical matters, such as telling respondents how much time will be expected for their participation.

5. *Disclose the purpose of the research* to the participants. In some cases the researcher does not want to indicate the full purpose, because this might contaminate the results by causing the respondents to provide less-than-truthful information. Even if the respondents try to be truthful, knowing too much about the project could bias the responses. However, the respondents or participants have the right to know at least the general purpose of the study. And participants generally can be told the purpose of the research when their role is ended.

6. *Disclose the identity of the researcher.* Active participants should know who you are and that you are conducting research.

7. *Disclose the identity of the research sponsor.* Would-be respondents and other participants have the right to know the name of the organization sponsoring and benefiting from the research. As with the item above about the purpose of the research, the identity of the research sponsor may be withheld until the conclusion of the study, so participants can act and provide information without bias.

8. *Inform participants of the research results.* By debriefing participants, the researcher can explain the study and allow each participant to see himself or herself in relation to the total sample. Especially if the researcher concealed information about the purpose or sponsor to ensure candid responses by the participants, explaining to them afterward can make up for the deception.

Ethical Use of Research Data

Three ethical considerations are paramount related to the use of research data for public relations and marketing research of the kind considered in this book. Different ethical principles would apply to more experimental or laboratory-based social research.

1. *Develop a fair research process.*   Draw samples with great care so that they are likely to represent the target population, and don't yield to the temptation to obtain simply an easy or quick sample. In reporting your research, acknowledge any shortcoming in the sampling process.

2. *Develop fair measurement tools.*   Questions and response items should be designed to elicit honest responses, and research participants should not be tricked into giving information they don't believe in. Manipulation and coercion have no place in research.

3. *Analyze and report data ethically.*   Treat each piece of data with great respect; never fudge or falsify any data. Discard any data that is unclear, indecipherable or otherwise contaminated. In analyzing the data, draw only those conclusions justified by the information obtained; never discount or misinterpret data in favor of your own bias or your client's wishes. Fully report the circumstances of the research project: its geography and time frame, sampling techniques and methodology. Include copies of questionnaires and other data-gathering tools.

Sampling

The purpose of research is to describe various characteristics (such as the level of information, the existence of attitudes or opinions, or the extent of certain behaviors) of a *population,* which is a large group of subjects that are of interest to the researcher. For example, depending on the interests of the researcher, the residents of Kansas could be a population; so too Asian athletes at Kansas colleges and universities, or restaurants with vegetarian menus in the Sunflower State. Individual *elements* of the population (also called *units of analysis*) usually are people, but they can also be organizations, products, media artifacts such as news reports or editorials, public relations artifacts such as news releases or brochures, or advertising artifacts such as television commercials or print ads. Each research activity also has a particular *time period* (usually defined in weeks, months or years) and an *extent* (a geographic location such as a region, state or neighborhood).

Sometimes we conduct a *census* by including every member of the population in our study, such as a small business that polls every employee about an issue of company-wide interest.

Other times, however, it is impractical to poll every member of a very large or scattered population. In such cases, a good alternative is **sampling:** the identification of a subset of the population of individuals (or objects) who reflect and represent the larger body. This subset is known as a **sample.** The value of sampling is that it saves time and money, and it allows researchers to study a small group and then use those findings to make predictions for a much larger population. Depending on how a sample is pulled together, it may or may not be based on the concept of *probability*, which means that every element in the population has an equal chance of being selected for the sample.

To help you understand sampling, consider the analogy of cooking stew. A cook mixes a variety of vegetables and herbs in a pot, then stirs—that's the key. Presumably the stirring has mixed all the ingredients evenly. The cook then dips the ladle and takes a taste. No need to eat the entire pot to determine if more seasoning is needed; one ladle from a well-stirred pot provides a true sampling of the entire stew.

Over the years, the accuracy of polling has improved tremendously. Consider three national presidential polls. In 1936 the influential *Literary Digest* forecast that Alf Landon would beat Franklin Roosevelt 57 to 43 percent. Instead, Roosevelt easily won re-election with a landslide 61 percent of the vote. In 1948, the Roper Poll predicted that Thomas Dewey would beat Harry Truman by a five-point margin in the presidential election. Instead, Truman won by five points. In contrast, in the 1996 presidential election, the Gallup Poll predicted that Bill Clinton would receive 52 percent of the vote; he received 50.1 percent.

The evolution of polling accuracy lies in the improved sampling techniques. The *Literary Digest* polled 2,000,000 people using a volunteer sampling frame including telephone listings (in 1936, phones were for the well-to-do) and country club memberships, favoring the wealthy and excluding the poor. The 1948 poll was a cluster sample of 20,000, weighted toward the rural, Republican voters rather than the urban, Democratic voters. The 1996 sample of about 1,200 respondents was more scientifically selected and thus more accurate. Note that progressively smaller but more representative samples yielded greater accuracy.

Sampling can be largely divided into nonprobability and probability techniques.

Nonprobability Sampling

Nonprobability sampling involves a variety of techniques in which samples are chosen simply, quickly and inexpensively. It allows subjects to be selected even if they cannot be identified ahead of time. However, because subjects are chosen with no great care as to their makeup, nonprobability sampling has limited effectiveness. Here are five types of nonprobability samples: convenience, volunteer, purposive, snowball and quota.

Convenience Sampling.   *Convenience sampling* draws subjects because they are readily available to the researcher, such as people walking through a shopping mall, students enrolled in a particular college course, or participants in so-called (but not really) "random" street-corner interviews by reporters. This type of sampling generally is an unreliable indicator of a larger population, unless that population is, for example, shoppers at a particular mall.

Volunteer Sampling.   Another sampling technique, *volunteer sampling,* uses subjects who ask to be included in the research study. One example of self-selected samples is magazines that invite readers to respond to a printed questionnaire; another is radio talk show hosts who invite listeners to phone in with their comments. The problem with volunteer sampling is that it sometimes is interpreted as being representative when it really isn't. What should we think about the situation in which the talk show callers overwhelmingly support a political candidate who nevertheless is soundly defeated at the polls? We should remember that the callers are not representative of the voters, perhaps not even of all the program's listeners. They merely are those listeners who felt strongly enough about the issue and took the time to express their opinion.

Purposive Sampling. *Purposive sampling* (sometimes called *judgment sampling*) includes research subjects chosen simply because they have certain characteristics. For example, they may be people who were patients in a particular hospital, or they may be individuals who drive a particular brand of automobile. But remember that they are not representative of the entire population of hospital patients or motorists.

Snowball Sampling. The technique of *snowball sampling* (also called *socio-samples*) begins with a small group of individuals with a certain characteristic who are asked to identify others to participate in the research. This technique often is used for populations where member lists do not exist and whose members are hard to identify, at least by outsiders.

Quota Sampling. *Quota sampling* is an attempt to be more representative of the population. It involves the selection of subjects to fit a predetermined percentage. For example, if 40 percent of a company's employees have college degrees, then 40 percent of the company's sample in a study of employee attitudes also should have college degrees. Appropriate quota categories include age, gender, ethnicity, religion, occupation, geography and other demographic factors. But like the purposive sampling, quota sampling is haphazard because it is not representative of the entire population under study; instead it reflects only one characteristic (or a couple of characteristics) that the researcher considers most important.

Advantages and Disadvantages of Nonprobability Sampling. The limitation of any type of nonprobability sample is that it gives no reasonable certainty that findings will be representative of the larger population. And to be useful, most sampling research must be applicable to the entire population rather than to only the relatively few people sampled.

Still, nonprobability sampling is not without its good side. These techniques do have a legitimate role for public relations and marketing research. You should consider using nonprobability sampling in the following situations:

- When the purpose of the study is to gain general, nonspecific insight into a particular group.
- When a high margin of error is not a major concern.
- When the budget does not allow for more costly probability sampling.
- When the schedule does not allow for more time-consuming probability sampling.

But remember: Avoid using a nonprobability sample when you want to be able to project the findings of your research onto a larger population.

Probability Sampling

Probability sampling techniques, which follow the guidelines of mathematical probability, generally gain higher respect among researchers. When the research study seeks to learn the attitudes, opinions or behaviors of a large number of people, probability sampling ensures that every element within the population has an equal and known chance of being selected. Thus, some researchers refer to probability sampling techniques as *EPSEM samples* (Equal Probability of Selection Method). By using probability sampling, the researcher can legitimately calculate how accurately the sampled findings reflect the entire population.

Probability sampling requires that the researcher is able to identify every *sampling unit,* which is the individual element to be analyzed. Sampling units reflect the range noted earlier for population elements; they usually are people but also may be organizations, products and artifacts. The actual listing of sampling units is called the *sampling frame.* Often these are membership rosters or other comprehensive directories. Some random samples have been based on telephone directories, though phone books generally are bad choices for general populations because they screen out people without phone service and those with unlisted numbers. This is an example of *sampling bias,* when the sampling technique itself introduces an element of weakness into the process.

Another example of sampling bias can be related to the timing of the data gathering. Consider, for example, a restaurant that has a busy professional lunch crowd, an early-bird dinner special that caters to college students and senior citizens, a formal and relatively upscale dinner crowd and a trendy after-theater clientele. A study that draws its sample from only the early-bird group would yield significantly different results than one drawing from each of the four customer groups.

Following are four types of probability sampling: simple random, systematic, stratified and cluster.

Simple Random Sampling.   The basic type of probability sampling is *simple random sampling,* exemplified by lottery-style drawings such as pulling names from a hat. Researchers often use a table of random numbers to select the subjects for their study. For example, if you are researching the behavior of 5,000 college students, you might work with a list from the registrar's office and assign every student a number, 0001 through 5000. Let's say you decide to have 250 respondents. Simply generate a list of 250 random four-digit numbers between one and 5,000, match them up to the numbered names, and interview the students.

The major advantage of random sampling is that it produces a sampling in which everyone in the population has an equal chance of being selected. This provides a generally unbiased group of respondents, which, in turn, is good for a research study seeking to project findings for the entire group. Random sampling is particularly good when a population is homogenous, with no significant divisions within it.

But simple random sampling has two major disadvantages. First, it requires a sampling frame, which may not be available for all target populations. Second, while random sampling gives every element within the population an equal chance of being selected, it does not necessarily produce a representative sampling if significant subsets exist within the population. For example, a sample of 250 students identified randomly out of a population of 5,000 could produce no students majoring in a foreign language. That could be a limitation, especially if the study dealt with something like international exchange programs, language requirements for graduation or student fees for language labs.

Systematic Sampling.   *Systematic sampling* (or *systematic interval sampling*) involves the selection of subjects spaced at equal intervals, such as every n^{th} name on a membership roster. Let's stay with the example of the survey of college students. If you do the simple math and divide 5,000 by 250, then you would select every 20th name from your sampling frame. To make the systematic sampling truly unbiased, use a systematic sampling with a random start. This involves a random selection of the starting number (in this case, a number from 1 to 20). Don't use systematic sampling if a particular order or recurring pattern exists within the ranking. For example, if a listing of sororities always begins with the names of officers, then a systematic sampling of every 15th name with a starting number of 2 would result in a sampling top-heavy with sorority vice presidents—not very random after all.

Stratified Sampling.   A modification of random and systematic techniques is *stratified sampling*. This sampling technique involves a ranking of elements on a list, such as four subset lists (freshmen, sophomores, juniors and seniors) for your study of college students. Other relevant demographic categories for research might include age, gender, income, religion, media use, academic major and product use. By stratifying the list by important characteristics, the researcher is able to ensure a greater likelihood that the sample will be representative of the population. One problem with stratified sampling is that the subsets may indicate more than they appear to. For example, subsets related to residency in different parts of a city may reflect not only geography but also different ethnic, occupational or socioeconomic patterns.

Stratified sampling may be *proportionate,* with research sizes based on their proportion in the population, such as a research project with a sample of 45 percent males and 55 percent females used for a college with a student population of the same gender proportions. Or it may be *disproportionate* (also called *weighted*) if particular attention is given to underrepresented members of a population. Using the college scenario, if the student population is 10 percent Hispanic, the researcher may want to have a sample of more than 10 percent Hispanics so a wider range of comments might be obtained from the research participants.

Cluster Sampling.   *Cluster sampling* (also called *multistage sampling*) is used when the researcher can't readily generate a list of the entire population but can obtain listings of particular groups within the population. For example, if your research population was all college and university students within your state, you could have a difficult time putting together a complete sampling frame listing every student in the state from which to draw a random, systematic or stratified sample. But using the cluster sampling technique, you first would identify several schools (either randomly or through a stratified technique based on criteria such as size or location), then select individual students (randomly, systematically or through stratified techniques) using separate sampling frames, such as enrollment lists obtained from each school identified in the first stage.

Sample Error and Size

In textbooks dedicated to research methodologies, you can find sophisticated information about research statistics. To simplify things here, let's consider a few key terms that deal with the inevitable limitations of sampling.

The *sampling error* (sometimes called the *margin of error*) is the extent to which the sample does not perfectly correspond with the target population. Sampling error usually is reported as a percentage. For example, a finding of 62 percent with a sampling error of ±3 percent indicates that the finding actually could fall between 59 percent and 65 percent. The statistic used to describe sampling error is called the *standard error* (more correctly, the *standard error of the mean*).

Since sampling is an imperfect reflection of the population, researchers always expect some sampling error. Researchers have sophisticated ways to calculate sampling error.

What is the ideal number of subjects for a research study? There is no single answer to this question, because so much depends upon what the researcher needs to accomplish. Focus groups use only a few people, generally five to 12 for each session. Surveys for pretest studies may use a sample of 15 to 30 subjects.

Two concepts about sample size often are difficult for non-researchers to grasp. First, a bigger sample doesn't necessarily mean better results. Second, the appropriate size of the sample is not based in any way on a percentage or fraction of the population. In general, samples of 200 to 400 are commonplace.

Roger Wimmer and Joseph Dominick (1999) note that researchers often use a sample of 100 subjects for each relevant demographic group likely have to distinctive characteristics (for example, 100 males and 100 females; or 100 each of undergraduates, graduate students and alumni). Walter K. Lindenmann (1977), then research director at Ketchum Public Relations, gave the following guidelines for samples with a 5 percent margin of error: 278 for a population of 1,000; 322 for 2,000; 355 for 5,000; 370 for 10,000; 381 for 50,000; 383 for 100,000; and 384 for an infinite number.

One thing is certain: Larger doesn't necessarily mean better. Very good research can be based on modest sample sizes. The idea underlying sampling is to use the smallest number of research subjects that can accurately predict characteristics of the population. A small but appropriate sample is better than a larger but haphazard one. Remember also that the smaller the sample size, the less expensive the study will be, the less time it will take and the easier it will be to calculate, analyze and report.

A common way of determining sample size is first to decide what margin of error you can tolerate in your sample. If the answer is "zero," you are headed for a census of the entire population, rather than a sampling. But think again, because research seldom requires perfect data. Even if your client or boss wants that, there probably isn't enough money in the budget to achieve it, unless the target population is very small.

Secondary Research

One of the first steps in conducting research is to conduct **secondary research**—that is, research conducted to find out what information already is available through existing sources. This is distinguished from **primary research,** which generates new data collected specifically for this investigation.

Advantages and Disadvantage of Secondary Information

Why use existing information? Because it's there, and thus less expensive to analyze than if you gather new data. Secondary research also is helpful in refining the research topic, building files of previous findings, keeping current with new developments in the field and providing a launch point for your own additional research.

When using secondary information, evaluate it carefully. Consider the circumstances surrounding the data, such as when and how it was gathered, for what purpose, by what researcher, with what sample; most especially, consider the objectivity with which it was gathered. All these factors can affect the usefulness of the information to your situation. However, if the data is relevant, it can save you much time and money. Even if you have to purchase the data from a commercial information service, it still may be more cost effective than mounting your own primary research activity.

Remember that even though you are interested in applied research for a particular client, you still can learn a lot from academic research. Because it is seeking insights into topics more than solutions to specific problems, academic research can provide valuable background information.

Types of Secondary Information

Secondary information is available in many different sources, including organizational files, trade and professional associations, public and academic libraries, government records, commercial information companies, and computer-assisted or online research sources. Let's look briefly at each.

Organizational Files.   Information in the organizational files of your employer or client can provide a wealth of information for researchers and practitioners. Many public relations offices include extensive files of news releases, brochures, annual reports and internal documents, as well as information files about relevant issues. Some organizations also have extensive archives with historical data and artifacts.

Trade and Professional Associations.   Industry groups may offer much useful information for public relations and marketing researchers. For example, the Public Relations Society of America has extensive files about various aspects of public relations that it makes available to members. The *Encyclopedia of Associations* lists thousands of professional groups that can be very helpful in obtaining information about a specific industry.

Public and Academic Libraries.   Public libraries in towns and cities as well as academic libraries on college and university campuses provide an accessible source of information. Information also may be available in specialized libraries such as those operated by companies, museums, industries, hospitals, professional organizations and so on. Materials available in libraries can be categorized as *one-step resources* that provide information directly (such as encyclopedias and textbooks) and *two-step resources* that direct the researcher to information in other sources (such as indexes and directories).

Government Records.   Information gathered by governmental agencies is available both in public and academic libraries and directly from the agencies themselves. Vast amounts of information are generated by the U.S. Census Bureau, which actually produces 11 different censuses (population, governments, agriculture, housing, transportation, manufacturing, mineral industries, selected construction industries, selected service industries, retail trade and wholesale trade). Other information is available from individual federal agencies dealing with commerce, education, labor, justice and so on. A useful guide to information available through the federal government is the monthly *American Statistics Index* compiled by the Congressional Information Service or the annual *Statistical Abstract of the United States;* both publications are available in most libraries.

Much information is available from state, county and city/local governments. Additionally, individual foreign nations have information available to varying degrees, and the United Nations provides information about countries and about various global issues.

Commercial Information Services.   Commercial sources of information include polling firms such as the Gallup Organization, Harris Polls, Roper Starch Worldwide and Yankelovich Partners. Other polling centers are associated with higher education, such as the National Opinion Research Center at the University of Chicago or the Marist College Bureau of Economic Research. Meanwhile, the Roper Center for Public Opinion Research at the University of Connecticut conducts no research of its own but instead serves as an archive (updated daily) for research from more than 125 research organizations. Trade and professional associations also are sources of syndicated data. Media-ratings companies such as Arbitron and A. C. Nielsen also have useful demographic data.

Stanford Research Institute pioneered the VALS system (Values and LifeStyles) of *psychographics,* which combines demographic and lifestyle data. Other companies have begun offering census-based marketing services using a technique called *geodemography,* which combines census and other demographic information with zip codes, census tracts and other data to describe the characteristics of particular neighborhoods and the people who live in them. Geodemography has proved very useful for marketing and fund-raising purposes. Sources of this information include PRIZM (Potential Rating Index Zip Markets) created by the Claritas Corporation, Strategic Mapping's ClusterPLUS, Equifax's MicroVision and ACORN by CACI.

Computer–Assisted or On-Line Research.   Information searches conducted via computer are becoming increasingly common. CD-ROM and on-line sources can provide data direct from sources such as the Census Bureau or through commercial

---

Internet Information Sites

A. C. Nielsen Corporation: www.acnielsen.com

Arbitron Company: www.arbitron.com

CACI Marketing systems/ACORN: www.caci.com

Claritas/PRIZM: www.claritas.com

Equifax: www.equifax.com

Gallup Organization: www.gallup.com

Harris Polls: www.harrispollonline.com

LEXIS/NEXIS: www.lexis-nexis.com

Marist Research: www.marist.edu/management/bureau

National Opinion Research Center: www.norc.uchicago.edu

Psychological Abstracts: www.apa.org/psycinfo

Roper Center for Public Opinion Research: www.ropercenter.uconn.edu

Roper Starch Worldwide: www.roper.com

Sociological Abstracts: www.socabs.org

Stanford Research Institute/VALS: www.future.sri.com/vals

U.S. Department of the Census: www.census.gov

Yankelovich Partners: www.yankelovich.com

---

databases. Sources for online information can be identified through directories such as the *Directory of On-Line Databases* and the *Directory of On-Line Portable Databases,* both published by Gale Research. The Cambridge Information Group publishes *FINDEX: The Directory of Market Research Reports, Studies, and Surveys,* and British Overseas Trade Board prepares *Marketsearch: International Directory of Published Market Research.* Some online resources helpful to public relations and marketing practitioners include *AMI* (Advertising and Marketing Intelligence), *LEXIS/NEXIS, Foundation Directory, National Newspapers Index, Wilson Index,* and the *Dow Jones News/Retrieval,* as well as *Psychological Abstracts* and *Sociological Abstracts.*

With its ability to connect you directly with the home pages of many businesses, nonprofits and other organizations, the Internet is a powerful research tool. However, there is also plenty of garbage and gossip on the Web. In judging the quality of information you find on the Internet, ask yourself the following questions:

- Is the source or sponsor of the information indicated?
- Is the information source respected?
- Is the information source knowledgeable about the subject?
- Is the information source free from bias on the subject?
- Is the information presented in an objective manner?
- Is the information documented and verifiable?
- Is the information up to date?
- Is the information consistent with information from other sources?
- Does the Web site present links to other sources of unbiased information?

How to Speak Boolean

Many computer-assisted information searches use the principles of *Boolean logic,* named for the 19th-century British mathematics teacher George Boole. This simply is a method of describing the relationship among several items. The basic Boolean operators are AND, OR and NOT. Your search for citations will be more effective if you communicate with the computer in terms it understands.

Use common terms. Remember that computers are very literal-minded. You may think "college" means about the same as "university," but the computer doesn't know this. Be prepared to modify your searches using different variations of your topic.

Here are the common Boolean operators used in searches:

- OR statements yield citations that include either term within a text. For example, "research OR survey" will give you a long list of items that include either but not necessarily both terms, so this is the operator that yields the largest number of citations. Another use for the Boolean OR is when words have more than one spelling, such as "online OR on-line OR on line," or when a term has synonyms, such as "survey OR poll."

- AND statements yield citations that include both terms. "Research AND survey" will give you a shorter list of items that feature both terms together.

- NOT statements will yield citations that include the first terms but exclude the second. "Research NOT survey" will give a list of items about research which do not mention surveys.

- NEAR statements are available with some search engines. They are like AND but more restrictive. NEAR locates items that appear within a certain proximity, but this varies. For example, NEAR means within 25 words for Lycos, but it means within 10 words for AltaVista.

- Most search engines have a way to keep two or more words together, such as "public relations" or "Edward Bernays." For some, single or double quotation marks or parentheses around the terms will keep them together. For others, Boolean AND is a default so you don't need any special notations (but a confusion about this is that a few search engines use OR as the default, so check to see how your system works).

- You can combine the various features in Boolean searches. "Research AND survey AND sampling" will generate citations that feature all three terms but not those with only one or two terms.

- You can force the order of a search by using parentheses around items you want cited before another operation occurs. Example: "(Public relations OR marketing) NOT advertising" will yield all citations dealing with either public relations or marketing but excluding anything dealing with advertising. The parentheses force the computer to generate the OR list first, then to extract from it any citations mentioning advertising. "Public relations OR (marketing NOT advertising)" would generate marketing listings, extract advertising mentions from this, then add all public relations listings, even those that mention advertising.

- Some search programs allow you to seek a root word and various endings. For example, "alum?" or "alum$"—the feature differs among search engines—might generate the various forms of alumnus, alumni, alumna and alumnae. But it also would give you unrelated words such as aluminum and alumroot, so you'd be better off using a root word "alumn" in your search.

If you can answer "yes" to the above questions, it is probably safe to assume that the information is trustworthy and accurate. However, let common sense prevail. Trust your instincts that suggest that some information may not be fully reliable. And remember always to attribute the source of information obtained from the Internet, just as you would any other information obtained from books, periodicals or other sources.

Interviews

Whatever you need to know, someone probably already knows it. Thus, as public relations and marketing research needs move beyond the information available through secondary research, **interviews** become a commonly used research tool. These meetings intended to obtain information can be conducted by phone, e-mail or videoconferencing, even by letter, though inperson interviews generally are the best. These have the added benefit of allowing the interviewer to "read" the body language of the person providing the information.

All interviews have a common purpose: to obtain information. Some are general and open-ended, allowing the interview to unfold according to the interaction of the participants and as the information rolls out. Others are more focused and in-depth, with the interviewer sticking to a prepared list of questions. The latter approach is especially good for comparative studies when you ask each interviewee more or less the same set of questions.

Asking Questions During an Interview

Interviews are a good way to get a lot of information quickly and easily. But good interviews need competence and cooperation by both parties. The quality of the information they yield can be limited by several factors, including poor rapport between the interviewer and the interviewee; an interviewer who does not understand the significance of the information; or an interviewee who is unable, unwilling or uncomfortable with providing information. Still, when interviews are done professionally, they can be excellent research tools.

Here are several suggestions for effective interviewing:

- *Plan the interview* by identifying the topic of your research, noting specifically what information you need to obtain and where you might obtain it.
- *Decide whom to interview* by asking yourself what person or persons are likely to have the information you need. Perhaps people within your own or your client's organization would be good information sources. Librarians, government or industry officials, regulators and professionals in the field also may have the information you need. Consider reporters or other public relations practitioners familiar with your topic of interest. Witnesses to events can be particularly helpful.
- *Write down what you already know* about the subject, then build from there. If you cannot identify specific sources of information, then try to identify knowledgeable people who could refer you to these information sources.

- *Learn as much as you can* before the actual interview. Study the topic by doing secondary research.
- *Write out questions* before the interview. Make sure these cover all the areas in which you need information. Be prepared to use these questions as a guide, but remain flexible to allow the discussion to move along its own natural course.
- *Take good notes.*   For lengthy interviews, consider tape recording the information, so you are freer to interact with the interviewee. Make certain the interviewee knows you are recording the conversation and has no objections to this.
- *Build a rapport with the interviewee* at the beginning of the interview. Show an interest in this person and the topic under discussion. Note what you might have in common with the interviewee. Explain the purpose of your interview, and briefly summarize the background information you have already obtained.
- *Build on information you already have.*   Instead of asking vaguely "What do you think about the location for the zoo?" show that you have done your homework by saying, for example, "The planning commission is expected to recommend moving the zoo to the waterfront redevelopment area. What do you think of such a move?"
- *Look for a window* if the interviewee closes a door. For example, if the head coach of a professional football team refuses to tell you why the contract has not been renewed for an assistant coach, ask what qualities the coach is looking for in a replacement. That might give you some insight into the firing.
- *Distinguish between knowledge and opinion questions* during the interview. You will need some facts. You might ask for explanations: "What happened?" "How does this work?" "What do you know about X?" Or you might ask for examples or anecdotes to clarify abstract points: "Can you give me an example of . . . ?" "Can you tell me about a specific case where . . . ?" But go beyond the basics, and probe for additional information by asking opinion questions: "Why did this happen?" "How is this useful?"
- *Consider the relevance of feeling questions.*   More than simple opinion items, affective or feeling questions seek to elicit how someone responds emotionally. "How does this make you feel?" may yield a different response than "What do you think about this?"
- *Distinguish between experience-based and hypothetical questions.*   For example, it may be important to know both what an interview subject did in a certain situation and what he or she might do in a speculative setting.
- *Don't rush into sensitive areas.*   Tread gently if you wish to guide the interview into topics dealing with touchy areas, especially if they may be illegal, immoral or otherwise antisocial, or if they could impact negatively on the interviewee. Unless the interviewee clearly wishes to discuss such topics, build up to them gradually. When you have established a level of trust, such issues will be easier to discuss. One technique is to frame a question as a hypothetical: "If someone you trust asked how to buy some cocaine, what would you tell her?"

- *Don't argue with your interviewee.*   Ask for clarification of anything you don't understand, and point it out if what you are hearing seems to run counter to other information you have.

- *Remain neutral and nonjudgmental* about the information you receive. Your role as an interviewer is somewhat akin to that of a psychologist. If the interviewee says something offensive or outrageous, don't yell "You did what?" or "Are you insane? I can't report that!" Refrain from commenting on what your interviewee says to you. Even positive feedback can be a problem. "That's good" or "I like what you are saying" could prompt the interviewee to focus on certain topics and avoid others.

- *Nudge additional information* from the interview subject through probing or follow-up questions. For example, use questions such as "Who else was involved?" "How did that come about?" and "What else was happening?" Use sentences such as "Tell me more about that" and "Give me an example."

- *Conclude by inviting the interviewee to provide any additional information that seems relevant to the topic.*   Ask if there is anything important that you didn't discuss. Review your notes and verify dates, spellings and other important details. Try to arrange a time when you can contact the interviewee to clear up any questions that may arise later.

Listening During an Interview

Good interviewing requires good listening skills. Consider the difference between merely hearing and actually listening:

- *Hearing* is the physiological process of sound waves making the eardrums vibrate, which in turn stimulate nerve impulses to the brain. Hearing is the result of something that happens to us.

- *Listening,* on the other hand, is something we choose to do. It is an interpersonal process in which you not only hear words but also interpret them, attempting to obtain essentially the same meaning in the words as the sender intended.

As the questioner during an interview, focus on what is being said. Avoid distractions, whether they are worries about your recording equipment or plans for your next question. Effective listening also involves understanding the speaker; try to achieve this, to the extent that one person can appreciate the background and experiences of another. As listening involves the interpretation of messages, it involves more than hearing words. Try to obtain information with your other senses. For example, listen with your eyes by observing the interviewee's body language and perhaps the surroundings as well.

Effective listening involves more than concentration. A person may pay close attention when someone speaks in a foreign language he has studied, though he still may not be able to understand the speaker very well.

Communicators talk about *active listening* or *strategic listening,* which goes beyond simply paying attention. Raymond Zeuschner (1993) identifies four steps for active listening: (1) getting physically and mentally prepared to listen, (2) staying involved physically and mentally with the communication, (3) keeping an open mind while listening and (4) reviewing and evaluating the information after it has been received.

In addition to one-on-one interviews, researchers sometimes obtain information from *intensive interviews* (also called *in-depth interviews*). These are lengthy and detailed interviews on a particular topic that are conducted individually with several respondents. Intensive interviewers often present a set of carefully designed parallel questions for each respondent, so that information more easily can be compared or blended together. Use this type of research technique when it is important both to give the research subject the opportunity to provide personal opinion and insight, but also to keep the subject on a narrow course. Another benefit of intensive interviews is that they reduce variation among different interviewers, since each is working from the same set of questions; follow-up questions are used mainly to probe more deeply along the prearranged line of questioning.

Focus Groups

A particular type of small-group discussion is a **focus group** (or less formally, a *group interview*), in which a researcher guides a conversation about an issue under study and, in doing so, enables the group members to stimulate each other with their comments. The result is a more interactive and complete discussion than would be possible through individual interviews. These controlled group discussions are recorded and later analyzed by the researcher.

Focus groups generate ideas, comments and anecdotes. These can help you gain insight into and understanding about an issue. Focus groups are good techniques for clients who want to know "why," "how" and "what if." Specifically, they are used by public relations and marketing practitioners to test concepts, copy and campaigns, or to evaluate potential logo designs, advertisements or even program and product names.

But focus groups are inappropriate if you need statistical data. If your client wants to know "how much" or "how many," conduct a survey instead. Remember also that focus groups are not decision-making or problem-solving sessions; don't expect the group participants to resolve the issue you are researching.

In some cases, focus groups are the primary research technique used. Other times, researchers use them to complement surveys, either as preliminary tools to gain a better understanding of the issue to be surveyed, or as follow-ups to shed light on the survey findings.

Advantages and Disadvantages of Focus Groups

Focus groups have the advantage of being quick, inexpensive, flexible and very practical. On the other hand, they can become expensive and more complex if the client requires videotaping and a special viewing room with one-way mirrors. Such a video setup is particularly associated with marketing research, which has been criticized as being somewhat of a show for clients who, unseen behind their mirrors, believe that they are privy to consumer revelations (see Rubenstein, 1995; Merton, 1987). Still, it can be a useful tool in the right research situation.

How a Focus Group Works

Here's how a focus group works. Assemble a small group of people who, as closely as possible, reflect your target population or a specific segment within the population. The group typically consists of between eight and 12 people, though some researchers find they get better interaction from groups as small as five.

The *moderator* (sometimes called a *facilitator*) generally introduces the topic, explains a few ground rules, then invites comments on the topic, often with an ice-breaking question. For example, in a focus group with college-bound high school students, the moderator might begin by asking each participant his or her name, areas of academic interest, and future career plans. After the introductions, the real research begins—gently, often wandering through the discussion topic. The session generally lasts 60 to 90 minutes.

Focus groups are meant to be flexible. The moderator has an agenda of topics and themes to present to the group, though not necessarily a specific list of questions. A good moderator is agile, allowing the discussion to flow gracefully through group inter-action and keeping obvious control of the discussion to a minimum. In some focus sessions, the moderator will give a high degree of direction; in others, the moderator will manage the group with so much flexibility that it does not feel manipulated.

Consider the following real-life situation: A researcher conducted a pair of focus groups for post-master's students (all of them mid-career educational professionals), discussing the ideal learning environment as part of a study commissioned by a university vice president for renovating classrooms. When the findings were shared with participants in a follow-up session, several said they were pleased to have felt unre-strained in their discussions. They confided that they had expected the focus groups merely to seek justification for foregone conclusions by the university. They were even more surprised when the researcher showed them a discussion outline, which included nearly every topic they had discussed. But instead of keeping a tight rein on their inter-action, the moderator had allowed the discussion to meander through various aspects of the topic so gently that they felt they were involved more in a casual conversation than a research study. The research goals were accomplished without a feeling of manipula-tion or control. Mission accomplished.

Conducting a Focus Group

Various researchers may have slightly different approaches for preparing and conduct-ing a focus group. Edmunds (1999), for example, identifies several variations on the standard focus group. These include telefocus groups, which are conducted via a tele-phone conference call; mini–focus groups, with only five or six participants; triads with only three participants; Internet focus groups; and video focus groups, conducted via teleconference. However, most researchers would find their personal techniques reflected in the following 11-step outline for conducting focus groups:

1. *Identify the topic of your research.*   Do enough secondary research to gain a good understanding of the topic. Redefine or narrow the topic if you are not convinced the information generated by the focus group will have practical significance for your organization or client or try a different research technique.

2. *Select the moderator.*   Professional focus-group moderators are available through marketing research firms and some public relations agencies, as well as through some colleges and universities. Look for someone who is unbiased about the issue under study, who has good communication skills (both listening and speaking), a strong ability to probe and analyze, a good memory and an engaging personality. The moderator must also be able to quickly learn new concepts. Usually a professional moderator can handle almost any topic, but in some sensitive areas, consider carefully who should be selected as moderator. For example, female participants in a focus group dealing with reconstructive surgery following breast cancer may be more comfortable with a moderator of their own gender, as might a group of men discussing products such as condoms.

   Should you facilitate your own focus group? It can save time and money, and you probably have more knowledge of the issue than an outside moderator. But the problem of bias, even an unconscious bias, can be difficult to overcome. Internal moderators may be tempted to explain and defend rather than merely elicit comments from participants. Meanwhile, participants may be less than candid with a focus group moderator who is professionally involved with the topic under discussion.

3. *Select the sample,* remembering that the small size of focus groups makes a truly representative sample unlikely. A focus group studying attitudes toward a proposed new chain of coffee bars might include veteran coffee drinkers, young professionals and retired persons. Some researchers find it useful to separate participants by age, gender or other important characteristics, especially if such homogeneity would enhance interaction within the group. To obtain a group that is as unbiased as possible, avoid populating it with friends, colleagues or people associated the client, such as donors, employees, customers and so on.

4. *Determine the number of groups needed* to obtain an adequate range of opinions. Because focus groups are so easily swayed by intragroup dynamics, it is wise to plan for at least a couple groups; some researchers prefer as many as five similar groups for a true reading.

5. *Select the participants* you will need, with perhaps a few extra to compensate for the inevitable no-shows. Some researchers recruit 20 percent more than they actually need. When the research is done for commercial marketing

purposes, it is customary to pay participants a participation fee. The rate varies, but currently $25 to $50 is common, with more for doctors, lawyers and others with professional degrees.

6. *Select the site* for the research sessions. These sometimes are held in special research labs equipped with video cameras, built-in microphones and a viewing room behind a one-way mirror. A cost-effective alternative is a professionally furnished conference room with a circular or rectangular table and comfortable chairs. Focus groups also can be conducted in classrooms or in a living room or around a kitchen table. Make sure the site is conveniently accessible to your participants and that it is comfortable for them.

7. *Arrange to record the session* with either audio- or videotaping, whichever is more appropriate. Though marketing-oriented focus groups often are videotaped, some researchers find the practice intrusive and instead prefer audiotaping (Morgan, 1997). Remember that the primary reason for taping focus groups is to generate a written transcript of the discussion, which means videotaping probably isn't necessary. Some focus group work done for public relations purposes can be accomplished with audiotaping; an omni-directional zone-type microphone can be set inconspicuously in the middle of a conference table, and a tape recorder on a side table will scarcely be noticed by participants. It is a good idea to make a back-up recording or at least to have a microcassette recorder available. Videotaping, meanwhile, allows a more careful review of body language and other nonverbal cues. It also allows researchers to edit the tape for presentations to clients, which can be more powerful than transcripts or quotes presented in a written report.

8. *Prepare the discussion guide* with an outline of the questions to be used, and organize any participant materials such as samples, brochures, photographs, advertising sketches, slides, etc.

9. *Conduct the focus group session.*   Note the various distinct roles for the research team conducting the session.

10. *Review and analyze the data.*   Immediately after the session, review the tape. If any parts of it were not recorded properly, write down everything you can remember. Even if the tape is complete, listen to it and review your notes. Add any additional observations or insights that you didn't have time to note during the session. Transcribe the tape.

11. *Report the data* for your client or your boss. The research report generally is prepared by the moderator. It should include a statement of the purpose of the research, an overview of the selection process for participants and a copy of the discussion guide. The body of the report generally includes both selected comments made by participants and recommendations gleaned by the researcher.

In the comment section both direct quotes and paraphrases are drawn from the discussion, often divided into subtopics. Researchers sometimes present participant comments in a cumulative fashion, simply by noting

Who's Who in a Focus Group?

The *research leader* is the person who articulates the topic, conducts appropriate secondary research, selects the participants and—most importantly—develops the discussion guide with its questions and agenda topics. After the session, the research leader prepares the formal written report.

The *moderator,* who often is also the research leader, is responsible for the flow of the discussion, especially keeping it on point. The moderator will use open-ended questions such as "What do you think about . . . ," "Tell me more about . . . ," and "Let's now talk about. . . ." The moderator encourages discussion by reserved participants and tempers the involvement of those who may be overly talkative or aggressive. The moderator must be emotionally detached from the issue under study; don't ask the public relations director to moderate a group about the effectiveness of the newsletter her own staff edits.

The *assistant moderator* or *host* greets and seats participants, offers refreshments if these are available, prepares nametags if this is appropriate and escorts any latecomers to their seats. The host is a liaison between the moderator and any viewers who might be present, sometimes delivering to the moderator questions that a viewer-client might wish to have discussed.

The *recorder* takes notes throughout the discussion, producing a log of the discussion and making it easier to obtain quotes from the transcript later on. Special sheets can be prepared for recording key words and phrases of participants; who said what; significant nonverbal activity such as body language, excitement, nods and so on; and personal observations or insights. The recorder also prepares the typed transcript that the researcher will use in preparing a final report. In some situations, the recorder may be out of view, but in most focus-group settings the participants easily ignore a recorder sitting off to the side.

The *technician* is in charge of audio- or videotaping. This person should be as unobtrusive as possible.

It is possible to combine these roles. Many setups involve two people: a research leader/moderator and an assistant moderator/recorder/technician. For very simple situations, the moderator might handle all the roles.

---

remarks and suggestions, or they may highlight those comments that were echoed by several different participants. For example, the research report may separate comments that enjoyed general endorsement from those that were mentioned by only one or two persons.

Some focus group reports end with a summary, others with observations by the researcher, still others with specific recommendations that the researcher feels flow from the comments and observations. The decision about including recommendations is based on the expectations and needs of the client, as well as the agreed-upon role of the researcher.

Case Studies

A type of research useful for public relations and marketing communication is the **case study** (sometimes called a *case history* or more generally, *field research*). A case study investigates a single event, product or situation, looking at how an organization has handled it. The purpose of this investigation is to understand and learn from a real-life example.

The underlying idea is a simple one: Let's see what we can learn from someone who has been there. A public relations director in Virginia might contact a colleague in Iowa

---

Sample Discussion Guide

Client: University recruiting marketing program
Participants: Six to ten high-school honors students (seniors)

I. Introduction

    A. Identify moderator, assistant moderator

    B. Explain focus group

        1. Purpose [marketing decisions]

        2. Ground rules [confidentiality, candor, mutual respect, equal participation]

II. Perceptions of Central University

    A. What would your family/friends say if you decided to attend CU?

    B. What do you know about Central University? How much?

    C. From what you do know, what does Central University do well?

    D. From what you know, what does Central University not do well?

III. College/University Selection

    A. What are students looking for in a college/university? [location, cost, courses, reputation, jobs, parties]

    B. What do your parents ask you to consider in choosing a college?

    C. What role do guidebooks (Peterson's, Barron's, etc.) play in your college/university choice?

IV. Comparisons

    A. What colleges/universities are you seriously considering attending? Why?

    B. How does Central University compare to these colleges/universities? [pros, cons]

    C. In one sentence, what is your impression of Central University?

V. Marketing Critique

    A. Discuss logos [hand out samples]

    B. Discuss newspaper/magazine ads [hand out samples]

    C. Discuss billboard ads [hand out samples]

    D. Discuss messages

---

about a crisis situation she had successfully managed a year or so earlier. That is a case study, learning from someone else's success. Case studies don't necessarily have to present successful cases. When Sisters Hospital in Buffalo, N.Y., faced so much community opposition that it had to cancel its plan to open a methadone clinic in a residential neighborhood, the failure became a good case study for other hospitals around the country planning to open similar off-site drug-treatment centers. Public relations practitioners could learn what not to do as well as what to do to avoid such community opposition.

Case studies often are labeled as qualitative research, meaning that they rely more on the researcher's insight than on hard facts. However, Robert Yin (1994) notes that both contemporary and historical case studies can rely on quantitative evidence.

Advantages and Disadvantages of Case Studies

Like any other research technique, case studies feature both advantages and disadvantages. On the plus side, they can suggest *why* something happened and can deal with a wide spectrum of evidence, such as documents, interviews, even surveys (Babbie, 1997). On the other hand, case studies can't easily be generalized, making it risky to presume that what happened in the observed case will necessarily predict what could happen in other situations.

Though case studies have some limitations, they nevertheless can be very useful. Many university professors have found that both graduate and undergraduate students appreciate the practical value of case studies. Practitioners and students alike can learn a lot about crisis communication by looking at the classic cases: Three Mile Island and the Nestlé boycott in the late 1970s, Tylenol and Exxon in the 1980s, Dow-Corning's breast-implant imbroglio and Pan American's downed Flight 800 in the 1990s, plus a host of perhaps lesser-known crisis cases dealing with embezzlement (United Way of America), scandal (Covenant House), consumer fraud (Sears Auto Centers), product tampering (Pepsi syringe hoax), product credibility (Intel Pentium), customer injury (McDonald's) and employee behavior (U.S. Navy "Tailhook" episode). And that's just a few cases dealing with crises. We can learn from thousands more dealing with employee communication, community relations, investor relations and so on.

Conducting a Case Study

As a research method, case studies offer much flexibility to the researcher. However, some common approaches are helpful. Here are 10 steps to conducting a case study.

1. *Identify the problem* within your organization that generates your research. Make sure the problem is one that can be addressed by making a comparison to another organization.

2. *Select a relevant case* to investigate. Make sure the organization associated with the case is at least somewhat comparable to your own or your client's organization, so that the comparison is a meaningful one.

3. *Identify the information you need.* A case study can yield a wide range of information, but you can make your study more efficient by first noting the parameters of what you need to find out. Remember that you are not seeking merely a journalistic report of events, but rather an insightful analysis of causes and effects, strategies and tactics.

4. *Identify the data sources,* which generally are personal observation, interviews or documentation such as news releases, press clippings and other published information as well as internal documents such as letters, organizational files, agendas, reports and surveys.

5. *Articulate the questions* that you will use with the data sources to obtain the information you seek.

6. *Develop a study protocol* for formal case studies to be reported in writing (optional). Create a document that identifies the study's purpose and procedures, definitions, data sources, questions and plan for analysis and reporting.

7. *Conduct a pilot study* to pretest and perhaps refine the questions for the eventual investigation.

8. *Gather the information,* using your skills as both an interviewer and a secondary researcher.

9. *Analyze the information,* looking not only at the individual facts but also at their relationship and potential interaction. Apply the information to your own organization.

10. *Report the information,* based on the appropriate audience (yourself only, professional colleagues, bosses or clients). This reporting may be verbal and informal, even conversational if you have conducted the case study for your own company, or it may be written as part of a formal series of research and recommendations for a client or as part of a major campaign.

Sampling for case studies usually involves nonprobability methods, particularly convenience, purposive and snowball sampling (discussed earlier in Nonprobability Sampling).

Also important to case studies is the role of the observer and the informant. The *observer* is you, the person doing the research, and you are neither unobtrusive nor disinterested. Your *informant,* meanwhile, is the person you are interviewing to obtain information about the case. This informant also is not disinterested. Good research calls for both the observer and the informant to be objective, fair and as unbiased as possible. Questions should not be slanted to elicit hoped-for answers, and responses should tell all relevant aspects of the story as they really happened, without reinterpretation or reshaping.

Basic Skills for a Case Study Researcher

Here are five basic research skills necessary for people involved in preparing case studies. The case study preparer should:

1. *Be able to ask good questions*—and to interpret the answers.

2. *Be a good "listener"* and not be trapped by his or her own ideologies or preconceptions.

3. *Be adaptive and flexible,* so that newly encountered situations can be seen as opportunities, not threats.

4. *Have a firm grasp on the issues being studied,* whether this is a theoretical or policy orientation, even if in an exploratory mode. Such a grasp focuses the relevant events and information to be sought to manageable proportions.

5. *Be unbiased by preconceived notions,* including those derived from theory. Thus a person should be sensitive and responsive to contradictory evidence.

Source: Yin, R. K. (1994). *Case study research: Design and methods* (2nd ed.). Applied Social Research Methods Series, No. 5. Thousand Oaks, CA: Sage.

Survey Research

One of the oldest and most common research techniques is the **survey,** which involves asking standard questions of many respondents and then comparing their responses. Surveys, also known as *polls,* have many advantages. They are appropriate for description, analysis and prediction—three major research needs. They are among the least expensive and quickest types of research. They can be applied to both large and small groups of people. They can be very accurate, and their findings are easy to compare. On the down side, surveys are subject to both the bias and limitations of the researcher, particularly through inadequate samples or poorly worded questions.

Surveys can be administered in a number of ways, each with certain built-in benefits and disadvantages. *Telephone surveys* are quick to administer but limited to easy-to-understand questions. With the ubiquity of both telemarketing and answering machines, it is becoming increasingly difficult to conduct phone surveys.

The most common type of surveys, *mail surveys* (also called *self-administered surveys*), are convenient for respondents but the response rate generally is lower than for more expensive telephone surveys. *Personal interviews* are most expensive of all because they are very time consuming, and they are subject to interpersonal variables not found in most other types of surveys. Meanwhile, *group administration* of surveys is easy to execute, but there often is a concern about the appropriateness of the group. An emerging technique, *computer-based surveys,* offers some benefits of mail surveys, but they often are focused on a volunteer sample, which may not be the most appropriate for the research needs.

Response rates vary considerably with surveys. Some research is reported on the basis of a response rate of 5 percent or less. The Hite report on female sexual behavior, a 1976 popular best seller, was based on a 3 percent response rate to a mail survey. Such low response rates raise serious doubts about findings. Earl Babbie (1997) considers a response rate of 50 percent as adequate, 60 percent as good and 70 percent as very good. You'll have to decide what an acceptable rate is for your research, realizing that higher response rates generally are more reliable.

Some researchers use payments or other incentives to increase the response rate. Sometimes the payment is merely a token amount, perhaps a dollar, even a couple pennies ("We want your two cents' worth"). Incentives may be pens, calendars, tickets or simple items associated with the sponsor. Some surveys offer a more elaborate gift through a raffle held among participants who return the questionnaires.

Most questionnaires are accompanied by a stamped, self-addressed return envelope to make it easier for the respondent to return the questionnaire. Fax response may be appropriate for questionnaires sent to professionals and dealing with nonpersonal topics. Likewise, e-mail surveys are becoming increasingly popular.

Much depends on how carefully you select the sample and how well you groom your chosen respondents. A general rule applies: The more involved the respondents are with the sponsoring organization or the more concerned they are with the issue, the higher the response rate. Some researchers have the head of the organization send a letter to respondents asking them to complete the questionnaire they will soon receive and noting the importance of the information to the organization.

Follow-up mailings can greatly improve the response rate, as well. The least expensive way is to send a reminder postcard or letter. More effective, however, is to send another copy of the questionnaire. If your client or boss is serious about wanting responses, the price of second or even third mailings is money well spent. Thomas Mangione (1995) reports that a second mailing usually generates half the percentage of response as the first mailing generated, and the third mailing half that of the second. Babbie (1997) recommends two or three follow-up mailings for the best response. He cites the experience of the Survey Research Office at the University of Hawaii, which found a consistent pattern of returns. It generally obtains a 40 percent response from its initial questionnaire mailing. A second mailing two weeks later brings in another 20 percent, and a third mailing yields an additional 10 percent.

Another way to ensure adequate numbers of responses is to use a larger than desired sample, on the notion that not everyone in the selected sample will respond. Though this adds to the mailing cost, it may be a legitimate way to obtain responses, especially if it reduces the need for follow-up mailings.

Conducting a Survey

Here is a simple step-by-step formula for conducting a survey. The format is general, though steps 7 through 10 deal specifically with mail surveys; modify these steps for surveys administered over the phone or in person. Following these general steps, we'll talk more specifically about questionnaires.

1. *Identify the topic of your research.*   Do enough secondary research to gain a good understanding of the topic. Redefine or narrow the topic if you are not convinced the information generated by the survey will have practical significance for your organization or client, or abandon the survey and use a different research technique.

2. *Select a sample* that is appropriate for your organization, in terms of reliability as well as time and cost.

3. *Write the items* to be included in the questionnaire, the written document that presents questions or statements to respondents. (We'll talk more about questionnaires shortly.) Review the wording for each item. Keep the questionnaire as brief as possible, because the more concise it is, the higher response rate you can expect.

4. *Print the questionnaire* on letterhead or with the logo of the sponsoring organization. Visually the questionnaire should be neat and user-friendly, with clear instructions, readable type and easy response formats. Try not to split items over pages or columns.

5. *Test the questionnaire,* preferably with a small group of people reflecting the characteristics of your sample.

6. *Modify the questionnaire,* based on what you learn from your pretest group.

7. For mail surveys: *Write and send a cover letter* that introduces the survey to respondents. Identify the sponsoring organization, explain its purpose, note

the level of confidentiality and encourage their participation. Some researchers prefer to use an advance letter in addition to the cover letter. This can be particularly useful when the questionnaires are going to people associated with the sponsoring organization, such as an advance letter from the director of a nonprofit organization announcing an upcoming questionnaire and encouraging participation. In the cover letter include a telephone number where respondents can contact the research office with questions or simply to verify the legitimacy of the survey.

8. For mail surveys: *Mail the surveys to participants*. Always use first-class postage. Include a return envelope with first-class postage, or use envelopes with a postage-paid business reply imprint. The latter costs more per piece when returned, but you pay for only those envelopes that are returned. On the other hand, there is a psychological advantage in using a postage stamp that respondents will know they are wasting if they don't use it in returning a completed questionnaire. Alternatively, e-mail the questionnaire if you know that your intended respondents are comfortable with using e-mail.

9. For mail surveys: *Monitor the returns*. Keep a daily count of the number of returns received.

10. For mail surveys: *Send a follow-up mailing* after about 10 days. If necessary and appropriate, send a second follow-up mailing after another two weeks.

11. *Analyze and report the data.* Survey results usually are reported with a degree of formality because they are serious research. Generally the written report will include a statement of the purpose of the research, an outline of the methods used to obtain and contact the sample, a copy of the questionnaire, a report on the number of responses received and a notation of any limitations or weaknesses in the survey. The heart of the survey report is an item-by-item account of what the respondents said; sometimes researcher comments are included within the item reporting, pointing to interesting correlations with other questions. Usually the researcher includes a set of recommendations flowing logically from the findings.

Questionnaires

A **questionnaire** is the tool used for surveys. It is a written document that features a series of items such as questions or statements that call for a response.

Whether the questionnaire is delivered in person, over the telephone or in print, the *introductory statement* sets the stage. This introduction should identify the researcher and the sponsoring organization, indicate the topic, explain why the respondent was selected, guarantee confidentiality and note the approximate time required of the respondent. Don't ask the respondent to participate, because this provides an opportunity for the respondent to decline. Instead provide the preliminary information and ask the first question.

Data in questionnaires fits into several categories. The main content items generally follow the same hierarchy as do public relations objectives: awareness (knowledge,

---

How Am I Doing?

With any survey, especially one that seeks to gauge the level of satisfaction by customers, readers, employees and other key publics, it is very important to ask the right question. Howard Waddell (1995) notes that most customer-satisfaction surveys ask variations on "How am I doing?" Several different scales address this question:

- *Performance scale:* poor, fair, good, excellent, superior
- *Expectation scale:* much more than expected, better than expected, as much as expected, less than expected, much less than expected

- *Requirement scale:* exceeded my requirements, met requirements, nearly met requirements, did not meet requirements
- *Satisfaction scale:* very satisfied, satisfied, neither satisfied nor dissatisfied, dissatisfied, very dissatisfied

Waddell suggests a better approach—an *improvement scale* (none, some, considerable) that presumes there is generally room for better performance.

---

understanding or retention of information); acceptance (interest or attitude); action (opinion or behavior). Additionally, demographic items deal with the respondent's background or environment, which is useful information for analyzing the data gathered.

General Tips.   Asking the right questions in the right way is basic to conducting a good survey. Following are some general tips for questionnaire items, whether they are statements or questions:

- Keep the items short. Using many short, specific items is better than using fewer items that are complex and confusing.
- Use clear and simple words and phrases familiar to the respondents. Avoid jargon unless the respondents share the language. Also avoid all but the most commonly used abbreviations.
- Be specific; avoid ambiguous words and phrases. For example, the seemingly simple question "Where do you live?" could actually generate a range of responses. Is the desired answer "United States"? Or is it "Cleveland," "23 Oriole Road," "In an apartment building" or "With my parents"? Likewise, a question such as "What do you think about the mayor's tax proposal?" is unclear. One respondent may focus on the timing, another on the amount of money to be collected, still another on the method of collection or the eventual use of the money raised.
- Don't let your curiosity run amok. Ask only questions that are relevant to the research topic.
- Place items in a logical order, usually easy to difficult. Group items dealing with a similar topic together. Demographic items about the respondents

should be kept together; mail surveys often place these items at the end, while telephone surveys may lead with these because they are easy for respondents to answer.

- Arrange sentences in positive constructions. For example, ask "Do you participate in group exercise or fitness programs?" instead of the more negative "Do you avoid group exercise or fitness programs?" Especially avoid double negatives, such as the awkward "Do you disagree that lack of exercise is unhealthful?" (Presuming you have an opinion on the issue, try figuring out how to respond to the last question.)

- Use words with clear meanings, because every respondent must understand and interpret the questionnaire items exactly the same way. For example, "Have you ever considered having an affair?" begs the question of what *consider* means in this context. And what is an "affair"? Instead, try asking: "While you were married, did you ever engage in sexual intercourse with someone other than your spouse?"

- Avoid "double-barreled" items, ones that include two different thoughts. For example, the question "Do you think Portland is a friendly and progressive community?" is difficult for respondents to answer if they think Portland is friendly but not very progressive. The relationship between the two modifiers is unclear; they don't belong in the same question.

Level of Information.   Items dealing with the respondent's level of information may offer a particular challenge to questionnaire writers.

- If necessary, include a brief definition of key terms.
- Make sure the topic is within the competence of average respondents. Don't ask a sample of people without a strong scientific background if fusion or fission a better process for nuclear energy? Any response would be little more than an uninformed guess.
- Carefully explain when you are testing the knowledge of respondents. Example: "A main purpose of this survey is to find out how much residents know about the bridge proposal. The following six items present multiple-choice items about the proposal. Circle the answers you think are correct. . . ."

Opinion/Attitude.   Some special guidelines apply to questionnaire items that seek to elicit the respondent's opinion or attitude.

- Don't ask for opinions on questions that are matters of fact. For example, don't ask "Do boys get higher grades in mathematics than girls do?" because that question doesn't call for an opinion. You can easily research the facts on math grades. But a legitimate opinion question might be "Why do you think boys get higher grades in mathematics than girls do?" especially if your questionnaire is being answered by teachers, parents, psychologists or others whose opinions might be relevant.

- Avoid speculative or hypothetical questions. Example: "Would you prefer to move to a colony under the sea or in outer space?" An exception to this is if the item deals with a potential activity of the sponsoring organization. Example: "Given the opportunity, would you consider purchasing a vacuum cleaner that also served as an air purifier?"

- Avoid terms that call for subjective judgment, which can vary from person to person. Example: "Is the current tax structure reasonable?" The word *reasonable* may be interpreted differently by various respondents. Instead ask more specifically: "Is the current tax structure affordable?" Or "equitable," or whatever else you really want to know.

- Be careful about mixing fact and opinion. If a national magazine has just ranked Austin as one of the Top 10 progressive cities in the United States, don't ask "Is Austin a progressive city?" It's unclear if you are asking about the respondent's awareness or opinion. Instead ask "Do you agree with a magazine ranking that Austin is progressive?"

Action/Behavior.   Items dealing with actions and behaviors, whether current or past, also can be particularly difficult for the questionnaire writer.

- Make sure you are asking for relevant behaviors. Example: "Do you ever shop at GreenGrocers?" *Ever?*

- Don't word the questions so that they presume a particular answer. Example: "How often do you smoke marijuana?" This wording presumes that you smoke it at least sometimes. This might be better handled with a primary and a contingency question. "Do you smoke marijuana?" Then the contingency: "If yes, how often?"

- Make sure the questions can reasonably be answered. Avoid asking for highly detailed information, such as "In the last six months, how many hours of television have you watched?" Instead, use a time frame easier for the respondent, such as "On an average weekday, how many hours of television do you usually watch?" or "On an average weekend, how many hours of television do you usually watch?"

- Make sure the topic is within the respondent's relevant experience. Asking women about how frequently they practice self-examination techniques for testicular cancer isn't a useful question. Either limit it to male respondents or replace it with a question dealing with the frequency of self-examination techniques for two easily detectable cancers (breast cancer or testicular cancer).

- Be careful with intrusive or potentially embarrassing questions, especially those that deal with legal, social or moral transgressions. "Are you always truthful on your income tax returns?" may result in a less-than-truthful answer, in part because the respondent may be concerned about the confidentiality of the study, and in part because the respondent may simply be unwilling to confess a crime, even to him- or herself.

Impartiality.   In general, researchers want questionnaires to be unbiased. Following are a few pointers in writing impartial questions.

- Keep your wording neutral, and avoid leading items that indicate to the respondent what the researcher apparently sees as the "correct" answer. Example: "Do you agree with most Americans that more violent criminals should receive the death penalty?" Telling the respondent that most Americans agree with this statement is biasing the response.
- Make sure the wording doesn't signal your own bias, such as "Do you prefer reading good literature or just popular novels?" *Good* literature? *Just* novels? No doubt about the preferred answer here.
- Take particular care with socially or politically charged words. Kenneth Rasinski (1989) analyzed the wording in several national surveys. He found, for example, that 63 percent of respondents said too little money was being spent on "assistance to the poor," but only 23 percent said too little was being spent on "welfare."
- Realize that commonly used social and political terms sometimes have different meanings. Example: "Are you pro-abortion?" Some respondents may consider themselves pro-choice but not pro-abortion, or they might be disinclined to answer such a complex question with a simple yes or no. Whenever respondents feel a need to explain their interpretation of a questionnaire item, it is poorly worded.
- Avoid a prestige bias by making associations with respected authorities or well-known figures. Example: "Do you agree with the mayor that property taxes are too high?" The same is true with disrespected figures. If the mayor has just been indicted for embezzlement and tax fraud, respondents may hedge on stating any agreement with a disgraced public official.
- Use leading questions if you are dealing with a potentially embarrassing or controversial issue or if you feel a need to "give permission" to respondents to be truthful. For example: "Recently several political leaders have admitted to adultery. Have you ever been involved in adultery?"

Demographics.   Demographic items also require careful attention by the questionnaire writer.

- Rather than ask a respondent's age or income, group such sensitive questions into ranges. Example: "Which best describes your family income last year? Less than $40,000. $40,001 to $80,000. More than $80,000."

Timing and Wording Affect Poll Results

The timing of polls and the way questions are worded can have a big impact on how people answer them. Here is an example related by Adam Clymer, a columnist with the *New York Times,* who reflected on the fact that several conflicting surveys were being reported about supposed public support for federal funding of human embryonic stem-cell research.

As the issue was heating up during the summer of 2001, an NBC News/*Wall Street Journal* poll said that 69 percent favor the research. A Gallup Poll for CNN and *USA Today* reported 54 percent in favor. A poll by ABC News and Beliefnet (a religious Web site) found 58 percent in favor. These three news-related polls had significant differences. Meanwhile, two less-than-disinterested parties had reported even more disparate results. A poll by the Juvenile Diabetes Foundation, which favors stem-cell research, said 70 percent of American favor the research. But the U.S. Conference of Catholic Bishops, which opposes the research, reported a survey that said only 24 percent of Americans approve.

Clymer noted that some of the variations in the polling could be traced to how the questions were phrased. The NBC/*Journal* poll used the phrase "potentially viable human embryos," while the bishops' poll said "the live embryos would be destroyed in their first week of development." The bishop's poll also referred to "experiments," while the others alluded to the goals of the research.

Perhaps more importantly, the polls were so dissimilar because many respondents were unfamiliar with the topic. All the polls asked long, involved questions. Only the Gallup poll allowed respondents to answer that they did not know enough about the issue to have an opinion, and 57 percent chose that response category.

Clymer quoted research experts that the polls were measuring "non-attitudes." One survey expert focused on the newness and complexity of the issue: "Americans are acquiescent so they'll give you an answer. [But] the mere fact that you've got to offer a lengthy summary implies that it's too early to sort it out."

The insightful columnist concluded with a warning for all of us: "Sometimes, the pollsters are measuring phantoms, and the politicians are calling on them for support."

Source: Clymer, A. (2001, July 22). The Nation: Wrong Number; The Unbearable Lightness of Public Opinion Polls. [Column]. *New York Times,* s.4, p.3)

- Tailor educational levels to your target population, and consider asking for the highest grade or degree completed. Example: "How much education have you completed? Less than high school. High school. Some college but no degree. Associate degree. Bachelor's degree. Graduate degree." If this was directed to academic professionals, the response choices might be "Bachelor's degree. Academic master's degree. Terminal master's degree (i.e., M.F.A., M.S.W.). Academic doctorate (Ph.D.). Professional doctorate (i.e., J.D., M.D., D.D.S.). Post-doctoral study."

- Be careful when asking about racial or ethnic background, and make sure all options are included. Also consider the wording of the question. The U.S. Census Bureau asks people to indicate the race they *consider themselves* to be, a subtle difference over the strictly matter-of-fact question, "What is your race?" Also, because a growing number of people identify themselves as biracial or multiracial, consider allowing respondents to indicate more than one category.

- Tailor the demographic information to the research needs. For example, for surveys conducted near the northern U.S. border, demographic items might include the name of the specific province for someone who indicates a Canadian background. Likewise, in the Southwest, items might include the names of specific Central or Latin American countries of perhaps Mexican states, if that information is relevant to the researcher.

Questionnaire design also must give attention to the response categories for the various items. First of all, make the options visually simple and consistent. Use checkmarks, circles, boxes or other simple marks.

One of the first considerations is the type of response categories. *Open-ended items* allow respondents to answer in their own words; *closed-ended items* provide for check-offs to predetermined response categories.

Types of Questionnaire Items

Researchers have devised several different types of items that can be used in questionnaires. Some of the more common types are multiple-choice items, checklist items, forced-choice items and rating scales. A questionnaire may include more than one type of item, though it's generally a good idea to group similar items.

Multiple-Choice Items.   *Multiple-choice items* are questions or statements with a limited number of responses. These allow respondents to choose from a predetermined set of choices. For example: "Indicate your favorite major television network: ABC, CBS, FOX, NBC." Often multiple-choice items include an "other" category.

Guidelines for Open-Ended Versus Closed-Ended Items

Here are some guidelines for when to use open-ended questions and when closed-ended questions are more appropriate. Remember that both can be used within the same questionnaire.

Use open-ended items if you . . .	Use closed-ended items if you . . .
Prefer that respondents answer in their own words	Prefer that respondents use predetermined choices
Want to make it easier for respondents by answering in own words	Want to make it easier for respondents by using predetermined choices
Don't know the range of response choices	Can anticipate the range of response choices
Are willing to consider dissimilar comments from respondents	Want to directly compare and correlate responses

Response categories for choice items must be both *comprehensive* and *mutually exclusive*. That is, each response category must provide a full range of potential responses so there is an appropriate response for each respondent (a comprehensive set of responses), and there must be only one possible response (each response being mutually exclusive from the other choices).

For example, on a demographic question asking the income of respondents, the response categories might be "$20,000 or less," "$20,000 to $40,000," "40,000 to $60,000," and "$60,000 or more." The categories are comprehensive, covering all the bases. But they are not mutually exclusive because they overlap—both the second and third choices are appropriate for someone earning exactly $40,000 a year. A better way to write response categories might be "less than $20,000," "20,000 to $39,999," "$40,000 to $59,999," and "$60,000 or more."

Checklist Items.   Sometimes it is more effective to allow respondents to indicate more than one response through a *checklist*. Example: "What kind of country music do you listen to most often? (Check all that apply.) Classic country, new country, bluegrass, country rock."

Forced-Choice Items.   *Forced-choice items* feature two or more statements, with directions for respondents to select the one that most closely reflects their opinion. Example: "Of the following statements, select the one that comes closer to your own belief. Voting is a privilege and thus should be optional. Voting is a responsibility and thus should be required."

Rating Scales.   Some items have the advantage of focusing on the intensity of the respondent's feelings rather than eliciting a simple yes or no response. These are *rating scales,* in which respondents are asked to rate the degree of their feeling or certainty about an item. Some rating scales are bipolar instruments because they move in both directions from a neutral center point to either positive or negative points. Others are unipolar instruments that range from low to high points.

The popular *Likert scale* (pronounced LICK-ert) is a bipolar scale that asks the intensity of respondents' agreement to a statement along a range of response categories, such as "strongly agree," "agree," "disagree" and "strongly disagree." The wording for the Likert scale can be modified, such as by asking "strongly approve," "strongly believe," "strongly interested" and so forth.

In some versions, the Likert scale includes a central or neutral option, and sometimes a "no opinion" item. For some issues, researchers use the neutral option; for others they would rather eliminate the midpoint and force the respondent to indicate a preference one way of the other.

Define response options carefully. Rating scales sometimes offer choices such as "excellent," "very good," "average," "fair," "poor" and so on. A problem with such scales is that too many response categories can leave respondents confused about the differences among the categories—for example, between "average" and "fair" or between "excellent" and "very good."

To avoid this ambiguity, some rating scales are presented numerically, as in the following example: "Indicate your preference for various flavors of ice cream (1 being dislike, 5 being like): Vanilla 1-2-3-4-5. Chocolate 1-2-3-4-5. Strawberry 1-2-3-4-5" (and so on). When rating scales are used numerically, it is logical to arrange them so that a low or negative response translates into low numbers. Example: "Rate the following on a scale of 1 to 5 (1 being low priority, 5 being high priority)." Reversing this, to rank low priority items with a 5 and high priority items with a 1, would be confusing to respondents.

Rating scales can even be presented visually, such as with smiley face caricatures for children's surveys, ranging from very sad through very happy.

Writing about questionnaires in a series of book on survey research, Arlene Fink (1995a) recommends five types of response options for rating scales:

- Endorsement: definitely true, true, don't know, false, definitely false
- Frequency: always, very often, fairly often, sometimes, almost never, never
- Intensity: none, very mild, mild, moderate, severe
- Influence: big problem, moderate problem, small problem, very small problem, no problem
- Comparison: much more than others, somewhat more than others, about the same as others, somewhat less than others, much less than others

The *semantic differential scale* asks respondents to select a point on a continuum between two opposing positions. The scale generally uses opposing adjectives, usually with a five-point or seven-point scale. Example: "What are your perceptions about professional football? Interesting/uninteresting. Enjoyable/unenjoyable." This scale also can be presented numerically. For example:

| Uninteresting | 1 | 2 | 3 | 4 | 5 | Interesting |
| Unenjoyable | 1 | 2 | 3 | 4 | 5 | Enjoyable |

Content Analysis

Some problems are inherent in focus groups and surveys. When you directly ask people their opinion, their response may not be genuine—it may be shaped by the fact that you asked in the first place, or it may be colored by their desire to give you what they think is the most acceptable answer.

For example, ask an acquaintance if he likes you and the answer may be "Yes, of course." But is he saying that just because you asked, because he'd be embarrassed to answer no or because he doesn't want to hurt your feelings? Instead of asking outright, you could observe what he says and does without being asked. List all the significant interactions the two of you have had in the last several weeks—conversations, shared experiences and so on. Then evaluate each activity as being either friendly or unfriendly.

If the friendly activities far outweigh the unfriendly ones, you can conclude that he likes you. If the unfriendly activities predominate, he doesn't like you, no matter what he might say.

That's the idea behind the research methodology known as **content analysis**—the objective, systematic and quantitative investigation of something that has been written down (or at least something that can be written down for research purposes). It's a situation of actions speaking louder than words. As a formal research methodology, content analysis has been used for years to study mass media. This research technique can be used to shed light on the messages of communication, assess the image of a group or organization and make comparisons between media and reality.

Using Content Analysis

Researchers involved in public relations and marketing communication have found that content analysis can be useful in several different ways. Here are a couple of examples of how content analysis can be used to study various practical issues that could be important to your organization or client.

Let's say your client, an insurance agency, has a new policy covering sports cars. You want to reach your public—sports car drivers—on radio, using both public relations and advertising techniques. As you plan your campaign, you determine that you need to identify the most popular radio stations among people who drive sports cars. You could survey the drivers, but that might be unwieldy, because obtaining a sampling frame would be difficult. Instead, you might ask mechanics at several maintenance and repair shops specializing in sports cars to keep a list of which stations the radios are tuned to when the cars are brought in. That's content analysis.

Or perhaps you are researching consumer issues for your company, a garment manufacturer. Specifically, you want to know what people think about the new line of lightweight, high-insulating winter coats. You could conduct a survey or a focus group if you had the time. Or instead, you might check the letters and phone calls received by the consumer affairs department and compare these with customer comments about other products. This, too, is an example of content analysis.

Remember that the various research methods we're dealing with in this appendix don't have to stand alone. Content analysis can be used to complement other types of research. Researchers in public relations and marketing communication sometimes compare the results of their content analysis with the information they are able to obtain from surveys or focus groups.

For instance, if you are evaluating the effectiveness of your internal newsletter as part of an overall program review of your employee relations program, you might begin with a content analysis of the last three years' issues to identify topics that have been covered. Then you could conduct a focus group or readership survey to find out what topics your employees want to read about. Finally, you might compare the results of the content analysis with the results of your questioning, and from that comparison create a more popular employee publication.

Let's look at one final example. You are a media relations manager for a large public utility. You know that many of your news releases have been ignored by the newspapers and broadcast media in your service area. At a "meet the editors" forum sponsored by the local PRSA chapter, you hear from editors and news directors that they prefer stories with a strong local flavor. You realize you should evaluate the content of your releases as they focus on information of apparent significance to each locality within your service area. So you decide to do a content analysis of your releases of the last two years. Specifically, you evaluate four aspects of each release: the extent of the local significance of the issue or activity (1) as you know it to be, (2) as evident in the body of the release, (3) as identified in the lead sentence or paragraph and (4) as specifically featured in the headline or title on the release. By combining the information you received from the media gatekeepers and your own analysis of local content, you can gain some helpful insight for both topics and effective writing techniques for your future releases.

Advantages and Disadvantages of Content Analysis

Content analysis has several advantages, including a low investment of time and money. It can be done by a person working alone with little equipment beyond a simple calculator or a computer with relatively inexpensive software. Content analysis is unobtrusive research done "after the fact," without any effect on the people or issues being studied. It also has the advantage of allowing you to look at the facts without being caught up by the heat of the moment, free of the passion and enthusiasm that often surrounds surveys or focus groups. Content analysis also has the advantage of allowing you to go back in time to examine past messages. It can be used to compare an organization with industry norms or with wider trends. Finally, it helps the researcher separate the routine from the unusual.

Another aspect of content analysis is the notion of *intercoder reliability*—the degree to which several coders agree on how to label the content being studied. Among the disadvantages of content analysis are its limitation to recorded (or recordable) information and its susceptibility to coder influence and bias, in part because content analysis deals with what researchers call *manifest content,* the obvious and apparent meanings and interpretations that, unfortunately, are not always equally obvious and apparent to everyone. Also, while content analysis can point to coincidences and concurrences, it can't establish cause-effect relationships.

Conducting a Content Analysis Study

Below is a step-by-step explanation of how to conduct a research study via content analysis. Included with the explanations is a running example of how a health-care company might use content analysis.

Step 1. *Select an appropriate topic.*   Content analysis has many applications for all the social sciences. For academic research, it has been used in studies dealing with media content such as sex and violence. As a tool of applied research in public relations and marketing communication, content analysis can be used by planners who want to know what people are saying about their organizations, or how what they are saying coincides with how they are acting. Consider the following possibilities for public relations/ marketing applications of content analysis:

- News coverage (topics, balance, frequency)
- Media artifacts (video news releases, radio actualities, photographs)
- Organizational reputation among various media or particular publics
- Letters to the editor (opinions, topics)
- Customer comments (letters, telephone calls)
- Competitors (claims, offerings, positioning, advertising themes)
- Trends in graphic design or publishing techniques
- Effectiveness of various persuasive appeals
- Public issues affecting an organization
- Preferences of various media (story type, political bias, editorial coverage)

Topics appropriate for your organization are those that deal with the content of artifacts that have already been written (reports, releases, publications, scripts and so on) or that can be put into writing for research purposes (lists of characteristics, conversations, speeches, etc.). The text may originate within your organization, or it may be rooted in the communication or activity of one of your significant publics. Ask yourself how accessible the texts will be for you. Also consider how the information will be useful to your organization, especially because content analysis can help you learn facts about the content but not reasons behind those facts.

Example of Step 1

You are public education manager for MetroHealth, a large statewide health maintenance organization. One of your job responsibilities is to promote a series of patient workshops on topics such as weight loss, nutrition, exercise and general fitness.

You want to get an accurate picture of how the larger daily newspapers in the state deal with these issues. Your purpose for gaining this information is to arm yourself for an eventual public-education campaign that will look to the newspapers for support. Before asking for this support, you decide that it will be helpful to know something about the newspapers' current and recent coverage of these topics.

Step 2. *Select a population for your study.*   This may be people, such as all your employees or just the employees with less than two years' experience on the job. Or it may involve artifacts, such as news releases, company publications, advertisements and so on. After you identify the population, decide on a census or a representative sample.

Example of Step 2

You identify the six largest newspapers in your state. Let's say you decide to limit your study to their news sections (local and national/international), as well as to relevant specialized sections such as lifestyle and science/health.

Because it would be impractical to study every newspaper for every day over the last few years, you select a sample that includes each of the six newspapers for the following varied schedule throughout last 12 months:

One daily edition each month: Monday, first week of January; Tuesday, second week of February; Wednesday, third week of March; Thursday, fourth week of April; Friday, first week of May; Saturday, second week of June; Monday, third week of July; Tuesday, fourth week of August; Wednesday, first week of September; Thursday, second week of October; Friday, third week of November; Saturday, fourth week of December.

Seven to nine Sunday editions each quarter: Every sixth week following the beginning week, indicated by a throw of a dice.

Step 3. *Determine the unit of analysis* by carefully defining terms related to what you want to study.   For purposes of public relations and marketing communication, the unit of analysis may relate to one of the following aspects of communication. Many research studies would involve several of the following approaches mixed together to provide a general view of the whole issue:

- Subject: sorted by themes and topics
- Communication element: headlines, leads, news articles, photo captions, letters to the editor, advertising illustrations and so on
- Incoming communication: sorted by various channels, such as newspapers, magazines, television, radio, direct mail, telephone calls, letters, coupons and e-mail
- Outgoing communication: sorted by various tactics such as newsletters, e-mail, brochures, advertising spots and Web pages
- Source of communication: sorted broadly by various publics or more narrowly by specific individuals or organizations or by subdivisions such as departments, work sites and so on
- Destination: sorted broadly or narrowly; the same as for the source of communication (above)
- Results: sorted by outcomes, effects and consequences

Develop categories for coding your tallies of these units of analysis. These categories must meet the same two major criteria as response categories for surveys—that is, they need to be comprehensive (by including all the possible responses) and mutually exclusive (by not duplicating other possible responses).

Incoming telephone calls, for example, may be categorized as being "positive," "negative," "neutral" or "other." Too many responses in the "other" category indicate faulty categories. Newspaper articles may be studied to count the number of references to your organization, by both name and implication, and then to assess these references as to how positive they are or how accurately they portray your organization and its products or services.

Example of Step 3

You search the newspapers, and count the number of articles and news briefs that deal with one of the topics of your interest (weight loss, nutrition, exercise, general fitness and so on), as you have defined them. These numbers will be compared to the total number of articles and briefs in the publication.

You then analyze each mention of these topics according to the following criteria:

- *Type of article:* Code each published story as an article or a news brief. Define these terms clearly. For example, you might define the difference in terms of length—a brief is up to three paragraphs and an article is longer, or a brief is less than 150 words while an article is longer.

- *Attitude:* Each article related to fitness will be coded as "positive," "negative" or "neutral," depending on how its tone relates to MetroHealth's message of encouraging fitness.

- *Accuracy:* Each article will be coded as "very accurate," "moderately accurate" or "inaccurate," based on how well it presents information that is currently accepted by medical and fitness professionals. Or you might count the number of factual inaccuracies and unwarranted conclusions within the brief or article.

- *Prominence:* Each article will be rated for a "prominent position" (any location on Page One of a section, or top-of-page placement on an inside page) or "non-prominent position" (placement elsewhere on a page).

- *Demographics:* Each article will be coded as to its evident appeal based on gender (men, women or both genders) and age (young, middle, older readers or all ages). This may be determined through criteria such as placement in a particular section (such as women's page, youth tab, etc.) or by the people shown in accompanying photographs or cited as examples within the article.

Step 4. *Develop the mechanics of the study* as a simple follow-up to the previous one. Create a standardized coding form that allows you to record the numbers in each category. Usually this involves simple forms with space for tick marks (/////).

If you will have other people work on this project with you—always a good idea to minimize *coder bias*—you will need to train these coders. Essentially this means writing out and explaining all your definitions so each coder approaches the item in the same way. Because some of the category selection is subjective, there may be some differences here: What is a positive reference to one person may be neutral to another. That's one of the shortcomings of content analysis. One way around this is to have three coders do each item and then record the majority response.

At this stage you also should pretest the coding instrument before actually doing the research. Go through a dozen or so items and see if the coding instrument works well. If not, go back and rethink your categories.

When all of these tasks are completed, you are ready to actually measure the information and record it for later analysis.

Example of Step 4

Let's say that in coding your categories, you arrive at the following results for three different newspapers (Npr): A, B and C:

	NEWS ARTICLES			**NEWS BRIEFS**		
Npr	**Total Articles**	**Fitness Articles**	**Percent Fitness**	**Total Briefs**	**Fitness Briefs**	**Percent Fitness**
A	1000	60	6%	400	40	10%
B	940	54	5.7%	640	50	7.8%
C	1060	25	2.4%	800	70	8.8%

Articles and News Briefs re: Fitness

Npr	Positive	Negative
A	80%	20%
B	82%	18%
C	53%	47%

Articles and News Briefs re: Fitness

Npr	Accurate	Inaccurate
A	95%	5%
B	88%	12%
C	62%	38%

(Additional data would follow.)

Step 5. *Analyze the data.* Data analysis may generate formal reports to your client organization or employer, or it simply may remain as scribbling on your notepad for your own perusal and pondering. That's up to you. Either way, you will want to keep the numbers simple so you can more easily draw insight from them.

As you might guess, researchers have developed some sophisticated statistical techniques for use with content analysis. If you want intricate statistics, contact a professional researcher or refer to a statistics textbook. But you don't have to deal heavily with statistics. Many excellent content analyses rely on simple percentages, which are more useful than raw numbers. You don't know much, for example, if you are told that 25 employees have made money-saving suggestions via the company suggestion box. Twenty-five out of 50 workers? Out of 5,000? But if you are told that those 25 employees represent one-third of the night shift, and that 75 percent of them work in the computer department, you have learned something very interesting and potentially very useful about the quality of ideas originating with night-time computer workers.

If you do choose to prepare a formal report, include an explanation of the reason for your research, information about your sample and a copy of the coding form. Report the results in raw numbers, percentages or usually both. Discuss generalities and insights that you glean from those findings. Many reports conclude with recommendations based on the findings and insights.

Example of Step 5

The research shows that Newspapers A and B provide similar amounts of coverage to fitness-related information, both as news stories and as news briefs. Newspaper C, however, offers significantly less coverage to fitness information in the form of news articles, though it devotes slightly more space than the other newspapers do to fitness-related news briefs.

Newspaper C has a higher number of negative articles and briefs, as this relates to MetroHealth's conclusion about how the articles are likely to promote an appreciation for fitness. This newspaper also has a higher percentage of inaccurate articles and briefs, based on MetroHealth's understanding of up-to-date reliable information.

Based on the data from Newspaper C, you might want to review your public relations procedures.

(Other findings would reflect additional data.)

Recommended Follow–Up.   A logical follow-up step to this content analysis would be to contact the editorial staff of Newspaper C and arrange a meeting between yourself as MetroHealth public education manager and editors of the various news and lifestyle sections. At this meeting, you might noncritically present your findings that indicate the newspaper's relative disinterest in fitness-related articles. Admitting that you are an advocate for fitness information, you might point to surveys indicating a growing interest within the general population (and thus newspaper readers), offering possible ways in which your organization could assist the newspaper in increasing its coverage of this topic. Perhaps you will learn that you could foster more articles by suggesting strong local angles to general fitness information or by offering experts from your organization as interview subjects.

Additionally, you might contact Newspapers A and B and share your findings concerning their performance, encouraging their continued attention to fitness matters.

For future research you might conduct a similar study in one or two years to note any changes in the media trends.

Citations and Recommended Readings

Babbie, E. (1997). *The practice of social research* (8th ed.). Belmont, CA: Wadsworth.

Edmunds, H. (1999). *The focus group research handbook.* Lincolnwood, IL: NTC Business.

Fink, A. (1995). *The survey kit: 2. How to ask survey questions.* Thousand Oaks, CA: Sage.

Fink, A. (1995). *The survey kit: 6. How to sample in surveys.* Thousand Oaks, CA: Sage.

Fletcher, A. D., & Bowers, T. A. (1991). *Fundamentals of advertising research* (4th ed.). Belmont, CA: Wadsworth.

Haskins, J., & Kendrick, A. (1993). *Successful advertising research methods.* Lincolnwood, IL: NTC Business.

Lindenmann, W. K. (1977). Opinion research: How it works, how to use it. *Public Relations Journal, 1,* 13.

Mangione, T. W. (1995). *Mail surveys: Improving the quality.* Applied Social Research Methods Series, No. 40. Thousand Oaks, CA: Sage.

Merton, R. K. (1987). The focused interview and focus groups: Continuities and discontinuities. *Public Opinion Quarterly, 51,* 550–566.

Morgan, D. L. (1997). *Focus groups as qualitative research* (2nd ed.). Qualitative Research Methods Series, Vol. 16. Thousand Oaks, CA: Sage.

Rasinski, K. A. (1989). The effect of question wording on public support for government spending, *Public Opinion Quarterly, 53,* 388–396.

Rubenstein, S. M. (1995). *Surveying public opinion.* Belmont, CA: Wadsworth.

Seitel F. P. (1998). *The practice of public relations* (7th ed.). Upper Saddle River, NJ: Prentice-Hall.

Singletary, M. (1994). *Mass communication research.* White Plains, NY: Longman.

Waddell, H. (1995). Getting a straight answer: CSM scales all ask the wrong question: "How am I doing?" *Marketing Research, 7 (3),* 5–8.

Wimmer, R. G., & Dominick, J. R. (1999). *Mass media research: An introduction* (6th ed.). Belmont, CA: Wadsworth.

Yin, R. K. (1994). *Case study research: Design and methods* (2nd ed.). Applied Social Research Methods Series, No. 5. Thousand Oaks, CA: Sage.

Zeuschner, R. (1993). *Communicating today.* Boston: Allyn & Bacon.

Appendix B

Ethical Standards

Public Relations Society of America
Member Code of Ethics

Approved by the PRSA Assembly. October, 2000

Preamble

- Professional Values
- Principles of Conduct
- Commitment and Compliance

This Code applies to PRSA members. The Code is designed to be a useful guide for PRSA members as they carry out their ethical responsibilities. This document is designed to anticipate and accommodate, by precedent, ethical challenges that may arise. The scenarios outlined in the Code provision are actual examples of misconduct. More will be added as experience with the Code occurs.

The Public Relations Society of America (PRSA) is committed to ethical practices. The level of public trust PRSA members seek, as we serve the public good, means we have taken on a special obligation to operate ethically.

The value of member reputation depends upon the ethical conduct of everyone affiliated with the Public Relations Society of America. Each of us sets an example for each other—as well as other professionals—by our pursuit of excellence with powerful standards of performance, professionalism, and ethical conduct.

Emphasis on enforcement of the Code has been eliminated. But, the PRSA Board of Directors retains the right to bar from membership or expel from the Society any individual who has been or is sanctioned by a government agency or convicted in a court of law of an action that is in violation of this Code.

Ethical practice is the most important obligation of a PRSA member. We view the Member Code of Ethics as a model for other professions, organizations, and professionals.

PRSA Member Statement of Professional Values

This statement presents the core values of PRSA members and, more broadly, of the public relations profession. These values provide the foundation for the Member Code of Ethics and set the industry standard for the professional practice of public relations. These values are the fundamental beliefs that guide our behaviors and decision-making process. We believe our professional values are vital to the integrity of the profession as a whole.

Advocacy

- We serve the public interest by acting as responsible advocates for those we represent.
- We provide a voice in the marketplace of ideas, facts, and viewpoints to aid informed public debate.

Honesty

- We adhere to the highest standards of accuracy and truth in advancing the interests of those we represent and in communicating with the public.

Expertise

- We acquire and responsibly use specialized knowledge and experience.
- We advance the profession through continued professional development, research, and education.
- We build mutual understanding, credibility, and relationships among a wide array of institutions and audiences.

Independence

- We provide objective counsel to those we represent.
- We are accountable for our actions.

Loyalty

- We are faithful to those we represent, while honoring our obligation to serve the public interest.

Fairness

- We deal fairly with clients, employers, competitors, peers, vendors, the media, and the general public.
- We respect all opinions and support the right of free expression.

PRSA Code Provisions

Free Flow of Information

<u>Core Principle</u>
Protecting and advancing the free flow of accurate and truthful information is essential to serving the public interest and contributing to informed decision making in a democratic society.

<u>Intent</u>

- To maintain the integrity of relationships with the media, government officials, and the public
- To aid informed decision-making

<u>Guidelines</u>

A member shall:

- Preserve the integrity of the process of communication
- Be honest and accurate in all communications
- Act promptly to correct erroneous communications for which the practitioner is responsible
- Preserve the free flow of unprejudiced information when giving or receiving gifts by ensuring that gifts are nominal, legal, and infrequent

<u>Examples of Improper Conduct Under this Provision</u>

- A member representing a ski manufacturer gives a pair of expensive racing skis to a sports magazine columnist, to influence the columnist to write favorable articles about the product.
- A member entertains a government official beyond legal limits and/or in violation of government reporting requirements.

Competition

<u>Core Principle</u>

Promoting healthy and fair competition among professionals preserves an ethical climate while fostering a robust business environment.

<u>Intent</u>

- To promote respect and fair competition among public relations professionals
- To serve the public interest by providing the widest choice of practitioner options

<u>Guidelines</u>

A member shall:

- Follow ethical hiring practices designed to respect free and open competition without deliberately undermining a competitor
- Preserve intellectual property rights in the marketplace

<u>Examples of Improper Conduct Under This Provision</u>

- A member employed by a "client organization" shares helpful information with a counseling firm that is competing with others for the organization's business.
- A member spreads malicious and unfounded rumors about a competitor in order to alienate the competitor's clients and employees in a ploy to recruit people and business.

Disclosure of Information

Core Principle

Open communication fosters informed decision making in a democratic society.

Intent

- To build trust with the public by revealing all information needed for responsible decision making

Guidelines

A member shall:

- Be honest and accurate in all communications
- Act promptly to correct erroneous communications for which the member is responsible
- Investigate the truthfulness and accuracy of information released on behalf of those represented
- Reveal the sponsors for causes and interests represented
- Disclose financial interest (such as stock ownership) in a client's organization
- Avoid deceptive practices

Examples of Improper Conduct Under this Provision

- Front groups: A member implements "grass roots" campaigns or letter-writing campaigns to legislators on behalf of undisclosed interest groups.
- Lying by omission: A practitioner for a corporation knowingly fails to release financial information, giving a misleading impression of the corporation's performance.
- A member discovers inaccurate information disseminated via a Web site or media kit and does not correct the information.
- A member deceives the public by employing people to pose as volunteers to speak at public hearings and participate in "grass roots" campaigns.

Safeguarding Confidences

Core Principle

Client trust requires appropriate protection of confidential and private information.

Intent

- To protect the privacy rights of clients, organizations, and individuals by safeguarding confidential information

Guidelines

A member shall:

- Safeguard the confidences and privacy rights of present, former, and prospective clients and employees

- Protect privileged, confidential, or insider information gained from a client or organization
- Immediately advise an appropriate authority if a member discovers that confidential information is being divulged by an employee of a client company or organization

Examples of Improper Conduct Under This Provision
- A member changes jobs, takes confidential information, and uses that information in the new position to the detriment of the former employer.
- A member intentionally leaks proprietary information to the detriment of some other party.

Conflicts of Interest

Core Principle
Avoiding real, potential or perceived conflicts of interest builds the trust of clients, employers, and the publics.
Intent
- To earn trust and mutual respect with clients or employers
- To build trust with the public by avoiding or ending situations that put one's personal or professional interests in conflict with society's interests

Guidelines
A member shall:
- Act in the best interests of the client or employer, even subordinating the member's personal interests
- Avoid actions and circumstances that may appear to compromise good business judgment or create a conflict between personal and professional interests
- Disclose promptly any existing or potential conflict of interest to affected clients or organizations
- Encourage clients and customers to determine if a conflict exists after notifying all affected parties

Examples of Improper Conduct Under This Provision
- The member fails to disclose that he or she has a strong financial interest in a client's chief competitor.
- The member represents a "competitor company" or a "conflicting interest" without informing a prospective client.

Enhancing the Profession

Core Principle
Public relations professionals work constantly to strengthen the public's trust in the profession.

Intent
- To build respect and credibility with the public for the profession of public relations
- To improve, adapt and expand professional practices

Guidelines
A member shall:
- Acknowledge that there is an obligation to protect and enhance the profession
- Keep informed and educated about practices in the profession to ensure ethical conduct
- Actively pursue personal professional development
- Decline representation of clients or organizations that urge or require actions contrary to this Code
- Accurately define what public relations activities can accomplish
- Counsel subordinates in proper ethical decision making
- Require that subordinates adhere to the ethical requirements of the Code
- Report ethical violations, whether committed by PRSA members or not, to the appropriate authority

Examples of Improper Conduct Under This Provision
- A PRSA member declares publicly that a product the client sells is safe, without disclosing evidence to the contrary.
- A member initially assigns some questionable client work to a non-member practitioner to avoid the ethical obligation of PRSA membership.

PRSA Member Code of Ethics Pledge

I pledge:

- To conduct myself professionally, with truth, accuracy, fairness, and responsibility to the public;
- To improve my individual competence and advance the knowledge and proficiency of the profession through continuing research and education;
- And to adhere to the articles of the Member Code of Ethics 2000 for the practice of public relations as adopted by the governing Assembly of the Public Relations Society of America.

I understand and accept that there is a consequence for misconduct, up to and including membership revocation.

And, I understand that those who have been or are sanctioned by a government agency or convicted in a court of law of an action that is in violation of this Code may be barred from membership or expelled from the Society.

Canadian Public Relations Society

Declaration of Principles

It is the purpose of The Canadian Public Relations Society, Inc., in setting forth its ethics of professional conduct:

(a) To affirm that the obligations of a public trust are inherent in the practice of public relations.

(b) To promote and maintain high standards of professional practice and conduct among members, so as to ensure that public relations shall be esteemed as an honourable profession.

(c) To safeguard good taste and truthfulness in all material prepared for public dissemination, and in all aspects of the public relations practitioner's operations.

(d) To ensure that membership in the Society represents surety of ethical conduct, skill, knowledge and competence in the practice of public relations.

(e) To foster increased attention to public relations as a course of study in Universities, Colleges, Institutes, and other similar education organizations, in order to further the proficiency, knowledge and training of men and women engaged in or interested in entering public relations.

Code of Professional Standards

Members of The Canadian Public Relations Society, Inc., are pledged to maintain the spirit and ideals of the following stated principles of conduct, and to consider them essential to the practice of public relations.

(a) A member shall act primarily in the public interest in the practice of public relations and shall neither act nor induce others to act in a way which may affect unfavourably the practice of public relations, the community, or the Society.

(b) A member shall adhere to the highest standards of honesty, accuracy, and truth and shall not knowingly disseminate false or misleading information.

(c) A member shall protect the confidences of present, former and/or prospective clients or employers.

(d) A member shall not represent conflicting or competing interests without the express consent of those concerned, given after a full disclosure of the facts.

(e) A member shall not engage in any practice which has the purpose of corrupting the integrity of channels of public communication.

(f) A member shall not knowingly and directly solicit the client of an-other member unless both agree that there is no conflict between the two engagements.

(g) A member shall uphold this Code, shall cooperate with fellow members in so doing and in enforcing decisions on any matter arising from its application. If a member has reason to believe that another member has engaged in unethical or unfair practices, including practices in violation of this Code, he or she shall inform the proper authorities of the Society for action in accordance with the procedure set forth in the Society Bylaws.

International Public Relations Association
International Code of Ethics (Code of Athens)

CONSIDERING that all Member countries of the United National Organisation have agreed to abide by its Charter which reaffirm "its faith in fundamental human rights, in the dignity and worth of the human person" and that having regard to the very nature of the profession, Public Relations practitioners in these countries should undertake to ascertain and observe the principles set out in this Charter;

CONSIDERING that, apart from "rights," human beings have not only physical or material needs but also intellectual, moral and social needs, and that their rights are of real benefit to them only in-so-far as these needs are essentially met;

CONSIDERING that, in the course of their professional duties and depending on how these duties are performed, Public Relations practitioners can substantially help to meet these intellectual, moral and social needs;

And lastly, CONSIDERING that the use of the techniques enabling them to come simultaneously into contact with millions of people gives Public Relations practitioners a power that has to be restrained by the observance of a strict moral code.

On all these grounds, all members of the International Public Relations Association agree to abide by this International Code of Ethics, and that if, in the light of evidence submitted to the Council, a member should be found to have infringed this Code in the course of his/her professional duties, he/she will be deemed to be guilty of serious misconduct calling for an appropriate penalty.

Accordingly, each member:

Shall Endeavor

1. To contribute to the achievement of the moral and cultural conditions enabling human beings to reach their full stature and enjoy the indefeasible rights to which they are entitled under the "Universal Declaration of Human Rights";

2. To establish communications patterns and channels which, by fostering the free flow of essential information, will make each member of the group feel that he/she is being kept informed, and also give him/her an awareness of his/her own personal involvement and responsibility, and of his/her solidarity with other members;

3. To conduct himself/herself always and in all circumstances in such a manner as to deserve and secure the confidence of those with whom he/she comes into contact;

4. To bear in mind that, because of the relationship between his/her profession and the public, his/her conduct—even in private—will have an impact on the way in which the profession as a whole is appraised;

Shall Undertake

5. To observe, in the course of his/her professional duties, the moral principles and rules of the "Universal Declaration of Human Rights";

6. To pay due regard to, and uphold, human dignity, and to recognise the right of each individual to judge for himself/herself;

7. To establish the moral, psychological and intellectual conditions for dialogue in its true sense, and to recognise the right of these parties involved to state their case and express their views;

8. To act, in all circumstances, in such a manner as to take account of the respective interests of the parties involved: both the interests of the organisation which he/she serves and the interests of the publics concerned;

9. To carry out his/her undertakings and commitments which shall always be so worded as to avoid any misunderstanding, and to show loyalty and integrity in all circumstances so as to keep the confidence of his/her clients or employers, past or present, and of all the publics that are affected by his/her actions;

Shall Refrain From

10. Subordinating the truth to other requirements;

11. Circulating information which is not based on established and ascertainable facts;

12. Taking part in any venture or undertaking which is unethical or dishonest or capable of impairing human dignity and integrity;

13. Using any "manipulative" methods or techniques designed to create subconscious motivations which the individual cannot control of his/her own free will and so cannot be held accountable for the action taken on them.

Code of Conduct (Code of Venice)

A. Personal and Professional Integrity

It is understood that by personal integrity is meant the maintenance of both high moral standards and a sound reputation. By professional integrity is meant observance of the Constitution rules and, particularly the Code as adopted by IPRA.

B. Conduct Towards Clients and Employers

A member has a general duty of fair dealing towards his/her clients or employers, past and present. A member shall not represent conflicting or competing interests without the express consent of those concerned. A member shall safeguard the confidences of both present and former clients or employers. A member shall not employ methods tending to be derogatory of another member's client or employer. In performing services for a client or employer a member shall not accept fees, commission or any other valuable consideration in connection with those services from anyone other than his/her client or employer without the express consent of his/her client or employee, given after a full disclosure of the facts. A member shall not propose to a prospective client or employer that his/her fee or other compensation be contingent on the achievement of certain results; nor shall he/she enter into any fee agreement to the same effect.

C. Conduct Toward the Public and the Media

A member shall conduct his/her professional activities with respect to the public interest and for the dignity of the individual. A member shall not engage in practice which tends to corrupt the integrity of channels of public communication. A member shall not intentionally disseminate false or misleading information. A member shall at all times seek to give a faithful representation of the organisation which he/she serves. A member shall not create any organization to serve some announced cause but actually to serve an undisclosed special or private interest of a member or his/her client or employer, nor shall he/she make use of it or any such existing organization.

D. Conduct Towards Colleagues

A member shall not intentionally injure the professional reputation or practice of another member. However, if a member has evidence that another member has been guilty of unethical, illegal or unfair practices, including practices in violation of this Code, he should present the information to the Council of IPRA. A member shall not seek to supplant another member with his employer or client. A member shall co-operate with fellow members in upholding and enforcing this Code.

Appendix C

Sample Campaigns

Following are four examples of public relations and integrated marketing campaigns. Each of these campaigns won a Silver Anvil award from the Public Relations Society of America.

These are not the fully articulated campaigns but rather the summaries and overviews provided to PRSA in the awards competition. Each Silver Anvil entry is limited to two pages of information it provides the following categories:

- *Research*: Quality of original or secondary research used to identify the problem or opportunity and the approaches likely to be successful.
- *Planning*: Objectives, originality and judgement in selecting strategy and techniques, accuracy of budget, and difficulties encountered.
- *Execution*: How the plan was implemented; materials used; in-progress adjustments to the plan; techniques in winning management's support; other techniques; difficulties encountered; and effectiveness of the program's employment dollar, personnel and other resources.
- *Evaluation*: Efforts made to identify, analyze and quantify results and to what degree a program has met its objectives.

Check out the PRSA Silver Anvil Web site (www.silveranvil.org) for outlines on all the competition winners since 1968. The Silver Anvil competition represents the best of the best, at least in terms of entries in the annual national contest.

Notice, however, that even the best are inexact in how they use some of the elements of a good campaign that have been presented in this book. For example, some Silver Anvil winners have a fuzzy approach to goals and objectives, others mislabel or blend strategy and tactics, and some use inappropriate evaluation criteria such as advertising equivalency. So when you review the Silver Anvil winners, take each one with a grain of salt. Determine for yourself what particular elements of the campaign are good models for you to follow.

The following examples have been selected to give you a model of a particularly effective use of at least one phase of the planning process.

Formative Research Phase

Defending FedEx's Reliability:
"Absolutely, Positively, Whatever It Takes"
(Category: Crisis Communications)

Author's Commentary: This campaign by Ketchum Public Relations is a good example of the formative research phase of the planning process, particularly noteworthy since crisis communication often is done with little formative or ongoing research. Note that some of the research information, particularly that dealing with key publics (called "audiences" in this competition entry) is included in both the Overview and Planning sections of this entry.

Overview

During the hectic pre-holiday business season, the threat of a pilots' strike at Federal Express Corporation jeopardized the very foundation of FedEx—its reliable service—and loomed over the company's relationship with four key audiences:

- With customers, who might be forced to divert volume from FedEx to protect their 1998 holiday business;
- With FedEx employees, who feared massive layoffs if the company was forced to restructure to survive a strike;
- With FDX [parent company of FedEx] shareholders, who foresaw the potential earnings drain of a prolonged job action;
- And with pilots, who were influenced by a formidable and negative campaign by the FedEx Pilots Association.

The stakes were high, and global. Working hand-in-hand with senior management and the negotiating team, the FedEx Corporate Communications Department faced a daunting task: To create an integrated communications plan that would reassure all key audiences and turn crisis into opportunity. By leveraging all resources (the external counsel of Ketchum Public Relations plus internal resources from media relations, employee communications, investor relations, and other FedEx divisions) the communications team moved quickly to favorably shape public opinion, which helped influence a timely resolution to a potentially damaging global business crisis.

Research

National and local research—both quantitative and qualitative—was conducted intensively from mid-October to mid-December, given obvious time pressures.

Customer Studies: Focus groups were held in Chicago, New York and Phoenix to gauge awareness of contract negotiations between FedEx and its pilots union. In mid-October, few customers had heard of a possible FedEx service disruption. However, customers who had been hindered by the previous summer's strike at UPS stressed the importance of advance, honest communication about any service problems. During November, telephone polls of express shippers continued to show low awareness of a potential strike at FedEx.

Memphis Polling: FedEx research specialists conducted weekly polls of residents in Memphis, the company's headquarters city and home to one-third of the pilot force. While early polls revealed a neutral stance toward FedEx and the union, later polls reflected a dramatic shift in favor of the company—the city's largest employer—and against a strike.

Industry Analysis: The team analyzed case studies of companies that had faced similar labor situations, specifically UPS, Northwest Airlines and Caterpillar, Inc. Key learning was applied to the FedEx communications strategy.

Media Monitoring: Several times a day, the team monitored media outlets, Web sites, chat rooms, and online newsgroups to track relevant commentary. This ongoing "litmus test" of public opinion helped the team continually fine-tune its strategies and messaging.

Planning

Anticipating the negative tactics of the FedEx Pilots Association, the team took a true campaign approach with a positive and disciplined communications plan that focused on the strengths of the FedEx organization. The campaign had to build a compelling case that FedEx had the resolve, financial muscle and additional resources to restructure, if necessary, in order to survive a pilots' strike—unlike UPS, which was shut down by a Teamsters' strike in the summer of 1997. Early in the planning process, the team set up a central "War Room," clearly defined all communications responsibilities, and met daily to map out key messages and strategy. Full-scale scenario planning also provided the flexibility to adapt to constantly changing conditions. Risk management was the overarching goal as the team identified all possible allies and leveraged research findings to determine the best strategy to reach each audience.

Target Audiences: Customers, non-pilot employees, shareholders and pilots.

Objectives:

1.   Retain customers and maintain package volume during peak shipping season.
2.   Keep morale and service levels high among 143,000+ non-pilot employees.
3.   Maintain stock price and shareholder confidence in FDX, parent company of FedEx.
4.   Persuade pilots to return to the bargaining table and reach an equitable agreement.

Strategies:

1. Reassure customers that FedEx would remain operational, no matter what.
2. Keep non-pilot employees informed and assured of their importance.
3. Reinforce strength of FDX network to shareholders via national financial media and analysts
4. Correct pilots' misperceptions by relaying details of the company's proposals

Budget: $300,000 in fees and $100,000 in other expenses.

Execution

The team conducted twice-a-day, cross-functional meetings attended by Customer Service, Legal, Marketing and Investor Relations, as well as Public Relations and Employee Communications. Based on this daily feedback, messages and positioning were constantly refined in order to keep the campaign fully aligned with corporate strategy. Throughout the crisis, the team also capitalized on media interest in FedEx to highlight the company's strengths, such as its superior information technology, unique employee culture, management depth, and operational adaptability as a subsidiary of FDX.

1. *Reassuring customers:* FedEx feared that even the threat of a pilots' strike—coming at the brink of its busiest season—could prompt customers to make irreversible shipping decisions. With "poaching" competitors increasing their capacity to handle new business, FedEx had to move quickly and decisively to reassure customers that it would continue to meet their shipping needs. To prevent widespread shipper panic, the national media strategy focused on the FedEx commitment to its customers and its ability to reconfigure the network to remain operational. The team used the high-traffic FedEx web site for customer communication and coordinated one-on-one messaging with Customer Service and the FedEx Global Sales staff. The team also used press releases, video news releases, and B-roll to drive national media coverage of this "business as usual" commitment. To secure third-party endorsements, the team held one-on-one contingency plan briefings with customer executives.

2. *Informing employees:* Facing potential paralysis as employees feared for their job security, FedEx mounted a comprehensive campaign to keep non-pilot employees informed and motivated. The "Absolutely, Positively, Whatever It Takes" theme reinforced the positive tone of the campaign and refocused employee spirit on meeting customer needs. The campaign theme was carried out on posters, buttons, banners, bumper stickers, T-shirts and sweatshirts, and was highlighted daily on FXTV, the company's digital broadcast network and on a special intranet "sitelet." Non-pilot employees were also reached externally via national and local media stories. In addition, the FedEx CEO and COO conducted 15 meetings in mid-November, speaking to

more than 6,000 employees in Memphis and Indianapolis—the company's two largest operations—with FXTV coverage that extended the reach around the world.

3. *Maintaining shareholder confidence:*   On the investor front, FedEx walked a fine line between offering a contract the pilots would accept and maintaining shareholder value. The team regularly contacted key buy-side and sell-side analysts to forestall any downgrading and to explain the financial implications of the FedEx offer and the union's demands. As negotiations progressed, the team also set up financial media interviews with the CFO of FDX to detail specifics of the company's contingency plans in the event of a strike.

4. *Convincing pilots:*   When the union leadership deliberately deprived its members of the details of the company's latest and best offer, FedEx was concerned that pilots would make ill-informed decisions and support a strike movement. After a neutral third-party analysis characterized FedEx's proposal as favorable, fair and industry leading, the company sent the proposal and analysis directly to pilots' homes. When union officials encouraged members not to read the information, the team appealed to pilots through frequent local media interviews. The local media strategy reached pilots and the 30,000 other Memphis-based employees, informing them about the harm a strike would cause—to the company, to the community, and to global businesses—and communicating with credibility that the company offered an industry-leading contract to its pilots. A critical communication from FedEx founder Fred Smith, sent directly to the pilots and their families, strongly suggested that they consider all possible ramifications because the company would proceed "with or without you," emphasizing that the company could not and would not disproportionately compensate any one work group at the expense of others.

Evaluation

During the volatile negotiation process, the communications team took its "seat at the table" to shape the communication strategy and help protect the company's relationships with customers, employees and shareholders. Few, if any, valued customers switched their shipping business. The company's stock price actually soared, instead of plummeting. And employees turned their "Absolutely, Positively, Whatever It Takes" spirit into a customer focus. Just weeks after the integrated communications program was launched, the union postponed any job action, went back to the negotiating table, and overwhelmingly approved an industry-leading contract.

1. *Retain customers and maintain package volume.*   Nightly package volume remained steady throughout the strike threat and eventually reached more than 4.5 million packages, up 12 percent versus prior year. Opportunistic media interviews resulted in broader discussions of the FedEx business in key national outlets, and FedEx customer confidence remained strong. In a live

CNBC interview, Pat Connolly of Williams-Sonoma, a large FedEx customer, repeatedly confirmed his faith in FedEx: "We rely on Federal Express. Ninety-eight percent of their people will be there on the job. We're very confident of their back-up and contingency plans."

2. *Maintain employee focus and morale.*   During the negotiations, FedEx internal service measurements were the highest in the company's history. An overwhelming number of employees demonstrated their "purple blood" loyalty via e-mails and letters to the editor of *The Commercial Appeal* in Memphis. Further, in a remarkable show of employee spirit and dedication to customers, approximately 3,500 FedEx employees attended a public rally organized by a group of FedEx employees on their own time—an event that sparked national coverage and attention.

3. *Maintain shareholder confidence and stock price.*   Targeted communications helped buoy the stock price throughout the threatened strike period. As contingency plans were laid out for analysts and financial media, the team emphasized a critical cost/benefit ratio: How the cost of long-term technology investments would benefit FedEx with continued success in the global marketplace. The analysts' assessments gradually changed from skepticism to understanding, and finally to belief in the company's "business-as-usual" position. When the union sent out strike ballots, the stock was at $43. News of the pilots' decision to postpone a strike sent the stock price up to the mid-$80's. By the end of 1998, the stock traded at $93 a share.

4. *Persuade pilots to return to the bargaining table.*   The two-pronged communication strategy—direct and third-party influence—helped increase pilot awareness of the company's desire to reach an equitable contract and its determination to keep FedEx operating. On November 19, the union leadership agreed to return to the negotiating table and not count strike ballots. On December 18, the union negotiators reached a tentative contract agreement with FedEx. On December 23, the FPA board voted (15-3) to recommend ratification to members. And on February 4—after five years of negotiations and two previous failed contract votes—the first pilot contract with FedEx was ratified by an incredible 87 percent of voting crew members.

Strategy Phase

Colorado Prepaid Tuition Fund: "Educate Our Kids" (Category: Marketing Consumer Services)

Author's Commentary: The "Educate Our Kids" campaign is a particularly good example of the Strategy section of the planning process, with carefully outlined objectives and strategies. Note that each objective has a measurement component that is reviewed as part of the evaluation phase of the campaign.

Overview

The Colorado Prepaid Tuition Fund, a state fund to assist families in investing toward future college expenses for their children, faced an uphill marketing challenge in its second year of operation. Highly successful in 1997, its first year, the fund attracted a total investment commitment of $60 million from Colorado families, partially due to pent-up demand.

Research

To determine how to maximize second year results, Kostka-Gleason Communications (KGC) and the Colorado Student Obligation Bond Authority (CSOBA) commissioned a March 1998 baseline public opinion telephone survey of Colorado residents from Talmey-Drake Research & Strategy. This research, plus statistics from the fund's first year, shaped both objectives and strategies.

1. *Demographics.* Research indicated that demographics are not dependable in determining whether a family is likely to invest. The fund appeals to families across all demographics for income, education, age and investment savvy. Likelihood to invest is stronger among non-sophisticated investors and non-risk-takers of all income levels, a target market. Students enrolled in the fund are newborn to 16 years, concentrated at ages 8–12 years.

2. *Awareness.* Ninety-seven percent of families interviewed believe it is important for children to go to college, but general awareness of the fund was 49 percent statewide.

3. *Media are key to reaching families.* Thirty-nine percent of families first heard about the fund from TV and another 87 percent from newspapers.

4. *Key messages move families to invest.* Research identified three messages that motivate families to invest, myths to be countered that demotivate investors, and the need to emphasize the fund's stabilization reserve which makes it more secure (according to 77 percent of people interviewed).

5. *Need to motivate calls to 800 number.* Informal research showed that other state college savings plans achieved up to 40 percent of first-year results in the

second year. Based on data from the first year, 40 percent growth in the fund (to $84 million) would require at least 8,500 new prospect calls to the fund's 800 number. A second survey in 1999 and statistics from the 1998 enrollment period were used to track results.

Planning

KGC designed a public relations and marketing plan with input and approval from CSOBA. The enrollment period (the annual nine-week window during which families are allowed to invest in the fund) was set for October 5–December 8. The main thrust of marketing communications activity was focused on the two weeks preceding the enrollment period and the enrollment period itself.

Objective #1:   Increase the fund by 40 percent to a total of $84 million during the 1998 Enrollment Period, based on the success of other state college funds.

Objective #2:   Generate 500 new calls to the fund's 800 number to increase the prospect base needed to achieve targeted growth.

Objective #3:   Increase statewide public awareness of the fund to more than 50 percent.

Strategy #1:   Develop a community relations' media campaign to reach families who want to save for college, but would not respond to traditional marketing of financial products. (Research supported using TV/newspapers and targeting unsophisticated investors.)

Strategy #2:   Use the campaign to motivate families to contact the fund's 800 number, building the prospect list for direct mail follow-up with a user-friendly enrollment kit, which highlights investor families and encourages calls to the 800 number for enrollment help.

Strategy #3:   Target the market messages that appeal to wide demographics of families who want to send their children to college, positioning the Fund with a family focus (rather than financial) to attract unsophisticated investors, motivate families to invest, dispel myths about the fund, and emphasize the stabilization reserve which reinforces safety of the investment. (All of these points were based on research.)

Strategy #4:   Create elementary school curriculum projects targeting 6 to 12-year olds (and their parents) and leverage into proactive news coverage to increase statewide awareness. (First-year results and data from other states showed strength of this age group and the need to increase awareness.)

We prepared an integrated, comprehensive public relations and marketing program and calendar for pre-enrollment kick-off and the nine-week enrollment period. The challenge was to create news media interest in the fund's second, less newsworthy year.

Execution

Addressing Strategy #1:   A state-wide community relations' campaign, "Educate Our Kids," encouraged families to save for college, engaged news media interest by minimizing the commercial aspect of the fund, and focused on families rather than finance. The fund served as the messenger for the campaign.

Addressing Strategy #2:   Prominent display of the 800 number and web site was used in news media activities, marketing materials and advertising. Direct mail follow-up to the 800 number/web site mailing list included the 1998 enrollment kit, newsletters and two deadline postcards.

Addressing Strategy #3:   Messages identified through research attracted families to the 800 number in news media activities and converted prospects to investors through marketing materials including an employer outreach program of payroll stuffers, on-site distribution of information, company newsletter articles and employee presentations, and on bookmarks distributed by libraries statewide. The family theme was used in public service announcements featuring Denver Bronco wide receiver Ed McCaffrey and his family that resulted in high volume TV and radio air time. The enrollment kit featured seven kids (enrolled in the fund) in grown-up, oversized "career" clothes and their families, with quotes on why they invested—to help other family's identify with the prospect of investing for college. The stabilization reserve message was reinforced by a high credibility, husband/wife financial planner and investment banker team who are investors in the fund. A limited print advertising budget featured three of the "dressed-up" kids and TV and radio ads supported the messages.

Addressing Strategy #4:   Three curriculum projects targeting students ages 8–12 were created for elementary school participation and leveraged into news media coverage. For the kick-off event, schools from each of Colorado's 63 counties decorated a huge puzzle piece of their county. A statewide news media interview tour was conducted to pick up puzzle pieces for photo opportunities and media interviews. The giant 17×25-foot puzzle was unveiled at the kick-off by 250 students, parents and teachers and Governor Roy Romer with TV, newspaper and radio coverage. The puzzle was displayed in downtown Denver during the enrollment period. Two promotions generating TV and newspaper coverage were sponsored by each of the state's top two TV stations and offered to elementary schools statewide: A Day in the Life of Education Photo Contest by the NBC affiliate and a Reach 4 Your Future Learning Series by the CBS affiliate.

Evaluation

Objective #1:   The fund increased total dollars committed to future college expenses by 58 percent to a total of $95 million, 18 percent or $11 million higher than the goal which was based on the successful efforts of other state college savings plans.

Objective #2:   The fund exceeded its goal of calls to its 800 number by 18 percent, with 10,365 calls, and the number of enrollment kits mailed to callers was 93 percent higher than during the same period one year earlier.

Objective #3:   Statewide awareness of the fund increased 6 percent to 55 percent, well ahead of the goal of 50 percent, based on a new public opinion survey following the 1998 enrollment period.

Tactics Phase

Department 56's Collectibles: "A Royal Celebration"
(Category: Special Events and Observances)

Author's Commentary: This campaign by Carmichael Lynch Spong public relations agency is a particularly good example of effective communication tactics. Note that this campaign generated a lot of activity around a single event.

Overview

If you build it, they will come. That's what Department 56 (D56), a leading manufacturer of miniature lighted village collectibles and holiday giftware, believed with the introduction of its new special edition Village piece.

The company wanted to create excitement for the special edition piece, Kensington Palace, which would only be available during D56's 1998 Homes for the Holidays national retail event, November 5–9.

Carmichael Lynch Spong (CLS) proposed hosting "A Royal Celebration," a grand unveiling event at the International Collectibles Exposition in Rosemont, Ill., the nation's largest collectibles show.

CLS developed and implemented "A Royal Celebration" as a tease and reveal campaign designed to generate interest, build anticipation and raise awareness for the unveiling on June 27, 1998.

Research

CLS researched previous special events conducted at collectibles shows to determine how D56 could steal the Rosemont show.

CLS researched collector shows across the country to determine which venue would be appropriate for D56 to make the most impact with key audiences.

CLS investigated competitor events scheduled at the 1998 Rosemont show.

CLS reviewed other related Princess Diana collectible pieces to make sure D56 would not be associated with negative publicity surrounding the anniversary of the Princess's death.

Planning
Objectives

- Build awareness of and anticipation for Kensington Palace among potential and existing collectors.
- Stimulate purchase of Kensington Palace at retail.

Strategies

1. Stimulate awareness of and anticipation for Kensington Palace through a high impact special event.
2. Implement a national media relations program to generate awareness of the new piece.
3. Drive consumer traffic to participating Homes for the Holidays retailers through pre-event activities.

Target Audiences

- Current D56 collectors
- Memorabilia collectors
- Rosemont attendees
- People with a propensity to collect

Budget

Total project budget was $200,000. $125,000 was allocated for out-of-pocket expenses including staging, talent, collateral, props, etc. $75,000 was allocated for agency fees.

Execution

Special Event

CLS conducted brainstorming sessions to best determine how to reach target audiences and "own" Rosemont. The group agreed the theme "A Royal Celebration" would effectively capture collector interest while hinting to the origin of the special piece. CLS also recommended hosting a sweepstakes to incent non-village collectors to visit the D56 booth and attend the special product unveiling event.

Sweepstakes

CLS designed a "must be present to win" sweepstakes to help generate additional interest with non-D56 collectors. The prize was an all-expense-paid trip to London. The winner and a guest would fly to New York where they would board the QE2, a luxury cruise ship that transported them across the Atlantic on a six-day cruise. In London, they would stay at the Savoy Hotel for three days and visit historic landmarks, including Kensington Palace. Finally D56 would send the winner home to America first class on the Concorde.

Attendees could register for the sweepstakes at the D56 booth. During the unveiling ceremony, 10 finalists would be chosen. These 10 people would have the opportunity to choose a key, one of which would open a safe which held the new mystery Village piece. One by one, finalists would approach the safe with their key until the safe was unlocked and the special edition piece was revealed. The finalist with the winning key would win the grand prize.

Generating Awareness

Postcard Mailing: CLS distributed teaser postcards to pre-registered and former Rosemont attendees. The postcards mailed in early June with "Who Holds The Key?" teaser messaging about the event. The postcards encouraged attendees to visit the D56 booth to learn more about the special piece and the sweepstakes.

Keys: Knowing that Rosemont attendees enjoy receiving freebies, and to generate booth traffic and spread word of mouth, gold keys and lanyards were distributed to Rosemont attendees as they entered the show floor. The keys held a tag containing information about the sweepstakes registration and product unveiling. Actors dressed as palace guards and British Bobbies distributed the keys.

A Royal Celebration

Guarding the Special Piece: The special piece (Kensington Palace) was hidden in a safe in the D56 booth. The safe was guarded by Royal Palace Guards until its unveiling at the "A Royal Celebration" event.

Changing of the Guards: A changing-of-the-guard skit was choreographed to music and took place every hour on the hour at the D56 booth. The changing skit was meant to be humorous as the guards would "break out" of their official guard persona into a James Bond-type adventurer.

The Royal Procession: CLS created an exciting procession of the safe (containing the special piece) from the D56 booth to the staging area. Sent off with heralders at the booth, the safe was escorted through the crowds of collectors by Bobbies (British police). Two bagpipe players led the way and a procession of attendees followed the safe into the auditorium. On stage, Scottish dancers in kilts provided entertainment until the safe was center stage.

Staging: CLS produced all the staging elements to bring the event to life. The props included a 12 × 40-foot backdrop photograph of a D56 Village setting and a life-size replica of the Kensington Palace gate. The 10 finalists were called on stage and asked to select a key. One by one the finalists tried their keys in the safe lock. All finalists received a Kensington Palace piece signed by the Village artist.

Goodie Bags: British-themed goodie bags were distributed to event attendees as they exited the auditorium. A Kensington Palace postcard inside the bag reminded attendees the special piece was only available during Homes for the Holidays. Other goodie bag items included tea bags and shortbread cookies.

Dealer Postcard: A second version of the Kensington Palace postcard was reproduced as a tool for dealers to use in their own marketing efforts.

Publicity

Pre-Event:

- Event announcement was distributed to collector publications in April.
- D56 web site featured "Who Holds the Key?" teaser messaging.
- The pre-event information was featured in D56's *Quarterly* magazine.

Post Event: Kensington Palace was the news hook for proactive national media relations conducted in conjunction with Homes for the Holidays, November 5–9. This included a news release, photography and matte release.

Ronald McDonald House: A portion of the sales from Kensington Palace was donated to Ronald McDonald House Charities to add to the $2 million that D56 had raised since 1995.

Evaluation

Objective 1:   Build Awareness of Kensington Palace

- 4,500 Rosemont attendees registered for the sweepstakes (of the 8,000 show attendees).
- More than 7,000 keys and lanyards were distributed to attendees as they entered the exhibit area.
- More than 2,000 people attended "A Royal Celebration" unveiling event (of the 6,000 attendees in the exhibition hall at that time).
- In May 1998, while the "Who Holds The Key" teaser messaging was active, the Web site received 307,000 page views; 30 percent more than were received in May 1997.
- The Web site received more than 23,000 page views on June 27.
- Dialogue monitored on internet chat groups speculated about the D56 piece.
- Rosemont executives claimed D56 "owned" the show with the event.
- D56's senior vice president of marketing shared the following feedback with CLS, "We asked you to help us steal the show at Rosemont and that's exactly what you did. The event was beautifully organized and flawlessly executed."

Objective 2:   Stimulate Purchase of Kensington Palace.

- D56 dealers compiled waiting lists prior to Kensington Palace's availability.
- Many dealer waiting lists exceeded their product supply.
- Sales representatives indicated that dealers sold out of Kensington Palace pieces during the Homes for the Holidays event.
- Department 56 reported its highest fourth-quarter earning results, up 11 percent from the previous year.

- Revenues for D56 were 16 percent higher than third quarter 1997, due to mid-year product introductions, including Kensington Palace.
- D56 realized $6.5 million in incremental sales from the sale of the special piece which was only for sale during a five day window (November 5–9).
- More than $420,000 was donated to Ronald McDonald Houses as a result of the Kensington Palace piece.
- News about the unveiling resulted in media coverage in virtually all target collector media publications.
- Homes for the Holidays media relations efforts generated 34.5 million gross impressions.
- 172 placements featuring Kensington Palace photography or key messages generated 28 million gross impressions.
- Broadcast highlights featuring Kensington Palace included "Fox and Friends" national morning cable show and "Today Show New York."
- Print placement highlights featuring product photography included: *Cincinnati Post, Tampa Tribune* and *San Jose Mercury News*.

Budget: "A Royal Celebration" event was implemented on budget.

Evaluation Research Phase

Ketchum Employee Benefits Program:
"Ketchum Goes Primetime"
(Category: Internal Communications)

Author's Commentary: The Ketchum Public Relations employee benefits campaign is a particularly good example of the Evaluation phase of the planning process. Note that the presentation for the evaluation phase is structured around the individual objectives.

Overview

When Ketchum's Human Resources Department decided to offer its U.S. employees a new slate of benefit options for 1999 because of difficulty with the current plan and cost, they turned to their Pittsburgh office to create a communications program that would effectively and creatively provide information to this savvy audience during the 1998 enrollment period. During both the 1996 and 1998 open enrollment periods, Ketchum employees were required to switch health insurance providers. In 1996, U.S. offices went from a choice of three or more health insurance options to one: Allmerica, a company most employees had never heard of. For 1999, Ketchum again limited the option to one provider: PrimarySelect, another relatively obscure insurer.

Communicating the news of the benefit changes presented several challenges:

1. Ketchum employees are extremely busy with client-related work and are under billability pressure to focus on income-generating work, leaving little time for administrative tasks, such as reviewing benefits information.

2. The PrimarySelect plan incorporated vastly different guidelines for coverage than the existing plan, necessitating detailed explanation of how to obtain maximum benefits; in addition, changes to all of the other benefits plans (life insurance, dental, vision, etc.) had to be communicated at the same time.

3. Ketchum employees have been resistant to change in the past and had openly voiced a desire for a choice of health insurance options.

Research

- *Primary:* Focus groups were conducted by benefits consultant MMC&P at a representative sample of Ketchum U.S. offices. A significant number of respondents indicated substantial dissatisfaction with the clarity and quality of employee benefit communications. Specifically, employees asked for better communication and discussion of benefits, possibly at staff meetings, benefit recaps on customized profiles of their benefits.

- *Secondary:*   A literature search revealed a study by William M. Mercer, Inc., an employee benefits consulting firm, which reported that the majority (57 percent) of companies of comparable size to Ketchum (those with more than 500 employees) offered at least two health insurance plans and many offered more in 1997. This showed Ketchum's decision to offer only one plan was not the norm, making communications more difficult.

Planning

Program Objectives

1. Improve satisfaction of the benefits communications among U.S. employees.
2. Minimize negative reaction to the PrimarySelect health insurance plan compared to the last benefits change.
3. Reduce benefits administration staff hours during open enrollment period.

Strategies

- Develop a themed communications program that creatively provides employees with benefits information in response to the need for more interesting communication.
- Employ a customized approach, as requested by employees.

Audiences

- 700 full- and part-time employees in Ketchum's U.S. offices.

Budget

Out-of-pocket costs were $38,000, or less than $55 per employee. All development, writing and coordination was done in-house.

Execution

From the initial meeting with Benefits Administration, Ketchum created and produced the following materials in just six weeks:

Theme

A "Primetime Television" theme was created to introduce the new benefits program spinning off the PrimarySelect name, since it was unknown to employees. Given Ketchum's line of business, the media theme was also one that every Ketchum employee could relate to.

Series Premiere Party

To excite employees and elicit a positive reaction toward the benefits change, employees were sent personalized invitations to attend a premiere party for the benefits announcement. Since benefits meetings historically tend to be standard business meetings, Ketchum wanted a more engaging atmosphere. Refreshments were provided and meetings took place within two days nationwide to ensure maximum system-wide consistency. The parties helped Benefits Administration celebrate new enhancements to the overall program. Talking points were prepared for office directors. The party also helped to personally introduce employees to the benefits in a group setting, thus limiting opportunities for misinformed word-of-mouth, which was prevalent during the 1996 enrollment period.

"Primetime Benefits Live" Video

A series premiere entitled "Primetime Benefits Live," an 11-minute video, was created to launch the premiere party and share preliminary information about the benefits. The video was a spoof of ABC's former newsmagazine "Primetime Live." "Sam Ronaldson" and "Diana Saucer," professional actors, investigated Ketchum's new program. The show was divided into segments to give an overview of the various benefits including health, dental, vision, life insurance, accidental death and dismemberment, long-term disability and other supplemental insurance programs. Various Ketchum employees were interviewed by the investigative reporter. An additional version of the video was created for each office for use during new employee orientation in 1999.

KB Guide

The *KB Guide* (Ketchum Benefits Guide) was produced to create a single written benefits resource. The *KB Guide* contained features similar to various columns found in *TV Guide,* including "Cheers and Jeers" letters and even a crossword puzzle. The crossword puzzle was designed as an employee contest as a fun way to reinforce key benefits information. The guide's compact size made it easy for employees to carry in a briefcase or purse, and it easily fit in a desk drawer or file. The gatefold, which contained open enrollment dates and deadlines, was perforated so that it could be removed in 1999 for new hires. The *KB Guides* were distributed, along with PrimarySelect pens (to do the crossword puzzle in ink), at special staff meetings in which employees were first shown a video entitled "Primetime Benefits Live." The *KB Guide* was designed to be used during open enrollment; to be referred to throughout 1999 by existing employees; and as a reference for new hires throughout 1999. Employees received a personalized copy of the *KB Guide* with their name and home address affixed by label on the front cover.

Ketchum Global Network (KGN)

Ketchum's Intranet served as a key communications tool, customizing the information for employees. An entire area on the site was devoted to "Ketchum Is Going Primetime." Each employee benefit was described in detail and links to the insurers' Web sites provided additional information to employees. Weekly feature articles also were featured throughout the enrollment period. An interactive question-and-answer page gave employees the opportunity to submit questions. Responses were posted on the site the next day. KGN also was used to alert employees to enrollment meetings and benefits deadlines. Online enrollment also was provided to employees. By simply selecting the enrollment form on the site, employees could make their benefits selection and submit the form. This process dramatically decreased the amount of paperwork, and benefits confirmations were provided to employees within two weeks. A notification schedule was created to correspond to each office's deadlines, and system wide e-mail was used to deliver the reminder to each office.

Enrollment Meetings

Enrollment meetings were conducted nationwide so employees could personally meet with benefits representatives. To further explain the changes, Ketchum developed a PowerPoint presentation that was shared with each office and reviewed the key information about each benefits program.

Evaluation

Objective #1:   Improve satisfaction of the benefits communications among U.S. employees. A post-enrollment period employee survey revealed:

- The overall quality of benefits communications was rated by employees as an 8.4 out of 10. Overall content was rated as 8.2 out of 10, where 10 was very useful in understanding the new benefits plans.
- Employees rated the *KB Guide* an 8.0 out of 10, where 10 was very useful in understanding Ketchum's new benefit plans.
- Benefits announcement meetings were rated a 7.8, open enrollment meetings an 8.3 and the Primetime video was rated a 7. 1.
- Only 13 percent of employees reported not reading the *KB Guide,* and because the information was so understandable, 30 percent of employees chose not to attend an open enrollment meeting.
- Among those employees who were employed by Ketchum in 1996 during the last period of benefits communications, 79 percent rated 1998 benefits communications as better or much better than communications in 1996.

Objective #2:   Minimize negative reaction to the PrimarySelect health insurance plan compared to the last benefits change.

- A post-enrollment period employee survey revealed that 48 percent of employees said the new benefits made them feel better or much better about working at Ketchum than the old choices; only 7 percent said the new plan made them feel worse or much worse.

- There were only a few "complaint" calls to Benefits Administration during open enrollment period, and the open enrollment meetings were positive question-and-answer exchange periods. This compares very favorably with the 1996 period when open enrollment meetings were openly hostile and written and verbal complaints were lodged with human resources.
- 3 percent more employees elected medical coverage under the new plan.

Objective #3:   Reduce benefits administration staff hours during open enrollment period.

- There was a more than 50 percent decrease in phone calls to Benefits Administration during open enrollment as compared to 1996.
- 100 percent of employees completed online sign-up, which was fully explained in the *KB Guide*. This resulted in each employee electronically completing only one form, which was then electronically submitted to each carrier. This replaced a manual process requiring employees to fill out up to seven paper forms, which would then have had to be typed into the computer system by Human Resources Department personnel and temporary secretarial staff, requiring hundreds of man hours. In addition, employees cited online enrollment as the third most popular item they liked most about the new benefits program.

Unexpected Results

- The project team received numerous phone calls and e-mails from Ketchum employees in other offices commenting on the high quality of the communications campaign.
- Both MMC&P, Ketchum's benefits consulting firm, and PrimarySelect have requested samples of the *KB Guide* and Primetime video to share with their other clients as examples of excellent benefits communications.

Index